CAMBRIDGE TEXTS IN THE
HISTORY OF POLITICAL THOUGHT

=====

EDMUND BURKE
Pre-Revolutionary Writings

CAMBRIDGE TEXTS IN THE
HISTORY OF POLITICAL THOUGHT

Series Editors:
RAYMOND GEUSS, *Columbia University*
QUENTIN SKINNER, *Christ's College, Cambridge*

The series will make available to students the most important texts required for an understanding of the history of political thought. The scholarship of the present generation has greatly expanded our sense of the range of authors indispensable for such an understanding, and the series will reflect those developments. It will also include a number of less well-known works, in particular those needed to establish the intellectual contexts that in turn help to make sense of the major texts. The principal aim, however, will be to produce new versions of the major texts themselves, based on the most up-to-date scholarship. The preference will always be for complete texts, and a special feature of the series will be to complement individual texts, within the compass of a single volume, with subsidiary contextual material. Each volume will contain an introduction on the historical identity and contemporary significance of the text concerned, as well as such student aids as notes for further reading and chronologies of the principal events in a thinker's life.

For a complete list of titles published in the series, see end of book

EDMUND BURKE

Pre-Revolutionary Writings

EDITED BY

IAN HARRIS

Lecturer in Political Theory, University of Leicester

 CAMBRIDGE
UNIVERSITY PRESS

Published by the Press Syndicate of the University of Cambridge
The Pitt Building, Trumpington Street, Cambridge CB2 1RP
40 West 20th Street, New York, NY 10011–4211, USA
10 Stamford Road, Oakleigh, Victoria 3166, Australia

© Cambridge University Press 1993

First published 1993

Printed in Great Britain at the University Press, Cambridge

A catalogue record for this book is available from the British Library

Library of Congress cataloguing in publication data
Burke, Edmund, 1729–1797.
Pre-Revolutionary Writings / Edmund Burke : edited by Ian Harris.
p.   cm. – (Cambridge texts in the history of political
thought)
Includes bibliographical references and indexes.
ISBN 0 521 36227 X (hardback)
1. Political science—Early works to 1800.   I. Harris, Ian.
II. Title.   III. Series.
JC176.B82529   1992   320.5'2'092– dc20   91–43453   CIP

ISBN 0 521 36227 X hardback

ISBN 0 521 36800 6 paperback

Contents

Preface	*page* vii
Acknowledgements	ix
Abbreviations	x
Chronological table	xiii
Introduction	xvi
A note on the texts	xxxiv
Biographica	xxxvii
Bibliography	lxviii

'Extempore Commonplace on The Sermon of Our Saviour on the Mount'

Introduction	1
Text	3

A Vindication of Natural Society

Introduction	4
Analysis	7
Text	8

A Philosophical Enquiry into the Origin of our Ideas of the Sublime and Beautiful

Introduction	58
Analysis	61
Text	63

v

'Religion'

Introduction	78
Analysis	81
Text	82

Tracts on the Popery Laws

Introduction	88
Analysis	93
Text	95

Thoughts on the Cause of the Present Discontents

Introduction	103
Analysis	114
Text	116

Conciliation with America

Introduction	193
Analysis	205
Text	206

'Almas Ali Khan'

Introduction	270
Analysis	275
Text	277

'Speech on the Army Estimates'

Introduction	298
Analysis	305
Text	306

Index of persons	321
Index of subjects and places	326

Preface

Edmund Burke is sometimes presented as an apostle of development. The description is apt in that his own work displays a continuous elaboration, sometimes theoretical and sometimes practical. The object of this collection is to illustrate its course by presenting a series of texts, dating from Burke's time as an undergraduate to his response to the French Revolution of 1789.

Burke's views embraced both theoretical disquisitions on theology, society and aesthetics, and practical reflections on Ireland, America, India and France. This profusion of themes in two modes of writing, one might feel, envelops ordered description in a cloud of complexity. The editor trusts that the apparatus of this small edition will do something to dispel that feeling. The introductory essay outlines Burke's interests and their connection. It considers the texts printed here (and some whose inclusion considerations of space forbade) as moments in Burke's story. The shorter introduction prefixed to each text says something more about its individual character, particularly about the political circumstances which called for the practical writings. The footnotes, the chronological table and the biographical entries are intended to assist the reader's progress by explaining historical and literary references in the text.[1]

[1] These have been kept brief for reasons of space. In particular the literary references have been confined mostly to the Bible, Shakespeare and Milton. An illuminating study of Burke's relation to Addison and indeed Bolingbroke could be written.

  One point of literary usage, however, does call for comment. In common with most writers of his day Burke often used the nouns 'man' and 'men' to refer to the species rather than the gender. This historical usage is maintained in the introduction only because the prose is often continuous with quotations from Burke: a sentence would be confused by verbal changes. The reader may care to exercise himself or herself on Burke's meaning.

vii

The edition aims to give a concise presentation of Burke's views before his *Reflections on the Revolution in France*.² Because brief it concentrates on matters fundamental to understanding his thought, excluding others which would claim attention in a more extended treatment (just as it does not comment on the literature about Burke, save for the remarks in the bibliography). The editor will make good this omission elsewhere.

Leicester
9 July 1990

[August 1991] Whilst there would be no propriety in dedicating an edition of this kind, I should like to declare a special intention:

Charles Wilson,
1914–1991
In memoriam

---

² As such it undertakes to explain rather than to criticize Burke's views. The reader need not suppose that the editor's opinions are identical with Burke's.

Acknowledgements

A work of this sort is made possible by many different kinds of support and assistance. This edition was prompted by the suggestion of Richard Tuck. The other editors of the series in which this volume appears commented on an earlier draft of the introduction. Amongst those who have scrutinized that essay, Maurice Cowling suggested that it be made more complicated and John Dunn remarked that it should be made simpler: I have pursued both pieces of advice. Paul Langford commented on a draft and further thanks are due to him for a number of other kindnesses. Brian Roots identified three classical quotations which had escaped my vigilance. Aubrey Newman drew my attention to a point which would otherwise have been overlooked. Any editor owes a debt to his predecessors, and this one should record that he has found the annotations of Langford, Marshall, Payne and Sewell especially useful. Reasons of space make this sort of help difficult to acknowledge, but special mention is made for points which depended on knowledge or information beyond my reach. No one except myself is responsible for whatever errors and omissions may be present. Richard Fisher has been a model of patience on behalf of Cambridge University Press. Even greater patience has been exercised by my parents, as ever.

Amongst institutional debts, thanks are due for various forms of indispensable assistance to the staffs of Cambridge University Library, Northamptonshire Record Office, Sheffield City Library and Trinity College, Dublin. For permission to print manuscripts, thanks are due to the trustees of the late Olive, Countess Fitzwilliam and to the Board of Trinity College, Dublin, and for the use of printed books to the Syndics of Cambridge University Library.

Abbreviations

Writings by Burke

AAK	*Speech on Almas Ali Khan*
AEH	*Abridgement of English History*
CA	*Speech on Conciliation with America*
Corr	*Correspondence of Edmund Burke*, ed. T. W. Copeland *et al.* (Cambridge, 1958–78)
IA	*Letters, Speeches and Tracts on Irish Affairs*, ed. Matthew Arnold (London, 1881); reissued with a new introduction by Conor Cruise O'Brien (1988)
Notebook	*A Notebook of Edmund Burke*, ed. H. V. F. Somerset (Cambridge, 1957)
PD	*Thoughts on the Origins of the Present Discontents*
PE	*A Philosophical Enquiry concerning the Origin of our Ideas of the Sublime and Beautiful*, ed. J. T. Boulton (London, 1958 and 1987)
R	'Religion'
Ref	*Reflections on the Revolution in France*, ed. W. B. Todd (1959), cited by the pagination of the printing at Harmondsworth, 1968 and reprints, with an introduction by Conor Cruise O'Brien
SAE	*Speech on the Army Estimates*

x

TPL	*Tracts on the Popery Laws*
VNS	*A Vindication of Natural Society*

See also

W	*The Works of Edmund Burke* (World's Classics edn) (Oxford, 1906–07)
WSEB	*Writings and Speeches of Edmund Burke*, ed. Paul Langford *et al.* (Oxford, 1981–)

and also:

Samuels	*The Early Life, Writings and Correspondence of... Edmund Burke*, by A. P. I. Samuels (Cambridge, 1923) which contains in appendices I and II much early material by Burke.

These are all cited by volume (where applicable) and page of the edition specified, with the following exceptions: (i) page references to AAK, CA, PD, PE, R, SAE, TPL and VNS are to the present edition, (ii) PE is cited primarily by book and section numbers: no page references to Boulton's edition have been given, in order to avoid confusion with the portion printed here; (iii) since AEH is not available in a critical edition it has been cited only by book and chapter number.

Other documents

AR	*Annual Register*
Bedford Correspondence	Lord John Russell (ed.), *The Correspondence of John, fourth duke of Bedford*, 3 vols. (1842–46)
CJ	*Journal of the House of Commons*
Grenville Papers	W. J. Smith (ed.), *The Grenville Papers: being the correspondence of Richard Grenville, Earl Temple... and George Grenville...*, 4 vols. (1852–53)

Johnson	*The Political Writings of Dr Johnson*, ed. J. P.
Political Writings	Hardy (1968)
LJ	*Journal of the House of Lords*
PH	*Parliamentary History*
Rockingham Memoirs	Earl of Albermarle, *Memoirs of the Marquis of Rockingham and his contemporaries* 2 vols. (1852)

Chronological table

1727   Accession of George II

1729 or 1730 Burke born in Dublin

1730   Tindal, *Christianity as Old as the Creation*

1741   Burke sent to school at Ballitore, thirty miles from Dublin, under Abraham Shackleton, a Yorkshire Quaker.

1742   Resignation of Sir Robert Walpole

1743   Burke enters Trinity College, Dublin

1744   Henry Pelham forms his administration

1745–46 Jacobite Rising

1748   Burke graduates BA

1749   Bolingbroke, *Patriot King*

1750   Burke settles in London, first as a student in the Middle Temple: abandonment of law for literature leads to a period of obscurity and poverty

1751   Deaths of Bolingbroke and Frederick, prince of Wales

1756   *Vindication of Natural Society*

1757   *Sublime and Beautiful*; elder Pitt secretary of state; Burke marries Jane Mary Nugent (1734–1812); resides at first in Battersea, then in Wimpole Street

1758   Burke begins connection with *Annual Register* and composition of *Abridgement of English History* (unfinished); birth of sons Richard (d. 1794) and Christopher (d. in infancy)

1760   Accession of George III

1761   Burke returns to Ireland as secretary to W. G. Hamilton, Chief Secretary to the Lord Lieutenant, Lord Halifax; Bute secretary of state; Pitt resigns

xiii

1762 Bute forms ministry; Wilkes commences *North Briton*
1763 Peace of Paris; George Grenville forms ministry; Wilkes prosecuted for *North Briton* no. 45 under a general warrant
1764 'The Club' founded; Burke breaks with Hamilton; Wilkes expelled from Commons
1765 Stamp Act; Burke becomes Secretary to Rockingham and MP for Wendover; Rockingham forms ministry
1766 Burke's Maiden Speech in Commons; Stamp Act repealed; General Warrants condemned; elder Pitt forms ministry
1767 Townshend Duties
1768 Burke borrows to buy estate at Beaconsfield; Wilkes elected for Middlesex; reimprisoned; riots in his favour; Corsica falls to France; elder Pitt resigns; Grafton continues ministry
1769 *Observations on 'the Present State of the Nation'*; Wilkes repeatedly re-elected but unseated by Commons
1770 *The Present Discontents*; North forms ministry
1771 Burke becomes Agent for New York Province; he supports bill for amendment of law of libel; favours ceding the press the right to report Commons' debates
1773 Burke visits Paris; Boston Tea Party
1774 *Speech on American Taxation*; Burke becomes MP for Bristol; Wilkes permitted to take seat; Warren Hastings becomes governor-general of Bengal
1775 *Speech on Conciliation with America*; War with American colonies
1776 American Declaration of Independence
1777 *Letter to the Sheriffs of Bristol*
1780 Burke proposes Economical Reform; declines poll at Bristol; MP for Malton; Gordon Riots
1782 Burke becomes Paymaster-General of the Forces in Rockingham's second ministry; Rockingham dies (July); Shelburne forms ministry
1783 Fox–North coalition; Burke becomes Paymaster-General of the Forces; Fox's India Bill rejected by Lords; younger Pitt forms ministry
1784 Lord Rector of Glasgow University
1785 *Speech on the Nabob of Arcot's Debts*
1786 Burke moves Impeachment of Warren Hastings (1787–95)

1788   George III temporarily unhinged; Regency Crisis; *Speech in Opening against Hastings*

1789   French Revolution begins

1790   *Speech on the Army Estimates; Reflections on the Revolution in France*

1791   *Letter to a Member of the National Assembly; Appeal from the New to the Old Whigs; Thoughts on French Affairs*

1792   *Letter to Sir Hercules Langrishe*

1793   Execution of Louis XVI; the Terror

1794   Burke concludes his part in trial of Hastings; retires from Parliament; first pension (£1,200)

1795   Grant of two further pensions to Burke; acquittal of Hastings

1796   *Letter to a Noble Lord*; publication of *Letters on a Regicide Peace* commences

1797   Death of Burke, 9 July, at Beaconsfield

Introduction

What sort of thinker was Edmund Burke? His mind was equal to a wide range of concerns – theology, aesthetics, moral philosophy, history, political theory and public affairs – a range which seems bewilderingly diverse to the cautious eyes of a later day. In fact, these interests were intimately connected. Burke's theoretical writings suggested that the world was patterned unequally, whilst his practical works explored the possibilities of political inequality and, in the case of *Reflections on the Revolution in France*, defended it. The object of this introduction is to show the steps by which Burke moved to these positions.

When Burke was an undergraduate at Trinity College, Dublin, he and his friends founded a society devoted, like many such before and since, to improving themselves and the world. We discover from the club's minute book and from the writings which Burke published at the same period that he concerned himself especially about three matters: the revealed word and its effectiveness; aesthetics and virtue; and the possibilities of power and wealth for the good of society.

The first concern was expressed in 'an extempore commonplace of the Sermon of Our Saviour on the Mount' and was amplified when Burke asserted 'the superior Power of Religion towards a Moral Life'. For the second, Burke assumed that the arts and virtue went together, as 'the morals of a Nation have so great Dependence on their taste . . . that the fixing the latter, seems the first and surest Method of establishing the former'.[1] Imagination and virtue were linked when

---

[1] *The Reformer*, no. 11, 7 April 1748, no. 1, 28 Jan. 1748; Samuels, p. 324, 297.

Burke praised painting because 'it greatly tends to the furtherance & improvement of virtue'; and soon we find him mentioning plays that 'discountenance Virtue and good Manners' but 'not doubting to make a thorough and lasting Reformation'.[2] Wealth and power entered into a debate on the merits of the lord lieutenant of Ireland, in which Burke observed that 'the opportunity a man can have of promoting ye good of his Fellow creatures, is proportionate to his wisdom, his wealth, or his power'. He dwelt later on the necessity of property – 'a man's property's his life' – and on how the gentry of Ireland could improve their estates and so benefit the whole community (whilst lamenting that they usually did not).[3] These concerns, diverse as they seem, came to be related in one theory.

Burke embraced these three into a single understanding through the idea of inequality. Let us start with the revealed word. How could revelation – of all things, one might ask – fit this description? The answer lies with deism.

Deism may be defined as the view that the information man requires as a condition of salvation is obtained from natural means alone. By natural was meant what could be collected through human faculties, especially reason, as distinct from revelation. It was revelation, in fact, about which the deists had qualms. For they assumed that God willed that everyone in principle could be saved. This implied that each person had the minimum means needed for salvation. This could not include revelation, for the Bible had not been available to all people at all times. It followed that the revealed word was at the very least superfluous to salvation and at worst not actually of divine authorship. The deists considered that man's own faculties, especially his reason, could supply him with the information he needed.

Burke found deism obnoxious. His observations on the Sermon on the Mount (see below, pp. 1–3) declared a preference for revelation, arguing that it was superior to reason as a means of salvation. Shortly afterwards he suggested that Dublin's deists were really enemies to morality.[4] For if revelation was integral to God's design of saving man, to deny its authenticity was a denial of His plan.[5] To deny God's

[2] *Minute Book*, 26 May 1747; *The Reformer*, no. 3, 11 Feb. 1748, in Samuels, pp. 248, 305.
[3] *Minute Book*, 2 June 1747; *ibid.* (3 July 1747); *The Reformer*, no. 7, 10 March 1748, in Samuels, pp. 263, 289, 317.
[4] *The Reformer*, no. 11, 7 April 1748; Samuels, p. 323.
[5] Cf. *Speech on Toleration Bill, 17th March 1773*, WSEB, II p. 387f.

providence might in itself be held to signify atheism, or scepticism about revelation might be felt to reflect a complete unbelief. At any rate whilst Burke could later distinguish deists from atheists,[6] he was not ultimately much concerned about the difference. Addressing himself to France in 1790, he would refer to 'those men . . . whom the vulgar, in their blunt, homely style, commonly call Atheists and Infidels', and then included deists in his list, 'Colins [*sic*], and Toland, and Tindal, and Chubb, and Morgan, and . . . Bolingbroke' (Ref, p. 185f). The distinction was perhaps to his mind an over-refinement, in the sense that the two doctrines had the same effect.

Both removed what Burke understood by God from the explanation of human concerns. For they involved a denial of at least some of what Christians understood as His government of the world. Burke developed a contrasting vision. He was keen to employ God in explanation, whether of man's aesthetic perceptions, of the social order, or of morality. Let us see how he came to apply this view to two other early concerns, the social order and the imagination.

To uphold revelation in the face of deism is to commit oneself to a pattern of divine conduct involving inequality. To make revelation necessary to salvation is to found it on a form of inequality, for historically revelation was diffused over only a limited part of the globe: God's favour was not extended equally to all. As such, revelation implies the concession that at least one part of God's government was conducted on unequal lines. Since that part, the business of salvation, was obviously the most important to man, (God being held to work in a constant fashion) we would expect that others would conform to the same pattern. Our expectation is fulfilled in Burke's views on imagination and virtue and on the social order.

God, as traditionally understood, was man's superior, for man was dependent on Him (for example, as the agent who did for man what he was too feeble a creature to do for himself – guide and preserve him). An explanation conducted in terms which required God or drew Him to the reader's attention would refer to His superiority and man's continued dependence on Him. God is important to Burke in both aesthetics and moral theory.

God's place in aesthetics is found in Burke's *Philosophical Enquiry into the Origin of our Ideas of the Sublime and Beautiful*. The sublime

---

[6] *Speech on Toleration Bill*, WSEB, II, p. 389.

and beautiful were the chief categories of contemporary aesthetics. Burke used the former to remind man of his inferiority. Whilst we think of God's power, Burke wrote, 'we shrink into the minuteness of our own nature, and are, in a manner, annihilated before him'. God's power indicated man's dependence:

> And though a consideration of his other attributes may relieve in some measure our apprehensions; yet no conviction of the justice with which it is exercised, nor the mercy with which it is tempered, can wholly remove the terror that naturally arises from a force which nothing can withstand. If we rejoice, we rejoice with trembling; and even whilst we are receiving benefits, we cannot but shudder at a power which can confer benefits of such mighty importance. (PE, ii.v)

But why should Burke use aesthetics to remind man of his relation to God?

The answer is that aesthetics had been linked to moral theory by one school of thought in a way which significantly reduced God's explanatory role in the latter. Where traditionally man's dependence had been used to explain how God was entitled to give him laws, the theory of moral sense forgot to treat man as dependent and regarded him mostly as a created being. God as creator was said to have endowed man with a sense of beauty and this sense provided also a basis for moral judgement. Man's dependence on God faded into the background. Burke stigmatized moral sense as 'whimsical' in its applications and judged that in general it had 'misled us both in the theory of taste and of morals' (PE, iii.xi). He reasserted God's superiority in order to explain the theory of morals.

Moral sense theories, he thought, had 'induced us to remove the science of our duties from their proper basis'. By this he understood 'our reason, our relations, and our necessities' (PE, iii.xi). He undertook to explain it theocentrically in 'Religion'. This essay starts out from man's relation to God – as a created and dependent being – and infers it is reasonable to think that man is bound to obey Him, and that man's necessities suggest that he has duties to others. 'Religion' is also theocentric in a specific way, for it suggests that reason points us towards an after-life and revelation. It is obvious enough that Burke, by suggesting that reason arrives at precisely this conclusion, was turning the deists' weapon on themselves, the more so as he went on to imply in the same essay that revelation was more certain than reason. But there is something more to 'Religion'. For Burke suggested that reason should be complemented by human feeling in understanding man's station and his duties. This leads us to the social order, for *A Philosophical Enquiry* shows how feeling involves a specific account of society.

Before turning to Burke's general view of society it is as well to turn to what he rejected. Again, deism figures, this time not merely for itself but in the logic Burke read into it. Deism, in his view, opened up unpleasant implications for society. One deist in particular might be read in this way. The posthumous publication of Bolingbroke's works was a literary event and one especially interesting to Burke. For to provide deism with a conceptual guarantee one had to reject God's particular Providence – His concern with individual destinies – for that obviously embraced revelation. Most deists were not so thorough: but Bolingbroke was.[7] His view was objectionable on wider grounds. Besides discounting revelation, it implied that God exercised no direction over specific cases. Individual events and institutions would not reflect His intentions. The social order, on this reading, need not answer to any beneficial purpose. Such a view would be unlikely to appeal to Burke, who at Trinity had sensed benevolent possibilities in the unequal order of his day.

Shortly after Bolingbroke's works were published there appeared an essay which seemed to suggest that precisely this form of society was the cause of human misery. Rousseau's *Discourse on the Origin and Foundation of Inequality* embodied two claims about modern European society. One was that its hierarchical form implied a perversion of man's moral feeling. That feeling, which by nature took the form of compassion (a regard for those less fortunate than ourselves), would be stifled by the regard for those above us engendered in the social order. The compassion which man had by nature would be lost in the emulation he assumed in society. Rousseau's second claim was that a society so constituted was unnatural, and therefore produced a range of economic and social miseries. Both claims condemned social inequality in the name of nature.

Burke's response in his *Vindication of Natural Society* offered an *ad*

---

[7] Bolingbroke, *Works*, 6 vols. (1754), V, p. 414: 'The truth is that we have not in philosophical speculation, in any history except that of the Bible, nor in our own experience, sufficient grounds to establish the doctrine of particular providences.'

hominem formula. It suggested that if one espoused deism one's logic led to Rousseau. To generalize, the rejection of the inequality involved in revealed religion stood on the same grounds as the rejection of hierarchy in civil society, that 'the same Engines which were employed for the Destruction of Religion, might be employed with equal Success for the Subversion of Government' (see below, p. 10). Revelation and the social order were vulnerable to the same logic. Yet a fuller response required a further stage. Burke had still to rebut the view that social inequality was unnatural.

A Philosophical Enquiry showed how nature gave rise to inequality. Burke did not dispute the standard view that men were by nature equal,[8] though he did little to illuminate it. He indicated instead how passions that were entirely natural would give rise to a graduated social order. For Burke divided the passions which 'served the great chain of society' under three heads – sympathy, imitation and ambition. These linked men in society, and linked them so as to make inequality natural. Sympathy was a 'bond' which made men never 'indifferent spectators of almost anything which men can do or suffer'. Sympathy by itself did not make for inequality, but it concurred with the passions which did. 'For as sympathy makes us take a concern in whatever men feel', Burke wrote, so imitation 'prompts us to copy whatever they do'; and imitation was complemented by ambition, which gave 'a satisfaction arising from the contemplation of excelling his fellows' to a man (PE, i.xii, xiii, xvi, xvii; see below, pp. 68–74). So it was natural for the ambitious to lead and for the imitative to follow. Hence, inequality in society would be established. The bonds of civil society were the causes of inequality: and inequality arose from nature.

An unequal society in Burke's view was not only natural but also progressive. If men were devoted to imitation alone, 'it is easy to see that there never could be any improvement amongst them' and it was 'to prevent this' that God instilled ambition into man (PE, i.xvii; below, p 73f). 'Improvement' implies human artifice, and Burke was quick to show how human invention lay in the pattern of nature. Nature could extend to artifice and to a specific form of artifice. For 'nature' in Burke's hands included the best adaptation of the artificial to the ends that man's nature suggested. The content of 'nature'

---

[8] *The Reformer*, no. 7, 10 March 1748, in Samuels, p. 316; AEH, i.ii.

would be presented to best advantage not in a primitive condition, as Rousseau had suggested, but in the perfection of artifice. 'Art is man's nature', Burke wrote, because 'man is by nature reasonable; and he is never perfectly in his natural state, but when he is placed where reason may be best cultivated'.[9] At one level this view enlarged upon the view that man required society to flourish, for 'without which civil society man could not by any possibility arrive at the perfection of which his nature is capable, nor even make a remote and faint approach to it' (Ref, p. 196). At another, it authorized the distinct version of civil society Burke intended. For the author of *A Philosophical Enquiry* believed that society could produce 'a true natural aristocracy'. Nature culminated in artifice. In Burke's own words, 'the state of civil society, which necessarily generates this aristocracy, is a state of nature'.[10]

There was a further variety of inequality implicit here, for the perfection of artifice was the work of time. As such, its benefits accrued more to the modern than to the ancient. When Burke acknowledged the artificial character of property he emphasized its growth over time and observed that 'inequality, which grows out of the *nature of things*' was nurtured through 'time, custom, succession, accumulation, permutation, and improvement of property'.[11] The progressive was the unequal.

Thus, Burke found no reason to think that modern society necessarily involved moral perversion. He wrote of humanity, without deliberation, that 'we love these beings & have a sympathy with them' (R, below, p. 82). But did society involve the misery of man? We may assume that social inequality could involve an unequal distribution of benefits. But the point is less a state of affairs than how it is considered. Burke, on occasion, was scarcely more restrained in his observations on contemporary ways than Rousseau: but he viewed society in a different light. He came to argue that society depended for its prosperity on inequality: so that to undermine the latter was to strike at whatever benefits the poor might receive.[12]

There was, in any case, a further inequality which indicated that the largest questions were not for man to answer. The human under-

[9] *An Appeal from the New to the Old Whigs* (1791), W, V, p. 101.
[10] *An Appeal from the New to the Old Whigs*, W, V, p. 101.
[11] Burke to John Bourke (November 1777), Corr, III, p. 403.
[12] *The Reformer*, no. 7, 10 March 1748, in Samuels, pp. 314–17; *Thoughts and Details on Scarcity* (written 1795), W, VI, pp. 4, 9, 11; cf. Ref, p. 372.

standing was unequal to understanding fully God's purposes. Burke had argued in 'Religion' that man's duty was intelligible through reason and passion, and had related the passions to God in his *Philosophical Enquiry*. But he insisted that the circle of man's comprehension was limited. His knowledge of causes was small, for 'when we go but one step beyond the immediately sensible qualities of things, we go out of our depth' (PE, IV.i). In general, his intellect was unsuited for speculation which took him out of common life, because then 'we can never walk sure but by being sensible of our Blindness' (VNS, see below, p. 11). God's Providence was included here. As Burke's favourite passage from Isaiah (55,8) expresses the matter, 'my thoughts *are* not your thoughts, neither *are* your ways my ways, saith the LORD.'

Man's task was not to question God's Providence. God was assumed to be wise, benevolent and powerful, so His actions would be well-calculated for a beneficial end and move certainly towards it, however unclearly to man's eyes. Thus, we read that Providence did not work 'but with a view to some great end, though we cannot perceive distinctly what it is' (PE, I.x, below, p. 67). It must be assumed to work efficiently towards the best; and we find Burke ending his lament for the death of his hopes with his son Richard by remarking that 'a Disposer whose power we are little able to resist and whose wisdom it behoves us not at all to dispute, has ordained it in another manner, and (whatever my querulous weakness might suggest) a far better'.[13] Because God's purpose was to the good of man however unpleasant its incidents and institutions might be, they were part of an unimpeachable plan.

We have seen that for Burke the divine worked through inequality. Revelation was an unequal mode of distributing information. It involved a further inequality, because God issued it, who was man's superior: and this superior directed man through his passions. 'Religion' showed that God was also the author of a morality discoverable by reason, just as *A Philosophical Enquiry* had emphasized the passions which tended to establish a social inequality. We could add that since the workings of Providence did not favour each equally, inequality could be seen there too. Man's intellect was not equal to understanding God's plan, let alone to criticizing it.

Thus, Burke's initial allegiances and the way in which he arti-

[13] *A Letter to A Noble Lord* (1796), W, VI, p. 63f.

culated them theoretically as responses to other views disclose a general political theory. A society founded on nature would develop inequality. This assumption of inequality provided a basis for other views. For instance, Burke's regard for wealth harmonized with it. For 'the characteristic essence of property . . . is to be *unequal*' (Ref, p. 140). So property, which the young Burke had seen as a source of possible benevolence, was in the same pattern as nature.

We need not suppose that Burke's general stance implies an indiscriminate approval of all graduated dispensations. He could say that 'all who administer in the government of men . . . stand in the person of God himself' (Ref, p. 189): but this scarcely implies that those who were like God in power were like Him also in goodness. To put the matter another way, some modes of inequality might be better than others. In order to distinguish which, Burke's focus had to move from the general to the particular. Most of his writings after *A Philosophical Enquiry* assess individual regimes. He turned first from his native Ireland in his *Abridgement of English History* and focussed on England's particular virtues.

When the undergraduate Burke discussed the possibilities of wealth for good, he had not forgotten power. In fact, he thought that power might be more important for good than wealth.[14] Power too required vindication, for among the inversions Burke attributed to the pseudo-Bolingbroke was the claim that any government, in its nature, was an instrument of evil (VNS, below, pp. 14–46). For just as Rousseau had told a story in which man was corrupted by society, Bolingbroke's account of history suggested that the liberty found amongst the Saxons in England was subsequently under threat from government and that one of its other enemies was the Church.

The accounts of Rousseau and Bolingbroke in their different ways suggested that the motif of history was decline, whether in the loss of virtue through society or in the problems of liberty after the Saxons. A writer offering an antidote might prefer to place his accent on progress. Where Bolingbroke's account questioned whether English liberties had grown since the Saxons and implied with a deistic sneer that the Church was against political liberty,[15] an alternative account would suggest that liberty had grown, not diminished, and that the

---

[14] *Minute Book*, 2 June 1747; Samuels, p. 264.
[15] Bolingbroke, *A Dissertation on Parties*, letter xvi; *Remarks on the History of England*, letter iv; *Letters on the Study and Use of History*, nos. v & vi.

Church had assisted it. Since Bolingbroke argued that the early middle ages had seen a virtual extinction of political liberty, it would also be fitting to suggest that it was then that it was established. There would have to be a carefully turned explanation of this story. For it was obviously counter-intuitive to the eighteenth century to find Norman and Angevin government or the Roman Church placing political liberty high amongst their deliberate ends. Liberty, like improvement, was the common coin of eighteenth-century thought. The significant matter is how they were explained; the choice of explanation reflected the preferences of the writer. With Hume the conflict of interests would bring about the blessings of the modern world through a process of accident. Robertson would describe an escape from the feudal order. Burke showed that it was Providence which secured England her liberty and improvement. Naturally enough, he found that Providence worked through the agencies of social inequality and revealed religion.

Burke's *Abridgement of English History*, written shortly after the publication of *A Philosophical Enquiry*, gave a providential narrative from the earliest times to *Magna Carta*. This did not suggest the direct intervention of God, save at one point, but showed how desirable results occurred gradually without any human having insight into His plans. By the same token, the results did not reflect deliberate human activity. Burke emphasized the themes of inequality, improvement and liberty. Fundamentally, he thought, the structure of Saxon and Norman society was sound in that it reflected nature by instancing inequality. Further, whether under the indistinct forms of Saxon society or under the feudalism of the Normans, the subordination of one man to another, reaching to the king, was uncoerced. Therefore, kings felt sufficiently secure, on the whole, to govern through laws rather than by force. These monarchs, too, favoured Christianity, which secured the benefits of improvement. Literacy and good manners were nurtured. So Burke could see the middle ages as the period in which the bearers of religious and social inequality secured blessings to England.

These reflections formed the basis of Burke's view of how government by opinion arose. Government by force ceased to be necessary when the ruler and the ruled could trust each other. This happened under the feudal system, which embodied the loyalty of subject to sovereign and which Burke would describe eventually as 'the old feudal and chivalrous spirit of *Fealty*, which, by freeing kings from fear, freed both kings and subjects from the precautions of tyranny' (AEH, esp. I.ii; II.i–ii, vii; III.iii, viii; Ref, p. 172). Under this condition, force would be replaced by opinion as a mode of government. This feudalism both necessitated and provided. It was necessary because leaders were followed freely (the sovereign 'was only a greater lord among great lords' (AEH, III.i)), and it was supplied by the code of honour feudalism embodied ('the soft collar of social esteem' (Ref, p. 170)).

Improvement flourished under the same conditions. Burke thought that 'the rudeness of the world was very favourable for the establishment of an empire of opinion' and the body most fitted to form opinion was the Church. As 'the asylum of what learning had escaped the general desolation' (AEH, III.i), the Church imparted knowledge to the world. Hence the 'ground-work' of intellectual improvement was a 'Gothic and monkish education', because the Church had been the agent 'preserving the accessions of science and literature, as the order of Providence should successively produce them' (Ref, p. 199). Thus, the agents of revelation complemented the beneficiaries of social hierarchy in God's design.

This story was common to Europe and England, for both had been feudal, but there was one feature peculiar to England. Political liberty arose through the coincidence of the growth of order, the church, and the precise structure of Norman society. Executive government extended its power. But it was balanced when the aristocracy was encouraged by the Church to resist. Since the aristocracy was not sufficiently strong on its own to prevail, it sought to enlist popular support by claiming liberty for all. In this fashion it was ensured that liberty was not merely won but won on a general basis (AEH, III.viii). We could perhaps say that because Burke's story gives out at *Magna Carta* it is unclear what would happen next; and that his story concerned chiefly England. But a passage in *Reflections* made it clear that to his mind the civilization and manners of modern Europe as a whole were the children of Church and hierarchy:

> Nothing is more certain, than that our manners, our civilization, and all the good things which are connected with manners, and with civilization, have ... depended for ages upon two principles; and were indeed the result of both combined; I mean the spirit of a gentleman, and the spirit of religion. (Ref, p. 173)

We can see a connection with his earlier views. For the middle ages built upon nature itself. The *Abridgement* explains how feudal society had been founded 'for the most part upon two principles in our nature', which were 'ambition, that makes one man desirous, at any hazard or expence, of taking the lead amongst others, – and imitation, which makes others equally desirous of following him'. 'These two principles', he concluded, 'strong, both of them in our nature, create a voluntary inequality' (AEH, II.vii). The voluntary character of obedience was the foundation of the civilization of Europe, for it implied that uncoerced order which gave an opportunity to liberty and improvement. It was not just England by itself which was significant for Burke's thinking about government.

This is true in another sense. We should bear in mind a contrast which Burke's experience impressed upon him. It lay between a providential development and the triumph of violent destruction. The contrast is exemplified in the difference between the country in which Burke was born and the one he adopted. He at once felt 'very warm good wishes for the place of my birth' and found 'the sphere of my duties' in England.[16] The differences between the two lands suggested a striking polarity.

Burke's *Tracts on the Popery Laws*, dating from the early 1760s, saw Ireland as a country which was marked by its conquest. The central fact was that Protestants had triumphed over Catholics and meant to maintain their ascendancy. But Burke understood the case in more general terms. For him, it was the negation of the uses of power and wealth for benevolence. Ireland was a country run for the benefit of the rulers rather than the governed. From bad principles flowed unhappy consequences. Liberty and improvement alike were depressed. The Ascendancy, because few in number, needed to fetter the many, so that Catholics enjoyed few civil liberties. The laws which prescribed these restrictions were enforced by penalties that weighed heavily on Catholic possessions, originally the bulk of Ireland's landed property. The depression of property hindered improvement gravely. In short, a regime which was morally wrong made Ireland unfree and unprogressive.

England, by contrast, had lost the marks of its conquest and displayed a more admirable political constitution. Burke's *Abridgement*

---

[16] *Speech in the Guildhall at Bristol, previous to the late election* (1780), IA, p. 128.

had shown the emergence during the middle ages of artificial institutions which reflected the natural order. Church and aristocracy, institutions characterized by inequality, formed the English polity. They protected improvement and liberty. These benefits were evidently not lost in Burke's own time. For he saw civilization in England: 'I Live and have Lived In Liberal and humanized company', he wrote in 1771. Those with wealth and power could continue their benevolent role, 'you if you are what you ought to be,' he told the duke of Richmond, 'are the great Oaks that shade a Country and perpetuate your benefits from Generation to Generation'.[17] England embodied a proper polity and enjoyed its benefits.

Thus, these two countries exemplified the significance of the proper order of things and its consequences. The proper order was one agreeable to man's social passions, in particular those which would fasten on subordination. That order, instantiated in various forms of inequality, could provide the means to secure the good of society, whether through the benefits of liberty or through those of improvement. Yet securing these goods depended upon those who ruled. The conduct of government could determine whether these benefits would be secured to the governed or lost. So the contrast between governments well and badly constituted and conducted became integral to Burke's thought.

The interests of his middle years meant that it was very prominent too. In his politics England bulked large during the sixties, America in the seventies and India in the eighties. In every case it was the conduct of government – whether by the English court, by the administration of Lord North or by the governor-general of Bengal – which seized his attention. In each case, too, the polarity is present in Burke's thinking. *Thoughts on the Origins of the Present Discontents* identified a threat to England's liberties from the Court and sought a remedy in the appeal of political virtue to public opinion. Burke argued in *On Conciliation with America* that the Americans were at bottom English and as such devoted to liberty. They therefore had to be either reduced to obedience by force or, better, governed according to their own opinions as free men. India excited him where it was, in sober fact, a country conquered. Burke became convinced that the subjugation of much of the sub-continent by the East India Company

---

[17] Burke to William Markham (after 9 Nov. 1771), Corr, II, p. 264; Burke to the duke of Richmond (after 15 Nov. 1772), Corr, II, p. 377.

implied the destruction of a civilization for the benefit of the oppressor.

Yet these themes are themselves general: it remains to explain why Burke conceived them in a specific way. It was a party stance that enabled him to particularize his political theory. His party position gave him a point of view on questions of the day and so enabled him to apply his view of government in a given way. In the England of the 1760s, for instance, George III could as plausibly seem the embodiment of hierarchy, and certainly claimed to be as much devoted to liberty as Lord Rockingham. Likewise, whilst some publicists saw the court threatening liberty, others identified aristocracy as its enemy. Burke was able to opt for the former view after he attached himself to Rockingham. This was, no doubt, a fragile contingency: yet once established it gave Burke a fixed point from which to examine political conduct. So the opponents of Rockingham, whether over England, America or India, became identified at appropriate junctures as the enemies of good government.

Equally, Burke's sense of the general provided the presuppositions of his particular views. This often distinguished him from his political colleagues. For he differed from them regularly: some felt his *Present Discontents* pointed too directly towards the king; some preferred a harder line against America; and most felt that India obsessed him beyond the limits of prudence. When Burke was unable, for whatever reason, to put matters in his own terms, he spoke with a rather less distinct voice. The Burke who harried Grenville and North, and spoke for the restoration of Lord Pigot, was a very clever publicist and debater.

Thus, political engagement both led Burke to apply his general views in a highly particularized way and imparted a distinctiveness to his views on specific questions. Was Goldsmith right to say that he was one

> whose genius was such,
> We scarcely can praise it, or blame it too much;
> Who, born for the Universe, narrowed his mind,
> And to party gave up what was meant for mankind[18]

or is there something besides to be said?

There is much that is obviously plausible in Goldsmith's view. The

---

[18] Oliver Goldsmith, *Retaliation*, ll. 29–32.

Burke whose mind ranged from the Sermon on the Mount to the subjugation of Ireland dealt with the most general questions and with the story of whole nations. Whilst his writings of the twenty-five years from 1765 show continuity of concern, they display a narrowing of focus and the specifications of party. But we must beware of attributing our sense of Burke's destiny to him. He was something rare, a man whose intellect was equal to his heart, and both were on a grand scale. He was also an Irish adventurer. Party politics took him a long way. He enjoyed the society he admired, as parliamentarian and privy counsellor; for a period, when he represented Bristol, he was a national figure; and he acquired wealth (or, more precisely, debts) befitting his new station. Yet beyond such personal amenities, there were gains which directed Burke's thought into the form we find in *Reflections on the Revolution in France*. Indeed, political *losses* helped to elicit his views. Because he had narrowed his mind he came to broaden it finally.

Burke identified the aristocracy as a bulwark of good rulership. He was not an enthusiast for aristocracy *per se* – he called it an 'an austere and insolent domination' (PD, below, p. 134f) – but he developed a decided view of its function: to govern virtuously. Early in Burke's career he had decided that human nature was marked by an ambition to lead and a desire to follow. He had described, a little later, how the English aristocracy had won political liberty when followed by their inferiors and how this popular support had induced them to diffuse liberty to all. He marked out a similar role for the modern aristocracy. When Rockingham died, Burke declared that the Marquess had endeavoured 'to give stability to the liberties of his country'.[19] Burke illustrated this point in many ways: the central point was that the man of established property was fitted to govern. His wealth could free him of any interest in keeping office, any temptation to subordinate private to public good. Government by the propertied was free to be virtuous. It should be added that property tended to political virtue more directly when held in land. For property in land was an irremovable part of the community – it was literally a stake in the country – and as such made its holder's interests part of his country's. Better still, it should be an hereditary wealth so that its possessor would be unmarked by the selfish arts that acquired substance and, instead,

---

[19] Albemarle, *Rockingham Memoirs*, II, pp. 486ff.

brought up to think of other questions: to think particularly of standards of probity and decency which would make him an example for lesser men to imitate. On Burke's view of human nature, the latter would follow their superiors. Aristocracy would acquire popular support. Such were the habits of political virtue, 'the temperate, permanent, hereditary virtue of the whole house of Cavendish'.[20]

At length, Burke returned to mankind what he had given to party, and that in part because he was a figure isolated in his party. The death of Rockingham in 1782, the rise of a younger generation of politicians, the failure of the Fox–North coalition in 1783, and his party's diminishing regard for the impeachment of Hastings contributed to Burke's lonely position in the later 1780s. He required a new loyalty and a new opportunity to re-establish himself as a central figure on the national stage. By a turn of events which was certainly providential for Burke, his life soon wore a new aspect. An event occurred in which Burke was in the deepest sense partial: he had a point of view.

Burke's views had dwelt on inequality in manifold forms. He had begun by emphasizing the importance of revelation, which was a message distributed unevenly. He had developed a view of man which stated that the inequality between leaders and followers was natural. Social hierarchy, property and government too stood on an unequal basis. The bearers of social and religious inequality, aristocracy and Church, had achieved liberty and improvement for England in the middle ages. After nearly twenty-five years in Parliament, Burke held that good government was still secured by some of the bearers of inequality. So when the French Revolution came it touched a live nerve. For Burke, a movement which made *égalité* its watchword implied the destruction of the conditions on which society existed and prospered. To his mind, it would involve not merely the destruction of legal privilege but the destruction of inequality in society and everything which went with it.

Reflections on the Revolution in France is divided into two parts, arranged in dramatic contrast with one another. The first contains an account of a properly regulated society, interwoven with a description of the attack upon it. It displays a providential order. The succeeding

---

[20] *A Letter to the Sheriffs of Bristol* (1777), W, ii, p. 283. On Burke's view of the function of aristocracy, see *Appeal*, W, v, p. 101.

part provides a sharp contrast, dwelling on the results of working by human foresight alone – inadequacy. Burke underlined the inadequate nature of the revolutionary institutions by giving an appreciation of British recognition of man's limitations and his proper reliance on God. The divine order and its opposite stood in pointed contrast. Let us turn to the earlier part, where Burke's premises are revealed.

The proper order had been challenged along lines obvious to one of Burke's experience. The opportunity for mischief came from the third estate. Its members lacked what Burke understood as a character proper to those who govern. They lacked social and financial ease: on the contrary, they had a dependent and unsettled character and one especially disposed to trade off property.

Their character was exploited by two cabals discontented with the present dispensation. One was men of commercial interests, whom the peculiarities of the French polity had prevented from bringing their property to rest in land. Since their ambition for a leading role in society could find no place in the existing order, they sought an alternative dispensation. The other consisted of men of letters, who were 'atheists' and hated God's order. They combined to attack inequality, whether the aristocracy (whose pinnacle was the monarchy) or the Church (the bearer of the revealed word) and the result was that France became as a country conquered (Ref, esp. pp. 128–32, 168–74, 185f, 209–12, 297f). It was the destruction of the proper order of things at the hands of people who lacked the character to govern well.

It was the inversion of Burke's preferences. But though the Revolution was his nightmare it was also his opportunity. In the light of Burke's preceding thought we can see what subsequent commentators have forgotten: why Burke's response was 'so intense, so eccentric, and so astonishingly perceptive'.[21] It was intense because the rebuttal of revolution was in a literal sense vital to Burke, for the foundations of society were at stake. It was not merely the society into which he had woven his affections and his ambition that was attacked – and attacked by 'atheists' – but the very society which Burke understood God to have prescribed. The Revolution in France was the worst of nightmares.

---

[21] John Dunn, 'Against Vanity', *The Times Literary Supplement*, no. 4,552 (29 June–5 July 1990), p. 691.

Yet by the same token it was the greatest opportunity to expound his views. It had never before fallen to him to deploy his political opinions in so concentrated a form. Are those views eccentric? All interesting political theory makes connections others have overlooked. This prize is likely to fall to one whose stance is out of the ordinary. Burke's point of view, formed we have seen out of an amalgam of inequalities and a view of character, was the fruit of a particular origin and experience. No doubt Burke's perspective is unfamiliar, but one of the objects of historical study is to explain how the unusual is plain enough in its own situation. At any rate, *Reflections* was Burke's greatest work, for his mental equipment, developed in youth and in political life, gave him a powerful instrument to interpret the Revolution. His pre-revolutionary thought is vital to understanding *Reflections*.

A note on the texts

Sources of texts

The editor's policy has been (i) to go to manuscript wherever possible (ii) to give preference to what embodies Burke's own attentions. In one case, 'Almas Ali Khan', known only through a contemporary newspaper report, we cannot be sure of the wording as distinct from the tenor of his speech. In another (the chapter from *Tracts on the Popery Laws*) we have to rely on a printed edition made from Burke's manuscript after his death. The other texts are printed from editions which, on the evidence of W. B. Todd, *A Bibliography of Edmund Burke* (1964; slightly augmented, 1982), are the latest to which he attended. Two exceptions have been made to this rule: (i) the second edition of PD is preferred to the third (which has already been printed in WSEB, II) in order to make a slightly different text generally available (ii) readings from the first collected edition (see below) have not been adopted. With all texts revised by Burke the earlier editions have been examined and variations have been noted in one or two places. It was not felt, however, that a register of them was necessary in an edition of this kind.

The sources are as follows:

(i) 'Extempore Commonplace' manuscript at Trinity College, Dublin (TCD MUN/SOC/HIST/81 pp. 27–9);
(ii) *A Vindication of Natural Society*, 2nd edn (London, 1757);
(iii) *A Philosophical Enquiry into the Origin of our Ideas of the Sublime and Beautiful*, 2nd edn (London, 1759);

(iv) 'Religion' manuscript at Sheffield City Library (WWM Bk.P.40 pp. 73–85);

(v) *Tracts relative to the Laws against Popery in Ireland*, in *The Works of ... Edmund Burke*, vol. 5 (London, 1812), pp. 271–80;

(vi) *Thoughts on the Cause of the Present Discontents*, 2nd edn (London, 1770), with subsequent MSS. annotations by Burke (Sheffield City Library, WWM Bk.31.47);

(vii) *Speech ... on Moving his Resolutions for Conciliation with the Colonies*, 3rd edn (London, 1775);

(viii) 'Speech on Almas Ali Khan', *Parliamentary Register*, xvi, pp. 289–98, 299–301, 302–11;

(ix) *Substance of the Speech ... in the Debate on the Army Estimates*, 3rd edn (London, 1790).

Textual citation

The citation of Burke's writings is something of a bibliographical nightmare, a situation which will be ended only when *The Writings and Speeches of Edmund Burke* [WSEB] (Oxford, 1981–), under the general editorship of Paul Langford, is complete. The first collected edition (London, 1792–1827) varies in standard from some textual authority (the earlier volumes were published during Burke's lifetime) to the cavalier and careless. It is the basis of both the large nineteenth-century compilations (Bohn: London, 1866, and Little, Brown: Boston, 1854 etc.), which in turn stand behind the World's Classics printing (Oxford, 1906–7).

The basic policy adopted here is to cite WSEB wherever possible. (The sole exception is that *Reflections* is cited from the text edited earlier by W. B. Todd (Harmondsworth, 1968) because this is more likely to be in the hands of students). WSEB, unfortunately, does not at present cover all the citations. Wherever possible a critical edition is cited, as J. T. Boulton's *Philosophical Enquiry* [PE] (London, 1958; 2nd edn, with unrevised text, 1987). Failing that, the reader's convenience has been consulted by citing the text thought to be most freely available, especially Matthew Arnold's selection from Burke on *Irish Affairs* [IA] (London, 1881, reprinted 1988). For this purpose the World's Classics text has been preferred to the larger nineteenth-century editions.

Burke's letters are cited from T.W. Copeland, general editor, *The Correspondence of Edmund Burke* [Corr] (10 vols., Cambridge, 1958–78).

See also the table of abbreviations (above, pp. x–xii).

Dates

All dates before Lord Chesterfield's Act are given according to the Old Style, except that the year is reckoned from 1 January.

Biographica

AGESILAUS (*c*.444–361 BC) was king of Sparta from *c*.398, though not strictly due to succeed. He distinguished himself in wars against the Persians in 396–5 and the Thebans in 395, but was less successful against the latter in 379–62. In order to finance hostilities, he accepted the commission of an Egyptian prince against Persia, where he met his death in 361.

ALEXANDER the GREAT (Alexander III of Macedon, 356–323 BC) was a pupil of Aristotle, but as king of Macedon from 336 neglected his tutor's view that war was merely a means to peace. Having consolidated his grasp on his hereditary kingdom and his father's acquisitions (Philip II of Macedon had established a hegemony in Greece), he devoted himself to conquering Persia. This he largely accomplished in a series of brilliant campaigns, briefly subjugating India too. Alexander was, however, more than a military genius. He aimed to treat his European and Asiatic subjects on an even footing and his campaigns were succeeded by an extension of Greek civilization into the East.

ALMAS ALI KHAN (d. 1808) was the most important *amil* (revenue official) in Oudh, controlling about a third of the Wazir of Oudh's revenues in two frontier areas (Doab and Kora). His loyalty to the Wazir became suspect by 1782, and Hastings (*qv*) ordered that he be disciplined.

ANAXAGORAS (*c*.500–*c*.428 BC) was the first philosopher to reside in Athens. He was the tutor and friend of Pericles (*qv*), by whose

xxxvii

enemies he was impeached for impiety; but with Pericles' aid he escaped to Lampascus, where he established a philosophical school and died an honoured citizen.

ANNE (1665–1714) was the younger daughter of James II (*qv*). At the Glorious Revolution of 1688–89, she was detached from her father by Marlborough (*qv*) and his wife. On the death of William III (*qv*) in 1702, Anne succeeded as queen. Her reign was marked by a flowering of English literature, the union of England and Scotland (1707) and the triumph of English arms under the direction of Marlborough in the War of the Spanish Succession. The paradox of Anne is that whilst her own inclinations were towards Toryism and a high view of the Church of England, her reign strengthened Whiggery. Her failure to produce a healthy heir (the longest-lived of her fourteen children, the duke of Gloucester, died aged twelve) allowed the Hanoverian line to succeed to the throne in 1714, inaugurating the long dominance of the Whigs in government.

ANTIOCHUS was the name of three Hellenistic rulers, of whom the most important was Antiochus III (*c*.242–187 BC), who acquired Armenia, Parthia and Bactria. Like Alexander (*qv*) he killed so many people that he was called 'the Great', but ran up against Rome, with whom, however, he had the rare distinction of making an advantageous peace.

ARCHELAUS (fl. 1st century BC) was a Greek in the service of Mithridates (*qv*). Although he overran Bithynia and much of central Greece from 88 BC, he was defeated twice by Sulla (*qv*) and negotiated peace with Rome (85). Under suspicion of treason, he subsequently deserted to Rome (83) and helped Lucullus to defeat Mithridates (74).

Whilst ARISTIDES (died after 467 BC) was a successful Athenian general and admiral, he is known chiefly for his exemplary honesty. His repute began in his own day, when he was contrasted with the subtle Themistocles (*qv*), through whose manoeuvres he was ostracized in 482. According to Plutarch, an illiterate citizen was helped by Aristides to record his hostile vote; on being asked if Aristides had ever harmed him, he replied 'No, but it vexes me to hear him everywhere called the Just'.

Tigranes I 'the Great', king of ARMENIA (d. 56 BC) greatly expanded his realm at the expense of Parthia and Syria. Unfortunately his alliance with Mithridates (*qv*), whose son-in-law he was, involved him in war with Rome from 69 BC: he lost all his possessions, except Armenia itself, and became an obedient vassal of Rome.

Richard ATKINSON (1738–85) was a director of the East India Company and a contractor for the British army during the American war. He was involved in the management of the 1784 General Election on behalf of the younger Pitt (*qv*).

Jean Sylvain BAILLY (1736–93), by training an astronomer, became a deputy in the estates-general of 1789, was elected president of the third estate on 4 June (he presided over the Tennis-court session and was first to take the oath) and on the 17th was nominated Mayor of Paris (a new office). He found difficulty in keeping order in the city and resigned in November 1791; but his efforts led to his death, under unusually atrocious conditions, during the Terror.

Allen BATHURST, first Earl Bathurst (1684–1775) was distinguished alike as the friend of Pope (*qv*), Swift, Congreve, Prior and Sterne and as a stout Tory, notable for his criticisms of Walpole (*qv*). He received marks of favour under George III (*qv*), including his elevation from a barony to an earldom (1772). His heir Henry (1714–94) was Lord Chancellor (1771–78) and Lord President (1779–82).

John Russell, fourth duke of BEDFORD (1710–71) began political life in opposition to Walpole (*qv*), but held office under Pelham (*qv*) from 1744, and became secretary of state in 1748. He resigned in 1751 through the jealousy of Newcastle (*qv*). He was friendly to most administrations which did not include the duke, serving under Devonshire, Bute and Grenville (*qqv*). After 1765 his chief aim was office not for himself but for his followers. The fifth duke (1765–1802), the addressee and victim of Burke's *Letter to a Noble Lord*, was his grandson.

Sir William BLACKSTONE (1723–80) discarded literature for the law with triumphant success, as author of *Commentaries on the Laws of England* and other works, which secured him great celebrity, and on the bench, where he secured an increase in judicial salaries.

Viscount BOLINGBROKE (1678–1751) was born Henry St John and

distinguished himself in the Commons as a Tory, becoming successively secretary for war (1704–08) and secretary of state (1710–14),
insisting on a peerage in 1712. Bolingbroke had high oratorical and
literary talent but his mismanagement of the succession at the death
of Queen Anne (*qv*) (1714) ensured his political extinction at the
hands of George I and the exclusion of his party from office for many
years. He occupied his enforced leisure (after a flirtation with Jacobitism) in political journalism and in speculation, both philosophical and
theological. The deistic content of the latter did as little for his fame
as his energetic private life: Voltaire learnt much from him. Bolingbroke's reputation illustrates Disraeli's dictum that England, being
subject to fogs and possessing a powerful middle class, requires grave
statesmen.

Rev. John BROWN (1715–66) author of *Essays* on the third earl of
Shaftesbury's moral philosophy and *An Estimate of the Manners and
Principles of the Times* (1757), a well-written variation on the appealing
theme of degeneracy, which was fortunate enough to have a strong
appeal at a moment of national depression. He was at least partially
deranged for some years and ended his own life.

John Stuart, third earl of BUTE (1713–92), described by Frederick,
Prince of Wales (*qv*) as 'a fine showy man who would make an
excellent ambassador in a court where there was no business',
acquired after the Prince's death an ascendancy over his widow and
the young Prince George. When the latter succeeded as George III
(*qv*) Bute was able to exercise extensive influence and acquire high
office, culminating in the premiership (1762–3); but only at the cost
of antagonizing the great Whig families (Newcastle, Grafton and
Rockingham (*qqv*) being dismissed from their lord-lieutenancies).
Bute, tired by the complexities of politics, recognized his own
unpopularity and retired in favour of George Grenville (*qv*). The
supposition, sincere or convenient, that he influenced the king continued in Whig circles for some time.

Gaius Julius CAESAR (100–44 BC) improved his impoverished if noble
lot by adroit political manoeuvring to become pontifex maximus (63)
and consul (59). He acquired Cisalpine and Transpadane Gaul for
his proconsular provinces, and proceeded to extend the empire in the
Gallic Wars (58–51), incidentally invading Britain twice. He

responded to senatorial pressure by invading Italy and defeating the Senate's armies decisively in Greece (48), Africa (46) and Spain (45) whilst consolidating his grip on Rome. His accumulation of powers, however, precipitated his assassination on the Ides of March, 44. His most enduring reform was the Julian calendar. His writings and his generalship alike reflect an elegant economy of means.

CALIGULA (more properly Gaius Caesar, AD 12–41), the third Roman Emperor (37–41), was initially popular, but after a serious illness (by which he may have been unhinged) alienated the Senate, governed through extensive executions and may have committed incest with his sister Drusilla. His alleged elevation of his horse to a consulship has provided posterity with a facile analogy for many political appointments.

Charles Pratt (1714–94), Earl CAMDEN (baron, 1765; earl, 1786) was a career lawyer, becoming attorney-general in 1757 and chief justice of the Common Pleas in 1761. He achieved wider political signifi-cance by deciding in the Wilkes case (1763) that general warrants were illegal and by declaring that the Stamp Act was unconstitutional. He was Lord Chancellor (1766–70), returning to office in 1782 as Lord President under Rockingham (*qv*) and resuming it from 1784 under the younger Pitt (*qv*).

Lucius Sergius CATILINA (d. 63 BC) was a thug of a type ordinary in the declining years of the Roman republic, but attained special notice when, disappointed of the consulship by Cicero (*qv*), he began an organized conspiracy. He was outmanoeuvred by Cicero and executed under circumstances of dubious legality.

Marcus Porcius CATO (95–46 BC), achieved a permanent reputation for principle by committing suicide at Utica rather than submit to Julius Caesar after the latter defeated the republicans at Thapsus. His preceding political career had been less inflexible, though marked by a degree of stubbornness.

Lord John CAVENDISH (1732–96) was the fourth son of the third duke of Devonshire and brother of the fourth duke (*qv*). MP from 1753, he adhered firstly to his brother and then to Rockingham (*qv*). Chancel-lor of the Exchequer, 1782 and 1783.

CHARLES II (1630–85) as king of England (*de jure* from 1649 and in practice from 1660) exhibited a mixture of personal charm and political astuteness which helped him to weather a life complicated in both its private and public spheres. These were related, for his inability to produce a legitimate heir made his brother James (*qv*) heir presumptive. Despite James' Catholicism, Charles was able to secure the succession for him. Charles' policy, which was marked by colonial expansion, uncertain foreign relations and subsidies from Louis XIV (*qv*), was distinguished more by technical virtuosity than fixity of purpose.

Etienne François, comte de Stainville (1719–75) and duc de CHOISEUL (1757) served Louis XV as ambassador to Rome (1753–8) and then as minister for foreign affairs (1758–70). In the latter capacity he negotiated a relatively advantageous end to the Seven Years' War and was, in effect, chief minister.

Thomas CHUBB (1679–1747) was enabled by patronage to abandon trade for letters, becoming first an Arian and then a deist. He attended church regularly and called himself a Christian. Chubb, who ate steadily and gave up walking, died suddenly.

Marcus Tullius CICERO (106–43 BC) rose through his oratorical skill with a measure of political luck to the consulship in 63. He achieved that office because, in a poor field, Optimate voters were alarmed about the intentions of Catilina (*qv*); but his zeal exceeded the law in executing the latter and his fellow conspirators without trial, thus making himself vulnerable to his opponent Clodius. Though Cicero escaped prosecution and, after a year at an expedient distance, returned to Rome he played no decisive part in the collapsing world of republican politics. He occupied his leisure in the fifties and during Julius Caesar's (*qv*) rule with literary activity. After Caesar's death he returned to public effectiveness, but his distinctive combination of verbal explicitness and political miscalculation led to his death at the behest of Mark Antony. Cicero's works – orations, rhetorica, letters and philosophical writings (in politics, theology and morals), not to mention poetry – make up a remarkable corpus and are one of Rome's chief bequests to posterity.

Sir Edward COKE, Baron Coke (1552–1634) acquired wealth, advancement in public life and lasting fame through the common law. At various times solicitor-general, speaker of the Commons, attorney-general and chief justice successively of common pleas and of the king's bench he did the government's bidding, assisting in the destruction of Ralegh (*qv*); but losing favour at court he became a vigorous proponent of anti-prerogative views. These (and others) are detailed in his *Reports* and *Institutes*. Of the latter Hobbes (*qv*) remarked, 'I have never read weaker reasoning in any author on the laws of England'.

Anthony COLLINS (1676–1729) explored the implications of some of Locke's (*qv*) views and developed a scepticism of his own. He questioned Christianity through historical criticism and wit, remarking that no one had doubted the existence of God until certain divines set out to prove it.

Henry Seymour CONWAY (1721–95) entered the army at an early age, rising very rapidly there and in public life. Having been dismissed at the behest of George III (*qv*) from his army command for voting against the government in 1764 he seemed a proper person to be secretary of state under Rockingham (*qv*). He remained in office under the elder Pitt (*qv*), hoping to link the ministry with the Rockinghams, but resigned in 1768 over America. When Rockingham returned in office in 1782, Conway became Commander-in-Chief with a seat in the Cabinet. Remaining there under Shelburne (*qv*), he effectively left politics with the coming of the Fox–North Coalition: but stayed as C-in-C until 1793.

William Augustus, Duke of CUMBERLAND (1721–65), the third son of George II (*qv*) was educated for the navy, but became a soldier from 1740, rising to major-general by 1742. Captain-General 1745–57 and 1765, he defeated the Jacobites at Culloden (1746) but was himself defeated at Lauffelt and Hastenbeck. His influence over his nephew, George III (*qv*), was extinguished only by death.

Sir John DAVIS or DAVIES (1569–1626) damaged his career in the law by breaking a cudgel over the head of a friend in the Middle Temple's dining hall, but redeemed his fortunes by writing a poem which gained the approval of Elizabeth I (*qv*) and so public office. James I also admired the poem and appointed him solicitor-general for Ireland. His *Discovery of the True Causes why Ireland was never Entirely Subdued* (1612) argued that England's government of Ireland was weak because it had not extended the benefit of English law to all its subjects.

George DEMPSTER (1732–1818) was distinguished as an agriculturalist and advocate before becoming an MP (1761–90). He became a director of the East India Company, but withdrew and supported Fox's East India Bill; he also promoted a society for the extension of Scottish fisheries. His works include *Magnetic Mountains of Cannay*.

William Cavendish, fourth duke of DEVONSHIRE (1720–64), was a natural candidate for office as a sane representative of a great Whig family. Newcastle (*qv*) made him lord lieutenant of Ireland in 1755. When Newcastle left office in dudgeon with the elder Pitt (*qv*), Devonshire was induced to serve as first lord of the treasury by George II (*qv*). He held this office briefly (1756–7) and was glad to become Lord Chamberlain when Pitt and Newcastle found it necessary to co-operate. Being handled ungenerously by George III (*qv*) he resigned his office and also his lord lieutenancy, the latter as a gesture of sympathy at Newcastle's and Rockingham's (*qqv*) deprivation. He was the shortest-lived of all Britain's prime ministers.

William DOWDESWELL (1721–75) was an independent-minded MP (1747–54 and 1761–75), who was persuaded to become Chancellor of the Exchequer under Rockingham (*qv*). Although Dowdeswell complained that he was wanted only for his talent, he rejected overtures from the elder Pitt (*qv*) and thenceforth was the major speaker for the Rockinghams in the Commons.

Henry DUNDAS (1742–1811), first Viscount Melville (1802) acquired the art of public speaking in the General Assembly of the Church of Scotland and practised it in the British House of Commons (from 1774), where he figured first as a powerful speaker for North (*qv*). He acquired considerable influence in India, as well as obtaining the management of all the government's Scottish patronage from 1782. He denounced Fox's (*qv*) India Bill and held a variety of offices under the younger Pitt (*qv*), whose close friend he was. Dundas was eventually impeached for diverting naval funds to domestic use (1806). He was acquitted but never held office again.

John Murray (1732–1809), fourth earl of DUNMORE (succ. 1756) was governor of New York from 1770 (to which he added Virginia). He was unable to manage the House of Assembly and repeatedly dissolved it. In 1775 he resorted to arms. He was governor of the Bahamas 1789–1796.

Jeremiah DYSON (1722–76) became a clerk of the Commons in 1748 and an MP in 1762. He appeared first as a supporter of George Grenville (*qv*) but was really a king's friend. He held many offices, and enjoyed a mastery of parliamentary procedure and a subtlety which won him the nickname 'the jesuit of the house'. He remained in office under Rockingham (*qv*), who attempted to dismiss him for insubordination. Dyson died in office.

EDWARD I (1239–1307) reigned as king of England from 1272. His career combined gallantry (he was on Crusade when his father Henry III (*qv*) died) and a certain hardheadedness. The latter was manifested in his financial exactions from his subjects (which led to an opposition to which he made concessions in 1297) and in his highly successful conquest of Wales. His dealings with Scotland were less successful, for though he conquered the country he never subdued it. Edward died on campaign against the Scots.

ELIZABETH I (1533–1603) was the daughter of Henry VIII (*qv*) by Anne Boleyn. She succeeded in surviving the reign of her Roman Catholic sister Mary and reigned as a decidedly Protestant queen of England 1558–1603. Her rule was distinguished by the hostility of Spain, a renaissance in English literature and a containment of the Commons' demands which her successors did not manage to continue. Retrospectively, the period acquired a rosy glow.

Sir Gilbert ELLIOT (1722–77) attained office in 1756 and kept it, partly through oratorical talent and partly through political dexterity. Originally a follower of the elder Pitt (*qv*) he next adhered to his fellow-Scotsman Bute (*qv*) and became a confidant of George III (*qv*), whose views he expressed in the Commons.

Charles James FOX (1749–1806) son of Henry Fox, (cr. first Baron Holland, 1763), who had rivalled the elder Pitt (*qv*) in the Commons during the fifties. Charles, true to the family's calling of service to and profit from the state, was initially a supporter of North (*qv*) but transferred his affections to Rockingham (*qv*). After the latter's death he went into coalition with North (*qv*) in order to defeat Shelburne (*qv*), George III's (*qv*) preferred minister. Reckoning without the determination of the king and the younger Pitt (*qv*), Fox remained in opposition for all but the last few months of his life, when he was foreign secretary in William Grenville's (*qv*) ministry (1806). Fox combined great oratorical skill with fecklessness about money and public reputation (for instance, he married his mistress secretly so that they continued to flaunt a condition they practised no longer). Fox's long period out of office, due also partly to his unseasonal sympathy with the French Revolution, allowed his followers to lay claim to the Ark of the Whig Covenant, an attitude enshrined in the life and writings of his nephew, the third Lord Holland.

Sir Philip FRANCIS (1740–1818) rose through diplomatic and secretarial service, acquiring a position on the Bengal Council under North's (*qv*) Regulating Act (1772). He quarrelled with Hastings (*qv*) and provided both information and venom for Burke (with whom, however, he differed on other matters). Francis is the most likely author of *The Letters of Junius*.

FREDERICK, Prince of Wales (1707–51) was the eldest son of George II (*qv*) and father of George III (*qv*). His poor relations with his parents (for which see Lord Hervey's *Memoirs*) led Frederick to make his residence at Leicester House a centre of political opposition. It was perhaps natural for George III and Bute (*qv*) to feel opposed to the ministers the new king inherited from his grandfather, as Newcastle and the elder Pitt (*qqv*).

Rose FULLER (*c*.1708–77) had a varied career in Leyden, Cambridge, Jamaica (where he was chief justice) and London. He was a supporter of Newcastle (*qv*). From 1774 he criticized the American policy of North's (*qv*) government.

Thomas GAGE (1721–87) commanded the British forces in the colonies (1763–75) after spending much of a lengthy and successful military career in North America. He served as a lieutenant-colonel from 1756, commanded the light infantry at Ticonderoga, led Amherst's rearguard and was governor of Montreal. As Commander-in-Chief in America he faithfully executed the orders of the British government, though well aware of the difficulties of conquering the country.

David GARRICK (1717–79) was Dr Johnson's (*qv*) pupil and wrote for the *Gentleman's Magazine* before performing at Drury Lane in 1740. He soon made a great reputation as an actor and flourished as playwright, producer and actor- manager.

GEORGE II (1683–1760) after a troubled relationship with his father (which he reproduced with his own heir, Frederick (*qv*)), succeeded as king in 1727. His reign witnessed the practical extinction of Jacobitism, the consolidation of Whig government (though George exercised his powers more effectively than was once thought) and closed in a blaze of glory with numerous British victories and extensive territorial gains in the Seven Years' War.

GEORGE III (1738–1820) sought a more positive role for the monarchy in the executive. He began with a (somewhat simple) distaste for party, which vented itself through the agency of Bute (*qv*) against the Whigs in the highest offices, as Newcastle and the elder Pitt (*qqv*). George's subsequent search for a minister who would be both obedient (unlike George Grenville (*qv*)) and effective (unlike the elder Pitt again, Grafton and Shelburne (*qqv*)) led him to North (*qv*) and then to the younger Pitt (*qv*). George's settled views – as his opposition to Catholic emancipation – led to trouble even with the latter. But because the king was persuasive, relentless and solvent he was largely successful in eluding the Whiggish bumptiousness of Rockingham (*qv*) and Fox (*qv*). From 1788, however, he suffered periods of disabling mental incapacity, culminating in a regency exercised by his son George from 1811.

Richard GLOVER (1712–85) is best-known for *Leonidas* and *London, or the Progress of Commerce*, but figured politically first as an opponent of Walpole (*qv*) and a follower of Frederick, Prince of Wales (*qv*). He became an MP in 1761 and supported Bute and then Grenville (*qqv*). He retired from Parliament in 1768 but appeared before the Commons to give evidence on commercial grievances (1774–75).

Sidney GODOLPHIN (1645–1712) began as a courtier of Charles II (*qv*), becoming secretary of state in 1684 and remaining in office under both James II (*qv*) and William III (*qv*); Charles is said to have remarked that he was never out of the way and never in it. His son married Marlborough's (*qv*) daughter in 1698: he was in effect head of the home government during Marlborough's campaigns. He was finally detached from office in 1710, having lost royal favour. Less Whiggish than Burke's treatment would suggest.

Oliver GOLDSMITH (1728–74) began an irregular adult life by education at Trinity College, Dublin, Edinburgh and Leyden before wandering in Europe. He practised as schoolmaster and physician before turning to literature. Famous as author of *The Deserted Village*, *The Traveller*, *The Vicar of Wakefield* and other works.

Granville Leveson-Gower (1721–1803), second Earl GOWER and Marquess of Stafford (1786) began political life as a follower of Bedford (*qv*) but was temperamentally an office-holder. He was given preferment by Bute (*qv*) in 1763 but resigned in 1765 rather than serve under Rockingham (*qv*). He did serve under both Grafton and North (*qqv*), but resigned in 1779 rather than prosecute the war against America. He returned to office under the younger Pitt (*qv*).

Augustus Henry Fitzroy, third Duke of GRAFTON (1735–1811) regarded the proceedings of Bute (*qv*) with scepticism, but did not embrace the creed of Rockingham (*qv*). A descendant of Charles II (*qv*) and an hereditary supporter of the Hanoverians (his grandfather was a close friend of George II (*qv*)), Grafton opposed Bute's peace policy and was deprived of his lord-lieutenancy with Newcastle and Rockingham (*qqv*). He served as secretary of state under Rockingham in 1765–6, but resigned when it proved impossible to strengthen the ministry by bringing in the elder Pitt (*qv*). He took office as first lord of the treasury under Pitt in 1766 and on the latter's withdrawal figured as Prime Minister (1767–70), a position which he succeeded in palming off to North (*qv*); under whom he then served, but resigned in 1775 over the coercion of America. He held office under both Rockingham and Shelburne (*qv*), avoided the Fox–North coalition and declined office from the younger Pitt (*qv*). Grafton, who was educated at Peterhouse, Cambridge, was the last prime minister to keep a mistress openly whilst in office.

George GRENVILLE (1712–70) began his political career in opposition to Walpole with his brother-in-law, the elder Pitt (*qv*), but achieved office under the Pelhams, went on to serve under Bute (*qv*) and was Prime Minister 1763–5. Grenville was an extremely pertinacious politician, with a special talent for finance and procedure; his motto should have been *esse est adminstrari*. His Whiggery achieved an edge through enmity towards Bute and George III (*qqv*), but his relations with both the elder Pitt (his brother-in-law) and Rockingham (*qqv*) were edgy for less avowable reasons.

William Wyndham GRENVILLE (1759–1834) was destined to a political career as a son of George Grenville (*qv*); he is supposed to have said that one of his brothers 'would be a good and popular Prime Minister' and certainly gave Cabinet office to another. Grenville (created Baron Grenville, 1790) himself held a series of high offices under his cousin, the younger Pitt (*qv*), going into opposition over the King's refusal to grant Catholic emancipation in 1801 and resigning as Prime Minister (1806–07) when George again made difficulties. Grenville appears to have derived more pleasure from his chancellorship of Oxford University (1809–34) than from his premiership.

Francesco GUICCARDINI (1483–1540) was a Florentine statesman and diplomat. Ambassador to Spain under both the republic and the Medici, he latterly served as governor of Modena, Reggio Parma and Bologna, as well as a general, before retiring from politics to write his *History of Italy*.

W. G. HAMILTON (1729–96) made a celebrated maiden speech in the Commons, 1755 ('Single-speech Hamilton') and rose steadily from commissioner of trade (1756) to chief secretary for Ireland (1761–64) and chancellor of the Irish exchequer (1763–84). *The Letters of Junius* were attributed to him and his genuine remains were published as *Parliamentary Logic*.

Thomas HARLEY (1730–1804), great-grandson of Lord Treasurer Oxford, was MP for the city of London from 1761 and was re-elected against Wilkes (*qv*) in 1768. As sheriff of London and Middlesex he caused no. 45 of the *North Briton* to be burnt in 1763. Lord Mayor of London in 1767–8, he repressed Wilkite disorder; for which he was made a privy counsellor in 1768 and mobbed in 1770.

James HARRINGTON (1611–77) was a political theorist, who sought to discover the relation between property and polity most likely to produce stable government. His views are outlined at length in his *Oceana* (1656).

Warren HASTINGS (1732–1818) despite a promising scholastic career at Westminister (where he was placed above Impey (*qv*)) entered the service of the East India Company aged eighteen. In India he rose rapidly through posts connected with Calcutta, before becoming second in council at Madras in 1769. In 1771 he was appointed governor of Bengal (governor-general from 1775) and instituted extensive reforms in the judiciary and administration. In 1777 he signified his intention 'to make the British nation paramount in India' and soon made war on the Mahrattas and others. He laid down his office in 1784 and returned to England the next year. By the interested indignation of Sir Philip Francis (*qv*; an enemy on the Bengal council) Burke and others were sufficiently excited to procure his impeachment (1787). His trial dragged on until 1795, leading Gibbon to remark that he had heard of eternal punishment but not eternal trial. Hastings was acquitted of all charges.

HENRY III (1207–1272) was the eldest son of King John (*qv*) whom he succeeded in 1216. His reign was marked by continued problems in foreign affairs and finance, which, however, he weathered rather better than his father.

HENRY VIII (1491–1547, reigned 1509–47) was an outstanding specimen of monarchical self-assertion, who extruded papal authority from England, married six times and executed most potential claimants to his throne (besides numerous others).

Wills Hill (1718–1793), second Viscount HILLSBOROUGH (succ. 1742; cr. Marquess of Downshire, 1789) rose steadily in politics under George II (*qv*) and held high office 1763–1772 (but resigned rather than serve under Rockingham (*qv*)) and again 1779–82. George II remarked that he did 'not know a man of less judgement than Lord Hillsborough'.

Thomas HOBBES (1588–1679) was diverted from expounding a universal scheme of knowledge by the onset of the English civil war. His political works (culminating in his *Leviathan* of 1651) aimed to abridge political conflict by making the sovereign juridically unchallengeable. Amongst the considerations necessary for men to agree rationally in this view was an insistence that without it they would be liable to perpetual conflict.

HOMER was believed by the Greeks to have composed both the *Iliad* and the *Odyssey*, but they knew no facts for certain about his life.

Modern scholarship occupies a somewhat less definite position, since there is not universal agreement that one person wrote both or either. But whatever our views may be on the authorship of the Homeric poems there can be no doubt of their quality.

Francis HUTCHESON (1694–1746) was professor of moral philosophy at Glasgow, 1729–46. One of the most influential philosophers of the eighteenth century, he developed the views of Shaftesbury by working out the theory and applications of the moral sense in aesthetics and moral theory. His son, also Francis, was a distinguished musician.

Thomas HUTCHINSON (1711–80) came of a family long settled in America and had a distinguished career in Massachussets (lieutenant-governor, 1758, governor 1771) ended in 1774 by pressure from radicals. He opposed the use of force against Boston and Massachusetts.

Sir Elijah IMPEY (1732–1809) was educated at Westminster with Hastings (*qv*), but unlike him rose through education (Fellow of Trinity College, Cambridge, 1757) and the law (barrister, 1756) to be Chief Justice of Bengal (1774–89). A loyal ally of Hastings against Francis (*qv*), he narrowly avoided impeachment 1787 and became an MP.

JAMES II (1633–1701) was the surviving brother and heir of Charles II (*qv*) and, thanks to Charles' luck and adroitness, was able to succeed him as king despite avowed Roman Catholicism. However, within four years (reigned 1685–88) James' perceived tendency towards absolute rule and his excessive preferment of his co-religionists had alienated the political nation sufficiently to allow his nephew, William III (*qv*), to replace him.

Charles JENKINSON, 1st earl of Liverpool (1727–1808) held office, with short intervals, from 1761 to 1802. His first loyalty was to the monarch rather than to any political leader (although he resigned his political office rather than serve under Rockingham (*qv*) in 1765, he moved to a post in the royal household). He achieved special, but unwelcome, prominence on Bute's (*qv*) retirement when he was recognized as leader of the King's friends in the Commons and again as Secretary at War (from 1778) in the later stages of the American War of Independence.

King JOHN (1167–1216, reigned 1199–1216) inherited a situation in foreign affairs and finance which was difficult and made it impossible, alienating many of his barons and clergy, as well as losing Normandy. His unsubtle methods led eventually to *Magna Carta* and an extremely bad press at the hands of ecclesiastical chroniclers.

Whilst popularly known as the overbearing intellectual thug of Boswell's *Life*, Samuel JOHNSON (1709–84) deserves a better fame both personally, as a man of unusual private tenderness and consistency of belief, and intellectually as critic, editor of Shakespeare and compiler of a *Dictionary of the English Language*. He received a royal pension through Bute (*qv*) and wrote a number of political pamphlets taking a line which helped the executive. Despite this, he greatly respected Burke, with whom he shared a number of fundamental convictions.

JUGURTHA (d. 104 BC) became king of Numidia (118 BC) only at the cost of losing half the realm to a rival. He regained it by war, but had the misfortune to fall foul of Rome. He was defeated eventually not by force of arms, despite repeated and costly effort, but by treachery.

JUSTIN is here Marcus Junianius, who made an epitome of Pompeius Trogus' *Historiae Philipicae*, probably in the third century AD.

Marie-Josephe Paul Yves Roche Gilbert du Motier, Marquis de LAFAYETTE (1757–1834) began his career as a volunteer on the American side of the War of Independence, in which he rose to high command. He complemented this dramatic role by becoming commander of the citizens' militia, the National Guard, at the beginning of the French Revolution. He succeeded in developing the Guard into a well-organized body, but by October 1789 the Guard's independence and power made it clear that though their leader he must follow them. Lafayette found it increasingly difficult at once to satisfy his followers and to protect the monarchy (and, indeed, himself). In August, 1792 he escaped the dilemma by surrendering to the Prussians. Fortunate as ever, his time in their hands preserved not only his life but also his reputation, for he escaped association with the less creditable episodes in the Revolution. He returned briefly to public life at the Revolution of 1830.

John LOCKE (1632–1704) was a British thinker, distinguished alike as the author of *Two Treatises of Government, A Letter concerning Toleration, An Essay concerning Human Understanding, Some Thoughts concerning Education* and *The Reasonableness of Christianity*.

LOUIS XIV (1638–1715, king of France 1643–1715) presided in boyhood over the strengthening of his monarchy by Richelieu and Mazarin. He exercised French power in a series of aggressive wars, directed not least against Holland, and, though militarily defeated, carried his point in the War of the Spanish Succession: his grandson became Philip V of Spain (reigned 1700–46).

Sir James LOWTHER (1736–1802), earl of Lonsdale (cr. 1784) inherited extensive properties and political influence in north-west England, which he increased resolutely. Lowther married Bute's (*qv*) daughter and so became the object of a Whiggish vendetta by Portland (*qv*). This, however, rebounded on the latter's head when his tenure of certain lands from the Crown was disputed successfully (on the *nullum tempus* question, see below, p. 138). Lowther opposed the American war and helped the younger Pitt's (*qv*) rise. He balanced economic improvement (as building up Whitehaven) with personal meanness (withholding debts from the Wordsworths, amongst others).

LYCURGUS is the name attributed to the legendary founder of Sparta. There are no decisive arguments against the existence of such a figure, whatever his name.

LYSANDER (*c.*390–325/4 BC) was an Athenian statesman, who after the city's defeat at Chaeronea (338) rectified her finances, reconstructed her navy and discouraged defeatism. He suffered the indignity of a life by Plutarch.

Niccolò MACHIAVELLI (1469–1527) was a Florentine diplomat and civil servant who devoted a number of works to the conditions of political stability, especially how states could survive or prosper in the face of threats, whether internal or external. His most sustained effort is his *Discourses*, but an exemplification of his views, referred to the question of how to extrude foreign rule from Italy, is found in his more famous *Prince*.

James Stuart MACKENZIE (1719?–1800) was the younger brother of

Bute (*qv*), from whose rise he prospered. Having been envoy extraordinary to Turin (1758–61) he acquired the management of the government's Scottish patronage. On Bute's resignation he secured for Mackenzie the Scottish Privy Seal, which the latter held until ejected by George Grenville (*qv*) against George III's (*qv*) wishes. He was reinstated by the elder Pitt (*qv*) and remained in office until his death.

John MACNAMARA (1756–1818) was MP for Leicester 1784–90 in the duke of Rutland's interest. He was a follower of the younger Pitt (*qv*), whom he protected from the mob on one occasion. His wealth derived partly from the West Indies.

John Churchill, first duke of MARLBOROUGH (1650–1722) was the son of the minor royalist writer, Sir Winston Churchill, and rose rapidly under Charles II and James II (*qqv*) through sexual charm and military competence. He acheived further advancement through detaching James' daughter Anne from her father and thus strengthening William III (*qv*) in 1688. His military career prospered under William; but its apogee came when Anne herself was queen, for then Marlborough defeated the French in four major battles during the war of the Spanish Succession (1701–13). Marlborough and Godolophin (*qv*), however, were outmanoeuvred at home; Marlborough's subsequent career was relieved chiefly by tricking his enemy Bolingbroke (*qv*) at a critical juncture for the latter.

MILTIADES (*c.*550–489 BC) was an Athenian nobleman who consolidated the city's rule over Thrace and acquired Lemnos. His rule over Thrace was more or less kingly, but survived charges of 'tyranny' and became politically influential at Athens. He won a decisive victory against Persia at Marathon (490 BC) and inaugurated a policy of naval expansion.

MINOS figures as king of Crete; the stories concerning him reflect the power of Minoan civilization. These include making war on Athens, and marrying a woman who copulated with a bull and by this singular method produced the minotaur. The stories are combined in the narrative of Athenian youth being given up to the minotaur, till Theseus (*qv*) dealt with it.

MITHRIDATES is the name of six kings of Pontus, of whom the best known is Mithridates VI (120–63 BC). He inaugurated his career by imprisoning his mother, marrying his sister and killing his brother; his expansionist policies (which were not entirely successful in themselves) attracted the enmity of Rome. Mithridates was the Romans' most formidable oriental opponent, but was successful neither in strategy nor in keeping the loyalty of his subordinates. Defeated, he discovered that a diet of prophylactics had made him immune to poison, and he died by the hand of a guard.

Sir Thomas MORE (1478–1535) was a prominent public servant under Henry VIII (*qv*), eventually becoming Lord Chancellor. He was unhappy about Henry's attitude to the pope; his reluctant reticence on this point led to his execution. He wrote many works, including *Utopia* (1516), a short volume of labyrinthine ambiguity.

Thomas MORGAN (d. 1743) was a poor Welshman who exchanged Christianity for deism, but described himself as a 'Christian deist'. No one took much notice of him.

MOSES was the great law-giver and leader of the Hebrews, whom he led from captivity in Egypt, formed as a nation under God, and conducted to the land promised to their forefathers.

NERO (more formally Nero Claudius Caesar, AD 37–68) was the fifth Roman emperor (54–68). He coupled artistic instincts with extravagance, vanity, sexual license and paranoia. His preference for Greece, financial gerrymandering, persecution of aristocrats and debasement of the coinage won little sympathy at Rome and he was overthrown by the military. A *poseur* to the end, his dying words were *quam artifex pereo*.

Thomas Pelham-Holles, Duke of NEWCASTLE (Newcastle-upon-Tyne, cr. 1715, Newcastle-under-Lyne, cr. 1756) (1693–1768), although said by George II (*qv*) to be unfit to be chamberlain to a petty German prince, held high office in Britain, with two short intermissions, from 1717 to 1762. With his brother Pelham (*qv*) he governed, in Gibbon's words, 'on the old basis of the Whig aristocracy' i.e. through money, influence at Court and patronage. After Pelham's death Newcastle's chief difficulty was finding someone to run the Commons. He eventually allied, despite personal differences, with the elder Pitt (*qv*). But the terms of politics were revised by the accession of George III (*qv*). In 1762 Newcastle felt constrained to resign; and within a year, in the company of Rockingham and Grafton (*qqv*), he was deprived of the three lord-lieutenancies he had held since the days of George I. He naturally shared Rockingham's point of view, serving as Lord Privy Seal in 1765–66.

NINUS see SEMIRAMIS

Frederic, Lord NORTH (1732–92) was the eldest son of the third Lord Guilford (created earl, 1752), a Lord of the Bedchamber to Frederick, Prince of Wales (*qv*) and for a short period governor of the young Prince George (George III, *qv*). Family background, personal ability and financial exigency (Guilford, who was mean with North, lived until 1790) made him a natural officeholder. He rose gradually, serving in every administration from 1759 to 1770 (save that he would not remain under Rockingham (*qv*)), until himself becoming Prime Minister (1770–82). North had no particular difficulty in maintaining a majority in Parliament until the loss of America was obvious. Later (1783), feeling that George had neglected him, he joined with his erstwhile opponent Fox (*qv*) (and with Burke) to defeat the King's chosen minister, Shelburne (*qv*). He underestimated George's determination, overlooked the younger Pitt (*qv*) and lost office. Failing health and financial security on his father's death diminished his interest in politics.

Robert Henley, first earl of NORTHINGTON (*c.*1708–72) combined boldness with legal knowledge. Originally an adherent of Frederick, Prince of Wales (*qv*) he received advancement from both the elder Pitt and George III (*qqv*), becoming Lord Keeper (1757–61), Lord Chancellor (1761–66) and Lord President (1766–67). He was the immediate cause of Rockingham's (*qv*) dismissal in 1766 when he announced he would no longer come to the Cabinet. Northington, who retired through ill-health, was a hard drinker; being afflicted with gout he remarked that had he known his legs would one day carry a lord chancellor he'd have taken better care of them.

Sir Fletcher NORTON, Lord Grantley (1716–89) as solicitor-general prosecuted Wilkes (*qv*) in 1763 and in 1764 discounted the parliamentary resolution declaring that general warrants were illegal. Rockingham (*qv*) dismissed him and in 1770 the ministry made him Speaker of the House of Commons. He gradually adopted a more critical view of the executive, which led to his ejection from office by North (*qv*) in 1780 and his elevation to a peerage by Rockingham in 1782. He combined intelligence with offensive manners.

NUMA Pompilius, reckoned as the second king of Rome (*c*.715–673 BC by tradition), was the archetype of a great rise from humble beginnings. A variety of religious and cultural reforms were attributed to him, some of which were supposed to have been suggested by the nymph Egeria. There may be a grain of truth in some of the stories about him.

ORPHEUS is famed in Greek myth as a singer and musician, who may or may not have been a real person. Orphism was a religious movement which displayed a cosmogony and anthropology, of which our knowledge depends on late sources.

Henry PELHAM (1695–1754) held a variety of offices under Walpole (*qv*), after whose fall he gradually emerged as prime minister (holding office, with one brief intermission, to his death). His tenure, which was largely though not ungrudgingly upheld by his brother Newcastle (*qv*), rested upon Whiggery, the disposal or conciliation of eloquent rivals (as the elder Pitt (*qv*)) and royal favour.

PERICLES (*c*.495–429 BC) combined a policy of popular conciliation in Athens with assertiveness towards Sparta, maintaining a long eminence through character, intelligent policy and outstanding oratory.

PHILIP II (1527–98) succeeded to the Spanish possessions of his father Charles V (i.e. Spain and the Spanish Netherlands). He married four times and produced eight children. His reign was not marked by political prosperity.

Sir George PIGOT, Baron Pigot (1719–77) arrived in Madras in 1737 and was governor 1755–63, during which period he defeated the French. As governor once more from 1775 he found himself at odds with the council over the restoration of the raja of Tanjore. He was arrested and died in confinement. His brother Admiral Hugh PIGOT (1721?–1792) entered the navy as an able seaman and became an admiral in 1775. A Lord of the Admiralty in 1782 he was made admiral of the blue and succeeded Rodney in command of the West Indies the same year.

PISISTRATUS, tyrant of Athens, seized power (561 BC) after the reforms of Solon (*qv*), whose relative he was, and kept it, with intermissions, till his death in 527. He inaugurated Athens' vigorous foreign policy.

William PITT the elder (cr. Earl of Chatham, 1766) (1708–78) discovered great powers of oratory in his opposition to Walpole (*qv*). This was an indispensable part of managing the Commons and (despite George II's (*qv*) resentment of his remarks about Hanover), Pelham (*qv*) insisted on his inclusion in the government; and, more reluctantly, Newcastle (*qv*) found he could not do without him. His direction of affairs was distinguished by British success in the Seven Years' War; and his desire to continue the war made it possible to remove him. He took advantage of shifts in affairs to form a ministry in 1766, but ill-health supervened and from the beginning of 1767 he took only an occasional part in public business.

William PITT the younger (1759–1806) was the younger son of the elder Pitt (*qv*). Like his father he was an outstanding speaker, which helped him to become Chancellor of the Exchequer at twenty-three under Shelburne (*qv*). In default of a rival acceptable to the king, it also made him premier when George disposed of Fox and North (*qqv*) in 1783. Pitt thus became Britain's youngest prime minister and, as it turned out, its longest serving (1783–1801, 1804–06) if we except Walpole. His tenure was distinguished at first chiefly by parliamentary, financial and administrative skill and from 1793 by resistance to revolutionary France. Pitt died on the twenty-fifth anniversary of the day he had first entered Parliament.

PLATO (*c*.427–347 BC) occupies a central place in the history of philosophy as the first Greek thinker whose work survives *in extenso*. Plato's doctrines, which span theology, metaphysics, epistemology, ethics and other subjects, are expressed in a style of infinite variety which has always helped his fame. His political views, expressed most famously in his *Republic*, present a model which is anti-democratic in the broadest sense.

PLUTARCH (before AD 50–after 120) was a Greek man of letters whose work embraces rhetorica, moral philosophy, metaphysics, antiquarianism and biography. His best-known writings are the *Parallel Lives*, which pair the lives and characters of distinguished Greeks and

Romans in order to exemplify private virtue (and occasionally vice) in their careers.

Alexander POPE (1688–1744) developed the heroic couplet for use in satiric, didactic and translated poetry. As with Tennyson, the perfection of his versification and the extent of his sales were not matched by his talent for conceptual thought. Pope fell under the influence of Bolingbroke (*qv*).

William Cavendish-Bentinck, third duke of PORTLAND (1738–1809) as both the representative of the Bentincks, who had come to England with William III (*qv*), and more particularly as the son-in-law of Devonshire (*qv*) took his place amongst the followers of Rockingham (*qv*), in whose first ministry he served as Lord Chamberlain and in whose second he was lord lieutenant of Ireland. He presided over the coalition of Fox and North (*qqv*) as first lord of the Treasury, but broke with Fox over the French Revolution after 1792. He held office under the younger Pitt (*qv*), disliked Catholic emancipation and, when the ministry of the younger Grenville (*qv*) fell on this issue, formed an administration (1807) over which he presided till his death.

Richard PRICE (1723–91) was a dissenting minister who wrote on a variety of financial, political and philosophical questions. He advocated a reduction of the national debt in 1771, opposed the American war from 1776, being invited by Congress in 1778 to emigrate, and is best known as author of *A Review of the Principal Questions in Morals*.

Sir Walter RAWLEIGH or RALEGH (*c.*1554–1618) has a career which defies summary as courtier, statesman, seaman, soldier, chemist, historian, poet, philosopher and theologian; as Aubrey says, 'he was no Slug'. He was imprisoned and executed by James I as part of his repudiation of Elizabeth's (*qv*) consistently anti-Spanish policy.

RICHARD II (1367–1400) reigned 1377–99, a period distinguished by a poll tax rising, parliamentary scepticism about the king's high view of his prerogative and invasions of Ireland and Scotland. His subjects, like posterity, did not find Richard entirely attractive. He was dethroned (and probably murdered) by his cousin Henry of Lancaster (Henry IV).

George RICE (1724–79), a local magnate in Carmarthenshire, (where he held various offices from mayor to lord lieutenant, including MP) obtained leverage in high politics when he married the Lord Steward's daughter in 1761. From 1761 to 1770 he was at the Board of Trade and at North's (*qv*) suggestion became treasurer of the king's chamber in 1770, holding office until he died.

Charles Lennox (1735–1806), third duke of RICHMOND (succ. 1750) distinguished himself at Minden and became ambassador to Paris (1765) before becoming secretary of state in succession to Grafton (*qv*) (1766–67). He objected to the treatment of America. He re-entered office with Rockingham (*qv*) as master-general of the Ordnance in 1782 and stayed there until 1795.

Richard RIGBY (1722–88) served successively Bedford, Grenville and Grafton (*qqv*). His career embodied great and prosperous corruption.

William ROBERTSON (1721–93) prospered equally through religion and learning, advancing to fame and wealth as the historian of Scotland, England, India and Charles V and to power as Principal of Edinburgh University (1762–92) and Moderator of the General Assembly of the Church of Scotland (1763–90).

William Henry Zulestein de Nassau, 4th earl of ROCHFORD (1717–81) inherited Whig views and obtained a lord lieutenancy in 1756. Groom of the Stole at the death of George II (*qv*) he acquired, as was the custom, the furniture of the room in which the king expired: a charitable interpretation of this maxim provided him with a quilt which long served as an altar cloth in St Osyth's Church. Successively ambassador at Madrid (1763–6) and Paris (1766–8), where he suffered a good deal from the ministry's indecision, his career ended as secretary of state (1768–75).

Charles Watson-Wentworth, second Marquess of ROCKINGHAM (1730–82) was born at a time and commanded a fortune which made him a natural exponent of Whiggish scepticism about George III. Rockingham's loyalty to the dynasty was unimpeachable – as a fifteen-year-old he had joined the government forces against the Jacobites – and at an early age enjoyed royal favour under George II, acquiring two lord lieutenancies and a lordship of the bedchamber before he was twenty-two and becoming KG in 1760. Owing to his position he was regarded as a leading Whig: when Devonshire (*qv*) was struck off the privy council he resigned his position at court and shortly after was dismissed from his lieutenancies, along with Newcastle and Grafton (*qqv*). Thereafter, abundantly rich, he devoted himself to inserting his own views into government. Becoming Prime Minister in 1765 (though the king complained 'I thought that I had not two men in my bedchamber of less parts than Lord Rockingham'), he discovered his purposes thwarted by placemen whose first loyalty was to George III. Thereafter, he aimed to limit royal influence in parliament. With the failure of North (*qv*) in 1782 he had his opportunity, but died shortly after assuming power. Rockingham never held any political office except the premiership – a unique distinction.

John ROLLE (1756–1842) was an MP 1780–96, during which time he abused Burke over India and over his apparent patronage of two delinquent clerks as paymaster-general.

Jean-Jacques ROUSSEAU (1712–78) had a varied career as composer, private secretary and mendicant genius, in the intervals of which he wrote a variety of works outlining the ills of society and suggesting remedies, both personal and political. His *Du Contrat Social* (1762) is in many ways the first modern work of political theory.

Sir George SAVILE (1726–84) was Member for Yorkshire 1759–83 and a man of independent disposition whose views often coincided with those of Rockingham (*qv*). He introduced the *Nullum Tempus* bill in 1768, deprecated the use of force against the colonists in 1775 and supported economical reform 1779.

SCIPIO was the cognomen of a prominent part of the *gens* Cornelius. Its two most distinguished bearers were Publius Cornelius Scipio Africanus (236–184/3 BC), who was the victor of the second Punic War, repeatedly defeating the Carthiginians in Spain and finally vanquishing them at Zama in North Africa (202), and his adoptive son Publius Cornelius Scipio Aemilianus Africanus Numantinus (185/4–129 BC) who defeated the Carthiginians in the third (and final) Punic War, sacking Carthage in 146. He subsequently defeated Numantia (133), having held a then-unprecedented second consulship.

Major John SCOTT (1747–1819) entered the service of the East India Company, *c.*1766, rose in the Bengal army and became ADC to Hastings (*qv*) in 1778. He was sent to England by Hastings in 1781 to act as his agent, but his injudicious zeal helped to precipitate impeachment. He used his pen and his position in Parliament (MP, 1784–93) to defend his patron from Burke's attacks. He assumed the name of Scott-Waring in 1798.

SEMIRAMIS in Greek legend was the wife of Ninus (*qv*) after whose death she ruled Assyria for many years, building Babylon and indulging in extensive wars. The historical figure behind this story may be Sammuramat, wife of the Assyrian monarch Shamshi-Adad V and regent (810–805 BC) during the minority of her son.

SESOSTRIS was a mythical king of Egypt, to whom are ascribed extensive conquests in Africa and Asia. His story, like so much else, is told at diffuse length by Herodotus.

William Petty Fitzmaurice (1737–1805), second earl of SHELBURNE and subsequently (1784) first Marquess of Lansdowne rose rapidly in politics thanks to his wealth and military reputation. His career commenced under the auspices of Bute (*qv*) and then George Grenville (*qv*), but he next attached himself to the elder Pitt (*qv*). He left Grafton's ministry (*qv*), opposing the use of force against America. After Pitt's death he succeeded to the leadership of his small following. He entered Rockingham's second ministry (*qv*) as secretary of state. He quarrelled with Fox (*qv*), who after Rockingham's death refused to serve under Shelburne when George III (*qv*) invited the latter to form a ministry. Shelburne's premiership ended when he resigned, unable to form a coalition (with either Fox or North (*qqv*)) adequate to maintain a Commons majority. Shelburne, who inspired distrust, was known as 'the Jesuit of Berkeley Square'. The younger Pitt (*qv*) promoted him in the peerage but denied him office.

Richard Brinsley SHERIDAN (1751–1816) had a dual career as writer and politician. Author of comedies from 1773 he acquired the ownership of Drury Lane theatre. When this burnt down in 1809 Sheridan was observed drinking and was heard to ask whether a man couldn't take a glass of wine at his own fireside. MP from 1780, he was Fox's (*qv*) under-secretary in 1782. His speech against Hastings (*qv*) in 1787 lasted nearly six hours. He upheld the French Revolution and was treasurer of the navy in 1806–7.

SOCRATES (469–399 BC) seems to have been interested in science in his early life, but later preferred to inquire into the right conduct of life, carried on by the method of cross-questioning those whom he met. Since this seems to have involved the deflation in public of many prominent men who had a high opinion of themselves, it was not unnatural that Socrates should be indicted (on the charge of corrupting the young). He refused to conciliate the jury, rejected plans for escape and was condemned to death. In effect he has been canonized as a martyr to free inquiry. The significance of his contribution to thought is a matter of debate.

SOLON (fl. *c.*600 BC) was an Athenian statesman and poet, who composed a code of laws which stabilized the political condition of Athens by economic measures, reformed the constitution and softened the penal code.

John Somers, first Baron SOMERS (1651–1716) rose from being a small attorney to the lord chancellorship. A stout Whig, he presided over the committee which formulated the Declaration of Rights. He was successively solicitor and attorney-general, obtaining the woolsack in 1697. He enjoyed the confidence of William III (*qv*) more than any other Englishman, but was forced to retire by parliamentary pressure in 1700. Under Queen Anne (*qv*) he devoted himself to furthering the Hanoverian succession and to the Union of England and Scotland.

Lucius Cornelius SULLA Felix (*c.*138–78 BC) after a youth distinguished by sexual, financial and military success became the most aggressive representative of Optimate views at Rome. He succeeded in maintaining the military command assigned to him against the will of the tribune Sulpicius through the simple expedients of murder and intimidation, waged war against Rome's enemies, exploited her eastern provinces, invaded Italy and established military rule in his own favour. He then increased the constitutional strength of the Optimates, massacred his opponents and retired serenely to private life.

Maximilien de Bethune, duc de SULLY (1559–1641) held a variety of offices in finance and warfare under Henry IV of France, whose trusted counsellor he was. He produced a plan for general peace at the end of his life.

Charles Spencer, third earl of SUNDERLAND (1674–1722) was distinguished alike as bibliophile and politician. Son-in-law of

Marlborough (*qv*), but renowned particularly as a Whig. Having held high office he was dismissed in 1710 and spent the next few years acquiring an influence in Hanover which stood him in good stead: after George I's accession in 1714 he returned to power, but was ousted by Walpole (*qv*) in 1721.

THEMISTOCLES (*c.*528–462 BC) was a successful party politician, who succeeded in manoeuvring Athens into building a large battle fleet and gaining command of it. In co-operation with Sparta, he forced the Persians to battle at Artemisium, thus exposing them to storm damage on the Thessalian coast, and defeated them decisively at Salamis. Subsequently power in Athens passed to his opponents; having retreated to the Peloponnese, Themistocles became suspect at Sparta and eventually fled to Asia, where he ended his life in an ironic posture – as governor of a Persian province.

THESEUS, the hero of Athens, distinguished himself by dealing with Minos (*qv*), succeeded his father as a local king and brought about the union of Attica into one state, with Athens as its capital.

Edward Thurlow (1731–1806), Baron THURLOW (cr. 1778) rose in the law by boldness and in politics by using the law to uphold the executive. He supported Wilkes' (*qv*) expulsion and the war with America. He was rewarded successively with the offices of solicitor-general (1770–71), attorney-general (1771–78) and lord chancellor (1778–83, 1783–92). He was a king's friend, but primarily his own.

TIBERIUS Julius Caesar Augustus (42 BC–AD 37) was the son of Ti. Claudius Nero and Livia. The latter's re-marriage to the Emperor Augustus placed Tiberius at the centre of the imperial family, but he succeeded as emperor only because Augustus' preferred candidates all died. His policy was marked by caution and financial rectitude, but disfigured by treason trials.

Matthew TINDAL (1653?–1733) held a variety of religious opinions, culminating in deism. He was a fellow of All Souls' (1678–1733) and won arguments at High Table because, though he ate much, he drank little. His most famous work was *Christianity as Old as the Creation* (1730).

TITUS Flavius Vespasianus (AD 39–81) was the elder son of Vespasian (*qv*), under whom he served in Judaea (capturing Jerusalem in 70) and succeeded as emperor in 79. His short principate was marked by the same affability that had characterized his father's; but Titus was succeeded by his less amiable brother Domitian.

John TOLAND (1670–1722) is said to have been the son of a Catholic priest and revenged the indignity upon Christian belief with his *Christianity not Mysterious* (1696), whose tendency is deist. Its notoriety enabled him to earn his living by his pen. Toland wrote his own epitaph: *Ipse vero aeturnum est resurrectus, et idem Tolandus nunquam.*

Charles TOWNSHEND (1725–67) first attained office in 1748 and rose smoothly until 1763, when Grenville (*qv*) refused to countenance his terms for accepting the Admiralty. But Townshend's talents as an orator made him too dangerous to neglect; Grenville re-employed him and he kept office under Rockingham (*qv*), though doing nothing for the ministry. He became chancellor of the exchequer under the elder Pitt (*qv*) in 1766, imposed unpopular revenue duties on America to provide Britain with income and promptly died.

M. Ulpius Traianus, known to posterity as TRAJAN (AD 53–117) was a popular general whom the emperor Nerva adopted as his son and successor. Trajan's foreign policy was marked by vigorous action in Dacia and Parthia. His administration was strict and seems to have been popular. He was succeeded by his adoptive son, M. Antoninus Pius.

T. Flavius Vespasianus (AD 9–79), known to history as VESPASIAN, rose steadily in a senatorial and military career, eventually being sent to Judaea by Nero (*qv*) in 67 to subdue the Jewish rebellion. Vespasian turned to advantage the large army this gave him after Nero's dethronement, to which he added the support of the Danubian legions, becoming emperor in 69. He restored discipline to Rome's armies, was financially prudent and popular with the Senate. Tacitus remarks that he was the only man improved by becoming emperor.

Sir Robert WALPOLE (1676–1745), first earl of Orford (1742) began his political career under Queen Anne, holding office as a Whig and being imprisoned at Tory behest. The accession of George I and the mistakes of Bolingbroke (*qv*) established the Whigs in power: the question was, which Whigs would enjoy it. Walpole and his brother-in-law Townshend, after early reverses, succeeded in ousting Sunderland (*qv*) and for twenty-one years (1721–42) Walpole was first lord of the treasury and chancellor of the exchequer. He succeeded in conciliating the court (winning over George I, George II and the latter's wife Caroline), managing the Commons (withdrawing unpopular measures, as his Excise Bill of 1733) and conciliating or ousting would-be rivals. By the end of the 1730s, however, his range of personal adversaries was wide enough to make withdrawal prudent. Walpole is reckoned conventionally as Britain's first prime minister and, if this may be misleading, it is certainly a tribute to his virtuosity. Henry Pelham (*qv*) emerged as the heir to his combination of Court and Whig support.

John WILKES (1727–97), libertine and FRS, was in politics originally a supporter of the elder Pitt (*qv*) and began a persecution of Bute (*qv*) in *The North Briton*. The government attempted to arrest him under a general warrant, a procedure whose whole validity then came to be questioned. Wilkes escaped by claiming privilege as an MP. Attempts were made to have him expelled, which succeeded on a technicality. The electors of Middlesex, however, returned him repeatedly as their member. He succeeded finally in taking his seat in 1774, after which he maintained his popularity in the city.

WILLIAM III (1650–1702) was the son of William II, Prince of Orange, and Mary, daughter of Charles I of England: his career reflects these two facts. He first established his sway not only over his hereditary principality but over the whole of the Netherlands. His next task was to defend Holland against the encroachments of Louis XIV (*qv*). Although he married his cousin Mary, daughter of the future James II (*qv*) and niece of Charles II (*qv*) he was not always successful in winning England's support. However in 1688–9 he was able to take advantage of James' unpopularity to oust him and succeeded in being crowned as monarch jointly with Mary. William expelled James from Ireland, being victorious at the Boyne (1690), and repelled an invasion attempt (1692). He was able to bend Britain's resources against Louis. William, although not especially partial to Whigs, figured retrospectively in their pantheon as the chief agent in the Revolution of 1688.

XERXES, king of Persia (reigned 486–465 BC) inherited from his father Darius the task of attacking Greece (in revenge for the Greeks' support of the Ionian revolt). Setting out in 480 he met with success – winning the naval battle of Artemisium, forcing the pass of Thermopylae, laying waste to Attica and forcing the Greeks back to the Isthmus of Corinth – until his navy was defeated at Salamis by Themistocles. Their supplies cut off, the Persians had to retreat to Asia. After his defeats Xerxes retired to his harem.

Bibliography

This list of books and articles covers studies of the matters discussed above, but is also intended to introduce the reader to scholarly writings on Burke's life and thought before 1790. In particular it lists both interpretative monographs on his thought and books and articles about his political career.

Life

There is an agreeable biography by Stanley Ayling, *Edmund Burke* (1988). The fullest study of Burke's life, Carl B. Cone, *The Life and Thought of Edmund Burke*, 2 vols. (1959–64), is in every sense a weightier production. Isaac Kramnick, *The Rage of Edmund Burke: Portrait of an Ambivalent Conservative* (1977) entertains without precisely enlightening. Alice P. Miller, *Edmund Burke and His World* (1979) offers a popular introduction. A.P.I. Samuels, *The Life, Correspondence and Early Writings of . . . Edmund Burke* (1923) prints much valuable material (including Burke's contributions to *The Reformer*), but should be used with caution on the Lucas controversy (see G.L. Vincintorio, 'Edmund Burke and Charles Lucas', *Proceedings of the Modern Language Association*, 68 (1953), pp. 1,047–55). John Morley, *Burke* (1882) is the best Victorian life and still repays attention. James Prior, *The Life of . . . Edmund Burke* (best edn is the second, 1826) is a compilation of very uneven value, but contains some information from sources no longer available. T.W. Copeland, *Our Eminent Friend Edmund Burke: Six Essays* (1949) has interesting matter on several aspects. Francis Canavan, 'Edmund Burke's College Study of Philosophy', *Notes and Queries* n.s. 4 (1957), pp. 538–43, and R.B.

McDowell and D.A. Webb, *Trinity College, Dublin* (1982) contain useful material relating to his early life.

General

Readers can take their pick amongst a variety of interpretations, most of which would have surprised Burke. The one concentrating on natural law is represented by Peter Stanlis, *Edmund Burke and the Natural Law* (1953), F.P. Canavan, *The Political Reason of Edmund Burke* (1960), and B.T. Wilkins, *The Problem of Burke's Political Philosophy* (1967), some of which bear the impress of Leo Strauss, *Natural Right and History* (1953). Canavan's book is the subtlest of the three. For the view that Burke was a utilitarian, see John Morley, *Burke: A Critical Study* (1867), Alfred Cobban, *Edmund Burke and the Revolt against the Eighteenth Century*[2] (1960), F.J.C. Hearnshaw 'Edmund Burke', pp. 72–99 of Hearnshaw (ed.), *The Social and Political Ideas of Some Representative Thinkers of the Revolutionary Era* (1931), and J.R. Dinwiddy, 'Natural Law and Utility in Burke's Thought', *Studies in Burke and his Time*, 16 (1974), pp. 105–28. For Burke as a bourgeois, see Kramnick's *Rage* and C.B. Macpherson, *Burke* (1980), but compare Ruth Bevan, *Marx and Burke* (1973); and for him as a conservative, see Geoffrey Butler, *The Tory Tradition* (1913), and Russell Kirk, *The Conservative Mind* (1953). For the views of J.G.A. Pocock, see his *The Ancient Constitution and the Feudal Law*[2] (1986) (compare Gisela Schell, 'Englisches Rechstdenken im Werk Edmund Burkes', PhD thesis, Frankurt-am-Main, 1955), *Politics, Language and Time* (1972), *Virtue, Commerce and History* (1985), and his edition of *Reflections* (1988). For Burke as a rather protean figure, see Frank O'Gorman *Edmund Burke: His Political Philosophy* (1973), which is to be contrasted with Charles Parkin, *The Moral Basis of Burke's Political Thought* (1956). Gertrude Himmelfarb, appropriately in the light of her view of J.S. Mill, is herself in two minds: see her *Victorian Minds* (1968), pp. 4–31. There is commentary on some of this literature in Paul Lucas, 'On Edmund Burke's Doctrine of Prescription', *Historical Journal*, 11 (1968) pp. 35–63, and F.A. Dreyer *Burke's Politics* (1979). John MacCunn, *The Political Philosophy of Burke* (1913), despite age and political ingenuousness, retains its value.

For some instructive monographs, see amongst literary studies J.T. Boulton, *The Language of Politics in the Age of Burke and Wilkes* (1963),

Paul Fussell, *The Rhetorical World of Augustan Humanism* (1965), Gerald W. Chapman, *Edmund Burke: The Practical Imagination* (1967) and Christopher Reid, *Edmund Burke and the Practice of Political Writing* (1985); for Burke and the enlightenment, see C.P. Courtney, *Montesquieu and Burke* (1963) and his 'Edmund Burke and the Enlightenment', pp. 304–22 of Anne Whiteman *et al.* (eds.), *Statesmen, Scholars and Merchants* (1973). For the question of representation, see James Hogan, *Election and Representation* (1945), pp. 157–203, Hannah F. Pitkin, *The Concept of Representation* (1967), L.S. Sutherland, 'Edmund Burke and the Relationship between Members of Parliament and Their Constituents', *Studies in Burke and his Time*, 10 (1968), pp. 1,005–21, and, more generally, H. Wellenreuther, *Representation und Grossgrundbesitz in England 1730–1770* (1979), and Paul Langford 'Property and "Virtual Representation" in Eighteenth-Century England', *Historical Journal*, 31 (1988), pp. 83–115. Burke is bracketed with Rousseau in A.M. Osborn, *Rousseau and Burke* (1940), and treated more soberly in D.R. Cameron, *The Social Thought of Rousseau and Burke* (1973). H.-G. Schumann, *Edmund Burkes Anschauungen vom Gleichgewicht in Staat und Staatensystem* (1964) studies Burke's view of balance in the state and between states.

Early Works

There is less than there might be about Burke's two earliest works. Murray Rothbard, 'A Note on Burke's *Vindication of Natural Society*', *Journal of History of Ideas*, 19 (1958), pp. 113–18 was challenged by J.C. Weston Jr., 'The Ironic Purpose of Burke's *Vindication* Vindicated', in the same journal, 19 (1958), pp. 435–41. R.B. Sewall Jr. wrote effectively about 'Rousseau's Second Discourse in England from 1755 to 1762', *Philological Quarterly*, 17 (1938), pp. 97–114. Burke's *Philosophical Enquiry* is well served by J.T. Boulton's introduction to his edition (1958; second edition, 1987) and its relation to his political thought less strikingly in Neal Wood, 'The Aesthetic Dimension of Burke's Political Thought', *Journal of British Studies*, 4 (1964), pp. 41–64. Something can be gleaned from general studies of aesthetics, as in S.H. Monk, *The Sublime* (1935), esp. pp. 84–100; W.J. Bate, *From Classic to Romantic* (1946); W.J. Hipple *The Beautiful, The Sublime and The Picturesque in Eighteenth-Century British Aesthetic Theory* (1957), esp. pp. 83–98; M.H. Nicholson, *Mountain*

Gloom and Mountain Glory (1959); and J. Cohn and T.H. Miles, 'The Sublime', *Modern Philology*, 74 (1977), pp. 289–304; and from the detailed treatments in V.M. Bevilacqua, 'Two Newtonian Arguments Concerning Taste', *Philological Quarterly*, 46 (1968), pp. 585–90; Paul Gottfried 'Kunst und Politik bei Burke und Novalis', *Zeitschrift für Aesthetik und allgemeine Kunstwissenschaft*, 19 (1974), pp. 240–51; Barbara Oliver, 'Edmund Burke's "Enquiry" and the Baroque Theory of the Passions', *Studies in Burke and his Time*, 12 (1970), pp. 1,661–76; Dixon Wecter, 'Burke's Theory of Words, Images and Emotions', *Publications of the Modern Language Association*, 55 (1940), pp. 167–81; and H.A. Wichelns, 'Burke's Essay on the Sublime and its Reviewers', *Journal of English and Germanic Philology*, 21 (1922), pp. 645–61. Burke's view of religion is considered by Jeffrey Hart and H.C. Mansfield, who offer argument, counter-argument and reply in 'Burke and Pope on Christianity', *Burke Newsletter*, 8 (1967), pp. 702–13; 'Burke on Christianity', *Studies in Burke and his Time*, 9 (1968–69), pp. 864–65; and 'Burke and Christianity', *ibid* pp. 866–7.

Ireland

The fullest and most sober general treatment is T.H.D. Mahony *Edmund Burke and Ireland* (1960). There are two stimulating essays on Burke as an Irishman by Conor Cruise O'Brien in his introductions to Ref and IA. For Ireland itself, T.W. Moody *et al.* (eds.), *A New History of Ireland: Eighteenth Century Ireland* (1985), and T. Bartlett and D.W. Hayton (eds.) *Penal Era and Golden Age: Essays in Irish History 1690–1800* (1979) are in different ways standard works. R.B. McDowell's *Ireland in the Age of Imperialism and Revolution 1760–1801* (1979) provides a massive account, whilst E.M. Johnston, *Ireland in the Eighteenth Century*[2] (1980) offers a manageable survey. Much can be learnt about Irish society from L.M. Cullen's *An Economic History of Ireland since 1660* (1972) and his *The Emergence of Modern Ireland 1600–1900* (1981). J.C. Beckett, *A Short History of Ireland*[6] (1979) and R.F. Foster, *A History of Modern Ireland 1660–1972* (1988) offer introductions on different scales.

For Burke's views on religious toleration, see especially Ursula Henriques, *Religious Toleration in England 1787–1833* (1961), ch. 4, and F.A. Dreyer, 'Burke's Religion', *Studies in Burke and his Time*, 17 (1976), pp. 199–212.

England

There is some matter on the *Abridgement* in J.C. Weston Jr., 'Edmund Burke's view of History', *Review of Politics*, 23 (1961), pp. 203–29, and more in R.J. Smith's important *The Gothic Bequest* (1987).

English history in the period is well treated in Paul Langford, *A Polite and Commercial People: England 1727–1783* (1990), which lays an accent on contemporary society and has a chapter on the constitution. More exclusively focussed on politics are J. Steven Watson, *The Age of George III, 1760–1820* (1960), and Ian Christie, *Wars and Revolutions: Britain 1760–1815* (1982). For a collection of essays on the period, see Jeremy Black (ed.), *British Politics and Society from Walpole to Pitt, 1742–89* (1990).

The Present Discontents are usually considered with an emphasis on party, as in John Brewer, 'Party and the Double Cabinet: Two Facets of Burke's *Thoughts*', *Historical Journal*, 14 (1971), pp. 479–501; Harvey C. Mansfield, *Statesmanship and Party Government* (1965); Frank O'Gorman, 'Party and Burke: The Rockingham Whigs', *Government and Opposition*, 3 (1967), pp. 92–119, and in his *The Rise of Party in England: The Rockingham Whigs, 1760–1782* (1975). For two literary studies, see Donald C. Bryant, 'Burke's *Present Discontents*', *Quarterly Journal of Speech*, 42 (1956), pp. 115–26, and J.J. Fitzgerald, 'The Logical Style of Burke's *Thoughts*', *Burke Newsletter*, 7 (1965), pp. 465–78. For contemporary views of party, see (e.g.) Marie Peters, ' "Names and Cant": Party Labels in English Political Propaganda, *c.*1755–1765', *Parliamentary History*, 3 (1984), pp. 103–27, and P.D.G. Thomas, 'Sir Roger Newdigate's Essays on Party, *c.*1760', *English Historical Review*, 102 (1987), pp. 394–400.

On Rockingham, his party and its fortunes, see Albemarle, *Memoirs of the Marquess of Rockingham and his Contemporaries*, 2 vols. (1852); R.J.S. Hoffman, *The Marquis: A Study of Lord Rockingham, 1730–1782* (1973); D.H. Watson, 'The Rise of the Opposition at Wildman's Club', *Bulletin of the Institute of Historical Research*, 44 (1971), pp. 55–77, and, more particularly, L.S. Sutherland, 'Edmund Burke and the First Rockingham Ministry', *English Historical Review*, 47 (1932), pp. 46–72; Paul Langford, *The First Rockingham Administration, 1765–1766* (1973) and above all his introduction to WSEB II (1981).

This bibliography does not pretend to deal with English politics in general, but works not specifically about Burke throw much light on him. Chief amongst these are John Brooke, *The Chatham Administration* (1956) and *George III* (1972); Herbert Butterfield, *George III and the Historians* (1957); John Cannon, *The Fox-North Coalition* (1969) and his *Aristocratic Century* (1984); Ian Christie, *The End of North's Ministry, 1780–82* (1958), *Myth and Reality in Late-Eighteenth Century British Politics* (1970), esp. pp. 27–54, 109–32 and 296–310; and three later articles by the same hand: 'George III and the Historians – Thirty Years On', *History* 71 (1986), pp. 205–21; 'Party in Politics in the Age of Lord North's Administration', *Parliamentary History*, 6 (1987), pp. 47–68, and 'The Composition of the Opposition in 1784', *Parliamentary History* 7 (1990), pp. 50–77; E.A. Smith, *Whig Principles and Party Politics* (1975); Richard Pares, *King George III and the Politicians* (1954), and some of the essays in his *The Historian's Business* (1961); John Derry, *The Whigs and the Regency Crisis* (1963) and his *Charles James Fox* (1972); and John Ehrman, *The Younger Pitt*, vol. 1 (1969).

With especial reference to Burke there is, B.W. Hill, 'Fox and Burke: The Whig party and the Question of Principles, 1784–1789', *English Historical Review*, 89 (1974), pp. 1–24; D.L. Keir, 'Economical Reform, 1779–1787', *Law Quarterly Review*, 30 (1934), pp. 368–85; N.C. Phillips, 'Edmund Burke and the County Movement, 1779–1780', *English Historical Review*, 76 (1961), pp. 254–78; E.A. Reitan, 'Edmund Burke and the Civil List', *Burke Newsletter* 7 (1966), pp. 604–618, and Caroline Robbins, 'Edmund Burke's Rationale of Cabinet Government', *Burke Newsletter*, 7 (1965), pp. 457–65.

America

Bernard Donoghue, *British Politics and the American Revolution* (1964), does a better job for its period than C.R. Ritcheson, *British Politics and the American Revolution, 1763–1783* (1954). See also G.H. Gutteridge *English Whiggism and the American Revolution* (1942). P.D.G. Thomas offers careful surveys of *The Stamp Act Crisis* (1975) and *The Townshend Duties Crisis* (1987), which together form the best history of the British response to the colonial question, 1763–73. Paul Langford effectively debunks the Rockinghams in 'The Rockingham Whigs and America', in Whiteman (ed.), *Statesmen, Scholars and Mer-*

chants, pp. 135–52. See also his 'Old Whigs, Old Tories and the American Revolution', *Journal of Imperial and Commonwealth History*, 8 (1980). On Burke's connection with Bristol, see Peter Underdown, *Bristol and Burke* (1961), with references to his earlier articles, and Ian Christie, 'Henry Cruger and the End of Edmund Burke's Connection with Bristol', *Transactions of the Bristol and Gloucestershire Archaeological Society*, 74 (1955), pp. 153–70. Burke's work as a colonial agent is examined usefully by R.J.S. Hoffman, *Edmund Burke: New York Agent* (1955).

India

Lucy S. Sutherland, *The East India Company in Eighteenth–Century Politics* (1952) remains central, as does K.N. Chaudhuri, *The Trading World of Asia and the English East India Company 1660–1760* (1978). P.J. Marshall, *Bengal the British Bridgehead* (1988) and, on a wider canvas, C.A. Bayly, *Indian Society and the Making of the British Empire* (1988) represent more recent work. See also L.S. Sutherland and J.A. Woods, 'The East India Speculations of William Burke', *Proceedings of the Leeds Philosophical and Literary Society*, 11 (1966), pp. 183–216. There is much of interest in R. Guha, *A Rule of Property for Bengal* (1963). For parallels between Ireland and India, see R. Janes, 'High-Flying', *Bulletin of Research in the Humanities* 82 (1979), pp. 185–89. S.K. Sen (ed.), *Edmund Burke on Indian Economy* (1969) should not be overlooked. A number of works by P.J. Marshall are vital to understanding Burke on India, especially his *Impeachment of Warren Hastings* (1965), *East India Fortunes* (1976) and his introduction to WSEB v (1981). Hastings' story is told at length in G.R. Gleig, *Memoirs of . . . Warren Hastings*, 3 vols. (1841) and with more literary grace by Keith Feiling, *Warren Hastings* (1954).

France

For Burke's isolation in his party, see L.G. Mitchell, *Charles James Fox and the Disintegration of the Whig Party, 1782–1794* (1971) and his introduction to WSEB viii (1989). See also Albert Goodwin, 'The Political Genesis of Edmund Burke's *Reflections*', *Bulletin of the John Rylands Library*, 50 (1968), pp. 336–64, and F.A. Dreyer, 'The Genesis of Burke's *Reflections*', *Journal of Modern History*, 50 (1978), pp. 462–79. For the question of why Britain lacked a revolution, see Ian Christie, *Stress and Stability in Late Eighteenth-Century Britain* (1984).

The present work ends in early 1790. For the remainder of Burke's life, much material is contained in Frank O'Gorman, *The Whig Party and the French Revolution* (1967); Peter Burley, *Witness to the Revolution: British and American Dispatches from France, 1788–1794* (1988); Seamus Deane, *The French Revolution and Enlightenment in England, 1789–1832* (1988); and H. T. Dickinson (ed.), *Britain and the French Revolution, 1789–1815* (1989). Those with a liking for secondary literature will be satisfied by Clara I. Gandy and Peter J. Stanlis, *Edmund Burke: A Bibliography of Secondary Studies to 1982* (1983), whose annotations should be treated with scepticism whenever Stanlis' own views are engaged.

'An Extempore Commonplace on The Sermon of Our Saviour on the Mount'

Introduction

The Sermon on the Mount is at the centre of Christian worship and morality. It contains both the Lord's prayer and the injunction to love not only neighbours but also enemies. Thus it makes a distinct statement about both Tables of the law.[1] However, it was less the content of Christian revelation than its moral standing which was the concern of Burke's time.

The deists argued that God's moral character could not be reconciled with the partial distribution of revelation. The standing assumption was that revelation was necessary to salvation. But as it was diffused slowly over time and that to only a few countries, it followed that the means of salvation were not available to all mankind – in fact, to a few only. If one wished to suggest that God was fair to everyone, it followed that revelation, at best, was superfluous to salvation. As one writer put it:

---

[1] The Ten Commandments were divided traditionally into Two Tables. The First Table grouped the commandments relating to the worship of God, whilst the Second concerned duties towards man. The two were summarized as 'love God; and thy neighbour as thyself', denoting respectively worship and morality. The acts of both Tables were supposed to be acceptable in God's sight only if they were truly manifestations of the disposition of love that their surface implied.

it has been demanded of me, Whether I should be convinc'd of my Opinion, and admit of supernatural Religion, in case the Gospel a supernatural Religion had been promulgated to all the World? I answer'd, I should; and was contented that the whole stress of the Dispute should be terminated in that one point.[2]

If revelation was irrelevant, what was offered as a substitute? The complement of deist criticism was the assertion that what man could discover through his own reason, unassisted by revelation, was sufficient for his salvation. Thus, deism implied an assessment of reason.

This assessment was not merely theoretical, but also practical. It was not merely the possibilities of reason, but also its actual achievements, which mattered. For if reason had been unable to provide for man's purposes as a matter of fact, it would not excel revelation by the very standard of sufficiency the deists had proposed. Joseph Butler made the point generally in his *Analogy of Religion*, which argued that the defects of revelation were paralleled by those of reason. The point could also be made particularly, by observing how little the ancients had been able to do for religion and morality before the coming of Christ or that reason's achievements were intellectually above most people's use.[3]

Burke took a low view of deism. A little after he gave his speech, he decided that some of its exponent really aimed their criticisms against all religion and morality.[4] It was natural for him to argue the superiority of Christianity over the pagans. That he should dwell on the moral efficiency of Christ's message, rather than its other features, reflects the terms of the controversy. But if the arguments were not novel, they show the allegiance Burke would soon develop in a more striking way.

[2] *The Miscellaneous Works of Charles Blount* (1695), p. 210.

[3] Joseph Butler, *The Analogy of Religion to the Constitution and Course of Nature* (1736). For heathen morality, see (e.g.) John Locke, *The Reasonableness of Christianity* (1695), pp. 265–73, and, for an Irish example, the '*Introduction* concerning the *mistaken Notions* which the *Heathens* had of the DEITY, and the *Defects* in their MORALITY, whence the *Usefulness* of REVELATION may appear' that John Maxwell prefixed to his translation of Richard Cumberland's *A Treatise of the Laws of Nature* (1727).

[4] He wrote of Dublin in April, 1748 that 'there are a set of Men not infrequent in this City, who tho' they allow of Morality, cry down reveal'd Religion, yet in their Practice, they make them equal, neglecting both' (Samuels, p. 323).

An Extempore Commonplace on The Sermon of Our Saviour on the Mount

Mr. Burke orderd to make an extempore common-place on the Sermon of our Saviour on the mount –

Taken occasion to observe how much the Christian morality [excels][1] the Best heathen by refining our passions, not only our acts[2] but their spring, the heart, our divine physician heals the corrupted source, the others but surgeons tampering wth the outward sores. very defective in that, when we stand in two grand relations the one to Society & the other to our Creator – it only teaches the first. that nothing Was better for Society. & that this its excellent policy insted of being an objection[3] to it, was one of the greatest proofs of its divinity. that the Heathens even the wisest & best were employ'd a long time in searching what was good or Virtue & consequently lost a good deal of practice – that ye most learned were much puzzled in their enquiry & the ignorant could know nothing at all. But the Gospel by subsituting faith wch the most ignorant can have gives us the preceptor & leaves us immediately to the practice. that the morality inculcated in this ecellent sermon conduced so admirably to the improvement of society that had its rules been observed we should have a heaven upon earth. but since men are so wicked that this cannot be those who do may be sure of finding it in a better place.

---

[1] **[excels]**   Samuels reads the verb as 'exceeds', but the MS. is scarcely legible
[2] **acts**   MS. very faint, but there does not seem to be room for Samuels' reading 'actions'
[3] **an objection**   'an obj' very faint

3

A Vindication of Natural Society

Introduction

Burke's first extended publication has baffled commentators over two centuries. For Thomas Burgh it was a juvenile squib.[1] To William Godwin, who exploited its material for his own ends, it was 'a treatise in which the evils of the existing political institutions are displayed . . . while the intention of the author was to show that these evils were to be considered as trivial', whilst to Lord Wedgwood it offered 'arguments against authority'.[2] To the less engaged mind of Sir George Clark it was 'an ironical book which still puzzles commentators who try to interpret its purpose'.[3] The work, viewed by itself, is evidently not easy to interpret.

Its purpose is more readily intelligible if we recollect Burke's position on religion and society. Deism, which he had rejected, suggested that revelation was inessential to the divine economy because its benefits were confined to a limited section of mankind. If we set this objection in a general form we have: any state of affairs whose goods are distributed irregularly lacks a properly divine warrant. *A Vindication* applies the formula to the social order. In particular it suggests

---

[1] Comment in Burgh's copy of VNS (Dublin, 1757), now in Cambridge University Library.

[2] William Godwin, *Enquiry concerning Political Justice*, ed. I. Kramnick (1976), I.ii, p. 88; Josiah Wedgwood and Allan Nevins, *Forever Freedom* (1940), p. 82.

[3] G.N. Clark, *The Wealth of England from 1496 to 1760* (1946), p. 188 who, unlike Godwin, notes Burke's concern at economic misery.

4

that political and social hierarchy – in the language of the piece *Subordination* – was responsible for man's ills.

Burke's argument is usually described as whimsical or ironical. It focusses upon the *reductio ad absurdum* of a single assumption, namely the sufficiency of nature. Deism suggested that man's natural faculties sufficed for his salvation and that revelation was superfluous or, indeed, an opportunity for evil.[4] Burke's piece looks to the consequences of applying the same assumption to society. It treats man's natural state as pre-political and finds the source of his misfortunes in government. For instance, just as the deists preferred natural theology to positive, so the piece prefers the claims of the state of nature (the natural society of the title) to those of civil (or 'artificial') society.

What was the occasion of Burke's interest? It lies in two events. The first was the publication of Bolingbroke's *Works* in March 1754. This was a literary event, for Bolingbroke's political stature and his intellectual association with Pope had bred high expectations. Burke was well-read in Pope and felt drawn to literature (rather than the law which he was supposed to be studying in the Middle Temple). That Bolingbroke in the event had rehashed the deism Burke disliked must have turned interest into opposition.

This intellectual distance involves no difference over the social order. Bolingbroke in fact asserted 'the justice of providence'.[5] This is compatible in itself with the hopes Burke had invested in the social order when at Trinity. Burke, indeed, may have been considering what to say about it in the *Philosophical Enquiry* which he had meditated for some years. Just as the distribution of revelation was skewed, so the order of society would be unequal. Whence, then, the *Vindication*'s emphasis on subordination? It lies partly in that Bolingbroke had pointedly denied the operation of a particular providence. If he asserted the justice of providence it was only general providence which he had chosen,

> I chuse rather to insist on the constant, visible, and undeniable course of a general providence which is sufficient for the purpose, than to assume a dispensation of particular providences . . . The truth is that we have not in philosophical specu-

---

[4] For the evils of priests, Charles Blount, *Religio laici* (1683), p. 25, John Toland, *Nazarenus* (1718), p. 70, Anthony Collins, *Priestcraft in Perfection* (1710), p. 46; the examples could be multiplied indefinitely.

[5] Bolingbroke, *Works*, v, p. 414.

lation, in any history except that of the Bible, nor in our own
experience, sufficient grounds to establish the doctrine of particular providences, and to reconcile it with that of a general
providence.[6]

This allowed one to suppose that the particular shape of the social
order was not an instrument in God's design. The other source of
Burke's emphasis was that someone explored just that avenue of
subversive thought.

The year after Bolingbroke's *Works* appeared, social inequality was
stigmatized with a force which has resonated to the present day.
Rousseau's *Discourse on the origin and foundation of inequality* identified
a decline in man's moral standing and happiness throughout his
progress – or rather, decline from a pre-political state to modern
European society. The cause of the decline was the establishment of a
graduated social order. So, like the deists, Rousseau displayed nature
(or, to be precise, a state of society without government) as his basis
and found that deviation from it was unfortunate.

Of course, this was the inversion of Burke's position. He had
already identified government and the social order as potentially
beneficial. The contrast with Rousseau is all the more fascinating
because the details of the *Discourse* accorded with Burke's own
observation. The youth of eighteen or so who had described a hovel of
Irish peasants as 'scarcely indistinguishable from a Dunghill'[7] could
have subscribed to much in Rousseau's description. But where Rousseau's presuppositions encouraged him to treat such matters as the
appropriate outcome of an unnatural regime, Burke was free to recognize other possibilities.

Deism and social equality Burke linked as partners in logic; and in
error, too. For just as deism was unattractive to many of Burke's
contemporaries, so too was an attack on hierarchy. It was reasonable
to anticipate that Rousseau's *Discourse* would meet with an unfavourable reception. The *Court Magazine* found disapproval of the work so
widespread by 1762 that it wondered whether Rousseau would escape
persecution 'even among his favourite Hottentots, or his more
favourite savages of North America'.[8] Burke could expect an audience

---

[6] For the denial of a particular providence, see Bolingbroke *Works*, v, p. 414; *cf.* pp. 416,
472.   [7] *The Reformer*, printed in Samuels, p. 315.
[8] *Court Magazine*, 1 (1762), 232. Adam Smith asked wryly of Hume whether Rousseau
had gone abroad 'because he cannot continue to get himself sufficiently persecuted in

for his views. Whether he would have expressed himself quite so robustly as a certain distinguished lady writer we cannot say, but his sentiments were not incompatible.[9]

Analysis

Preface: Bolingbroke's works undermine religion and virtue (pp. 8–9), especially divine providence (p. 9). Burke's object is to show that the logic of Bolingbroke's arguments against (revealed) religion could be applied with equal success against government (pp. 9–12).

Text: Nature is better than man's artifice (pp. 12–13). Nature placed man in a condition without government, a state of nature (pp. 13–14). Man instituted political society, i.e. government (pp. 14–15). If we examine this closely, we shall find that artificial religion supports government (pp. 15–16).

The consequences of government can be divided under two heads, namely internal and international (pp. 16–17). In the latter aspect history shows from start (p. 16) to finish (p. 28) a continuous chain of misery and destruction.

These ills are not accidental, but flow from the subordination implicit in society under government (pp. 29–30). We can use our natural faculties to judge every type of government (p. 30). We see that despotism (pp. 30–3), aristocracy (pp. 33–5) and democracy (pp. 36–41) alike are forms of tyranny. The same is true of a balanced mixture of them (pp. 41–6). There is no refuge from misery in law (pp. 46–50) and there is much misery in the division between rich and poor society involves (pp. 50–4).

We may conclude that artificial institutions are as great a problem as artificial (revealed) religion (pp. 54–7).

Great Britain?' *Correspondence of Adam Smith*, ed. E.C. Mossner and I.S. Ross (1977) no. 103, p. 125 (7 June 1767). Burke seems to have been a little too quick off the mark in issuing VNS in 1756, for the anti-Rousseauvian reaction gathered head slightly later.
[9] 'She shew'd him her Commode, with false back of books, the works of Pope ... and Bolinbroke [*sic*]: she said she knew them well. They were the greatest Rascals, but she had the satisfaction of shitting on them every day.' Robert Halsband. 'New Anecdotes of Lady Mary Wortley Montagu', in René Wellek and Alvaro Ribeiro (eds.), *Evidence in Literary Scholarship: Essays in Memory of James Marshall Osborn* (1979), pp. 241–6, at p. 245.

A
Vindication
of
Natural Society:
or,
A View of the Miseries and Evils
sharing to Mankind from every Species
of Artificial Society.
In a Letter to Lord****
By a late Noble Writer.
(Second edition, 1757)

Preface

Before the Philosophical Works of Lord BOLINGBROKE had appeared,
great Things were expected from the Leisure of a Man, who from the
splendid Scene of Action, in which his Talents had enabled him to
make so conspicuous a Figure, had retired to employ those Talents in
the Investigation of Truth. Philosophy began to congratulate herself
upon such a Proselyte from the World of Business, and hoped to have
extended her Power under the Auspices of such a Leader. In the
Midst of these pleasing Expectations, the Works themselves at last
appeared in *full Body*,[1] and with great Pomp. Those who searched in
them for new Discoveries in the Mysteries of Nature; those who
expected something which might explain or direct the Operations of
the Mind; those who hoped to see Morality illustrated and inforced;
those who looked for new Helps to Society and Government; those

---

[1] *full body* Bolingbroke's *Works* were published in six volumes on 6 March 1754 by
David Mallet, who seems to have issued some works by stages during the preceding two
years.

who desired to see the Characters and Passions of Mankind delineated; in short, all who consider such Things as Philosophy, and require some of them at least, in every philosophical Work, all these were certainly disappointed; they found the Land-marks of Science precisely in their former Places: And they thought they received but a poor Recompence for this Disappointment, in seeing every Mode of Religion attacked in a lively Manner, and the Foundation of every Virtue, and of all Government, sapped with great Art and much Ingenuity. What Advantage do we derive from such Writings? What Delight can a Man find in employing a Capacity which might be usefully exerted for the noblest Purposes, in a sort of sullen Labour, in which, if the Author could succeed, he is obliged to own, that nothing could be more fatal to Mankind than his Success?

I cannot conceive how this sort of Writers propose to compass the Designs they pretend to have in view, by the Instruments which they employ. Do they pretend to exalt the Mind of Man, by proving him no better than a Beast?[2] Do they think to enforce the Practice of Virtue, by denying that Vice and Virtue are distinguished by good or ill Fortune here, or by Happiness or Misery hereafter? Do they imagine they shall increase our Piety, and our Reliance on God, by exploding his Providence, and insisting that he is neither just nor good?[3] Such are the Doctrines which, sometimes concealed, sometimes openly and fully avowed, are found to prevail throughout the Writings of Lord BOLINGBROKE; and such are the Reasonings which this noble Writer and several others have been pleased to dignify with the Name of Philosophy. If these are delivered in a specious Manner, and in a Stile above the common, they cannot want a Number of Admirers of as much Docility as can be wished for in Disciples. To these the Editor of the following little Piece has addressed it: there is no Reason to conceal the Design of it any longer.

The Design was, to shew that, without the Exertion of any con-

---

[2] **Beast** Bolingbroke had argued that however great man's attainments, 'they do not take us out of the class of animality ... the metaphysician ... will feel hunger and thirst'. This provoked Mrs Carter to suggest that Bolingbroke employed the highest degree of human understanding to prove himself a brute (*Letters from Mrs Elizabeth Carter to Mrs Montagu* (ed. M. Pennington, 1817), I, p. 115). See Burke's *Philosophical Enquiry*, I.ix (below, p. 66) for an explanation of how humans differ from beasts in one significant respect. See also 'Some Scattered Hints', *Notebook*, p. 91 and WSEB, II 388.

[3] **just nor good** i.e. if God made revelation, available only to some, a condition of salvation, His providence would not be fair by human canons.

siderable Forces, the same Engines which were employed for the Destruction of Religion, might be employed with equal Success for the Subversion of Government; and that specious Arguments might be used against those Things which they, who doubt of every thing else, will never permit to be questioned. It is an Observation which I think *Isocrates*[4] makes in one of his Orations against the Sophists, That it is far more easy to maintain a wrong Cause, and to support paradoxical Opinions to the Satisfaction of a common Auditory, than to establish a doubtful Truth by solid and conclusive Arguments. When Men find that something can be said in favour of what, on the very Proposal, they have thought utterly indefensible, they grow doubtful of their own Reason; they are thrown into a sort of pleasing Surprize; they run along with the Speaker, charmed and captivated to find such a plentiful Harvest of Reasoning, where all seemed barren and unpromising. This is the Fairy Land of Philosophy.[5] And it very frequently happens, that those pleasing Impressions on the Imagination, subsist and produce their Effect, even after the Understanding has been satisfied of their unsubstantial Nature. There is a sort of Gloss upon ingenious Falsehoods, that dazzles the Imagination, but which neither belongs to, nor becomes the sober Aspect of Truth. I have met with a Quotation in Lord *Coke*'s Reports that pleased me very much, though I do not know from whence he has taken it: '*Interdum fucata falsitas*, (says he) *in multis est probabilior, et sæpe rationibus vincit nudam veritatem*.'[6] In such Cases, the Writer has a certain Fire and Alacrity inspired into him by a Consciousness, that let it fare how it will with the Subject, his Ingenuity will be sure of Applause; and this Alacrity becomes much greater if he acts upon the offensive, by the Impetuosity that always accompanies an Attack, and the unfortunate Propensity which Mankind have to the finding and exaggerating Faults. The Editor is satisfied that a Mind which has no Restraint from a Sense of its own Weakness, of its subordinate Rank in the Creation, and of the extreme Danger of letting the Imagination

---

[4] **Isocrates** Cf. *Kata ton Sophiston*, 19 and for a more temperate view, *Antidosis*, 220.

[5] **Fairy Land of Philosophy** 'A satire upon civilized society, a satire upon learning, may make a tolerable sport for an ingenious fancy; but if carried farther, it can do no more (and that in such a way is surely too much) than to unsettle our notions of right and wrong, and lead by degrees to universal scepticism' (*Annual Register*, 2 (1759), p. 479, reviewing Rousseau's, *Lettre à D'Alembert*).

[6] **veritatem** sometimes a painted lie is more probable in many ways, and often overcomes the unadorned truth by force of argument.

loose upon some Subjects,[7] may very plausibly attack every thing the most excellent and venerable; that it would not be difficult to criticise the Creation itself; and that if we were to examine the divine Fabricks by our Ideas of Reason and Fitness, and to use the same Method of Attack by which some Men[8] have assaulted Revealed Religion, we might with as good Colour, and with the same Success, make the Wisdom and Power of God in his Creation appear to many no better than Foolishness. There is an Air of Plausibility which accompanies vulgar Reasonings and Notions taken from the beaten Circle of ordinary Experience, that is admirably suited to the narrow Capacities of some, and to the Laziness of others. But this Advantage is in great measure lost, when a painful, comprehensive Survey of a very complicated Matter, and which requires a great Variety of Considerations, is to be made; when we must seek in a profound Subject, not only for Arguments, but for new Materials of Argument, their Measures and their Method of Arrangement; when we must go out of the Sphere of our ordinary Ideas, and when we can never walk sure but by being sensible of our Blindness.[9] And this we must do, or we do nothing, whenever we examine the Result of a Reason which is not our own.[10] Even in Matters which are, as it were, just within our Reach, what would become of the World if the Practice of all moral Duties, and the Foundations of Society, rested upon having their Reasons made clear and demonstrative to every Individual?[11]

The Editor knows that the Subject of this Letter is not so fully handled as obviously it might; it was not his Design to say all that could possibly be said. It had been inexcusable to fill a large Volume

---

[7] **upon some Subjects** 'It has been the misfortune (not as these gentlemen think it, the glory) of this age, that every thing is to be discussed', and Burke referred next to government, 'as if the constitution of our country were to be always a subject rather of altercation than enjoyment' (Ref, p. 188).

[8] **some Men** i.e. the Deists.

[9] **Blindness** Cf. *Philosophical Enquiry*, IV.i: 'When we go but one step beyond the immediately sensible qualities of things, we go out of our depth.'

[10] **not our own** Cf. *Isaiah* 55:8: 'For my thoughts *are* not your thoughts, neither *are* your ways my ways, saith the LORD' and see 'Introduction', above, p. xxiii and PE, below, p. 67, with note.

[11] **every Individual** Burke suggested that English society got by happily without this: 'These . . . are, were, and I think long will be the sentiments of not the least learned and reflecting part of this kingdom. They who are included in this description, form their opinions on such grounds as such persons ought to form them. The less enquiring receive them from an authority which those whom Providence dooms to live on trust need not be ashamed to rely on' (Ref, p. 195f).

with the Abuse of Reason; nor would such an Abuse have been tolerable even for a few Pages, if some Under-plot, of more Consequence than the apparent Design, had not been carried on.

Some Persons have thought that the Advantages of the State of Nature ought to have been more fully displayed.[12] This had undoubtedly been a very ample Subject for Declamation; but they do not consider the Character of the Piece. The Writers against Religion, whilst they oppose every System, are wisely careful never to set up any of their own.[13] If some Inaccuracies in Calculation, in Reasoning, or in Method be found, perhaps these will not be looked upon as Faults by the Admirers of Lord BOLINGBROKE; who will, the Editor is afraid, observe much more of his Lordship's Character in such Particulars of the following Letter, than they are like to find of that rapid Torrent of an impetuous and overbearing Eloquence, and the Variety of rich Imagery for which that Writer is justly admired.

A LETTER TO LORD * * * *.

Shall I venture to say, my LORD, that in our late Conversation, you were inclined to the Party which you adopted rather by the Feelings of your good Nature, than by the Conviction of your Judgment? We laid open the Foundations of Society; and you feared, that the Curiosity of this Search might endanger the Ruin of the whole Fabrick. You would readily have allowed my Principle, but you dreaded the Consequences; you thought, that having once entered upon these Reasonings, we might be carried insensibly and irresistably farther than at first we could either have imagined or wished. But for my part, my LORD, I then thought, and am still of the same Opinion, that Error, and not Truth of any kind, is dangerous;[14] that ill Conclusions can

---

[12] **fully displayed** Cf. 'Les Philosophes qui ont examiné les fondemens de la société, ont tous senti la nécessité de remonter jusqua' à l'état de Nature, mais aucun d'eux n'y est arrivé' (Rousseau, *Discours sur . . . l'inégalité* (1755), p. 4). Many of the parallel passages quoted here were collected by R. B. Sewall Jr., see Bibliography, above, p. lxx.

[13] **of their own** Deism involves the subtraction of elements from Christianity rather than a newly generated theology; Rousseau had yet to publish his third discourse (1758) and *Du contrat social* (1762).

[14] **is dangerous** 'C'est de l'homme que j'ai à parler; & la question que j'examine m'apprend que je vais parler à des hommes, car on n'en propose point de semblables quand on craint d'honorer la vérité' (*Discours*, p. 1).

only flow from false Propositions; and that, to know whether any Proposition be true or false, it is a preposterous Method to examine it by its apparent Consequences.

These were the Reasons which induced me to go so far into that Enquiry; and they are the Reasons which direct me in all my Enquiries. I had indeed often reflected on that Subject before I could prevail upon myself to communicate my Reflections to any body. They were generally melancholy enough; as those usually are which carry us beyond the mere Surface of Things; and which would undoubtedly make the Lives of all thinking Men extremely miserable, if the same Philosophy which caused the Grief, did not at the same Time administer the Comfort.

On considering political Societies, their Origin, their Constitution, and their Effects, I have sometimes been in a good deal more than Doubt, whether the Creator did ever really intend Man for a State of Happiness. He has mixed in his Cup a Number of natural Evils, (in spite of the Boasts of Stoicism they are Evils) and every Endeavour which the Art and Policy of Mankind has used from the Beginning of the World to this Day, in order to alleviate, or cure them, has only served to introduce new Mischiefs, or to aggravate and inflame the old. Besides this, the Mind of Man itself is too active and restless a Principle ever to settle on the true Point of Quiet. It discovers every Day some craving Want in a Body, which really wants but little.[15] It every Day invents some new artificial Rule to guide that Nature which if left to itself were the best and surest Guide. It finds out imaginary Beings prescribing imaginary Laws; and then, it raises imaginary Terrors to support a Belief in the Beings, and an Obedience to the Laws. Many Things have been said, and very well undoubtedly, on the Subjection in which we should preserve our Bodies to the Government of our Understanding; but enough has not been said upon the Restraint which our bodily Necessities ought to lay on the extravagant Sublimities, and excentrick Rovings of our Minds. The Body, or as some love to call it, our inferior Nature, is wiser in its own plain Way, and attends its own Business more directly than the Mind with all its boasted Subtilty.

In the State of Nature, without question, Mankind was subjected to many and great Inconveniencies. Want of Union, Want of mutual

---

[15] **but little**   Rousseau argued that most wants were unnatural and superfluous.

Assistance,[16] Want of a common Arbitrator[17] to resort to in their Differences. These were Evils which they could not but have felt pretty severely on many Occasions. The original Children of the Earth lived with their Brethren of the other Kinds in much Equality.[18] Their Diet must have been confined almost wholly to the vegetable Kind; and the same Tree, which in its flourishing State produced them Berries, in its Decay gave them an Habitation.[19] The mutual Desires of the Sexes uniting their Bodies and Affections, and the Children, which were the Results of these Intercourses, introduced first the Notion of Society, and taught its Conveniences. This Society, founded in natural Appetites and Instincts, and not in any positive Institution, I shall call *Natural Society*. Thus far Nature went, and succeeded; but Man would go farther. The great Error of our Nature is, not to know where to stop, not to be satisfied with any reasonable Acquirement; not to compound with our Condition; but to lose all we have gained by an insatiable Pursuit after more. Man found a considerable Advantage by this Union of many Persons to form one Family; he therefore judged that he would find his Account proportionably in an Union of many Families into one Body politick. And as Nature has formed no Bond of Union to hold them together, he supplied this Defect by *Laws*.

This is *Political Society*. And hence the Sources of what are usually called States, civil Societies, or Governments; into some Form of which, more extended or restrained, all Mankind have gradually fallen. And since it has so happened, and that we owe an implicit Reverence to all the Institutions of our Ancestors, we shall consider these Institutions with all that Modesty with which we ought to conduct ourselves in examining a received Opinion; but with all that Freedom and Candour which we owe to Truth wherever we find it, or however it may contradict our own Notions, or oppose our own Interests. There is a most absurd and audacious Method of reasoning

---

[16] **Assistance**   the Rousseauvian savage needs none, which Burke ignores. See the passage beginning 'Le corps de l'homme sauvage étant le seul instrument qu'il conaisse' (*Discours*, p. 25).

[17] **Arbitator**   Cf. Locke, *Two Treatises of Government*, II.ix.125.

[18] **much Equality**   'L'Inégalité est à peine sensible dans l'état de Nature, & ... son influence y est presque nulle' (*Discours*, p. 91).

[19] **an Habitation**   'trouvant son lit au pied du meme arbre qui lui a fourni son repas; & voilà ses besoins satisfaits' (*Discours*, p. 12).

avowed by some Bigots and Enthusiasts,[20] and through Fear assented to by some wiser and better Men; it is this. They argue against a fair Discussion of popular Prejudices, because, say they, tho' they would be found without any reasonable Support, yet the Discovery might be productive of the most dangerous Consequences.[21] Absurd and blasphemous Notion! as if all Happiness was not connected with the Practice of Virtue, which necessarily depends upon the Knowledge of Truth; that is, upon the Knowledge of those unalterable Relations[22] which Providence has ordained that every thing should bear to every other. These Relations, which are Truth itself, the Foundation of Virtue, and consequently, the only Measures of Happiness, should be likewise the only Measures by which we should direct our Reasoning. To these we should conform in good Earnest; and not think to force Nature, and the whole Order of her System, by a Compliance with our Pride, and Folly, to conform to our artificial Regulations. It is by a Conformity to this Method we owe the Discovery of the few Truths we know, and the little Liberty and rational Happiness we enjoy. We have something fairer Play than a Reasoner could have expected formerly; and we derive Advantages from it which are very visible.

The Fabrick of Superstition has in this our Age and Nation received much ruder Shocks than it had ever felt before; and through the Chinks and Breaches of our Prison, we see such Glimmerings of Light, and feel such refreshing Airs of Liberty, as daily raise our Ardor for more. The Miseries derived to Mankind from Superstition, under the Name of Religion, and of ecclesiastical Tyranny under the Name of Church Government,[23] have been clearly and usefully

---

[20] **Enthusiasts** for the term's pejorative overtones, cf. S.I. Tucker *Enthusiasm* (1972), esp. chs. 3, 5–8.

[21] **dangerous Consequences** 'Whatever unsettles the foundations of government, affects the well-being of society, or *any way disturbs the peace and quiet of the world*, is of very destructive consequence; and the man who should retrieve fifty such truths . . . would . . . be a very pernicious member of society' (Francis Blackburne, *The Confessional* (1767), p. 349).

[22] **Relations** reminds us of Samuel Clarke's view that good and evil could be described as relations in the nature of things, rather than Bolingbroke's view; see *Works*, IV, p. 284, cf. v, pp. 55, 93 and his criticism of Clarke, v, pp. 42ff, cf. p. 435.

[23] **Church government** since deism implied the uselessness of revelation it followed that churches, the purveyors of revelation, were at best superfluous; and if their existence was attributed to a deceitful design, self-interested; cf. Charles Blount, *Great is Diana of the Ephesians* (1695), p. 8f on pagan priests, who 'turn'd Religion into a Trade' and 'under pretence of wishing well to others, enrich and advantage themselves: They not being like the Pastors of the Christian Church'.

exposed. We begin to think and to act from Reason and from Nature alone. This is true of several, but still is by far the Majority in the same old State of Blindness and Slavery; and much is it to be feared that we shall perpetually relapse, whilst the real productive Cause of all this superstitious Folly, enthusiastical Nonsense, and holy Tyranny, holds a reverend Place in the Estimation even of those who are otherwise enlightened.

Civil Government borrows a Strength from ecclesiastical; and artificial Laws receive a Sanction from artificial Revelations. The Ideas of Religion and Government are closely connected; and whilst we receive Government as a thing necessary, or even useful to our Well-being, we shall in spite of us draw in, as a necessary, tho' undesirable Consequence, an artificial Religion of some kind or other. To this the Vulgar will always be voluntary Slaves; and even those of a Rank of Understanding superior, will now and then involuntarily feel its Influence. It is therefore of the deepest Concernment to us to be set right in this Point; and to be well satisfied whether civil Government be such a Protector from natural Evils, and such a Nurse and Increaser of Blessings, as those of warm Imaginations promise. In such a Discussion, far am I from proposing in the least to reflect on our most wise Form of Government; no more than I would in the freer Parts of my philosophical Writings, mean to object to the Piety, Truth and Perfection of our most excellent Church. Both I am sensible have their Foundations on a Rock. No Discovery of Truth can prejudice them. On the contrary, the more closely the Origin of Religion and Government are examined, the more clearly their Excellencies must appear. They come purified from the Fire. My Business is not with them. Having entered a Protest against all Objections from these Quarters, I may the more freely enquire from History and Experience, how far Policy has contributed in all Times to alleviate those Evils which Providence, that perhaps has designed us for a State of Imperfection, has imposed; how far our physical Skill has cured our constitutional Disorders; and whether, it may not have introduced new ones, cureable perhaps by no Skill.

In looking over any State to form a Judgment on it; it presents itself in two Lights, the external and the internal. The first, that Relation which it bears in point of Friendship or Enmity to other States. The second, that Relation its component Parts, the Governing, and the Governed, bear to each other. The first Part of the external View of all States, their Relation as Friends, makes so trifling a Figure in History, that I am very sorry to say, it affords me but little Matter on which to expatiate. The good Offices done by one Nation to its Neighbour (a); the Support given in publick Distress; the Relief afforded in general Calamity; the Protection granted in emergent Danger; the mutual Return of Kindness and Civility, would afford a very ample and very pleasing Subject for History. But, alas! all the History of all Times, concerning all Nations, does not afford Matter enough to fill ten Pages, though it should be spun out by the Wire-drawing Amplification of a *Guicciardini* [25] himself. The glaring Side is that of Enmity. War is the Matter which fills all History, and conse-quently the only, or almost the only View in which we can see the External of political Society, is in a hostile Shape; and the only Actions, to which we have always seen, and still see all of them intent, are such, as tend to the Destruction of one another.[26] War,[27] says *Machiavell*, ought to be the only Study of a Prince; and by a Prince, he means every fort of State however constituted. He ought, says this great political Doctor, to consider Peace only as a Breathing-time, which gives him Leisure to contrive, and furnishes Ability to execute military Plans.[28] A Meditation on the Conduct of political Societies made old *Hobbes* imagine, that War was the State of Nature;[29] and truly, if a Man judged of the Individuals of our Race by their Conduct when united and packed into Nations and Kingdoms, he might imagine that every sort of Virtue was unnatural and foreign to the Mind of Man.[30]

The first Accounts we have of Mankind are but so many Accounts of their Butcheries. All Empires have been cemented in Blood; and in those early Periods when the Race of Mankind began first to form

---

(a) Had his Lordship lived to our Days, to have seen the noble Relief given by this Nation to the distressed *Portuguese*,[24] he had perhaps owned this Part of his Argument a little weakened, but we do not think ourselves intitled to alter his Lordship's Words, but that we are bound to follow him exactly.

[24] **distressed Portuguese** an allusion to the Lisbon earthquake of 1755, for which see T. D. Kendrick, *The Lisbon Earthquake* (1955).

[25] **Guicciardini** His *History of Italy* runs to twenty books.

[26] **Destruction of one another** 'history; which is, indeed, little more than the register of the crimes, follies and misfortunes of mankind' (Gibbon, *Decline and Fall*, ch. 3).

[27] **War** Machiavelli, *Il principe*, ch. 14, cf. 12.

[28] **military Plans** *ibid.*, ch. 14.　　　　[29] **Nature** e.g. *Leviathan*, ch. 13.

[30] **Mind of Man** 'Hobbes prétend que l'homme est naturellement intrépide, & ne cherche qu' a attaquer' (*Discours*, p. 16).

17

themselves into Parties and Combinations, the first Effect of the Combination, and indeed the End for which it seems purposely formed, and best calculated, is their mutual Destruction. All antient History is dark and uncertain. One thing however is clear. There were Conquerors, and Conquests, in those Days; and consequently, all that Devastation, by which they are formed, and all that Oppression by which they are maintained. We know little of *Sesostris*, but that he led out of *Egypt* an Army of above 700,000 Men; that he over-ran the *Mediterranean* Coast as far as *Colchis*; that in some Places, he met but little Resistance, and of course shed not a great deal of Blood; but that he found in others, a People who knew the Value of their Liberties, and sold them dear. Whoever considers the Army this Conqueror headed, the Space he traversed, and the Opposition he frequently met; with the natural Accidents of Sickness, and the Dearth and Badness of Provision to which he must have been subject in the Variety of Climates and Countries his March lay through, if he knows any thing, he must know, that even the Conqueror's Army must have suffered greatly; and that, of this immense Number, but a very small Part could have returned to enjoy the Plunder accumulated by the Loss of so many of their Companions, and the Devastation of so considerable a Part of the World. Considering, I say, the vast Army headed by this Conqueror, whose unwieldy Weight was almost alone sufficient to wear down its Strength, it will be far from Excess to suppose that one half was lost in the Expedition. If this was the State of the Victorious, and from the Circumstances, it must have been this at the least; the Vanquished must have had a much heavier Loss, as the greatest Slaughter is always in the Flight, and great Carnage did in those Times and Countries ever attend the first Rage of Conquest. It will therefore be very reasonable to allow on their account as much as, added to the Losses of the Conqueror, may amount to a Million of Deaths, and then we shall see this Conqueror, the oldest we have on the Records of History, (though, as we have observed before, the Chronology of these remote Times is extremely uncertain), opening the Scene by a Destruction of at least one Million of his Species, unprovoked but by his Ambition, without any Motives but Pride, Cruelty and Madness, and without any Benefit to himself; (for *Justin* expressly tells us, he did not maintain his Conquests) but solely to make so many People, in so distant Countries, feel experimentally, how severe a Scourge Providence intends for the human Race, when he gives one Man the Power over many, and arms his naturally impotent, and feeble Rage, with the Hands of Millions, who know no common Principle of Action, but a blind Obedience to the Passions of their Ruler.

The next Personage who figures in the Tragedies of this ancient Theatre is *Semiramis*: For we have no Particulars of *Ninus*, but that he made immense and rapid Conquests, which doubtless were not compassed without the usual Carnage. We see an Army of above three Millions employed by this martial Queen in a War against the *Indians*. We see the *Indians* arming a yet greater; and we behold a War continued with much Fury, and with various Success. This ends in the Retreat of the Queen, with scarce a third of the Troops employed in the Expedition; an Expedition, which at this rate must have cost two Millions of Souls on her part; and it is not unreasonable to judge that the Country which was the Seat of War, must have been an equal Sufferer. But I am content to detract from this, and to suppose that the *Indians* lost only half so much, and then the Account stands thus: In this War alone, (for *Semiramis* had other Wars) in this single Reign, and in this one Spot of the Globe, did three Millions of Souls expire, with all the horrid and shocking Circumstances which attend all Wars, and in a Quarrel, in which none of the Sufferers could have the least rational Concern.

The *Babylonian*, *Assyrian*, *Median*, and *Persian* Monarchies must have poured out Seas of Blood in their Formation, and in their Destruction. The Armies and Fleets of *Xerxes*, their Numbers, the glorious Stand made against them, and the unfortunate Event of all his mighty Preparations, are known to every body. In this Expedition, draining half *Asia* of its Inhabitants, he led an Army of about two Millions to be slaughtered, and wasted, by a thousand fatal Accidents, in the same Place where his Predecessors had before by a similar Madness consumed the Flower of so many Kingdoms, and wasted the Force of so extensive an Empire. It is a cheap Calculation to say, that the *Persian* Empire in its Wars, against the *Greeks*, and *Sythians*, threw away at least four Millions of its Subjects, to say nothing of its other Wars, and the Losses sustained in them. These were their Losses abroad; but the War was brought home to them, first by *Agesilaus*, and afterwards, by *Alexander*.[31] I have not, in this Retreat, the Books

---

[31] *Alexander* for Alexander, like Charles XII of Sweden, as a military lunatic, see Pope, *Essay on Man*, IV. 217–22:

necessary to make very exact Calculations; nor is it necessary to give more than Hints to one of your Lordship's Erudition. You will recollect his uninterrupted Series of Success. You will run over his Battles. You will call to mind the Carnage which was made. You will give a Glance of the Whole, and you will agree with me; that to form this Hero no less than twelve hundred thousand Lives must have been sacrificed; but no sooner had he fallen himself a Sacrifice to his Vices, than a thousand Breaches were made for Ruin to enter, and give the last hand to this Scene of Misery and Destruction. His Kingdom was rent and divided; which served to employ the more distinct Parts to tear each other to Pieces, and bury the whole in Blood and Slaughter. The Kings of *Syria* and of *Egypt*, the Kings of *Pergamus* and *Macedon*, without Intermission worried each other for above two hundred Years; until at last a strong Power arising in the West,[32] rushed in upon them and silenced their Tumults, by involving all the contending Parties in the same Destruction. It is little to say, that the Contentions between the Successors of *Alexander* depopulated that Part of the World of at least two Millions.

The Struggle between the *Macedonians* and *Greeks*, and before that, the Disputes of the *Greek* Commonwealths among themselves, for an unprofitable Superiority, form one of the bloodiest Scenes in History. One is astonished how such a small Spot could furnish Men sufficient to sacrifice to the pitiful Ambition of possessing five or six thousand more Acres, or two or three more Villages: Yet to see the Acrimony and Bitterness with which this was disputed between the *Athenians*[33] and *Lacedemonians*; what Armies cut off; what Fleets sunk, and burnt; what a Number of Cities sacked, and their Inhabitants slaughtered, and captived; one would be induced to believe the Decision of the Fate of Mankind at least, depended upon it! But these Disputes

Look next on Greatness; say where Greatness lies
'Where, but among the Heroes and the Wise?'
Heroes are much the same, the point's agreed,
From Macedonia's madman to the Swede;
The whole strange purpose of their lives, to find
Or make, an enemy of all mankind!
cf. *ibid.*, I. ll. 160, and Henry Fielding *Jonathan Wild*, I. 3; see also 'New Anecdotes of Alexander the Great', in M.D. Conway (ed.), *The Writings of Thomas Paine*, 4 vols. (1894–96), I, pp. 26–8, and *The American Crisis*, no. 5, in the same edition, I, p. 248.

[32] **West** alluding to Rome, which devoted her imperial energies to the east after subjugating Carthage.

[33] **Athenians** i.e. the Peloponnesian War 431–404 BC, which saw Athens and her allies ranged against Sparta and Corinth.

ended as all such ever have done, and ever will do; in a real Weakness of all Parties; a momentary Shadow, and Dream of Power in some one; and the Subjection of all to the Yoke of a Stranger, who knows how to profit of their Divisions. This at least was the Case of the *Greeks*; and sure, from the earliest Accounts of them, to their Absorption into the *Roman* Empire, we cannot judge that their intestine Divisions, and their foreign Wars, consumed less than three Millions of their Inhabitants.

What an *Aceldama*,[34] what a Field of Blood *Sicily*[35] has been in antient times, whilst the Mode of its Government was controverted between the republican and tyrannical Parties, and the Possession struggled for by the Natives, the *Greeks*, the *Carthaginians*, and the *Romans*, your Lordship will easily recollect. You will remember the total Destruction of such Bodies as an Army of 300,000 Men. You will find every Page of its History dyed in Blood, and blotted and confounded by Tumults, Rebellions, Massacres, Assassinations, Proscriptions, and a Series of Horror beyond the Histories perhaps of any other Nation in the World; though the Histories of all Nations are made up of similar Matter. I once more excuse myself in point of Exactness for want of Books. But I shall estimate the Slaughters in this Island but at two Millions; which your Lordship will find much short of the Reality.

Let us pass by the Wars, and the Consequences of them, which wasted *Grecia-Magna*,[36] before the *Roman* Power prevailed in that Part of *Italy*. They are perhaps exaggerated; therefore I shall only rate them at one Million. Let us hasten to open that great Scene which establishes the *Roman* Empire, and forms the grand Catastrophe of the antient Drama. This Empire, whilst in its Infancy, began by an

---

[34] *Aceldama*   from the Aramaic for field of blood, via the Greek *Akeldama*, see Acts 1–19.

[35] *Sicily*,   like much of the Greek world, developed 'tyrannies' (i.e. seizures of power by individuals in the face of existing aristocratic or democratic rule). Tyranny in Sicily was threatened by the tenacity of the aristocracy ('the republican' party) and from interventions from neighbouring powers (Carthage, Athens and Rome): hence the frequency of wars. Burke alludes especially, no doubt, to the Carthaginian disaster at Himera (480 BC), the Athenian failure at Syracuse (415–13 BC), and the Roman conquest during the First Punic War (264–241 BC); but the military history of the island in antiquity defies brief summary: see E.A. Freeman, *History of Sicily*, 4 vols. (1890–94), and M.I. Finley *Ancient Sicily: To the Arab Conquest* (1968).

[36] *Grecia-Magna*   the southern parts of Italy, with Sicily, were the first great areas of Greek colonization (from before *c.*750 BC), since the colonists sought areas with a climate similar to the one they knew.

Effusion of human Blood scarcely credible. The neighbouring little States teemed for new Destruction: The *Sabines*,[37] the *Samnites*,[38] the *Æqui*,[39] the *Volsci*,[40] the *Hetrurians*,[41] were broken by a Series of Slaughters which had no Interruption, for some hundreds of Years; Slaughters which upon all sides consumed more than two Millions of the wretched People. The *Gauls* rushing into *Italy* about this Time,[42] added the total Destruction of their own Armies to those of the antient Inhabitants. In short, it were hardly possible to conceive a more horrid and bloody Picture, if that which the *Punic* Wars that ensued soon after did not present one, that far exceeds it. Here we find that Climax of Devastation, and Ruin, which seemed to shake the whole Earth. The Extent of this War which vexed so many Nations, and both Elements, and the Havock of the human Species caused in both, really astonishes beyond Expression, when it is nakedly considered, and those Matters which are apt to divert our Attention from it, the Characters, Actions, and Designs of the Persons concerned, are not taken into the Account. These Wars, I mean those called the *Punic* Wars,[43] could not have stood the human Race in less than three Millions of the Species. And yet this forms but a Part only, and a very small Part, of the Havock caused by the *Roman* Ambition. The War with *Mithridates* was very little less bloody; that Prince cut off at one Stroke 150,000 *Romans* by a Massacre. In that War *Sylla* destroyed 300,000 Men at *Cheronea*.[44] He defeated *Mithridates*' Army under

---

[37] **Sabines**   lived north-east of Rome in the Apennines and were subjugated in 290 BC.

[38] **Samnites**   held out longer than most against Rome and were gradually subjugated in a series of wars from 343 BC, losing heavily through the Second Punic War and latterly being either slaughtered or Romanized by Sulla.

[39] **Aequi**   inhabited Himela, Toleus and the upper Anio vallies: they were exterminated after 304 BC.

[40] **Volsci**   established themselves in the middle Liris valley and south-east of the Alban Hills; defeated and Romanized by 304 BC.

[41] **Hetrurians**   or, more accurately, Etruscans, were Rome's principal early rival for hegemony in central Italy: but by the end of the third century BC most of Etruria was in Roman hands.

[42] **about this Time**   the Gallic invasion of Rome, part of a larger celtic diffusion towards the Mediterranean, is traditionally ascribed to 390 BC.

[43] **Punic Wars**   the three conflicts in which Rome gradually superseded Carthage as the dominant power in the Western Mediterranean occurred 264–241, 218–201 and 149–146 BC.

[44] **Cheronea**   i.e. Chaeronea in Macedonia, where Archelaus, the greatest of Mithridates' generals, was beaten (i) in three successive battles by Bruttius Sura and (ii) by Sulla, who had sent a legion to protect Chaeronea, at an action at Thurium (rather than Chaeronea strictly). The latter was a far heavier defeat for Archelaus. Sulla also defeated Archelaus at Orchomenus.

Dorilaus,[45] and slew 300,000. This great and unfortunate Prince lost another 300,000 before *Cyzicum*.[46] In the course of the War he had innumerable other Losses; and having many Intervals of Success, he revenged them severely. He was at last totally overthrown; and he crushed to Pieces the King of *Armenia*[47] his Ally by the Greatness of his Ruin. All who had Connexions with him shared the same Fate. The merciless Genius of *Sylla* had its full Scope; and the Streets of *Athens*[48] were not the only one which ran with Blood. At this Period, the Sword, glutted with foreign Slaughter, turned its Edge upon the Bowels of the *Roman* Republick itself; and presented a Scene of Cruelties and Treasons enough almost to obliterate the Memory of all the external Devastations. I intended, my LORD, to have proceeded in a sort of Method in estimating the Numbers of Mankind cut off in these Wars which we have on Record. But I am obliged to alter my Design. Such a tragical Uniformity of Havock and Murder would disgust your Lordship as much as it would me; and I confess I already feel my Eyes ake by keeping them so long intent on so bloody a Prospect. I shall observe little on the *Servile*, the *Social*, the *Gallic*, and *Spanish* Wars;[49] nor upon those with *Jugurtha*, nor *Antiochus*, nor many others equally important, and carried on with equal Fury. The Butcheries of *Julius Cæsar* alone, are calculated by some body else;[50] the Numbers he has been a means of destroying have been reckoned at 1,200,000. But to give your Lordship an Idea that may serve as a Standard, by which to measure, in some degree, the others; you will

---

[45] **Dorilaus** presumably an error for Archelaus.

[46] **Cyzicum** or, more accurately, Cyzicus was a Milesian colony in Bithynia (part of modern Turkey) which put up a courageous resistance to Mithridates in 74 BC, during the third Mithridatic War, which enabled Lucullus to cut off Mithridates' army from its supplies and then destroy it; for which Rome rewarded the city with an increase to its territories.

[47] **Armenia** i.e. Tigranes I 'the Great'.

[48] **Athens** had been forced to side with Mithridates by the tyrant Aristion; Sulla captured the city and let his troops run riot in it; later, having defeated Archelaus, he returned to Italy, defeated and proscribed his enemies.

[49] **Servile, Social, Gallic and Spanish Wars** respectively: the revolt of Spartacus, who led numerous Thracian, German and Celtic renegades (at the most about 90,000) from 73 BC and beat several Roman armies, but was defeated decisively by Crassus in 71; the war against the Italian allies (*socii*) of Rome, who resented her predominance (91–87 BC), which Rome won by granting citizenship to her adversaries; the conquest of Gaul (58–51 BC) by Julius Caesar; and the gradual expansion of Roman control over the Iberian Peninsula, beginning with the ejection of the Carthiginians in 206 BC and concluding with the campaigns of Augustus.

[50] **some body else** Plutarch, *Caesar*, ch. 15 estimates the Gauls' casualties at one million dead and another million captured.

turn your Eyes on *Judea*; a very inconsiderable Spot of the Earth in itself, though ennobled by the singular Events which had their Rise in that Country.[51]

This Spot happened, it matters not here by what means, to become at several times extremely populous, and to supply Men for Slaughters scarcely credible, if other well-known and well-attested ones had not given them a Colour. The first settling of the *Jews* here, was attended by an almost entire Extirpation of all the former Inhabitants. Their own civil Wars, and those with their petty Neighbours, consumed vast Multitudes almost every Year for several Centuries; and the Irruptions of the Kings of *Babylon* and *Assyria* made immense Ravages. Yet we have their History but partially, in an indistinct confused manner;[52] so that I shall only throw the strong Point of Light upon that Part which coincides with *Roman* History, and of that Part only on the Point of Time when they received the great and final Stroke which made them no more a Nation; a Stroke which is allowed to have cut off little less than two Millions of that People. I say nothing of the Loppings made from that Stock whilst it stood; nor from the Suckers that grew out of the old Root ever since. But if in this inconsiderable Part of the Globe, such a Carnage has been made in two or three short Reigns, and that this Carnage, great as it is, makes but a minute Part of what the Histories of that People inform us they suffered; what shall we judge of Countries more extended, and which have waged Wars by far more considerable?

Instances of this Sort compose the Uniform of History. But there have been Periods when no less than universal Destruction to the Race of Mankind seems to have been threatened. When the *Goths*, the *Vandals*, and the *Huns*[53] poured into *Gaul*, *Italy*, *Spain*, *Greece*, and

[51] **that Country** the pseudo-Bolingbroke avoids an explicit reference to the life of Christ.

[52] **confused manner** a passing sneer at the Old Testament. It was assumed by Christian writers in the seventeenth century that there were no contradictions or incoherences between different scriptural passages. This makes consistency and coherence a measure of intellectual worth; anti-Christian writers found a favourite gambit in arguing that the Bible did not meet it.

[53] **Goths … Vandals … Huns** the Goths were a Germanic people who moved on the Black Sea AD 150–200, and by 238 had begun to raid the Roman Empire. One section, the Visigoths, established themselves in Dacia, whilst the remainder, the Ostrogoths, founded an Empire in the Ukraine. Both were driven to invade the Roman Empire by the pressure of the Huns on them. In 489 the Ostrogoths marched on Italy; the Visigoths had already devastated Greece and Italy, settling in Spain and southern France. The Vandals likewise moved southwards, from southern Scandanavia, and, again under

Africa,[54] carrying Destruction before them as they advanced, and leaving horrid Desarts every where behind them. *Vastum ubique silentium, secreti colles; fumantia procul tecta; nemo exploratoribus obvius*, is what *Tacitus* calls *facies Victoriæ*.[55] It is always so; but was here emphatically so. From the North proceeded the Swarms of *Goths*, *Vandals*, *Huns*, *Ostrogoths*, who ran towards the South into *Africa* itself, which suffered as all to the North had done. About this Time, another Torrent of Barbarians, animated by the same Fury, and encouraged by the same Success, poured out of the South, and ravaged all to the North-east and West, to the remotest Parts of *Persia* on one hand, and to the Banks of the *Loire* or further on the other; destroying all the proud and curious Monuments of human Art, that not even the Memory might seem to survive of the former Inhabitants.[56] What has been done since, and what will continue to be done whilst the same Inducements to War continue, I shall not dwell upon. I shall only in one Word mention the horrid Effects of Bigotry and Avarice,[57] in the Conquest of *Spanish America*;[58] a Conquest on a low Estimation effected by the Murder of ten Millions of the Species. I shall draw to a Conclusion of this Part, by making a general Calculation of the Whole. I think I have actually mentioned above thirty-six Millions. I have not particularized any more. I don't pretend to Exactness; therefore for the sake of a general View, I shall lay together all those actually slain in Battles, or who have perished in a no less miserable manner by the other destructive Consequences of War, from the Beginning of the World to this Day, in the four Parts of it, at a

pressure from the Huns, moved into Gaul and Spain at the beginning of the fifth century. The Huns, whose origin is unknown, as well as causing other barbarians to invade the western empire, levied large amounts of tribute from the eastern.

[54] *Africa* was conquered by the Vandals in AD 429.

[55] *Victoriae* 'everywhere the silence of desolation, lonely hills; houses smoking in the distance; and our scouts met no one . . . the spectacle of victory' (Tacitus, *Agricola*, c.38 (the case of *facies* altered)).

[56] **former Inhabitants** alluding to the Mohammedan conquests of the Middle East, northern Africa and Spain, in succession to the barbarians who had vanquished Rome.

[57] **Bigotry and Avarice** Bernal Diaz del Castillo remarked 'We came here to serve God and the king, and also to get rich': the Spanish conquerors were true to this high calling. 'Bigotry' sneers at the introduction of Christianity into South America.

[58] *Spanish America* the founding of Panama and Cortes' landing in Mexico (both 1519) marked an upswing in Spanish interest in South America (hitherto largely in the West Indies, though a settlement had already been established in Colombia). Cortes arranged for the defeated Aztec ruler of Mexico, Montezuma, to make an 'imperial donation' and proclaimed Charles V as emperor of 'New Spain'. Pizarro reproduced Cortes' victory (1519) when he conquered the empire of the Incas (1531–33).

thousand times as much; no exaggerated Calculation, allowing for Time and Extent. We have not perhaps spoke of the five-hundredth Part; I am sure I have not of what is actually ascertained in History; but how much of these Butcheries are only expressed in Generals, what Part of Time History has never reached, and what vast Spaces of the habitable Globe it has not embraced, I need not mention to your Lordship. I need not enlarge on these Torrents of silent and inglorious Blood which have glutted the thirsty Sands of *Afric*, or discoloured the polar Snow, or fed the savage Forests of *America* for so many Ages of continual War; shall I, to justify my Calculations from the Charge of Extravagance,[59] add to the Account those Skirmishes which happen in all Wars, without being singly of sufficient Dignity in Mischief, to merit a Place in History, but which by their Frequency compensate for this comparative Innocence; shall I inflame the Account by these general Massacres which have devoured whole Cities and Nations; those wasting Pestilences, those consuming Famines, and all those Furies that follow in the Train of War? I have no need to exaggerate; and I have purposely avoided a Parade of Eloquence on this Occasion. I should despise it upon any Occasion; else in mentioning these Slaughters, it is obvious how much the whole might be heightened, by an affecting Description of the Horrors that attend the wasting of Kingdoms, and sacking of Cities. But I do not write to the Vulgar, nor to that which only governs the Vulgar, their Passions. I go upon a naked and moderate Calculation, just enough, without a pedantical Exactness, to give your Lordship some Feeling of the Effects of political Society. I charge the whole of these Effects on political Society. I avow the Charge, and I shall presently make it good to your Lordship's Satisfaction. The Numbers I particularized are about thirty-six Millions. Besides those killed in Battles I have something, not half what the Matter would have justified, but something I have said, concerning the Consequences of War even more dreadful than that monstrous Carnage itself which shocks our Humanity, and almost staggers our Belief. So that allowing me in my Exuberance one way, for my Deficiencies in the other, you will find me not unreasonable. I think the Numbers of Men now upon Earth are computed at 500 Millions at the most. Here the Slaughter of Mankind, on what

---

[59] **Extravagance**   even a passing comparison with the first edition would show that Burke greatly increased many of the casualty figures in the second.

you will call a small Calculation, amounts to upwards of seventy times the Number of Souls this Day on the Globe. A Point which may furnish matter of Reflection to one less inclined to draw Consequences than your Lordship.

I now come to shew, that Political Society is justly chargeable with much the greatest Part of this Destruction of the Species. To give the fairest Play to every side of the Question, I will own that there is a Haughtiness, and Fierceness in human Nature, which will cause innumerable Broils, place Men in what Situation you please; but owning this, I still insist in charging it to political Regulations, that these Broils are so frequent, so cruel, and attended with Consequences so deplorable. In a State of Nature, it had been impossible to find a Number of Men, sufficient for such Slaughters, agreed in the same bloody Purpose; or allowing that they might have come to such an Agreement, (an impossible Supposition) yet the Means that simple Nature has supplied them with, are by no means adequate to such an End; many Scratches, many Bruises undoubtedly would be received upon all hands; but only a few, a very few Deaths. Society, and Politicks, which have given us these destructive Views, have given us also the Means of satisfying them. From the earliest Dawnings of Policy to this Day, the Invention of Men has been sharpening and improving the Mystery of Murder, from the first rude Essays of Clubs and Stones, to the present Perfection of Gunnery, Cannoneering, Bombarding, Mining, and all these Species of artificial, learned, and refined Cruelty, in which we are now so expert, and which make a principal Part of what Politicians have taught us to believe is our principal Glory.[60]

How far mere Nature would have carried us, we may judge by the Example of those Animals, who still follow her Laws, and even of those to whom she has given Dispositions more fierce, and Arms more terrible than ever she intended we should use. It is an incontestible Truth, that there is more Havock made in one Year by Men, of Men, than has been made by all the Lions, Tygers, Panthers, Ounces, Leopards, Hyenas, Rhinoceroses, Elephants, Bears, and Wolves,

---

[60] **principal Glory**   see the extraordinary passage in John Edwards, *Polupoikilos Sophia. A compleat history or survey of all the dispensations and methods of religion, from the beginning of the world to the consummation of all things; as represented in the Old and New Testament*, 2 vols. (1699), II, pp. 622–34, on the 'unspeakable Advantages that have accrued to Mankind', as gunpowder, which gives 'a more compendious and speedy, a more thrifty and frugal way of killing our Enemies'.

upon their several Species, since the Beginning of the World; though these agree ill enough with each other, and have a much greater Proportion of Rage and Fury in their Composition than we have. But with respect to you, ye Legislators, ye Civilizers of Mankind! ye Orpheus's, Moseses, Minoses, Solons, Theseuses, Lycurguses, Numas! with Respect to you be it spoken, your Regulations have done more Mischief in cold Blood, than all the Rage of the fiercest Animals in their greatest Terrors, or Furies, has ever done, or ever could do!

These Evils are not accidental. Whoever will take the pains to consider the Nature of Society, will find they result directly from its Constitution. For as *Subordination*, or in other Words, the Reciprocation of Tyranny, and Slavery, is requisite to support these Societies, the Interest, the Ambition, the Malice, or the Revenge, nay even the Whim and Caprice of one ruling Man among them, is enough to arm all the rest, without any private Views of their own, to the worst and blackest Purposes;[61] and what is at once lamentable, and ridiculous, these Wretches engage under those Banners with a Fury greater than if they were animated by Revenge for their own proper Wrongs.

It is no less worth observing, that this artificial Division of Mankind, into separate Societies, is a perpetual Source in itself of Hatred and Dissention among them. The Names which distinguish them are enough to blow up Hatred, and Rage. Examine History; consult present Experience; and you will find, that far the greater Part of the Quarrels between several Nations, had scarce any other Occasion, than that these Nations were different Combinations of People, and called by different Names; – to an *Englishman*, the Name of a *Frenchman*, a *Spaniard*, an *Italian*, much more a *Turk*, or a *Tartar*, raise of course Ideas of Hatred, and Contempt. If you would inspire this Compatriot of ours with Pity or Regard, for one of these; would you not hide that Distinction? You would not pray him to compassionate the poor *Frenchman*, or the unhappy *German*. Far from it; you would speak of him as a *Foreigner*, an Accident to which all are liable. You would represent him as a *Man*; one partaking with us of the same common Nature, and subject to the same Law. There is something so averse from our Nature in these artificial political Distinctions, that we need no other Trumpet to kindle us to War, and Destruction. But

---

[61] **blackest purposes** 'Il me suffit d'avoir prouvé que ce n'est point l'état originel de l'homme, & que c'est le seul ésprit de la Société, et l'inegalité qu'elle engendre, qui changent & alterent ainsi toutes nos inclinations naturelles' (*Discours*, p. 182).

there is something so benign and healing in the general Voice of Humanity, that maugre all our Regulations to prevent it, the simple Name of Man applied properly, never fails to work a salutary Effect.

This natural unpremeditated Effect of Policy on the unpossessed Passions of Mankind, appears on other Occasions. The very Name of a Politician, a Statesman, is sure to cause Terror and Hatred; it has always connected with it the Ideas of Treachery, Cruelty, Fraud and Tyranny; and those Writers who have faithfully unveiled the Mysteries of State-freemasonry, have ever been held in general Detestation, for even knowing so perfectly a Theory so detestable. The Case of *Machiavel* seems at first sight something hard in that Respect. He is obliged to bear the Iniquities of those whose Maxims and Rules of Government he published. His Speculation is more abhorred than their Practice.[62]

But if there were no other Arguments against artificial Society than this I am going to mention, methinks it ought to fall by this one only. All Writers on the Science of Policy are agreed, and they agree with Experience, that all Governments must frequently infringe the Rules of Justice to support themselves; that Truth must give way to Dissimulation; Honesty to Convenience; and Humanity itself to the reigning Interest. The Whole of this Mystery of Iniquity is called the Reason of State. It is a Reason, which I own I cannot penetrate. What Sort of a Protection is this of the general Right, that is maintained by infringing the Rights of Particulars? What sort of Justice is this, which is inforced by Breaches of its own Laws? These Paradoxes I leave to be solved by the able Heads of Legislators and Politicians. For my part, I say what a plain Man would say on such an Occasion. I can never believe, that any Institution agreeable to Nature, and proper for Mankind, could find it necessary, or even expedient in any Case whatsoever to do, what the best and worthiest Instincts of Mankind warn us to avoid. But no wonder, that what is set up in Opposition to the State of Nature, should preserve itself by trampling upon the Law of Nature.[63]

To prove, that these Sort of policed Societies are a Violation offered to Nature, and a Constraint upon the human Mind, it needs only to look upon the sanguinary Measures, and Instruments of Vio-

---

[62] **Practice**   the young Frederick the Great wrote an *Anti-Machiavel*.
[63] **Law of Nature**   'comme pour établir L'Escalavage il a fallu faire violence à la Nature, il a fallu la changer pour perpetuer ce Droit' (*Discours*, p. 155).

lence which are every where used to support them. Let us take a Review of the Dungeons, Whips, Chains, Racks, Gibbets, with which every Society is abundantly stored, by which hundreds of Victims are annually offered up to support a dozen or two in Pride and Madness, and Millions in an abject Servitude, and Dependence. There was a Time, when I looked with a reverential Awe on these Mysteries of Policy; but Age, Experience, and Philosophy have rent the Veil; and I view this *Sanctum Sanctorum*,[64] at least, without any enthusiastick Admiration. I acknowledge indeed, the Necessity of such a Proceeding in such Institutions; but I must have a very mean Opinion of Institutions where such Proceedings are necessary.

It is a Misfortune, that in no Part of the Globe natural Liberty and natural Religion are to be found pure, and free from the Mixture of political Adulterations. Yet we have implanted[65] in us by Providence Ideas, Axioms, Rules, of what is pious, just, fair, honest, which no political Craft, nor learned Sophistry, can entirely expel from our Breasts. By these we judge, and we cannot otherwise judge of the several artificial Modes of Religion and Society, and determine of them as they approach to, or recede from this Standard.

The simplest Form of Government is *Despotism*, where all the inferior Orbs of Power are moved merely by the Will of the Supreme, and all that are subjected to them, directed in the same Manner, merely by the occasional Will of the Magistrate. This Form, as it is the most simple, so it is infinitely the most general. Scarce any Part of the World is exempted from its Power. And in those few Places where Men enjoy what they call Liberty, it is continually in a tottering Situation, and makes greater and greater Strides to that Gulph of Despotism which at last swallows up every Species of Government. This Manner of ruling being directed merely by the Will of the weakest, and generally the worst Man in the Society, becomes the most foolish and capricious Thing, at the same time that it is the most terrible and destructive that well can be conceived. In a Despotism the principal Person finds, that let the Want, Misery, and Indigence of his Subjects, be what they will, he can yet possess abundantly of every thing to gratify his most insatiable Wishes. He does more. He finds that these Gratifications increase in proportion to the Wretchedness

[64] *Sanctus Sanctorum*   holy of holies.
[65] **implanted**   but Bolingbroke, who admired Locke's *Essay*, was not an innatist. But cf. Rousseau's *pitié* which, however, was not knowledge.

and Slavery of his Subjects. Thus encouraged both by Passion and Interest to trample on the publick Welfare, and by his Station placed above both Shame and Fear, he proceeds to the most horrid and shocking Outrages upon Mankind. Their Persons become Victims of his Suspicions. The slightest Displeasure is Death; and a disagreeable Aspect is often as great a Crime as High-treason. In the Court of *Nero* a Person of Learning, of unquestioned Merit, and of unsuspected Loyalty, was put to Death for no other Reason than that he had a pedantick Countenance which displeased the Emperor.[66] This very Monster of Mankind appeared in the Beginning of his Reign to be a Person of Virtue.[67] Many of the greatest Tyrants on the Records of History have begun their Reigns in the fairest Manner. But the Truth is, this unnatural Power corrupts both the Heart, and the Understanding. And to prevent the least Hope of Amendment, a King is ever surrounded by a Crowd of infamous Flatterers, who find their Account in keeping him from the least Light of Reason, till all Ideas of Rectitude and Justice are utterly erased from his Mind. When *Alexander* had in his Fury inhumanly butchered one of his best Friends, and bravest Captains; on the Return of Reason he began to conceive an Horror suitable to the Guilt of such a Murder. In this Juncture, his Council came to his Assistance. But what did his Council? They found him out a Philosopher who gave him Comfort. And in what Manner did this Philosopher comfort him for the Loss of such a Man, and heal his Conscience, flagrant with the Smart of such a Crime? You have the Matter at Length in *Plutarch*. He told him; *'that let a Sovereign do what he will, all his actions are just and lawful, because they are his.'* [68] The Palaces of all Princes abound with such courtly Philosophers. The Consequence was such as might be expected. He grew every Day a Monster more abandoned to unnatural Lust, to Debauchery, to Drunkenness, and to Murder. And yet this was originally a great Man, of uncommon Capacity, and a strong Propensity to Virtue. But unbounded Power proceeds Step by Step, until it has eradicated every laudable Principle. It has been remarked, that there is no Prince so bad, whose Favourites and Ministers are not worse. There is hardly any Prince without a Favourite, by whom he is

---

[66] **Emperor** Suetonius, *Nero*, 37; but Nero had other 'reasons' for disposing of P. Clodius Thresea Paetus – see esp. Tacitus, *Annals*, XVI.21.

[67] **Virtue** see Tacitus, *Annals*, XIII e.g. 4, 51.

[68] **his** the story is based on Plutarch, *Alexander*, 50–2.

governed in as arbitrary a Manner as he governs the Wretches subjected to him. Here the Tyranny is doubled. There are two Courts, and two Interests; both very different from the Interests of the People. The Favourite knows that the Regard of a Tyrant is as unconstant and capricious as that of a Woman;[69] and concluding his Time to be short, he makes haste to fill up the Measure of his Iniquity, in Rapine, in Luxury, and in Revenge. Every Avenue to the Throne is shut up. He oppresses, and ruins the People, whilst he persuades the Prince, that those Murmurs raised by his own Oppression are the Effects of Disaffection to the Prince's Government. Then is the natural Violence of Despotism inflamed, and aggravated by Hatred and Revenge. To deserve well of the State is a Crime against the Prince. To be popular, and to be a Traitor, are considered as synonimous Terms. Even Virtue is dangerous, as an aspiring Quality, that claims an Esteem by itself, and independent of the Countenance of the Court. What has been said of the chief, is true of the inferior Officers of this Species of Government; each in his Province exercising the same Tyranny, and grinding the People by an Oppression, the more severely felt, as it is near them, and exercised by base and subordinate Persons. For the Gross of the People; they are considered as a mere Herd of Cattle; and really in a little Time become no better; all Principle of honest Pride, all Sense of the Dignity of their Nature, is lost in their Slavery. The Day, says *Homer*,[70] which makes a Man a Slave, takes away half his Worth; and in fact, he loses every Impulse to Action, but that low and base one of Fear. – In this kind of Government human Nature is not only abused, and insulted, but it is actually degraded and sunk into a Species of Brutality.[71] The Consideration of this made Mr *Locke*[72] say, with great Justice, that a Government of this kind was worse than Anarchy; indeed it is so abhorred, and detested

---

[69] **Woman**   Tacitus, *Annals*, I, 4 for *muliebri inpotentia*.

[70] *Homer*, *Odyssey*, XVII. 322–3 cf. CA, below, p. 224–5. For a similar idea about poverty, see [John Trenchard and Thomas Gordon], *Cato's Letters: or, Essays on Liberty, Civil and Religious*[6] (1755): 'Poverty dejects the Mind, fashions it to Slavery, and renders it unequal to any generous Undertaking, and incapable of opposing any bold Usurpation' (letter of 18 Feb. 1720, I, p. 113); and about dependence, Adam Smith, *Lectures on Jurisprudence*, ed. R.L. Meek, D.D. Raphael and P.G. Stein (1978), p. 333 (report of 1762–3).

[71] **Brutality**   'C'est du sein de ce désordre & de ces révolutions que le Despotisme élevant par dégrés sa tête hideuse, & dévorant tout ce qu'il auroit apperçu de bon et de sain dans toutes les parties de l'Etat' (*Discours*, p. 174).

[72] *Locke*   a reminiscence of *Two Treatises of Government*, II.xi.137.

by all who live under Forms that have a milder Appearance, that there is scarce a rational Man in *Europe*, that would not prefer Death to *Asiatick* Despotism. Here then we have the Acknowledgment of a great Philosopher, that an irregular State of Nature is preferable to such a Government; we have the Consent of all sensible and generous Men, who carry it yet further, and avow that Death itself is preferable; and yet this Species of Government, so justly condemned, and so generally detested, is what infinitely the greater Part of Mankind groan under, and have groaned under from the Beginning. So that by sure and uncontested Principles, the greatest Part of the Governments on Earth must be concluded Tyrannies, Impostures, Violations of the Natural Rights of Mankind, and worse than the most disorderly Anarchies. How much other Forms exceed this, we shall consider immediately.

In all Parts of the World, Mankind, however debased, retains still the Sense of *Feeling*; the Weight of Tyranny, at last, becomes insupportable; but the Remedy is not so easy; in general, the only Remedy by which they attempt to cure the Tyranny, is to change the Tyrant. This is, and always was the Case for the greater Part. In some Countries however, were found Men of more Penetration; who discovered, '*that to live by one Man's Will, was the Cause of all Men's Misery.*'[73]. They therefore changed their former Method, and assembling the Men in their several Societies, the most respectable for their Understanding and Fortunes, they confided to them the Charge of the publick Welfare. This originally formed what is called an *Aristocracy*. They hoped, it would be impossible that such a Number could ever join in any Design against the general Good; and they promised themselves a great deal of Security and Happiness, from the united Counsels of so many able and experienced Persons. But it is now found by abundant Experience, that an *Aristocracy*, and a *Despotism*, differ but in Name; and that a People, who are in general excluded from any Share of the Legislative, are to all Intents and Purposes, as much Slaves, when twenty, independent of them, govern, as when but one domineers. The Tyranny is even more felt, as every Individual of the Nobles has the Haughtiness of a Sultan; the People are more miserable, as they seem on the Verge of Liberty,

---

[73] *Misery* 'Or dans les relations d'homme à homme, le pis qui puisse arriver à l'un étant de se voir à la discrétion de l'autre' (*Discours*, p. 145). The source is Hooker *of the Lawes of Ecclesiastical Politie* I. x. 5 (slightly altered).

from which they are for ever debarred; this fallacious Idea of Liberty, whilst it presents a vain Shadow of Happiness to the Subject, binds faster the Chains of his Subjection. What is left undone, by the natural Avarice and Pride of those who are raised above the others, is compleated by their Suspicions, and their Dread of losing an Authority, which has no Support in the common Utility of the Nation. A *Genoese*, or a *Venetian* Republick,[74] is a concealed *Despotism*; where you find the same Pride of the Rulers, the same base Subjection of the People, the same bloody Maxims of a suspicious Policy. In one respect the *Aristocracy* is worse than the *Despotism*. A Body Politick, whilst it retains its Authority, never changes its Maxims; a *Despotism*, which is this Day horrible to a Supreme Degree, by the Caprice natural to the Heart of Man, may, by the same Caprice otherwise exerted, be as lovely the next; in a Succession, it is possible to meet with some good Princes. If there have been *Tiberius's*, *Caligula's*, *Nero's*, there have been likewise the serener Days of *Vespasian's*, *Titus's*, *Trajan's*, and *Antonine's*;[75] but a Body Politick is not influenced by Caprice or Whim; it proceeds in a regular Manner; its Succession is insensible; and every Man as he enters it, either has, or soon attains the Spirit of the whole Body. Never was it known, that an *Aristocracy*, which was haughty and tyrannical in one Century, became easy and mild in the next. In effect, the Yoke of this Species of Government is so galling, that whenever the People have got the least Power, they have shaken it off with the utmost Indignation, and established a popular Form. And when they have not had Strength enough to support themselves, they have thrown themselves into the Arms of *Despotism*, as the more eligible of the two Evils. This latter was the Case of *Denmark*,[76] who sought a Refuge from the Oppression of its Nobility, in the strong Hold of arbitrary Power. *Poland* [77] has at

---

[74] **Venetian Republick**   alluding to the closed hegemonies that in fact ruled these states, which were republican only in that they lacked a king.

[75] **Antonine's**   presumably refers to both Antoninus Pius and Marcus Aurelius.

[76] **Denmark**   Frederick III became hereditary king of Denmark after the Danes had been defeated by Charles X of Sweden in 1657–58 and increased the power of the monarchy as part of a series of measures designed to modernize the government, law and administration.

[77] **Poland**   was predominantly a land of peasants, but had a nobility which amounted to about 10 per cent of its population. The latter occupied vast estates and the more important political offices, as well as controlling the policy of the state (often with diverting results). At the time of writing the Polish monarchy had failed to establish either a strong central government or representative institutions.

present the Name of Republick, and it is one of the *Aristocratick* Form; but it is well known, that the little Finger of this Government, is heavier than the Loins of arbitrary Power in most Nations. The People are not only politically, but personally Slaves, and treated with the utmost Indignity. The Republick of *Venice* is somewhat more moderate; yet even here, so heavy is the *Aristocratick* Yoke, that the Nobles have been obliged to enervate the Spirit of their Subjects by every Sort of Debauchery; they have denied them the Liberty of Reason, and they have made them amends, by what a base Soul will think a more valuable Liberty, by not only allowing, but encouraging them to corrupt themselves in the most scandalous Manner. They consider their Subjects, as the Farmer does the Hog he keeps to feast upon. He holds him fast in his Stye, but allows him to wallow as much as he pleases in his beloved Filth and Gluttony. So scandalously debauched a People as that of *Venice*, is to be met with no where else. High, Low, Men, Women, Clergy, and Laity, are all alike. The ruling Nobility are no less afraid of one another, than they are of the People; and for that Reason, politically enervate their own Body by the same effeminate Luxury, by which they corrupt their Subjects. They are impoverished by every Means which can be invented; and they are kept in a perpetual Terror by the Horrors of a State-inquisition; here you see a People deprived of all rational Freedom, and tyrannized over by about two Thousand Men; and yet this Body of two Thousand, are so far from enjoying any Liberty by the Subjection of the rest, that they are in an infinitely severer State of Slavery; they make themselves the most degenerate, and unhappy of Mankind, for no other Purpose than that they may the more effectually contribute to the Misery of an whole Nation. In short, the regular and methodical Proceedings of an *Aristocracy*, are more intolerable than the very Excesses of a *Despotism*, and in general, much further from any Remedy.

Thus, my Lord, we have pursued *Aristocracy* through its whole Progress; we have seen the Seeds, the Growth, and the Fruit. It could boast none of the Advantages of a *Despotism*, miserable as those Advantages were, and it was overloaded with an Exuberance of Mischiefs, unknown even to *Despotism* itself. In effect, it is no more than a disorderly Tyranny. This Form therefore could be little approved, even in Speculation, by those who were capable of thinking, and could be less borne in Practice by any who were capable of feeling.

However, the fruitful Policy of Man was not yet exhausted. He had yet another Farthing-candle to supply the Deficiencies of the Sun. This was the third Form, known by political Writers under the Name of *Democracy*. Here the People transacted all publick Business, or the greater Part of it, in their own Persons: their Laws were made by themselves, and upon any Failure of Duty, their Officers were accountable to themselves, and to them only. In all appearance, they had secured by this Method the Advantages of Order and good Government, without paying their Liberty for the Purchace. Now, my LORD, we are come to the Master-piece of *Grecian* Refinement, and *Roman* Solidity, a popular Government. The earliest and most celebrated Republic of this Model, was that of *Athens*. It was constructed by no less an Artist, than the celebrated Poet and Philosopher, *Solon*. But no sooner was this political Vessel launched from the Stocks, than it overset, even in the Life-time of the Builder. A Tyranny immediately supervened; not by a foreign Conquest, not by Accident, but by the very Nature and Constitution of a *Democracy*. An artful Man[78] became popular, the People had Power in their Hands, and they devolved a considerable Share of their Power upon their Favourite; and the only Use he made of this Power, was to plunge those who gave it into Slavery. Accident restored their Liberty, and the same good Fortune produced Men of uncommon Abilities and uncommon Virtues amongst them. But these Abilities were suffered to be of little Service either to their Possessors or to the State. Some of these Men, for whose Sakes alone we read their History, they banished; others they imprisoned; and all they treated with various Circumstances of the most shameful Ingratitude.[79] Republicks have many Things in the Spirit of absolute Monarchy, but none more than this; a shining Merit is ever hated or suspected in a popular Assembly, as well as in a Court; and all Services done the State, are looked upon as dangerous to the Rulers, whether Sultans or Senators. The *Ostracism*[80] at *Athens* was built upon this Principle. The giddy People, whom we have now under Consideration, being elated with some Flashes of Success, which they owed to nothing less than any Merit of their own, began to tyrannize over their Equals, who had associated

---

[78] **an artful Man**   Pisistratus.
[79] **Ingratitude**   e.g. Aristides and Themistocles.
[80] *Ostracism*   in Athens, a method of banishing unpopular citizens for ten years, which involved neither subsequent disgrace nor disability.

with them for their common Defence. With their Prudence they renounced all Appearance of Justice. They entered into Wars rashly and wantonly. If they were unsuccessful, instead of growing wiser by their Misfortune, they threw the whole Blame of their own Misconduct on the Ministers who had advised, and the Generals who had conducted those Wars; until by degrees they had cut off all who could serve them in their Councils or their Battles. If at any time these Wars had an happier Issue, it was no less difficult to deal with them on account of their Pride and Insolence. Furious in their Adversity, tyrannical in their Successes, a Commander had more Trouble to concert his Defence before the People, than to plan the Operations of the Campaign. It was not uncommon for a General, under the horrid *Despotism* of the *Roman* Emperors, to be ill received in proportion to the Greatness of his Services. *Agricola* is a strong Instance of this. No Man had done greater Things, nor with more honest Ambition. Yet on his Return to Court, he was obliged to enter *Rome* with all the Secrecy of a Criminal. He went to the Palace, not like a victorious Commander who had merited and might demand the greatest Rewards, but like an Offender who had come to supplicate a Pardon for his Crimes. His Reception was answerable: '*Brevi osculo, & nullo sermone exceptus, turbæ servientium immissus est.*'[81] Yet in that worst Season of this worst of monarchical *Tyrannies, Modesty, Discretion, and a Coolness of Temper, formed some kind of Security even for the highest Merit. But at *Athens*, the nicest and best studied Behaviour was not a sufficient Guard for a Man of great Capacity. Some of their bravest Commanders were obliged to fly their Country, some to enter into the Service of its Enemies, rather than abide a popular Determination on their Conduct, left, as one of them said, their Giddiness might make the People condemn where they meant to acquit; to throw in a black Bean, even when they intended a white one.

The *Athenians* made a very rapid Progress to the most enormous Excesses. The People under no Restraint soon grew dissolute, luxur-

---

* Sciant quibus moris illicita mirari, posse etiam sub malis principibus magnos viros,[82] & c. See 42 to the End of it.

[81] ***immissus est*** 'he was received with a hasty kiss and without a word, lost amidst the courtier crowd' (Tacitus, *Agricola*, c. 40).

[82] **viros** 'let it be clear to those who admire forbidden conduct, that even under bad rulers men can be great' (*Agricola*, c. 40).

ious, and idle. They renounced all Labour, and began to subsist themselves from the publick Revenues. They lost all Concern for their common Honour or Safety, and could bear no Advice that tended to reform them. At this time Truth became offensive to those Lords the People, and most highly dangerous to the Speaker. The Orators no longer ascended the *Rostrum*,[83] but to corrupt them further with the most fulsome Adulation. These Orators were all bribed by foreign Princes on the one Side or the other. And besides its own Parties, in this City there were Parties, and avowed ones too, for the *Persians*, *Spartans* and *Macedonians*, supported each of them by one or more Demagogues pensioned and bribed to this iniquitous Service. The People, forgetful of all Virtue and publick Spirit, and intoxicated with the Flatteries of their Orators (these Courtiers of Republicks, and endowed with the distinguishing Characteristicks of all other Courtiers) this People, I say, at last arrived at that Pitch of Madness, that they coolly and deliberately, by an express Law, made it capital for any Man to propose an Application of the immense Sums squandered in publick Shows, even to the most necessary Purposes of the State. When you see the People of this Republick banishing or murdering their best and ablest Citizens, dissipating the publick Treasure with the most senseless Extravagance, and spending their whole Time, as Spectators or Actors, in playing, fidling, dancing and singing, does it not, my LORD, strike your Imagination with the Image of a fort of a complex *Nero?* And does it not strike you with the greater Horror, when you observe, not one Man only, but a whole City, grown drunk with Pride and Power, running with a Rage of Folly into the same mean and senseless Debauchery and Extravagance? But if this People resembled *Nero* in their Extravagance, much more did they resemble and even exceed him in Cruelty and Injustice. In the Time of *Pericles*, one of the most celebrated Times in the History of that Commonwealth, a King of *Egypt*[84] sent them a Donation of Corn. This they were mean enough to accept. And had the *Egyptian* Prince intended the Ruin of this City of wicked Bedlamites, he could not have taken a more effectual Method to do it, than by such an ensnaring Largess. The Distribution of this Bounty caused a Quarrel; the

---

[83] **Rostrum** strictly a Roman term; for an account of the agora of Athens, see Pausanias, Bk. I, 2–17.

[84] **King of Egypt** see Plutarch, *Pericles*, 37 for the whole episode; the figure of five thousand is faithful to the source.

Majority set on foot an Enquiry into the Title of the Citizens; and upon a vain Pretence of Illegitimacy, newly and occasionally set up, they deprived of their Share of the royal Donation no less than five thousand of their own Body. They went further; they disfranchised them; and having once begun with an Act of Injustice, they could set no Bounds to it. Not content with cutting them off from the Rights of Citizens, they plundered these unfortunate Wretches of all their Substance; and to crown this Master-piece of Violence and Tyranny, they actually sold every Man of the five thousand as Slaves in the publick Market. Observe, my LORD, that the five thousand we here speak of, were cut off from a Body of no more than nineteen thousand; for the entire Number of Citizens was no greater at that Time. Could the Tyrant who wished the *Roman* People but one Neck; could the Tyrant *Caligula* himself have done, nay, he could scarcely wish for a greater Mischief, than to have cut off, at one Stroke, a fourth of his People?[85] Or has the Cruelty of that Series of sanguine Tyrants, the *Cæsar's*, ever presented such a Piece of flagrant and entensive Wickedness? The whole History of this celebrated Republick is but one Tissue of Rashness, Folly, Ingratitude, Injustice, Tumult, Violence, and Tyranny, and indeed of every Species of Wickedness that can well be imagined. This was a City of Wisemen, in which a Minister could not exercise his Functions; a warlike People, amongst whom a General did not dare either to gain or lose a Battle; a learned Nation, in which a Philosopher[86] could not venture on a free Enquiry. This was the City which banished *Themistocles*, starved *Aristides*, forced into Exile *Miltiades*, drove out *Anaxagoras*, and poisoned *Socrates*. This was a City which changed the Form of its Government with the Moon; eternal Conspiracies, Revolutions daily, nothing fixed and established. A Republick, as an antient Philosopher has observed, is no one Species of Government, but a Magazine of every Species; here you find every Sort of it, and that in the worst Form. As there is a

[85] **fourth** Plutarch records that after the legislation, 14,040 Athenians remained as citizens.
of his People Caligula is supposed to have exclaimed, 'Utinam populus Romanus unam cervicem haberet!'; see Suetonius, *Caligula*, c. 30.

[86] **Philosopher** Plato, *Republic*, VIII.557.b-d cf. 561.e obser/es that all varieties of constitution and character will be found under democracy; but suggests that tyranny can be worse than it.

The entire account of Athens should be compared with Bolingbroke's *On the Policy of the Athenians*, which suggests that Athens enjoyed glory and prosperity until subverted by Pericles.

perpetual Change, one rising and the other falling, you have all the Violence and wicked Policy, by which a beginning Power must always acquire its Strength, and all the Weakness by which falling States are brought to a complete Destruction.

Rome has a more venerable Aspect than *Athens*; and she conducted her Affairs, so far as related to the Ruin and Oppression of the greatest Part of the World, with greater Wisdom and more Uniformity. But the domestic Oeconomy of these two States was nearly or altogether the same. An internal Dissention constantly tore to Pieces the Bowels of the *Roman* Commonwealth. You find the same Confusion, the same Factions which subsisted at *Athens*, the same Tumults, the same Revolutions, and in fine, the same Slavery. If perhaps their former Condition did not deserve that Name altogether as well. All other Republicks were of the same Character. *Florence*[87] was a Transcript of *Athens*. And the modern Republicks, as they approach more or less to the Democratick Form, partake more or less of the Nature of those which I have described.

We are now at the Close of our Review of the three simple Forms of artificial Society, and we have shewn them, however they may differ in Name, or in some slight Circumstances, to be all alike in effect; in effect, to be all Tyrannies. But suppose we were inclined to make the most ample Concessions; let us concede *Athens*, *Rome*, *Carthage*, and two or three more of the antient, and as many of the modern Commonwealths, to have been, or to be free and happy, and to owe their Freedom and Happiness to their political Constitution. Yet allowing all this, what Defence does this make for artificial Society in general, that these inconsiderable Spots of the Globe have for some short Space of Time stood as Exceptions to a Charge so general? But when we call these Governments free, or concede that their Citizens were happier than those which lived under different Forms, it is merely *ex abundanti*.[88] For we should be greatly mistaken, if we really thought that the Majority of the People which filled these Cities, enjoyed even that nominal political Freedom of which I have spoken so much already. In reality, they had no Part of it. In *Athens* there were usually from ten to thirty thousand Freemen: This was the utmost. But the

---

[87] **Florence** under the Medici had been divided by rivalries between the classes and the greater families; whilst the latter monopolized the chief magistracy, they failed to develop a coherent policy and so created an opportunity for opposition.

[88] **ex abundanti** from the surplus.

Slaves usually amounted to four hundred thousand, and sometimes to a great many more. The Freemen of *Sparta* and *Rome* were not more numerous in proportion to those whom they held in a Slavery, even more terrible than the *Athenian*. Therefore state the Matter fairly: The free States never formed, though they were taken all together, the thousandth Part of the habitable Globe; the Freemen in these States were never the twentieth Part of the People, and the Time they subsisted is scarce any thing in that immense Ocean of Duration in which Time and Slavery are so nearly commensurate. Therefore call these free States, or popular Governments, or what you please; when we consider the Majority of their Inhabitants, and regard the natural Rights of Mankind, they must appear in Reality and Truth, no better than pitiful and oppressive Oligarchies.

After so fair an Examen, wherein nothing has been exaggerated; no Fact produced which cannot be proved, and none which has been produced in any wise forced or strained, while thousands have, for Brevity, been omitted; after so candid a Discussion in all respects; what Slave so passive, what Bigot so blind, what Enthusiast so head-long, what Politician so hardened, as to stand up in Defence of a System calculated for a Curse to Mankind? a Curse under which they smart and groan to this Hour, without thoroughly knowing the Nature of the Disease, and wanting Understanding or Courage to apply the Remedy.

I need not excuse myself to your Lordship, nor, I think, to any honest Man, for the Zeal I have shewn in this Cause; for it is an honest Zeal, and in a good Cause. I have defended Natural Religion against a Confederacy of Atheists and Divines.[89] I now plead for Natural Society against Politicians, and for Natural Reason against all three. When the World is in a fitter Temper than it is at present to hear Truth, or when I shall be more indifferent about its Temper; my Thoughts may become more publick. In the mean time, let them repose in my own Bosom, and in the Bosoms of such Men as are fit to be initiated in the sober Mysteries of Truth and Reason. My Anta-gonists have already done as much as I could desire. Parties in Reli-

---

[89] **Atheists and Divines** Bolingbroke had in fact argued that the divines who used the unmerited distribution of good and evil in this world to argue for a fair one in the next were little better than atheists (*Works*, v pp. 323, 355–6, 364, 378, 394–5, 487ff, 491, 542).

gion and Politics make sufficient Discoveries concerning each other, to give a sober Man a proper Caution against them all.[90] The Monarchic, Aristocratical, and Popular Partizans have been jointly laying their Axes to the Root of all Government, and have in their Turns proved each other absurd and inconvenient. In vain you tell me that Artificial Government is good, but that I fall out only with the Abuse. The Thing! the Thing itself is the Abuse! Observe, my LORD, I pray you, that grand Error upon which all artificial legislative Power is founded. It was observed, that Men had ungovernable Passions, which made it necessary to guard against the Violence they might offer to each other. They appointed Governors over them for this Reason; but a worse and more perplexing Difficulty arises, how to be defended against the Governors? *Quis custodiet ipsos custodes?*[91] In vain they change from a single Person to a few. These few have the Passions of the one, and they unite to strengthen themselves, and to secure the Gratification of their lawless Passions at the Expence of the general Good. In vain do we fly to the Many. The Case is worse; their Passions are less under the Government of Reason, they are augmented by the Contagion, and defended against all Attacks by their Multitude.

I have purposely avoided the mention of the mixed Form of Government, for Reasons that will be very obvious to your Lordship. But my Caution can avail me but little. You will not fail to urge it against me in favour of Political Society. You will not fail to shew how the Errors of the several simple Modes are corrected by a Mixture of all of them, and a proper Ballance of the several Powers in such a State. I confess, my LORD, that this has been long a darling Mistake of my own;[92] and that of all the Sacrifices I have made to Truth, this has been by far the greatest. When I confess that I think this Notion a Mistake, I know to whom I am speaking, for I am satisfied that Reasons are like Liquors, and there are some of such a Nature as none but strong Heads can bear. There are few with whom I can communicate so freely as with *Pope*. But *Pope* cannot bear every Truth. He has a Timidity which hinders the full Exertion of his

---

[90] **Parties ... them all** Burke's *Present Discontents* is devoted partly to showing an exception.

[91] *ipsos custodes* who will guard the guards themselves (Juvenal *Satires*, VI.347–8 (in traditional lineation)).

[92] **of my own** see Bolingbroke, *Remarks on the History of England*, I.

Faculties, almost as effectually as Bigotry cramps those of the general Herd of Mankind. But whoever is a genuine Follower of Truth, keeps his Eye steady upon his Guide, indifferent whither he is led, provided that she is the Leader. And, my LORD, if it be properly considered, it were infinitely better to remain possessed by the whole Legion of vulgar Mistakes, than to reject some, and at the same time to retain a Fondness for others altogether as absurd and irrational. The first has at least a Consistency, that makes a Man, however erroneously, uniform at least; but the latter way of proceeding is such an inconsistent Chimæra and Jumble of Philosophy and vulgar Prejudice, that hardly anything more ridiculous can be conceived. Let us therefore freely, and without Fear or Prejudice, examine this last Contrivance of Policy. And without considering how near the Quick our Instruments may come, let us search it to the Bottom.

First then, all Men are agreed, that this Junction of Regal, Aristocratic, and Popular Power, must form a very complex, nice, and intricate Machine, which being composed of such a Variety of Parts, with such opposite Tendencies and Movements, it must be liable on every Accident to be disordered. To speak without Metaphor, such a Government must be liable to frequent Cabals, Tumults, and Revolutions, from its very Constitution. These are undoubtedly as ill Effects, as can happen in a Society; for in such a Case, the Closeness acquired by Community, instead of serving for mutual Defence, serves only to increase the Danger. Such a System is like a City, where Trades that require constant Fires are much exercised, where the Houses are built of combustible Materials, and where they stand extremely close.

In the second Place, the several constituent Parts having their distinct Rights, and these many of them so necessary to be determined with Exactness, are yet so indeterminate in their Nature, that it becomes a new and constant Source of Debate and Confusion. Hence it is, that whilst the Business of Government should be carrying on, the Question is, who has a Right to exercise this or that Function of it, or what Men have Power to keep their Offices in any Function. Whilst this Contest continues, and whilst the Ballance in any sort continues, it has never any Remission; all manner of Abuses and Villanies in Officers remain unpunished, the greatest Frauds and Robberies in the publick Revenues are committed in Defiance of Justice; and Abuses grow, by Time and Impunity, into Customs; until they prescribe against the Laws, and grow too inveterate often to admit a Cure, unless such as may be as bad as the Disease.

Thirdly, the several Parts of this Species of Government, though united, preserve the Spirit which each Form has separately. Kings are ambitious; the Nobility haughty; and the Populace tumultuous and ungovernable. Each Party, however in appearance peaceable, carries on a Design upon the others; and it is owing to this, that in all Questions, whether concerning foreign or domestick Affairs, the Whole generally turns more upon some Party-Matter than upon the Nature of the Thing itself; whether such a Step will diminish or augment the Power of the Crown, or how far the Privileges of the Subject are like to be extended or restricted by it. And these Questions are constantly resolved, without any Consideration of the Merits of the Cause, merely as the Parties who uphold these jarring Interests may chance to prevail; and as they prevail, the Ballance is overset, now upon one side, now upon the other. The Government is one Day, arbitrary Power in a single Person; another, a juggling Confederacy of a few to cheat the Prince and enslave the People; and the third, a frantick and unmanageable Democracy. The great Instrument of all these Changes, and what infuses a peculiar Venom into all of them, is Party. It is of no Consequence what the Principles of any Party, or what their Pretensions are; the Spirit which actuates all Parties is the same; the Spirit of Ambition, of Self-Interest, of Oppression, and Treachery. This Spirit entirely reverses all the Principles which a benevolent Nature has erected within us; all Honesty, all equal Justice, and even the Ties of natural Society, the natural Affections. In a word, my LORD, we have all *seen*, and if any outward Considerations were worthy the lasting Concern of a wise Man, we have some of us *felt*, such Oppression from Party Government as no other Tyranny can parallel. We behold daily the most important Rights, Rights upon which all the others depend, we behold these Rights determined in the last Resort, without the least Attention even to the Appearance or Colour of Justice; we behold this without Emotion, because we have grown up in the constant View of such Practices; and we are not surprised to hear a Man requested to be a Knave and a Traitor, with as much Indifference as if the most ordinary Favour were asked; and we hear this Request refused, not because it is a most unjust and unreasonable Desire, but that this

Worthy has already engaged his Injustice to another. These and many
more Points I am far from spreading to their full Extent. You are
sensible that I do not put forth half my Strength; and you cannot be at
a Loss for the Reason. A Man is allowed sufficient Freedom of
Thought, provided he knows how to chuse his Subject properly. You
may criticise freely upon the *Chinese* Constitution, and observe with as
much Severity as you please upon the absurd Tricks, or destructive
Bigotry of the Bonzees.[93] But the Scene is changed as you come
homeward, and Atheism or Treason may be the Names given in
Britain, to what would be Reason and Truth if asserted of *China*. I
submit to the Condition, and though I have a notorious Advantage
before me, I wave the Pursuit. For else, my LORD, it is very obvious
what a Picture might be drawn of the Excesses of Party even in our
own Nation.[94] I could shew, that the same Faction has in one Reign
promoted popular Seditions, and in the next been a Patron of
Tyranny; I could shew, that they have all of them betrayed the publick
Safety at all Times, and have very frequently with equal Perfidy made
a Market of their own Cause, and their own Associates. I could shew
how vehemently they have contended for Names, and how silently
they have passed over Things of the last Importance. And I could
demonstrate, that they have had the Opportunity of doing all this
Mischief, nay, that they themselves had their Origin and Growth from
that complex Form of Government which we are wisely taught to look
upon as so great a Blessing. Revolve, my LORD, our History from the
Conquest.[95] We scarce ever had a Prince, who by Fraud, or Violence,
had not made some Infringement on the Constitution. We scarce ever
had a Parliament which knew, when it attempted to set Limits to the
Royal Authority, how to set Limits to its own. Evils we have had
continually calling for Reformation, and Reformations more grievous
than any Evils. Our boasted Liberty sometimes trodden down,
sometimes giddily set up, and ever precariously fluctuating and
unsettled; it has been only kept alive by the Blasts of continual Feuds,
Wars, and Conspiracies. In no Country in *Europe* has the Scaffold so
often blushed with the Blood of its Nobility. Confiscations, Banish-

---

[93] **Bonzees**   bonzee is a term appropriated by Europeans to the Buddhist clergy of Japan
and Asia.
[94] **even in our own Nation**   see Bolingbroke, *Dissertation on Parties*, esp. xvii–xix.
[95] **our History from the Conquest**   see Bolingbroke, *Remarks on the History of England*,
IV onwards, and latterly, *Letters on the Study and Use of History*, VI–VIII.

ments, Attainders, Executions, make a large Part of the History of such of our Families as are not utterly extinguished by them. Formerly indeed Things had a more ferocious Appearance than they have at this Day. In these early and unrefined Ages, the jarring Parts of a certain chaotic Constitution supported their several Pretensions by the Sword. Experience and Policy have since taught other Methods.

Res vero nunc agitur tenui pulmone rubetæ.[96]

But how far Corruption, Venality, the Contempt of Honour, the Oblivion of all Duty to our Country, and the most abandoned publick Prostitution, are preferable to the more glaring and violent Effects of Faction, I will not presume to determine. Sure I am that they are very great Evils.

I have done with the Forms of Government. During the Course of Enquiry you may have observed a very material Difference between my Manner of Reasoning and that which is in Use amongst the Abetors of artificial Society. They form their Plans upon what seems most eligible to their Imaginations, for the ordering of Mankind. I discover the Mistakes in those Plans, from the real known Consequences which have resulted from them. They have inlisted Reason to fight against itself, and employ its whole Force to prove that it is an insufficient Guide to them in the Conduct of their Lives. But unhappily for us, in proportion as we have deviated from the plain Rule of our Nature, and turned our Reason against itself, in that Proportion have we increased the Follies and Miseries of Mankind. The more deeply we penetrate into the Labyrinth of Art, the further we find ourselves from those Ends for which we entered it. This has happened in almost every Species of Artificial Society, and in all Times. We found, or we thought we found, an Inconvenience in having every Man the Judge of his own Cause. Therefore Judges were set up, at first with discretionary Powers. But it was soon found a miserable Slavery to have our Lives and Properties precarious, and hanging upon the arbitrary Determination of any one Man, or Set of Men. We flew to Laws as a Remedy for this Evil. By these we persuaded

---

[96] **rubetae** but now the business is done with a slice of toad's lung (Juvenal, *Satires*, VI.659, i.e. with poison); Juvenal contrasts modern methods of murdering husbands with the axes used in earlier and less subtle times.

ourselves we might know with some Certainty upon what Ground we stood. But lo! Differences arose upon the Sense and Interpretation of these Laws. Thus we were brought back to our old Incertitude. New Laws were made to expound the old; and new Difficulties arose upon the new Laws; as Words multiplied, Opportunities of cavilling upon them multiplied also. Then Recourse was had to Notes, Comments, Glosses, Reports, *Responsa Prudentum*,[97] learned Readings: Eagle stood against Eagle: Authority was set up against Authority. Some were allured by the modern, others reverenced the antient. The new were more enlightened, the old were more venerable. Some adopted the Comment, others stuck to the Text. The Confusion increased, the Mist thickened, until it could be discovered no longer what was allowed or forbidden, what Things were in Property, and what common. In this Uncertainty, (uncertain even to the Professors, an *Ægyptian*[98] Darkness to the rest of Mankind) the contending Parties felt themselves more effectually ruined by the Delay than they could have been by the Injustice of any Decision. Our Inheritances are become a Prize for Disputation; and Disputes and Litigations are become an Inheritance.

The Professors of Artificial Law have always walked hand in hand with the Professors of Artificial Theology. As their End, in confounding the Reason of Man, and abridging his natural Freedom, is exactly the same, they have adjusted the Means to that End in a Way entirely similar. The Divine thunders out his *Anathemas* with more Noise and Terror against the Breach of one of his positive Institutions, or the Neglect of some of his trivial Forms, than against the Neglect or Breach of those Duties and Commandments of natural Religion, which by these Forms and Institutions he pretends to enforce. The Lawyer has his Forms, and his positive Institutions too, and he adheres to them with a Veneration altogether as religious. The worst Cause cannot be so prejudicial to the Litigant, as his Advocate's or Attorney's Ignorance or Neglect of these Forms. A Law-suit is like an ill-managed Dispute, in which the first Object is soon out of Sight, and the Parties end upon a Matter wholly foreign to that on which they began. In a Law-suit the Question is, who has a Right to a certain House or Farm? And this Question is daily determined, not upon the Evidences of the Right, but upon the Observance or Neglect of some

---

[97] **Responsa Prudentum**   opinions of legal authorities.
[98] *Aegyptian*   alluding to Exodus 10:21–3.

Forms of Words in use with the Gentlemen of the Robe, about which there is even amongst themselves such a Disagreement, that the most experienced Veterans in the Profession can never be positively assured that they are not mistaken.

Let us expostulate with these learned Sages, these Priests of the sacred Temple[99] of Justice. Are we Judges of our own Property? By no means. You then, who are initiated into the Mysteries of the blindfold Goddess, inform me whether I have a Right to eat the Bread I have earned by the Hazard of my Life, or the Sweat of my Brow? The grave Doctor answers me in the Affirmative. The reverend Serjeant replies in the Negative; the learned Barrister reasons upon one side and upon the other, and concludes nothing. What shall I do? An Antagonist starts up and presses me hard. I enter the Field, and retain these three Persons to defend my Cause. My Cause, which two Farmers from the Plough[100] could have decided in half an Hour, takes the Court twenty Years. I am however at the end of my Labour, and have in Reward for all my Toil and Vexation, a Judgment in my Favour. But hold – a sagacious Commander, in the Adversary's Army has found a Flaw in the Proceeding. My Triumph is turned into Mourning. I have used *or*, instead of *and*, or some Mistake, small in Appearance, but dreadful in its Consequences, and have the whole of my Success quashed in a Writ of Error. I remove my Suit; I shift from Court to Court; I fly from Equity to Law, and from Law to Equity; equal Uncertainty attends me every where: And a Mistake in which I had no Share, decides at once upon my Liberty and Property, sending me from the Court to a Prison, and adjudging my Family to Beggary and Famine. I am innocent, Gentlemen, of the Darkness and Uncertainty of your Science. I never darkened it with absurd and contradictory Notions, nor confounded it with Chicane and Sophistry. You have excluded me from any Share in the Conduct of my own Cause; the Science was too deep for me; I acknowledged it; but it was too deep even for yourselves: You have made the way so intricate, that you are yourselves lost in it: You err, and you punish me for your Errors.

The Delay of the Law is, your Lordship will tell me, a trite Topic, and which of its Abuses have not been too severely felt not to be often complained of? A Man's Property is to serve for the Purposes of his

---

[99] **Temple** cf. Ref, p. 187.
[100] **from the Plough** the archetypal figure of unsophistication.

Support; and therefore to delay a Determination concerning that, is the worst Injustice, because it cuts off the very End and Purpose for which I applied to the Judicature for Relief. Quite contrary in Case of a Man's Life, there the Determination can hardly be too much protracted. Mistakes in this Case are as often fallen into as in any other, and if the Judgment is sudden, the Mistakes are the most irretrievable of all others. Of this the Gentlemen of the Robe are themselves sensible, and they have brought it into a Maxim. *De morte hominis nulla est cunctatio longa.*[101] But what could have induced them to reverse the Rules, and to contradict that Reason which dictated them, I am utterly unable to guess. A Point concerning Property, which ought, for the Reasons I just mentioned, to be most speedily decided, frequently exercises the Wit of Successions of Lawyers, for many Generations. *Multa virûm volvens durando sæcula vincit.*[102] But the Question concerning a Man's Life, that great Question in which no Delay ought to be counted tedious, is commonly determined in twenty-four Hours at the utmost. It is not to be wondered at, that Injustice and Absurdity should be inseparable Companions.

Ask of Politicians the End for which Laws were originally designed; and they will answer, that the Laws were designed as a Protection for the Poor and Weak, against the Oppression of the Rich and Powerful. But surely no Pretence can be so ridiculous; a Man might as well tell me he has taken off my Load, because he has changed the Burthen. If the poor Man is not able to support his Suit, according to the vexatious and expensive manner established in civilized Countries, has not the Rich as great an Advantage over him as the Strong has over the Weak in a State of Nature? But we will not place the State of Nature, which is the Reign of God, in competition with Political Society, which is the absurd Usurpation of Man. In a State of Nature, it is true, that a Man of superior Force may beat or rob me; but then it is true, that I am at full Liberty to defend myself, or make Reprisal by Surprize or by Cunning, or by any other way in which I may be superior to him. But in Political Society, a rich Man may rob me in another way. I cannot defend myself; for Money is the only Weapon with which we are allowed to fight. And if I attempt to avenge myself, the whole Force of that Society is ready to complete my Ruin.

---

[101] *cunctatio longa* 'a human death makes no pause lengthy' (Juvenal, 6.221).
[102] *saecula vincit* 'it survived many centuries, outliving generations of men' (*Georgics*, 2.295).

A good Parson once said, that where Mystery begins, Religion ends. Cannot I say, as truly at least, of human Laws, that where Mystery begins, Justice ends? It is hard to say, whether the Doctors of Law or Divinity have made the greater Advances in the lucrative Business of Mystery. The Lawyers, as well as the Theologians, have erected another Reason besides Natural Reason; and the Result has been, another Justice besides Natural Justice. They have so bewildered the World and themselves in unmeaning Forms and Ceremonies, and so perplexed the plainest Matters with metaphysical Jargon, that it carries the highest Danger to a Man out of that Profession, to make the least Step without their Advice and Assistance. Thus by confining to themselves the Knowledge of the Foundation of all Mens Lives and Properties, they have reduced all Mankind into the most abject and servile Dependence. We are Tenants at the Will of these Gentlemen for every thing; and a metaphysical Quibble is to decide whether the greatest Villain breathing shall meet his Deserts, or escape with Impunity, or whether the best Man in the Society shall not be reduced to the lowest and most despicable Condition it affords. In a word, my LORD, the Injustice, Delay, Puerility, false Refinement, and affected Mystery of the Law are such, that many who live under it come to admire and envy the Expedition, Simplicity, and Equality of arbitrary Judgments. I need insist the less on this Article to your Lordship, as you have frequently lamented the Miseries derived to us from Artificial Law, and your Candor is the more to be admired and applauded in this, as your Lordship's noble House has derived its Wealth and its Honours from that Profession.

Before we finish our Examination of Artifical Society, I shall lead your Lordship into a closer Consideration of the Relations which it gives Birth to, and the Benefits, if such they are, which result from these Relations. The most obvious Division of Society is into Rich and Poor; and it is no less obvious, that the Number of the former bear a great Disproportion to those of the latter. The whole Business of the Poor[103] is to administer to the Idleness, Folly, and Luxury of the Rich; and that of the Rich, in return, is to find the best Methods of confirming the Slavery and increasing the Burthens of the Poor. In

---

[103] **of the Poor** 'Les riches ... connurent à peine le plaisir de dominer, qu'ils dédaignerent bientôt tous les autres; & se servant de leurs anciens Esclaves pour en soumettre de nouveaux, ils ne songérent qu'a subjuger & asservir leurs voisins' (*Discours*, p. 130).

a State of Nature, it is an invariable Law, that a Man's Acquisitions are in proportion to his Labours. In a State of Artificial Society, it is a Law as constant and as invariable, that those who labour most, enjoy the fewest Things;[104] and that those who labour not at all, have the greatest Number of Enjoyments. A Constitution of Things this, strange and ridiculous beyond Expression. We scarce believe a thing when we are told it, which we actually see before our Eyes every Day without being in the least surprized. I suppose that there are in *Great-Britain* upwards of an hundred thousand People employed in Lead, Tin, Iron, Copper, and Coal Mines; these unhappy Wretches scarce ever see the Light of the Sun; they are buried in the Bowels of the Earth; there they work at a severe and dismal Task, without the least Prospect of being delivered from it; they subsist upon the coarsest and worst sort of Fare; they have their Health miserably impaired, and their Lives cut short, by being perpetually confined in the close Vapour of these malignant Minerals. An hundred thousand more at least are tortured without Remission by the suffocating Smoak, intense Fires, and constant Drudgery necessary in refining and managing the Products of those Mines. If any Man informed us that two hundred thousand innocent Persons were condemned to so intolerable Slavery, how should we pity the unhappy Sufferers, and how great would be our just Indignation against those who inflicted so cruel and ignominious a Punishment? This is an Instance, I could not with a stronger, of the numberless Things which we pass by in their common Dress, yet which shock us when they are nakedly represented. But this Number, considerable as it is, and the Slavery, with all its Baseness and Horror, which we have at home, is nothing to what the rest of the World affords of the same Nature. Millions daily bathed in the poisonous Damps and destructive Effluvia of Lead, Silver, Copper, and Arsenic. To say nothing of those other Employments, those Stations of Wretchedness and Contempt in which Civil Society has placed the numerous *Enfans perdus*[105] of her Army. Would any rational Man submit to one of the most tolerable of these Drudgeries, for all the artificial Enjoyments which Policy has made to result from them? By no means. And yet need I suggest to your Lordship, that those who

---

[104] **fewest Things**   as Burke himself recognized, 'The body of the people . . . must labour to obtain what by labour can be obtained; and . . . they find . . . the success disportioned to the endeavour' (*Reflections*, p. 372).

[105] *Enfans perdus*   lost infants.

find the Means, and those who arrive at the End, are not at all the same Persons. On considering the strange and unaccountable Fancies and Contrivances of artificial Reason, I have somewhere called this Earth the Bedlam of our System. Looking now upon the Effects of some of those Fancies, may we not with equal Reason call it likewise the Newgate, and the Bridewell of the Universe.[106] Indeed the Blindness[107] of one Part of Mankind co-operating with the Frenzy and Villany of the other, has been the real Builder of this respectable Fabric of political Society: And as the Blindness of Mankind has caused their Slavery, in Return their State of Slavery is made a Pretence for continuing them in a State of Blindness; for the Politician will tell you gravely, that their Life of Servitude disqualifies the greater Part of the Race of Man for a Search of Truth, and supplies them with no other than mean and insufficient Ideas. This is but too true; and this is one of the Reasons for which I blame such Institutions.

In a Misery of this Sort, admitting some few Lenities, and those too but a few, nine Parts in ten of the whole Race of Mankind drudge through Life. It may be urged perhaps, in palliation of this, that, at least, the rich Few find a considerable and real Benefit from the Wretchedness of the Many. But is this so in fact?[108] Let us examine the Point with a little more Attention. For this Purpose the Rich in all Societies may be thrown into two Classes. The first is of those who are Powerful as well as Rich, and conduct the Operations of the vast political Machine. The other is of those who employ their Riches wholly in the Acquisition of Pleasure. As to the first Sort, their continual Care, and Anxiety, their toilsome Days, and sleepless Nights, are next to proverbial.[109] These Circumstances are sufficient almost to level their Condition to that of the unhappy Majority; but there are other Circumstances which place them in a far lower Condition. Not only their Understandings labour continually, which is the severest Labour, but their Hearts are torn by the worst, most trouble-

---

[106] **Bedlam ... Newgate ... Bridewell**   the first was a lunatic asylum, the others prisons: there was not always much to chosen between them.

[107] **Blindness**   'Les politiques ... attribuent aux hommes ⋅ un penchant naturel à la servitude, par la patience avec laquelle ceux qu'ils sous les yeux supportent la leur' (*Discours*, p. 146).

[108] **so in fact**   Cf. Rousseau's view that the rich were as miserable as the poor; and for a similar sense of equality, see Ref, p. 124.

[109] **proverbial**   e.g. Milton, *Lycidas*, l.72.

some, and insatiable of all Passions, by Avarice, by Ambition, by Fear and Jealousy. No part of the Mind has Rest. Power gradually extirpates from the Mind every humane and gentle Virtue. Pity, Benevolence, Friendship are Things almost unknown in high Stations. *Veræ amicitiæ rarissime inveniuntur in iis qui in honoribus reque publica versantur*,[110] says *Cicero*. And indeed, Courts are the Schools where Cruelty, Pride, Dissimulation and Treachery are studied and taught in the most vicious Perfection. This is a Point so clear and acknowledged, that if it did not make a necessary Part of my Subject, I should pass it by entirely. And this has hindered me from drawing at full length, and in the most striking Colours, this shocking Picture of the Degeneracy and Wretchedness of human Nature, in that Part which is vulgarly thought its happiest and most amiable State. You know from what Originals I could copy such Pictures. Happy are they who know enough of them to know the little Value of the Possessors of such Things, and of all that they possess; and happy they who have been snatched from that Post of Danger which they occupy, with the Remains of their Virtue; Loss of Honours, Wealth, Titles, and even the Loss of one's Country, is nothing in Balance with so great an Advantage.

Let us now view the other Species of the Rich, those who devote their Time and Fortunes to Idleness and Pleasure. How much happier are they? The Pleasures which are agreeable to Nature are within the reach of all, and therefore can form no Distinction in favour of the Rich. The Pleasures which Art forces up are seldom sincere, and never satisfying. What is worse, this constant Application to Pleasure takes away from the Enjoyment, or rather turns it into the Nature of a very burthensome and laborious Business. It has Consequences much more fatal. It produces a weak valetudinary State of Body, attended by all those horrid Disorders, and yet more horrid Methods of Cure, which are the Result of Luxury on one hand, and the weak and ridiculous Efforts of human Art on the other. The Pleasures of such Men are scarcely felt as Pleasures; at the same time that they bring on Pains and Diseases, which are felt but too severely. The Mind has its Share of the Misfortune; it grows lazy and enervate, unwilling and unable to search for Truth, and utterly uncapable of knowing, much less of relishing real Happiness. The Poor by their excessive Labour,

---

[110] **versantur**   true friendship is a great rarity amongst those who compete for honours and office (Cicero, *De Amicitia*, 64.1–2).

and the Rich by their enormous Luxury, are set upon a Level, and rendered equally ignorant of any Knowledge which might conduce to their Happiness. A dismal View of the Interior of all Civil Society. The lower Part broken and ground down by the most cruel Oppression; and the Rich by their artificial Method of Life bringing worse Evils on themselves, than their Tyranny could possibly inflict on those below them. Very different is the Prospect of the Natural State. Here there are no Wants which Nature gives, and in this State Men can be sensible of no other Wants, which are not to be supplied by a very moderate Degree of Labour; therefore there is no Slavery. Neither is there any Luxury, because no single Man can supply the Materials of it. Life is simple, and therefore it is happy.[111]

I am conscious, my LORD, that your Politician will urge in his Defence, that this unequal State is highly useful. That without dooming some Part of Mankind to extraordinary Toil, the Arts which cultivate Life could not be exercised. But I demand of this Politician, how such Arts came to be necessary? He answers, that Civil Society could not well exist without them. So that these Arts are necessary to Civil Society, and Civil Society necessary again to these Arts. Thus running in a Circle, without Modesty, and without End, and making one Error and Extravagance an Excuse for the other. My Sentiments about these Arts and their Cause, I have often discoursed with my Friends at large. *Pope* has expressed them in good Verse, where he talks with so much Force of Reason and Elegance of Language in Praise of the State of Nature:

> Then was not Pride, nor Arts that Pride to aid,
> Man walk'd with Beast, Joint-tenant of the Shade.[112]

On the whole, my LORD, if Political Society, in whatever Form, has still made the Many the Property of the Few;[113] if it has introduced Labours unnecessary, Vices and Diseases unknown, and Pleasures incompatible with Nature; if in all Countries it abridges the Lives of Millions, and renders those of Millions more utterly abject and miserable, shall we still worship so destructive an Idol, and daily sacrifice to

---

[111] **happy** Rousseau suggested that luxury was not found before the coming of sophisticated society.

[112] **shade** Pope, *Essay on Man*, III.ll.151–52, slightly altered.

[113] **Property of the Few** Cf. 'party-spirit, which at best is but the madness of the many for the gain of a few' (Pope to E. Blount, 28 August 1714 in George Sherburn (ed.), *The Letters of Alexander Pope*, 5 vols. (1956), I, p. 247).

it our Health, our Liberty, and our Peace? Or shall we pass by this monstrous Heap of absurd Notions, and abominable Practices, thinking we have sufficiently discharged our Duty in exposing the trifling Cheats, and ridiculous Juggles of a few mad, designing, or ambitious Priests? Alas! my LORD, we labour under a mortal Consumption, whilst we are so anxious about the Cure of a fore Finger. For has not this Leviathan of Civil Power[114] overflowed the Earth with a Deluge of Blood, as if he were made to disport and play therein? We have shewn, that Political Society, on a moderate Calculation, has been the Means of murdering several times the Number of Inhabitants now upon the Earth, during its short Existence, not upwards of four thousand Years in any Accounts to be depended on. But we have said nothing of the other, and perhaps as bad Consequence of these Wars, which have spilled such Seas of Blood, and reduced so many Millions to a merciless Slavery. But these are only the Ceremonies performed in the Porch of the political Temple. Much more horrid ones are seen as you enter it. The several Species of Government vie with each other in the Absurdity of their Constitutions, and the Oppression which they make their Subjects endure. Take them under what Form you please, they are in effect but a Despotism, and they fall, both in Effect and Appearance too, after a very short Period, into that cruel and detestable Species of Tyranny; which I rather call it, because we have been educated under another Form, than that this is of worse Consequences to Mankind. For the free Governments, for the Point of their Space, and the Moment of their Duration, have felt more Confusion, and committed more flagrant Acts of Tyranny, than the most perfect despotic Governments which we have ever known. Turn your Eye next to the Labyrinth of the Law, and the Iniquity conceived in its intricate Recesses. Consider the Ravages committed in the Bowels of all Commonwealths by Ambition, by Avarice, Envy, Fraud, open Injustice, and pretended Friendship; Vices which could draw little Support from a State of Nature, but which blossom and flourish in the Rankness of political Society. Revolve our whole Discourse; add to it all those Reflections which your own good Understanding shall suggest, and make a strenuous Effort beyond the Reach of vulgar Philosophy, to confess that the Cause of Artificial Society is more defenceless even than that of Artificial Religion; that it is as

---

[114] **Leviathan of Civil Power** a passing tilt at Hobbes; for the original image, see Job 41.

derogatory from the Honour of the Creator, as subversive of human Reason, and productive of infinitely more Mischief to the human Race.

If pretended Revelations have caused Wars where they were opposed, and Slavery where they were received, the pretended wise Inventions of Politicians have done the same. But the Slavery has been much heavier, the Wars far more bloody, and both more universal by many Degrees. Shew me any Mischief produced by the Madness or Wickedness of Theologians, and I will shew you an hundred, resulting from the Ambition and Villainy of Conquerors and Statesmen. Shew me an Absurdity in Religion, I will undertake to shew you an hundred for one in political Laws and Institutions. If you say, that Natural Religion is a sufficient Guide without the foreign Aid of Revelation, on what Principle should Political Laws become necessary? Is not the same Reason available in Theology and in Politics? If the Laws of Nature are the Laws of God, is it consistent with the Divine Wisdom to prescribe Rules to us, and leave the Enforcement of them to the Folly of human Institutions? Will you follow Truth but to a certain Point?

We are indebted for all our Miseries to our Distrust of that Guide, which Providence thought sufficient for our Condition, our own natural Reason, which rejecting both in human and divine Things, we have given our Necks to the Yoke of political and theological Slavery. We have renounced the Prerogative of Man, and it is no Wonder that we should be treated like Beasts. But our Misery is much greater than theirs, as the Crime we commit in rejecting the lawful Dominion of our Reason is greater than any which they can commit. If after all, you should confess all these Things, yet plead the Necessity of political Institutions, weak and wicked as they are, I can argue with equal, perhaps superior Force concerning the Necessity of artificial Religion; and every Step you advance in your Argument, you add a Strength to mine. So that if we are resolved to submit our Reason and our Liberty to civil Usurpation, we have nothing to do but to conform as quietly as we can to the vulgar Notions which are connected with this, and take up the Theology of the Vulgar as well as their Politics. But if we think this Necessity rather imaginary than real, we should renounce their Dreams of Society, together with their Visions of Religion, and vindicate ourselves into perfect Liberty.

You are, my LORD, but just entering into the World; I am going out of it. I have played long enough to be heartily tired of the Drama. Whether I have acted my Part in it well or ill, Posterity will judge with more Candor than I, or than the present Age, with our present Passions, can possibly pretend to. For my part, I quit it without a Sigh, and submit to the Sovereign Order without murmuring. The nearer we approach to the Goal of Life, the better we begin to understand the true Value of our Existence,[115] and the real Weight of our Opinions. We set out much in love with both; but we leave much behind us as we advance. We first throw away[116] the Tales along with the Rattles of our Nurses; those of the Priest keep their Hold a little longer; those of our Governors the longest of all. But the Passions which prop these Opinions are withdrawn one after another; and the cool Light of Reason at the Setting of our Life, shews us what a false Splendor played upon these Objects during our more sanguine Seasons. Happy, my LORD, if instructed by my Experience, and even by my Errors, you come early to make such an Estimate of Things, as may give Freedom and Ease to your Life. I am happy that such an Estimate promises me Comfort at my Death.

[115] **of our Existence** 'life can little more supply / Than just to look about us and to die' (Pope, *Essay on Man*, I.3–4).

[116] **throw away** for the ensuing passage, cf. Pope, *Essay on Man*, II. ll.275–82:

Behold the child, by Nature's kindly law,
Pleased with a rattle, tickled with a straw:
Some livelier play-thing gives his youth delight,
A little louder, but as empty quite:
Scarfs, garters, gold amuse his riper stage,
And beads and pray'r books are the toys of age:
Pleas'd with this bauble still, as that before;
Till tir'd he sleeps, and Life's poor play is o'er.

A Philosophical Enquiry into the Origin of our Ideas of the Sublime and Beautiful

Introduction

The 'Extempore Commonplace' and *A Vindication of Natural Society* suggested that revelation was recognizably part of the divine order. The earlier text had praised revelation for informing moral conduct, whilst the later work suggested that the logic of deism admitted a view of the social order unacceptable to most minds in eighteenth-century England. By the same token, *A Vindication* implied some approval of society as presently constituted. A further form of inequality had found its way onto Burke's agenda. His attachment to an unequal social order had been expressed at Trinity, when he adverted to its potential for good. That position now achieved a theoretical elaboration.

The *Enquiry* employed the idiom of nature and did so with a determinate purpose. As 'Nature' was attractive to the eighteenth century, the content attributed to it varied with a writer's object. Deists had emphasized nature as reason. Rousseau had found nature in the simplest of lives. Burke himself set out to show that natural passion was God's medium of expression and suggested that nature grounded inequality.

To understand Burke's case we should consider another of his interests. At Trinity he had declared himself not only about religion and property, but also about taste. Burke took the view that the province of the imagination was important for forming good morals. It followed that the beliefs people entertained about aesthetics had a

58

bearing upon their conduct. Burke, indeed, felt at odds not only with the deists and Rousseau but also with certain aesthetic theories. He construed nature in terms of pleasure and pain, in a way which undermined the theory of moral sense. Bolingbroke had implied that the prime exponents of this theory, Shaftesbury and Hutcheson, were atheists.[1] Whatever Burke thought on *that* point, he took a congruent view of the tendency of their work. His treatment of pleasure and pain directed the reader to God.

The aesthetics of Shaftesbury underpinned a moral philosophy. Shaftesbury held that the eye of man, perceiving 'the Shapes, Motions, Colours, and Proportions' of objects and actions, formed an aesthetic judgement, for from these 'there necessarily results a Beauty or Deformity'.[2] Something besides beauty was found in proportion: beauty was held to imply goodness. 'What is beautiful is harmonious and proportionable; what is harmonious and proportionable is true; and what is at once both beautiful and true is, of consequence, agreeable and good', Shaftesbury tells us.[3] The moral sense tended to make ethics autonomous in relation to theology. It drew attention to nature as distinct from God. Shaftesbury and Hutcheson insisted, in fact, that God's willing something disclosed no moral properties in it: on the contrary, good or evil was disclosed through man's sense of the nature of things.

Burke could scarcely like this 'whimsical theory'. Whilst it suggested that the imagination and virtue were linked, it did so in a way which explained virtue without direct reference to God. As William Dennis, a college friend of Burke's, put it 'Hutchinson's [*sic*] treatise is an establishment of morals from the Beauty, order, fitness and rectitude of actions, and this indirectly saps religion by representing virtue independent of it'.[4] By contrast, Burke's 'Commonplace' had shown the dependence of virtue on revelation, which was God's direct act. How did Burke propose to amend the aesthetic error and show the centrality of God to the imagination?

God's power is emphasized in the *Philosophical Enquiry*. Burke's God used His power to contrive the effects which He thought it good

[1] *Works*, IV, p. 286.
[2] Shaftesbury, *An Inquiry concerning Virtue, or Merit*, ed. D.E. Walford (1977), I.ii.3, p. 16.
[3] Shaftesbury, *Characteristics of Men, Manners, Opinions, Times*, ed. J.M. Robertson, 2 vols. (1900), VI.iii.2 (vol. II, p. 268f).
[4] William Dennis to Richard Shackleton, March 1758 in Samuels, *Early Life*, p. 212.

to impress on man's consciousness. In this manner He was sure to induce man to follow His will. Burke put it thus:

> whenever the wisdom of our Creator intended that we should be affected with any thing, he did not confine the execution of his design to the languid and precarious operation of our reason; but he endued it with powers and properties that prevent the understanding, and even the will, which, seizing upon the senses and imagination, captivate the soul.[5]

So man's imagination would lead him to God's purposes.

How did Burke conceive this arrangement? His *Enquiry* draws attention to the ideas of sublime and beautiful. These were the two primary categories of current aesthetic thought. It was Burke's task to capture them for his own theory. He suggested that the sublime should be related to ideas of pain and the beautiful to ideas of pleasure. Pleasure and pain, in their turn were related respectively to hope and fear. These themselves related to God who, as the source of power, could satisfy hope and excite fear. In short, Burke meant to show that since 'the imagination' was 'the most extensive province of pleasure and pain, as it is the region of our fears and our hopes',[6] God would use it to direct man to specific ends.

Those ends were the ones traditionally understood as man's duty. For instance, the duty of self-preservation was central to thinking about natural law.[7] Entering into society and upholding it also figured strongly.[8] These tasks, however, were usually supposed to lie in the direction of natural drives rather than to be merely duties unanswered by instinct. Burke took up the naturalness of these duties and interpreted it in terms of his theory. Man was led to them, not by judgement but by his ideas of pleasure and pain:

> Most of the ideas which are capable of making a powerful impression on the mind, whether simply of Pain or Pleasure, or of the modifications of those, may be reduced very nearly to these two heads, *self-preservation* and *society*;

---

[5] PE, III.vii.

[6] PE, I.vii, xviii; below, p. 63f, 74f; cf. viii, introduction. (quote).

[7] Hobbes need hardly be mentioned in this connection, but see also John Locke, *Two Treatises of Government*, II.ii.6, and for Grotius, see Richard Tuck, 'The Modern Theory of Natural Law', in Anthony Pagden (ed.), *The Languages of Political Theory in Early-Modern Europe* (1987).

[8] See Aquinas, *Summa Theologica*, e.g. Ia IIae q. 94 a. 2 for one reference amongst others.

'to the ends of one or the other of which', Burke concluded, 'all our passions are calculated to answer'. He left no doubt that the 'final cause' which had so 'connected', 'annexed' and 'calculated' man's passions to these ends was God Himself.[9]

So if the imagination related to virtue, that sphere was re-mapped in terms very different from those proposed by the moral sense. But what of society? If society was God's work, operating through nature, the latter term would have to be reclaimed from Rousseau. In other words it remained to be shown that an hierarchical and progressive society was natural. The passions which related to society in general Burke thought complicated, but he saw them branching out into three principal forms: sympathy, imitation and ambition. Imitation and ambition together suggested that by nature some would lead and others follow. For if ambition 'drives men to all the ways we see in use of signalizing themselves', imitation 'prompts us to copy' what others do.[10] Sympathy 'makes us take a concern in whatever men feel' and so to have an interest in others, 'united by the bond of sympathy'.[11] The passions suggested progress, for ambition and imitation pointed towards improvement. God had calculated ambition to prevent men from remaining as 'they were in the beginning of the world'; imitation ensured improvement would be taken up, for it 'forms our manners, our opinions, our lives'.[12] Where Rousseau had found the natural in the equal and primitive, Burke located it in the hierarchical and progressive.

Burke had shown to his own satisfaction that a graduated and a progressive society were rooted in man's natural passions and that nature was God's instrument. Shaftesbury and Hutcheson, as much as Rousseau, were beside the point. One aspect, however, had yet to be treated. Burke had given no explicit account of moral theory. That was treated in 'Religion'.

Analysis

Most ideas of pleasure, pain and their modifications can be referred to either self-preservation or society. Those concerning self-preservation turn mostly on pain. Whatever excites ideas of pain is a source of the sublime.

---

[9] PE, i.vi; iv.i; introduction; i.vi.
[10] PE, i.xvii, xvi; below, pp. 72–4.
[11] PE, i.xv, xiv; below, pp. 69–72.
[12] PE, i.xvii, xvi; below, pp. 72–4.

Before considering those concerning society, we should divide society under two heads, the society of the sexes (which answers to propagation) and general society. The former is attended with ideas of pleasure. Because the propagation of the species is an extremely important purpose the pleasure which attends it is very great. Man, unlike the beasts, is constant to one mate because he has the idea of beauty. General society also is attended frequently by pleasure.

The passions relating to general society can be divided into three principal groups. These serve to maintain society in various ways. The groups are sympathy, imitation and ambition. Sympathy makes us enter into the concerns of others and, in particular, leads us to feel for their distresses. Imitation leads us to follow the example of others. Ambition or preference, on the other hand, leads some to wish to excel their fellows. Conclusion.

A Philosophical Enquiry
into the
Origin of our Ideas
of the
Sublime and Beautiful

(second edition, 1759)
[Part One, Sections VI–XIX]

SECT. VI.
Of the passions which belong to
SELF-PRESERVATION.

MOST of the ideas which are capable of making a powerful impression on the mind, whether simply of Pain or Pleasure, or of the modifications of those, may be reduced very nearly to these two heads, *self-preservation* and *society*; to the ends of one or the other of which all our passions are calculated to answer. The passions which concern self-preservation, turn mostly on *pain* or *danger*. The ideas of *pain, sickness,* and *death,* fill the mind with strong emotions of horror; but *life* and *health,* though they put us in a capacity of being affected with pleasure, they make no such impression by the simple enjoyment. The passions therefore which are conversant about the preservation of the individual, turn chiefly on *pain* and *danger,* and they are the most powerful of all the passions.

SECT. VII.
Of the SUBLIME.

WHATEVER is fitted in any sort to excite the ideas of pain, and danger, that is to say, whatever is in any sort terrible, or is conversant about terrible objects, or operates in a manner analogous to terror, is a source of the *sublime*; that is, it is productive of the strongest emotion which the mind is capable of feeling. I say the strongest emotion, because I am satisfied the ideas of pain are much more powerful than those which enter on the part of pleasure. Without all doubt, the torments which we may be made to suffer, are much greater in their effect on the body and mind, than any pleasures which the most learned voluptuary could suggest, or than the liveliest imagination, and the most sound and exquisitely sensible body could enjoy. Nay I am in great doubt, whether any man could be found who would earn a life of the most perfect satisfaction, at the price of ending it in the torments, which justice inflicted in a few hours on the late unfortunate regicide in France.[1] But as pain is stronger in its operation than pleasure, so death is in general a much more affecting idea than pain; because there are very few pains, however exquisite, which are not preferred to death; nay, what generally makes pain itself, if I may say so, more painful, is, that it is considered as an emissary of this king of terrors. When danger or pain press too nearly, they are incapable of giving any delight, and are simply terrible; but at certain distances, and with certain modifications, they may be, and they are delightful, as we every day experience. The cause of this I shall endeavour to investigate hereafter.

SECT. VIII.
Of the passions which belong to SOCIETY.

THE other head under which I class our passions, is that of *society*, which may be divided into two sorts. 1. The society of the *sexes*, which answers the purposes of propagation; and next, that more *general society*, which we have with men and with other animals, and which we may in some sort be said to have even with the inanimate world. The passions belonging to the preservation of the individual, turn wholly on pain and danger; those which belong to *generation*, have their origin

---

[1] **France**   Robert Francis Damiens (1714–57), having tried in vain to assassinate Louis XV in January 1757, was tortured and executed by being torn limb from limb. See Goldsmith, *The Traveller*, l.436, 'Damien's bed of steel', for another contemporary allusion. 'When Damiens ... was arraigned ... a council of anatomists was summoned to deliberate how a human being might be destroyed with the longest protracted and most diversified agony.' Godwin, *Enquiry*, l.ii, p. 87.

in gratifications and *pleasures*; the pleasure most directly belonging to this purpose is of a lively character, rapturous and violent, and confessedly the highest pleasure of sense; yet the absence of this so great an enjoyment, scarce amounts to an uneasiness; and except at particular times, I do not think it affects at all. When men describe in what manner they are affected by pain and danger; they do not dwell on the pleasure of health and the comfort of security, and then lament the *loss* of these satisfactions: the whole turns upon the actual pains and horrors which they endure. But if you listen to the complaints of a forsaken lover,[2] you observe, that he insists largely on the pleasures which he enjoyed, or hoped to enjoy, and on the perfection of the object of his desires; it is the *loss* which is always uppermost in his mind. The violent effects produced by love, which has sometimes been even wrought up to madness, is no objection to the rule which we seek to establish. When men have suffered their imaginations to be long affected with any idea, it so wholly engrosses them as to shut out by degrees almost every other, and to break down every partition of the mind which would confine it. Any idea is sufficient for the purpose, as is evident from the infinite variety of causes which give rise to madness: but this at most can only prove, that the passion of love is capable of producing very extraordinary effects, not that its extraordinary emotions have any connection with positive pain.

SECT. IX.
The final cause of the difference between the passions belonging to SELF-preservation, and those which regard the SOCIETY of the SEXES.

THE final cause of the difference in character between the passions which regard self-preservation, and those which are directed to the multiplication of the species, will illustrate the foregoing remarks yet further; and it is, I imagine, worthy of observation even upon its own account. As the performance of our duties of every kind depends upon life, and the performing them with vigour and efficacy depends upon health, we are very strongly affected with whatever threatens the destruction of either; but as we were not made to acquiesce in life and health, the simple enjoyment of them is not attended with any real

---

[2] **lover**   this may be drawn from life; see Samuels, pp. 50–2.

pleasure, lest satisfied with that, we should give ourselves over to indolence and inaction. On the other hand, the generation of mankind is a great purpose,[3] and it is requisite that men should be animated to the pursuit of it by some great incentive.[4] It is therefore attended with a very high pleasure; but as it is by no means designed to be our constant business, it is not fit that the absence of this pleasure should be attended with any considerable pain. The difference between men and brutes[5] in this point, seems to be remarkable. Men are at all times pretty equally disposed to the pleasures of love, because they are to be guided by reason in the time and manner of indulging them. Had any great pain arisen from the want of this satisfaction, reason, I am afraid, would find great difficulties in the performance of its office. But brutes who obey laws, in the execution of which their own reason has but little share, have their stated seasons; at such times it is not improbable that the sensation from the want is very troublesome, because the end must be then answered, or be missed in many, perhaps for ever; as the inclination returns only with its season.

SECT. X.
Of BEAUTY.

THE passion which belongs to generation, merely as such, is lust only; this is evident in brutes, whose passions are more unmixed, and which pursue their purposes more directly than ours. The only distinction they observe with regard to their mates, is that of sex. It is true, that they stick severally to their own species in preference to all others. But this preference, I imagine, does not arise from any sense of beauty which they find in their species, as Mr. Addison supposes,[6] but from a law of some other kind to which they are subject; and this we may

---

[3] **great purpose**   cf. Locke, *Two Treatises*, I.vi.59: 'the main intention of Nature, which willeth the increase of Mankind'.

[4] **incentive**   *Two Treatises*, I.vi.54: 'God in his infinite Wisdom has put strong desires of Copulation into the Constitution of Men, thereby to continue the race of Mankind'; cf. *Notebook*, p. 92: 'I rather thank providence that has so happily united the subsistence of my body with its satisfaction'.

[5] **brutes**   the difference between man and animal is pointed in VNS, preface, above p. 9 with note.

[6] **supposes**   see *Spectator*, no. 413, 24 June 1712 (ed. D.F. Bond, 5 vols. (1965), III, pp. 544–47); Burke's writing, both intellectually and stylistically, reveals a close study of Addison.

fairly conclude, from their apparent want of choice amongst those objects to which the barriers of their species have confined them. But man, who is a creature adapted to a greater variety and intricacy of relation, connects with the general passion, the idea of some *social* qualities, which direct and heighten the appetite which he has in common with all other animals; and as he is not designed like them to live at large, it is fit that he should have something to create a preference, and fix his choice; and this in general should be some sensible quality; as no other can so quickly, so powerfully, or so surely produce it's effect. The object therefore of this mixed passion which we call love, is the *beauty* of the *sex*. Men are carried to the sex in general, as it is the sex, and by the common law of nature; but they are attached to particulars by personal *beauty*. I call beauty a social quality; for where women and men, and not only they, but when other animals give us a sense of joy and pleasure in beholding them, (and there are many that do so) they inspire us with sentiments of tenderness and affection towards their persons; we like to have them near us, and we enter willingly into a kind of relation with them, unless we should have strong reasons to the contrary. But to what end, in many cases, this was designed, I am unable to discover; for I see no greater reason for a connection between man and several animals who are attired in so engaging a manner, than between him and some others who entirely want this attraction, or possess it in a far weaker degree. But it is probable, that providence did not make even this distinction, but with a view to some great end, though we cannot perceive distinctly what it is, as his wisdom is not our wisdom, nor our ways his ways.[7]

SECT. XI.
SOCIETY and SOLITUDE.

THE second branch of the social passions, is that which administers to *society in general*. With regard to this, I observe, that society, merely as society, without any particular heightenings, gives us no positive pleasure in the enjoyment; but absolute and entire *solitude*, that is, the total and perpetual exclusion from all society, is as great a positive pain as can almost be conceived. Therefore in the balance between the pleasure of general *society*, and the pain of absolute solitude, *pain*

---

[7] **his ways** alluding to *Isaiah* 55:8 – see Introduction, above p. xxiii, and VNS, above p. 11, as well as WSEB, II p. 362.

is the predominant idea. But the pleasure of any particular social enjoyment outweighs very considerably the uneasiness caused by the want of that particular enjoyment; so that the strongest sensations relative to the habitudes of *particular society*, are sensations of pleasure. Good company, lively conversations, and the endearments of friendship, fill the mind with great pleasure; a temporary solitude on the other hand, is itself agreeable. This may perhaps prove, that we are creatures designed for contemplation as well as action; since solitude as well as society has its pleasures; as from the former observation we may discern, that an entire life of solitude contradicts the purposes of our being, since death itself is scarcely an idea of more terror.

SECT. XII.
SYMPATHY, IMITATION, and AMBITION.

UNDER this denomination of society, the passions are of a complicated kind, and branch out into a variety of forms agreeable to that variety of ends they are to serve in the great chain of society. The three principal links in this chain are *sympathy, imitation*, and *ambition*.

SECT. XIII.
SYMPATHY.

IT is by the first of these passions that we enter into the concerns of others; that we are moved as they are moved, and are never suffered to be indifferent spectators of almost any thing which men can do or suffer. For sympathy must be considered as a sort of substitution, by which we are put into the place of another man, and affected in many respects as he is affected; so that this passion may either partake of the nature of those which regard self-preservation, and turning upon pain may be a source of the sublime; or it may turn upon ideas of pleasure; and then, whatever has been said of the social affections, whether they regard society in general, or only some particular modes of it, may be applicable here. It is by this principle chiefly that poetry, painting, and other affecting arts, transfuse their passions from one breast to another, and are often capable of grafting a delight on wretchedness, misery, and death itself. It is a common observation, that objects which in the reality would shock, are in tragical, and such like representations, the source of a very high species of pleasure. This taken as a fact, has been the cause of much reasoning.[8] The satisfaction has been commonly attributed, first, to the comfort we receive in considering that so melancholy a story is no more than a fiction; and next, to the contemplation of our own freedom from the evils which we see represented. I am afraid it is a practice much too common in inquiries of this nature, to attribute the cause of feelings which merely arise from the mechanical structure of our bodies, or from the natural frame and constitution of our minds, to certain conclusions of the reasoning faculty on the objects presented to us; for I should imagine, that the influence of reason in producing our passions is nothing near so extensive as it is commonly believed.

SECT. XIV.

The effects of SYMPATHY in the distresses of others.

To examine this point concerning the effect of tragedy in a proper manner, we must previously consider, how we are affected by the feelings of our fellow creatures in circumstances of real distress. I am convinced we have a degree of delight, and that no small one, in the real misfortunes and pains of others; for let the affection be what it will in appearance, if it does not make us shun such objects, if on the contrary it induces us to approach them, if it makes us dwell upon them, in this case I conceive we must have a delight or pleasure of some species or other in contemplating objects of this kind. Do we not read the authentic histories of scenes of this nature with as much pleasure as romances or poems, where the incidents are fictitious? The prosperity of no empire, nor the grandeur of no king, can so agreeably affect in the reading, as the ruin of the state of Macedon, and the distress of its unhappy prince.[9] Such a catastrophe touches us in history as much as the destruction of Troy does in fable.[10] Our delight in cases of this kind, is very greatly heightened, if the sufferer

---

[8] **reasoning**   see Addison, *Spectator*, no. 418, 30 June 1712 (III, pp. 566–70) and cf. Aristotle, *Poetics*, VI.2.

[9] **prince**   Perseus, king of Macedon (179–168 BC) was defeated decisively by Aemilius Paullus at Pydna (168) and led in triumph at Rome. For a graphic account of his misfortunes, see Plutarch, *Aemilius*, esp. 26, 4–6.

[10] **fable**   see Vergil, *Aeneid*, II, for the most affecting version; Burke quoted some lines in his *Speech on the Army Estimates*, below, p. 308f.

be some excellent person[11] who sinks under an unworthy fortune. Scipio and Cato are both virtuous characters, but we are more deeply affected by the violent death of the one, and the ruin of the great cause he adhered to, than with the deserved triumphs and uninterrupted prosperity of the other;[12] for terror is a passion which always produces delight when it does not press too close, and pity is a passion accompanied with pleasure, because it arises from love and social affection. Whenever we are formed by nature to any active purpose, the passion which animates us to it, is attended with delight, or a pleasure of some kind, let the subject matter be what it will; and as our Creator has designed we should be united by the bond of sympathy, he has strengthened that bond by a proportionable delight; and there most where our sympathy is most wanted, in the distresses of others. If this passion was simply painful, we would shun with the greatest care all persons and places that could excite such a passion; as, some who are so far gone in indolence as not to endure any strong impression actually do. But the case is widely different with the greater part of mankind; there is no spectacle we so eagerly pursue, as that of some uncommon and grievous calamity; so that whether the misfortune is before our eyes, or whether they are turned back to it in history, it always touches with delight. This is not an unmixed delight, but blended with no small uneasiness. The delight we have in such things, hinders us from shunning scenes of misery; and the pain we feel, prompts us to relieve ourselves in relieving those who suffer; and all this antecedent to any reasoning, by an instinct that works us to its own purposes, without our concurrence.

SECT. XV.
Of the effects of TRAGEDY.

IT is thus in real calamities. In imitated distresses the only difference is the pleasure resulting from the effects of imitation; for it is never so perfect, but we can perceive it is an imitation, and on that principle are somewhat pleased with it. And indeed in some cases we derive as much or more pleasure from that source than from the thing itself. But then I imagine we shall be much mistaken if we attribute any

[11] **excellent person**   see, above all, the passage in *Reflections*, pp. 168ff on Louis XVI and Marie Antoinette for an exemplification.
[12] **other**   it is unclear which of the two famous Scipiones Burke means here: for both, see Biographica, above p. lxi.

considerable part of our satisfaction in tragedy to a consideration that tragedy is a deceit, and its representations no realities. The nearer it approaches the reality, and the further it removes us from all idea of fiction, the more perfect is its power. But be its power of what kind it will, it never approaches to what it represents. Chuse a day on which to represent the most sublime and affecting tragedy we have; appoint the most favourite actors; spare no cost upon the scenes and decorations; unite the greatest efforts of poetry, painting and music; and when you have collected your audience, just at the moment when their minds are erect with expectation, let it be reported that a state criminal of high rank is on the point of being executed in the adjoining square;[13] in a moment the emptiness of the theatre would demonstrate the comparative weakness of the imitative arts, and proclaim the triumph of the real sympathy.[14] I believe that this notion of our having a simple pain in the reality, yet a delight in the representation, arises from hence, that we do not sufficiently distinguish what we would by no means chuse to do, from what we should be eager enough to see if it was once done. We delight in seeing things, which so far from doing, our heartiest wishes would be to see redressed. This noble capital, the pride of England and of Europe, I believe no man is so strangely wicked as to desire to see destroyed by a conflagration or an earthquake, though he should be removed himself to the greatest distance from the danger.[15] But suppose such a fatal

[13] **square** may refer to the trial and execution (9 April 1747) of Simon Fraser (*c.*1667–1747), 12th Lord Lovat, for his part in the '45. The Club at TCD debated Lovat's fate on 28 April 1747 (see Samuels, p. 231).

[14] **real sympathy** for an example, cf. *Reflections* p. 175, explaining his attitudes:

> because it is *natural* I should; because we are so made as to be affected at such spectacles with melancholy sentiments upon the unstable condition of mortal prosperity, and the tremendous uncertanty of human greatness; because in those natural feelings we learn great lessons; because in events like these our passions instruct our reason; because when kings are hurl'd from their thrones by the Supreme Director of this great drama, and become the objects of insult to the base, and of pity to the good, we behold such disasters in the moral, as we should behold a miracle in the physical order of things. We are alarmed into reflexion; our minds (as it has long since been observed) are purified by terror and pity; our weak unthinking pride is humbled, under the dispensations of a mysterious wisdom.

For purification by terror, see, of course, Aristotle, *Poetics*, VI.2, *Rhetoric*, II.8 and *Politics*, VIII.7.

[15] **danger** earthquakes were felt in London during February and March 1750. Thomas Sherlock, Bishop of London took the occasion to castigate contemporary

accident to have happened, what numbers from all parts would croud to behold the ruins, and amongst them many who would have been content never to have seen London in its glory? Nor is it either in real or fictitious distresses, our immunity from them which produces our delight; in my own mind I can discover nothing like it. I apprehend that this mistake is owing to a sort of sophism, by which we are frequently imposed upon; it arises from our not distinguishing between what is indeed a necessary condition to our doing or suffering any thing in general, and what is the *cause* of some particular act. If a man kills me with a sword, it is a necessary condition to this that we should have been both of us alive before the fact; and yet it would be absurd to say, that our being both living creatures was the cause of his crime and of my death. So it is certain, that it is absolutely necessary my life should be out of any imminent hazard before I can take a delight in the sufferings of others, real or imaginary, or indeed in anything else from any cause whatsoever. But then it is a sophism to argue from thence, that this immunity is the cause of my delight either on these or on any occasions. No one can distinguish such a cause of satisfaction in his own mind I believe; nay when we do not suffer any very acute pain, nor are exposed to any imminent danger of our lives, we can feel for others, whilst we suffer ourselves; and often then most when we are softened by affliction; we see with pity even distresses which we would accept in the place of our own.

SECT. XVI.
IMITATION.[16]

THE second passion belonging to society is imitation, or, if you will, a desire of imitating, and consequently a pleasure in it. This passion arises from much the same cause with sympathy. For as sympathy makes us take a concern in whatever men feel, so this affection

morals in his *Letter from the Bishop of London to the Clergy and people of London and Westminster on account of the late earthquakes.* A third earthquake was expected in April, leading to a mass exodus. After it failed to happen, there was published a *Full and True Account of the dreadful and melancholy earthquake which happened . . . on . . . the fifth instant* which noted that 'the very first man that was sunk by this earthquake was the B of L. It seems he might have escaped, but his zeal was so great in distributing copies of his letter'. The idea could have been reinforced or suggested by the Lisbon earthquake, see VNS, above, p. 17.

[16] **Imitation**   cf. Aristotle, *Poetics*, IV.2.

prompts us to copy whatever they do; and consequently we have a pleasure in imitating, and in whatever belongs to imitation merely as it is such, without any intervention of the reasoning faculty, but solely from our natural constitution, which providence has framed in such a manner as to find either pleasure or delight according to the nature of the object, in whatever regards the purposes of our being. It is by imitation far more than by precept that we learn every thing; and what we learn thus we acquire not only more effectually, but more pleasantly. This forms our manners, our opinions, our lives. It is one of the strongest links of society; it is a species of mutual compliance which all men yield to each other, without constraint to themselves, and which is extremely flattering to all. Herein it is that painting and many other agreeable arts have laid one of the principal foundations of their power. And since by its influence on our manners and our passions it is of such great consequence, I shall here venture to lay down a rule, which may inform us with a good degree of certainty when we are to attribute the power of the arts, to imitation, or to our pleasure in the skill of the imitator merely, and when to sympathy, or some other cause in conjunction with it. When the object represented in poetry or painting is such, as we could have no desire of seeing in the reality; then I may be sure that its power in poetry or painting is owing to the power of imitation, and to no cause operating in the thing itself. So it is with most of the pieces which the painters call still life. In these a cottage, a dunghill, the meanest and most ordinary utensils of the kitchen, are capable of giving us pleasure. But when the object of the painting or poem is such as we should run to see if real, let it affect us with what odd sort of sense it will, we may rely upon it, that the power of the poem or picture is more owing to the nature of the thing itself than to the mere effect of imitation, or to a consideration of the skill of the imitator however excellent. Aristotle has spoken so much and so solidly upon the force of imitation in his poetics, that it makes any further discourse upon this subject the less necessary.

SECT. XVII.
AMBITION.

ALTHOUGH imitation is one of the great instruments used by providence in bringing our nature towards its perfection, yet if men gave themselves up to imitation entirely, and each followed the other, and

73

so on in an eternal circle, it is easy to see that there never could be any improvement amongst them. Men must remain as brutes do, the same at the end that they are at this day, and that they were in the beginning of the world. To prevent this, God has planted in man a sense of ambition, and a satisfaction arising from the contemplation of his excelling his fellows in something deemed valuable amongst them. It is this passion that drives men to all the ways we see in use of signalizing themselves, and that tends to make whatever excites in a man the idea of this distinction so very pleasant. It has been so strong as to make very miserable men take comfort that they were supreme in misery; and certain it is, that where we cannot distinguish ourselves by something excellent, we begin to take a complacency in some singular infirmities, follies, or defects of one kind or other. It is on this principle that flattery is so prevalent; for flattery is no more than what raises in a man's mind an idea of a preference which he has not. Now whatever either on good or upon bad grounds tends to raise a man in his own opinion, produces a sort of swelling and triumph that is extremely grateful to the human mind; and this swelling is never more perceived, nor operates with more force, than when without danger we are conversant with terrible objects, the mind always claiming to itself some part of the dignity and importance of the things which it contemplates. Hence proceeds what Longinus[17] has observed of that glorying and sense of inward greatness, that always fills the reader of such passages in poets and orators as are sublime; it is what every man must have felt in himself upon such occasions.

SECT. XVIII.
The RECAPITULATION.

To draw the whole of what has been said into a few distinct points. The passions which belong to self-preservation, turn on pain and danger; they are simply painful when their causes immediately affect us; they are delightful when we have an idea of pain and danger, without being actually in such circumstances; this delight I have not called pleasure, because it turns on pain, and because it is different enough from any idea of positive pleasure. Whatever excites this

---

[17] **Longinus** *On the Sublime*, 7, though Longinus refers to hearing rather than reading.

delight, I call *sublime*. The passions belonging to self-preservation are the strongest of all the passions.

The second head to which the passions are referred with relation to their final cause, is society. There are two sorts of societies. The first is, the society of sex. The passion belonging to this is called love, and it contains a mixture of lust; its object is the beauty of women. The other is the great society with man and all other animals. The passion subservient to this is called likewise love, but it has no mixture of lust, and its object is beauty; which is a name I shall apply to all such qualities in things as induce in us a sense of affection and tenderness, or some other passion the most nearly resembling these. The passion of love has its rise in positive pleasure; it is, like all things which grow out of pleasure, capable of being mixed with a mode of uneasiness, that is, when an idea of its object is excited in the mind with an idea at the same time of having irretrievably lost it. This mixed sense of pleasure I have not called *pain*, because it turns upon actual pleasure, and because it is both in its cause and in most of its effects of a nature altogether different.

Next to the general passion we have for society, to a choice in which we are directed by the pleasure we have in the object, the particular passion under this head called sympathy has the greatest extent. The nature of this passion is to put us in the place of another in whatever circumstance he is in, and to affect us in a like manner; so that this passion may, as the occasion requires, turn either on pain or pleasure; but with the modifications mentioned in some cases in sect. II. As to imitation and preference nothing more need be said.

SECT. XIX.
The CONCLUSION.

I believed that an attempt to range and methodize some of our most leading passions, would be a good preparative to such an enquiry as we are going to make in the ensuing discourse. The passions I have mentioned are almost the only ones which it can be necessary to consider in our present design; though the variety of the passions is great, and worthy in every branch of that variety of an attentive investigation. The more accurately we search into the human mind, the stronger traces we every where find of his wisdom who made it. If a discourse on the use of the parts of the body may be considered as an hymn to the Creator; the use of the passions, which are the organs of the mind, cannot be barren of praise to him, nor unproductive to ourselves of that noble and uncommon union of science and admiration, which a contemplation of the works of infinite wisdom alone can afford to a rational mind; whilst referring to him whatever we find of right, or good, or fair in ourselves, discovering his strength and wisdom even in our own weakness and imperfection, honouring them where we discover them clearly, and adoring their profundity where we are lost in our search, we may be inquisitive without impertinence, and elevated without pride; we may be admitted, if I may dare to say so, into the counsels of the Almighty by a consideration of his works. The elevation of the mind ought to be the principal end of all our studies, which if they do not in some measure effect, they are of very little service to us. But besides this great purpose, a consideration of the rationale of our passions seems to me very necessary for all who would affect them upon solid and sure principles. It is not enough to know them in general; to affect them after a delicate manner, or to judge properly of any work designed to affect them, we should know the exact boundaries of their several jurisdictions; we should pursue them through all their variety of operations, and pierce into the inmost, and what might appear inaccessible parts of our nature,

Quod latet arcanâ non enarrabile fibrâ.[18]

Without all this it is possible for a man after a confused manner sometimes to satisfy his own mind of the truth of his work; but he can never have a certain determinate rule to go by, nor can he ever make his propositions sufficiently clear to others. Poets, and orators, and painters, and those who cultivate other branches of the liberal arts, have without this critical knowledge succeeded well in their several provinces, and will succeed; as among artificers there are many machines made and even invented without any exact knowledge of the principles they are governed by. It is, I own, not uncommon to be wrong in theory and right in practice; and we are happy that it is so. Men often act right from their feelings, who afterwards reason but ill on them from principle; but as it is impossible to avoid an attempt at such reasoning, and equally impossible to prevent its having some influence on our practice, surely it is worth taking some pains to have

---

[18] **fibrâ** 'the incommunicable feelings of my heart strings' (Persius, *Satires*, v.29).

it just, and founded on the basis of sure experience. We might expect that the artists themselves would have been our surest guides; but the artists have been too much occupied in the practice; the philosophers have done little, and what they have done, was mostly with a view to their own schemes and systems; and as for those called critics, they have generally sought the rule of the arts in the wrong place; they sought it among poems, pictures, engravings, statues and buildings. But art can never give the rules that make an art. This is, I believe, the reason why artists in general, and poets principally, have been confined in so narrow a circle; they have been rather imitators of one another than of nature; and this with so faithful an uniformity, and to so remote an antiquity, that it is hard to say who gave the first model. Critics follow them, and therefore can do little as guides. I can judge but poorly of any thing whilst I measure it by no other standard than itself. The true standard of the arts is in every man's power; and an easy observation of the most common, sometimes of the meanest things in nature, will give the truest lights, where the greatest sagacity and industry that slights such observation, must leave us in the dark, or what is worse, amuse and mislead us by false lights. In an enquiry, it is almost everything to be once in a right road. I am satisfied I have done but little by these observations considered in themselves; and I never should have taken the pains to digest them, much less should I have ever ventured to publish them, if I was not convinced that nothing tends more to the corruption of science than to suffer it to stagnate. These waters must be troubled before they can exert their virtues. A man who works beyond the surface of things, though he may be wrong himself, yet he clears the way for others, and may chance to make even his errors subservient to the cause of truth. In the following parts I shall enquire what things they are that cause in us the affections of the sublime and beautiful, as in this I have considered the affections themselves. I only desire one favour; that no part of this discourse may be judged of by itself and independently of the rest; for I am sensible I have not disposed my materials to abide the test of a captious controversy, but of a sober and even forgiving examination; that they are not armed at all points for battle; but dressed to visit those who are willing to give a peaceful entrance to truth.

'Religion'

Introduction

Burke seems to have turned to this subject after finishing his *Philosophical Enquiry*, published in 1757. His second edition of 1759 criticized the theory of moral sense as one which had 'misled us both in the theory of taste and of morals', specifying that it 'induced us to remove the science of our duties from their proper basis, (our reason, our relations, and our necessities).'[1] 'Religion' gave Burke's 'proper basis' to moral theory in the course of developing a wider argument.

Why should the paper be called 'Religion'? The common feature of moral sense and deism, two of the objects of Burke's enmity, was to his eyes an insufficient regard for God. The former had no explanatory role for Him in aesthetic or moral theory. Whilst the latter did not involve that omission, it made another by discounting His revealed word. Burke, having attended to aesthetics, turned to morals and revelation in order to relate them both to his understanding of God.

How did Burke's moral explanation use 'our reason, our relations, and our necessities'? Relation and reason are important at the most general level. Burke used them to explain duty. He took it that we 'cannot conceive that a reasonable Creature can be placed in any Relation that does not give rise to some Duty'. Relation, a term of scholastic origin, denotes the comparing of two ideas. For instance, we might conceive God as powerful and man as weak. The relation, if God acts in respect of man, would be one of dependence. On the

---

[1] see *Philosophical Enquiry*, III, xi.

78

other hand, comparing one man with another might suggest a relation of equality of power. How could relation give rise to duty? Here there are two questions: firstly, how could the conviction arise that there might be a duty? and, secondly, how could this conviction actually be a duty? To answer the first question, let us turn to an example of action. One person performs a service for another. We may say that there is a natural impulse to requite benefits and a conviction that this is a duty. Take the latter view, that the good done to a person ought to be requited by him, and leave out reference to individuals: we have the statement that good actions ought to be requited. So the relation of doing good to another suggests a duty. Whether or no this is a duty, in fact, is quite another matter, but a matter which the explanation of the content of Burke's argument does not require, for he took the alternative to be inconceivable.

Burke confined relations giving rise to duties to 'reasonable Creatures'. This suggests that he thought that reason disclosed duty. Consider an example which he gave, that 'if we require help, 'tis reasonable we should give help'. To make sense of this claim certainly requires some reasoning. Burke had in fact prefaced his statement by observing that man required the help of others like himself to obtain his ends. This suggests a relation of equal power. If two individuals are equal in relevant respects, then no distinction can be adduced which would make a difference to how each should be treated. So because they must be subject to the same rules, it follows that there is no rational ground for A to expect B to perform services for him which A will not undertake to perform for B. So far Burke is certainly a rationalist in ethics.

This, however, is reasoning in moral philosophy rather than moral theory. It reasons about conduct rather than showing that reason discloses the content of the rules in question or their obligatory force. For instance, it tells nothing about how the conviction that good should be returned is formed. The content of 'Religion' indicates how good comes to be done as a matter of fact – Burke says that 'we love' our fellow man and 'if we love, 'tis natural to do good to those whom we love' – but this is not identical with saying that a similar feeling explains the duty to requite the good done or that the initial act was a duty in virtue of a non-rational explanation. If either of these were true Burke would be a sentimentalist. Sentimentalism need not be identified with moral sense, for the latter was only one way in which sentiment could be related to ethics. For instance, most relevantly, sympathy might explain moral distinctions. Burke may well have read Hume and his response to Smith's *Theory of Moral Sentiments* was enthusiastic. But the matter is not broached here and Burke's political utterances were hardly an appropriate place to give theoretical disquisitions. Since this is nothing if not a department where precision is essential it would be unwise to speculate. It would be attempting merely to locate Burke accurately where the co-ordinates are not available to map him.

The paper, at any rate, outlines two relations, meant to show the foundations of religion and morality respectively. The former resides in man's relation to God. The good that God has done him cannot be returned, as Burke assumed would be appropriate, by action: for 'man has received several Benefits but can return none'. Man's response to God was found rather in worship. Together God's action and worship formed the basis of religion. The basis of morality involved man's necessities, as well as reason and relation. Man was not only weak in comparison with God, but also in respect of his own needs. He required the help of others men to meet them, and by that token it would be reasonable for each man to help others. It was not only reasonable, but also natural. Man's love and sympathy for his fellows provided an impulse to aid them. Reason and affection thus provided an account of moral conduct.

Whilst these two relations considered separately do not make God integral to moral explanation, they may be combined and supplemented in a way that does. Burke next argued that religion included morality. God had placed man in his posture of dependence on others, thus involving him in duty, and 'if God has placed us in a Relation attended with Duties, it must be agreeable to him that we perform those Duties.' What flowed from God's approval? Burke argued that an after-life could be posited. If we adduce once more the idea that doing good should be rewarded, it would follow (unless virtue were rewarded in this life, as Burke insisted it was not) that 'our Actions here are made the *Causes* of our future happiness'. So God and His works were indispensable to a proper understanding of ethics, where they were not in the moral sense theory.

Burke's moral explanation, because rational, used the instrument which the deists had employed against revealed theology: but his argument turned reason to a different end. It showed the reasons for a

revelation. Deism suggested reason was adequate to man's salvation –
for instance, that he could discover not only his duties and the after-
life but also the existence and attributes of God through his natural
faculties. Bolingbroke, for instance, argued at length that man had a
knowledge of God; arguments to the same effect are found in Collins
or Tindal; and Warburton observed that the deists were not disposed
to argue against God's being and attributes. Burke built on this point
to rebut their treatment of revelation.

The fundamental challenge to revelation was its inequity by the
canons of reason. Revelation on this reading was hardly good. If
revelation were not good, then one might doubt the value of the
miracles supposedly performed to attest it – the acts of power involved
might not be God's. Burke did not need to argue the latter point. His
tactic was to argue that a revelation properly attested would produce
more conviction than reason. If God had communicated some knowledge of Himself to man, he reasoned, it was unreasonable to exclude
the possibility that He might communicate more. The best means
would be human testimony, since the mutual aid needed by men
involved 'a principal of Credit, or faith, in Man to Man'. For this
reason testimony at its best did not leave doubt (it seems reasonable to
understand Burke to mean, consciousness of doubt). Indeed, it left
'less doubt' than reason. Reason, the deists' weapon, was hardly well
placed to assault revelation when the latter was more firmly lodged in
the human mind. On Burke's account, human testimony could offer
an incontestable attestation of God's acts.

Analysis

If God made man there a relation between them. Man has received
benefits and so ought to be grateful: which he expresses in worship.
Man is bound by need and by sentiment to others: which is the basis
of morality. Moral duties are included in religion and enforced by it.
Man and his attributes answer to an end beyond the temporal. Man
may be immortal; this life is a preparation for the next. It is therefore
important that we should know what God wills us to do in order to
reach the next life. God has provided evidence of His will in the form
of human testimony, which is more certain than a demonstration.
There should be books to record God's will and a society devoted to
teaching it.

'Religion'[1]

If there be a God such as we conceive, he must be our Maker.

If he is our Maker, there is a Relation between us.

If there be a Relation between us some Duty must arise from that Relation, since we cannot conceive that a reasonable Creature can be placed in any Relation that does not give rise to some Duty. This Relation betwixt God & Man, is that Man has received several Benefits but can return none./

that he may suffer all Manner of Mischief but can return none, or by himself avert none.

Therefore by no *act* can he perform this Duty but he can by the Sentiments of his Mind.

Where we have received good tis natural[2] to Praise.

where we hope good it is natural to pray.

Where we fear Evil. tis natural to deprecate it.

This is the foundation of Religion

We have a relation to other Men.

We want many things compassable only by the helps of other beings like ourselves.[3]

They want things compassable within our Help.

We love these beings & have a sympathy[4] with them.

If we require help tis reasonable we should give help.

If we love tis natural to good to those whom we love/

Hence one Branch of our Duties to our fellow Creatures is active – Hence Benevolence.

This is the foundation of Morality.

---

[1] Sheffield City Archives, WMM, Bk.P.40, pp. 73–85.
   The piece is printed exactly as it stands in the MS., save that the long s has been reduced to modern usage and that in three places, where writing beyond the ordinary starting place on the left of the line has been justified. Erasures have not been reproduced. In one place a word has been added; this is placed in square brackets [ ].
   Somerset's printing of the document (*Notebook*, pp. 69–75) revises the punctuation, but also makes several unacknowledged alterations, as correcting the spelling and supplying at least one word without notice.

[2] **natural**   Burke is keen to prove his case as natural theology.

[3] **ourselves**   it was usually assumed in natural law thinking that the individual is insufficiently strong to satisfy all his own wants: see e.g. VNS, above pp. 14f.

[4] **sympathy**   cf. *Philosophical Enquiry*, I.xiii–xiv, above, pp. 68–70.

Morality does not necessarily include Religion since it concerns only our Relation with Men But Religion necessarily includes Morality because the Relation of God as a Creator is the same to other Men as to us.

If God[5] has placed us in a Relation attended with Duties it must be agreable to him that we perform those Duties.

Hence Moral Duties are included in Religion & enforced by it.

If God has provided fatally for all things: we may honour him but we can neither love him, fear him, nor hope in him. for there is no object for those Passions.

This would reduce all worship to praise only & Gratitude.[6]

Gratitude is an inert Principle, because it concerns only things done.

Hope & fear are the Springs of every thing in us because they look to the future about which only Mankind can be sollicitous./

To take away Providence[7] would therefore be to take away Religion.

The Argument against a Providence are from our *Reasonings*,[8] observing a certain order in the works of God.

there is nothing at all in our natural feelings against it.

There is a great deal in our natural feelings for it.

All Dependent[9] Beings that have a Sense of their Dependence naturally cry out to their Superiour for assistance.

No Man can act uniformly as if a fatality governed every thing.

Men do not naturally conceive that when they are strongly actuated to call upon a Superior that they cannot be heard. they do not conceive that they have Passions which have [no] Purpose.

They naturally measure their Duties to the Divinity by their own wants & their feelings & not by abstract Speculations, in the one they cannot be deceived, in the other they may./

[5] **If God** Burke's conditional clause passes over the question of whether it could be shown that God gave moral laws apprehensible as such through reason.

[6] **Gratitude** for the benefits man has received could not be returned in kind (God being self-sufficient) and would be marked instead by praise.

[7] **Providence** involves the idea that man will be rewarded or punished after his death for his terrestrial conduct: so that hope and fear enter into his view of God. Cf. PE, II.v, and see above p. 60.

[8] **Reasonings** referring to deist attempts to undermine reliance on revelation cf. VNS, preface p. 9.

[9] **Dependent** as man is dependent on God he answers to His ends. Cf. Locke (*Ethica B*, MS.Locke c. 28 fol. 141 in Bodleian Library: modernized): 'The original and foundation of all Law is dependency. A dependent intelligent being is under the power and direction and dominion of him on whom he depends and must be for the ends appointed him by that superior being.'

One is taken from the Nature of God which we do not understand the other from our own which we understand better.

Metaphysical or Physical Speculations neither are or ought to be the Grounds of our Duties because we can arrive at no certainty[10] in them they have a weight when they concur with our own natural feelings, very little when against them.

The ends of a transitory Animal may be answered without any knowledge of a God. they are so answered in Beasts.[11]

Men have some knowledge of God –

Hence we presume other Ends are to be answered

Man has Ideas of Immortality & wishes for it he does not think he has Ideas & Wishes, for no End.

Hence he presumes he may be Immortal

Man is sensible he has Duties,/

That the Performance of these Duties must be agreable to God.

That, being agreable to God is the way to be happy.

Experience shews him that the Performance of these Duties does not give him happiness in Life – therefore

He concludes that they must make him happy after Death, & that for that Reason something in him must survive.

He sees that this Notion is favourable to the performance of all his Duties & that the Contrary notion is unfavourable to it.

He observes that this Notion tends to perfect his Nature, that the contrary tends to sink him to a level of Inferiour Natures.

In Disputed Questions those Notions that tend to make him better & happier, to bind him to his fellow Creatures & to his Creator & to make him a more excellent / Creature are true rather than the Contrary[12] these Arguments are taken from within the others are foreign.

If his Soul survives after Death it does not appear why it should not live forever:

If the Soul lives for ever the space of time spent in this Life is inconsiderable.

[10] **no certainty** for physical speculations, cf. 'When we go but one step beyond the immediately sensible qualities of things, we go out of our depth' (*Philosophical Enquiry*, iv.i); for metaphysical, see also 'Introduction', above p. 81.

[11] **Beasts** the image of God, peculiar amongst created life to man, was supposed to consist partly in reason.

[12] **the Contrary** cf. *Notebook*, p. 85: 'the End of all Knowledge ought to be the bettering us in some manner'.

It is therefore reasonable that it should take up but the smallest part of our Attention.

We do not know how far our relation to other Men shall continue after Death.

We know that our Relation to God must continue the same after Death.

We know therefore that our Duty to God is of more Moment than our Attention to ourselves or others.

It is natural to suppose that what goes first in the order of Nature should produce what follows it.

It is therefore reasonable to conclude that/our Performance of our Duty here must make our fate afterwards.

It is reasonable that the smallest part of any thing should be destined for the Uses of the whole rather than that the whole should be employed for the purposes of a part.

It is therefore reasonable to suppose that our Actions here are made the *Causes* of our future happiness or Misery & not that our future Misery & Happiness are designed as the sanctions of our Duties here.

Hence it is that this life is a Preparation for the next.

Hence it is that we ought not to immerse our selves too much in the things which make us consider this Life as our all.

Hence it is that for this Purpose we ought to deny ourselves, since an Indulgence in Pleasures here removes our Attention from further Objects & weakens our/Desire for them.

We may have observed that the Passions which arise from self love, frequently clash with those Duties, which arise from our Relation to other Men

But less mischeif arises from a restraint on our desires than from indulging them to the prejudice of others.

Thus self Denial becomes the second of the Pillars of Morality[13]

This is the more austere part of our Duty & the most difficult.

If [14] we depend upon a Superior being it is but just that we should pray to him, because we have no other means of sufficiently express-

---

[13] **Pillars of Morality** that this religion is Christanity is clear enough if we recollect *First Letter on a Regicide Peace* on Christianity as 'that religion of social benevolence, and of individual self-denial'.

[14] **If** the ensuing paragraphs offer an argument for the reasonableness of a revelation.

ing our Dependance, though he should already be sufficiently apprised of our wants & willing to supply them.

If we depend upon any Superior being it is reasonable that we should trust in him though we do not see the Motives/ & tendencies of his Actions. Good Will even among Men could not be supported otherwise.

If we have Reason to suppose that he has proposed any thing, we ought to beleive it firmly, though we should not thoroughly comprehend the Nature of the things proposed, otherwise we break off our Dependance as much as we should if we should our Connexion with Men if we refused them all Credit.

God has given us a knowledge of him self & we beleive that knowledge to be of some Importance to us.

We therefore ought not to imagine it impossible that he may be willing to give us some further knowledge of his Nature or his Will.

Neither is it reasonable that we should judge it impossible for him to find fit means of communicating this knowledge/

If he intends to communicate such knowledge the best Proofs of such a Design are such acts of Power as can leave us no Doubts of their coming from God[15] for thus[16] it is we know that he exists, & that he is all powerful & all wise.

God has for the most Parts made Men the Instruments of all the Good he does to Men.

Most of their strength is from mutual Assistance.

Most of their knowledge from mutual Instruction.

There is a principle of Credit or faith in Man to Man without which this Assistance & Instruction would be impracticable.

Therefore Human Testimony is the strongest Proof we can have of any thing & leaves no doubt when it is very strong./

That there is such a City as Rome is a Proposition of which we can doubt less than that the Square of the Hypothenuse is equal to the Squares of the two sides when the latter is demonstrated. the highest Degree of testimony leaves less doubt than Demonstration:[17]

---

[15] **from God** i.e. miracles. Burke takes the view that miracles evidence the divine credentials of a mission.

[16] **for thus** for power as a striking attribute of God, see *Philosophical Enquiry*, II.v.

[17] **Demonstration** in Locke's classification of knowledge, demonstration (the connection of our ideas) gave certainty; see *An Essay concerning Human Understanding*, IV.xvii.15; what we derived from testimony could be at best probable (IV.xv.1).

Besides the force of it is more easily & generally comprehended.[18]

If God has revealed any thing by evident Proof from his Power & that these Proofs of Power are conveyed to us by as high a Degree a Testimony as the thing can bear we ought to beleive it.

If the thing conveyed be intended to last in the world there must be means taken to make them last, there must be Men appointed to teach them. and Books written to record.[19]/

There should be some evident marks of the Designation of such Men that all may know, who they are that teach this Doctrine.

These Men should be compellable to teach it lest the knowledge of these truths might depend upon Caprice.

There must therefore be a Society for this Purpose.

Burke does not challenge this ordering, but suggests that because of man's reliance on testimony it produces a higher degree of conviction in him than demonstration.

[18] **comprehended**   a standard gambit in favour of revelation, cf. 'Extempore Commonplace', above p. 3.

[19] **record**   these needs obviously answer to the Hebrew and early Christian priests and to the Bible, just as the next sentences point to the continuing need for a church.

Tracts on the Popery Laws

Introduction

When Burke reminisced about Ireland in 1780, after fifteen years devoted largely to the politics of England and America, he claimed that on first entering Parliament 'What was first and uppermost' in his thoughts was the hope 'to be somewhat useful to the place of my birth and education, which in many respects, internal and external, I thought ill and impolitically governed'.[1] This is likely enough, for Ireland preoccupied Burke from his teens. His earliest speeches and writings, composed as an undergraduate, provide many criticisms of Irish society, especially its disregard for good taste, its low morals and economic backwardness. These points focussed, in the end, on the failure of the propertied order of Irish society to provide the leadership which their station made possible.[2]

Did Burke react against that order? He had a sense of its potential for good. He mentioned the case of one gentleman who had benefited his tenants greatly by a benevolent policy of improving his estate. The example was not entirely isolated. Another observer suggested that 'a man has a figure in his country in proportion to the improvements he makes'. When Arthur Young toured Ireland a little later (in 1776) he found a number of agricultural improvers at work.[3] A few years before

---

[1] *Letter to Thomas Burgh* (1780), IA, p. 314.
[2] See *The Reformer*, nos. 4, 6, 7 in Samuels, p. 307, 313, 316.
[3] *The Reformer*, no. 7, in Samuels, p. 317. Cf. no. 6, in Samuels, p. 314 for another sphere of improvement; E. Willes (writing about 1760) cited in R.B. McDowell, *Ireland in the Age of Imperialism and Revolution 1760–1801* (1979), p. 6f; Arthur Young, *Tour of Ireland* (1892), ii pp. 104, 22, 93.

Burke himself had arranged that 'one of the finest bull calves . . . of the short-horned Holderness breed'[4] should be sent to a cousin's farm. Again, he had general reasons for thinking an unequal order attractive. He reacted not against property, but against the political dispensation which frustrated the operation he intended for it in Ireland.

Burke looked to the landed classes not least because he saw no alternative for Ireland. 'You had none but a landed interest', he wrote in 1762, 'which had any strength or body in Ireland'. This was accurate enough, for agriculture was the foundation of Irish wealth; and such industry as there was, was itself largely based on agriculture. Burke was probably also right to look to the wealthy, for the country's income pattern, so far as it can be discovered, was sharply pyramidal. Landed property, besides, was not merely secure but conferred status and respect on its owner. But the political structure of Ireland hindered such leadership by putting brakes on landed wealth. Her government saw with denominational eyes. The Protestant ascendancy depended upon keeping Catholics under disabilities, and penal legislation had been framed to depress their political power. In part, this meant barring access to public life, but, 'framed upon a principle, generally true that influence follows property',[5] disabilities were imposed to prevent Catholics from becoming or remaining landowners. They could not purchase land and could not inherit it from a Protestant. They could not take a lease for more than thirty-one years. When a Catholic died, his estate was broken up amongst his sons. Since the vast majority of the Irish were Catholic, it followed that their industry and landed property could scarcely provide a basis for social and political leadership.

Protestant opinion when Burke began to consider Ireland was often suspicious of Catholicism. Henry Brooke, writing in 1745, referred back to the days of James II and asked 'where then was trade, where was art, where was industry, where was the law, the religion and the liberty?' Another writer suggested that 'the greatest part of the estates . . . would be lost to the protestant possessors, if popery should

---

[4] Corr, I, p. 329.
[5] Burke to Charles O'Hara, 30 Dec. 1762, Corr, I, p. 162; 'property' is cited in McDowell, *Ireland*, p. 177. Burke himself seems to have subscribed to this view for some time, see PD, below p. 134, with note. There is a summary of the penal legislation in T. H. D. Mahony, *Edmund Burke and Ireland* (1960), appendices I–VI.

prevail'.[6] Yet it was also possible to ask, with Bishop Berkeley, whether even the Protestants of Ireland could prosper whilst keeping the Catholics under disabilities: 'whether it be not a vain attempt to project the flourishing of our protestant gentry exclusive of the bulk of the natives'; or, as a chief secretary for Ireland put it sometime later, to remove the penal laws would make two million people flourish.[7]

Burke and others interested in developing Irish land and society had thus to ask questions about the penal laws. In part these would be questions about the laws' oppressive effect and in part about the political reliability of Catholics. Burke supposed that Catholics could be trusted – indeed, the protestancy of the Burke family before Edmund himself was recessive, to say the least[8] – and that the papacy would no more intrude its authority into Ireland than any other country.[9] But the most important question to his mind was the injustice and impolicy of the penal laws. The two aspects of the question, agriculture and rightness, came together in the literature of the late 1750s and early 1760s, when questions of improvement and, more especially, popery were prominent themes in pamphlet literature.[10] The latter especially so, for a series of attacks on landed property and tithe collectors in Munster (the Whiteboys disturbances) were blamed on Catholics. Burke, who at the time was secretary to W. G. Hamilton, Chief Secretary for Ireland, described the results, writing to a friend in 1762 that

---

[6] Henry Brooke, *A Friendly Call* (1757), p. 11; Anon., *Lord Taaffe's Observations Examined and Confuted* (1767), p. 25.

[7] George Berkeley, *The Querist*, no. 255, in A. A. Luce and T. E. Jessop (eds.), *The Works of Bishop Berkeley*, 9 vols. (1948–57), VI, 126; Sir George Macartney, *An Account of Ireland* (1773), p. 24. Burke's *Fourth Regicide* refers to 'the mode of stating the most decided opinions in the form of questions ... since the excellent queries of the excellent Berkeley', W, VI, p. 335.

[8] One Richard Burke, who is thought to have been Edmund's father, conformed in 1722; but Richard Burke was a common name. Burke's mother, Mary Nagle, was a Catholic.

[9] See below, p. 101.

[10] On the issue of improvement, see: Anon., *Thoughts on the general improvement of Ireland, with a scheme of a society for carrying out all improvements* (1758); John Long, *The golden fleece: or some thoughts on the clothing trade of Ireland* (1762). On the issue of anti-popery, see: Anon., *A protestant's address to the protestants of Ireland wherein some sure methods are laid down, by which their number may be increased and that of the papists diminished* (1757); *The protestant interest considered relatively to the operation of the popery acts in Ireland* (1757); [Charles O'Conor], *The danger of popery to the present government examined* (1761); Anon., *Some reasons against raising an army of Roman catholics in Ireland* (1762); James Caldwell, *A brief examination of the question whether it is expedient, either in a religious or political view, to pass an act to enable papists to take real securities for money which they may lend* (1764).

[11] Burke to Charles O'Hara, before 23 Aug. 1762, Corr, I, p. 147f.

Happy & wise are those poor Natives in avoiding yr. great World; that they are unacquainted with the unfeeling Tyranny of a mungril Irish Landlord, or with the Horrors of a Munster Circuit. I have avoided this subject whenever I wrote to you; & shall now say no more of it; because it is impossible to preserve ones Temper on the view of so detestable a scene. God save me from the power, (I shall take care to keep myself from the society) of such monsters of Inhumanity[11]

and remembered the period from 1761 to 1764 for its cruelty; Lord Charlemont described the government behaving as if towards a rising of foreign slaves.[12] Burke himself helped to mount an official inquiry, which found that 'however industriously the opposite has been promoted, Papist and Protestant were promiscuously concerned' and that the causes of the disturbances were less religious than economic.[13]

Burke's response to Ireland's plight is the unfinished piece we know as *Tracts on the Popery Laws*. He intended to display the penal laws against Catholics as a chief cause of Ireland's problems. He found in them a system of hardship imposed on the bulk of the population. He thought that their effect was to depress both morals and industry. The document, as we have it, is incomplete (chapters 1 and 5 are missing, whilst 4 is unfinished), but enough survives to make the steps of Burke's argument clear. He turned first to the laws 'which relate to the possession and inheritance of landed property in Popish hands'[14] and devoted the bulk of his second chapter to it.

Property was important here as an instrument in the larger design of improvement. Burke objected to the legal status quo because it frustrated Catholics 'in every road of industry', threw 'almost all sorts of obstacles in their way':[15] and not merely industry, but industry devoted to developing their property. Of the Catholic landowner whose offspring, converting to Protestantism, bring the force of law against him, Burke writes that there was 'no respite from the persecution of his children, but by totally abandoning all thoughts of improvement and acquisition.'[16] He showed also how the law regarding education and religious practice tended in the same direction. In short, the legal settlement discouraged economic development 'as

---

[11] Burke to Charles O'Hara, before 23 Aug. 1762, Corr, I, p. 147f.
[12] *HMC Charlemont*, I, p. 20 & note.   [13] Corr, I, p. 39f.
[14] *Tracts on the Popery Laws*, ch. 2, IA, p. 3.
[15] *Tracts*, p. 13.   [16] *Tracts*, p. 8.

directly as if the law had said in express terms, "Thou shalt not improve" [17]

What did 'improvement' involve? It might be viewed in two ways, one narrow and the other broader. In the former sense, improvement meant a better farming techniques: in the latter it conjured the consequences of prosperity, such as a larger population and that, indeed, with a better moral character. Burke's *Tracts* aimed to show that the penal laws frustrated not just agricultural improvement but its desirable results.

The standard by which Burke judged was twofold. 'There are two, and only two foundations of law,' he wrote, '. . . equity and utility'.[18] The standard of equity was divine law, specifically here the law of nature, which suggested that civil laws should treat people in the same manner: here was a mode of equality Burke approved – equality of consideration. Utility, the assessment of conduct with respect to happiness, was meant by Burke to refer to the happiness of the whole community. The two standards are conceptually distinct, but would imply a united condemnation of the penal laws. For these both disregarded equity, by raising 'artificial difference between men . . . in order to induce a consequential inequality in the distribution of justice', and violated utility, by consulting the good only of a few. Burke assumed that injustice would produce unfortunate consequences. Just as his *Abridgement* witnessed the happy results of following Providence for England, so the *Tract* intended to show that the Irish settlement 'is unjust, impolitic, and inefficacious; that it has the most unhappy influence on the prosperity, the morals, and the safety of that country; that this influence is . . . the necessary and direct consequence of the laws themselves'.[19]

Ireland, as Burke declared later, saw 'all the means given by Providence to make life safe and comfortable . . . perverted into instruments of terror and torment.'[20] This statement dates from 1780, but the same assumption is present in his *Tract*. The penal laws, he thought, 'tamper with the natural foundations of society.'[21] Many proper forms of inequality were levelled or even inverted. The superiority of parents over children was threatened[22] and, as Burke later

[17] See below, p. 97.
[18] *Tracts*, ch. 3. 1, IA, p. 27.   [19] *Tracts*, p. 21.
[20] *Speech at the Guildhall, in Bristol, previous to the late election* (1780), IA, p. 149.
[21] See below, p. 102.   [22] *Tracts*, ch. 2, IA, p. 6f.

added, the penal laws made 'the very servant who waits behind your chair the arbiter of your life and fortune'.[23] Above all, there was the dispersion of landed property. It was not available to most of the population, for 'by the express words of the law all possibility of acquiring any species of valuable property, in any sort connected with land, is taken away,'[24] and it could not be transmitted in large amounts, for statute dictated an equal division of property amongst possible heirs. Under these conditions the sort of order which Burke had seen approvingly in England could hardly develop.

Many years later he lamented the absence from Catholic Ireland of 'an aristocratic interest, that is, an interest of property and education'.[25] In his period at Trinity he had outlined the leadership such a body might give in establishing the character and prosperity of the people, whether by example or conduct. In his *Tracts* he showed why such leadership was hard to find in Ireland. Instead, Burke found it in England. Burke had in effect emigrated to England after graduating at Trinity, seeking a career, whether in law, literature or politics. He had found one in literature, with his *Vindication* and *Philosophical Enquiry* (and, of course, his connection with the *Annual Register*). In the 1760s he embarked on a political life, first with Hamilton, then with Charles Townshend and, from 1765, with the Marquess of Rockingham. In his case, as in so many, 'the mind of Ireland is to be found in a colony of refugees'[26] (or, as Bernard Shaw was to remark, 'as long as Ireland produces men with sense enough to leave her, she does not exist in vain').

Chapter 4 is printed here. It encapsulates briefly Burke's objections to the penal laws in respect of improvement. The text (which does not seem to survive in manuscript) is fragmentary and shows every sign of being unfinished: but even so it embodies the author's case concisely.

Analysis

The first three chapters of the *Tracts* have looked at the injustice to the community implied in the penal laws, but in the fourth chapter we

---

[23] *Guildhall*, IA, p. 149. [24] *Tracts*, ch. 2, IA, p. 13.
[25] *A Letter to Sir Hercules Langrishe* (1792), IA, p. 211.
[26] Anon., *A review of the strictures on the declaration of the catholic society* (1792), p. 18. Burke's political position may help to explain why the *Tracts* were neither finished nor published in his lifetime. For another explanation, see the transactions described by Mahony, *Edmund Burke*, p. 355f.

turn to their consequences for national prosperity (p. 95). The penal laws depress the resources for improvement found in industry (p. 95–98), skill, morals, justice and government [incomplete]; it is supposed that Catholics are untrustworthy, but any disloyalty springs not from religion but oppression (pp. 98–102).

Tracts on the Popery Laws

CHAPTER IV

IN the foregoing book we considered these Laws in a very simple point of view, and in a very general one; merely as a system of hardship imposed on the body of the community; and from thence and from some other arguments inferred the general injustice of such a procedure. In this we shall be obliged to be more minute; and the matter will become more complex as we undertake to demonstrate the mischievous and impolitick consequences, which the particular mode of this oppressive system and the instrument, which it employs, operating as we said on this extensive object, produces on the national prosperity, quiet, and security.

The stock of materials, by which any nation is rendered flourishing and prosperous, are its industry; its knowledge or skill; its morals; its execution of justice; its courage; and the national union in directing these powers to one point and making them all center in the publick benefit. Other than these I do not know, and scarcely can conceive any means, by which a community may flourish.

If we show that these Penal Laws of Ireland destroy not one only, but every one of these materials of publick prosperity, it will not be difficult to perceive that Great Britain, whilst they subsist, never can draw from that Country all the advantages, to which the bounty of Nature has entitled it.

To begin with the first great instrument of national happiness, strength and industry, I must observe that although these Penal Laws do indeed inflict many hardships on those, who are obnoxious to them, yet their chief, their most extensive, and most certain operation is upon property. These civil Constitutions, which promote industry, are such as facilitate the acquisition; secure the holding; enable the fixing and suffer the alienation of property. Every Law, which obstructs it in any part of this distribution, is in proportion to the force and extent of the obstruction a discouragement to industry. For a Law against property, is a Law against industry, the latter having always the former, and nothing else, for its object. Now as to the acquisition of landed property, which is the foundation and support of all the other kinds,[1] the Laws have disabled three-fourths of the inhabitants of Ireland from acquiring any estate of inheritance for life or years, or any charge whatsoever on which two-thirds of the improved yearly value is not reserved for 50 years.[2]

This confinement of landed property to one set of hands, and preventing its free circulation[3] through the community, is a most leading article of ill policy; because it is one of the most capital discouragements to all that industry which may be employed on the lasting improvement of the soil, or is any way conversant about land. A tenure of 30 years is evidently no tenure upon which to build; to plant; to raise enclosures; to change the nature of the ground; to make any new experiment which might improve agriculture; or to do any thing more than what may answer the immediate and momentary calls of rent to the landlord and leave subsistence to the tenant and his family. The desire of acquisition is always a passion of long views; confine a man to momentary possession, and you at once cut off that laudable avarice which every wise State has cherished, as one of the first principles of its greatness. Allow a man but a temporary possession, lay it down as a maxim, that he never can have any other, and you immediately and infallibly turn him to temporary enjoyments; and these enjoyments are never the pleasures of labour and free industry, and whose quality it is to famish the present hours, and squander all upon prospect and futurity; they are, on the contrary, those of a thoughtless, loitering, and dissipated life. The people must be inevitably disposed to such pernicious habits, merely from the short duration of their tenure which the Law has allowed. But it is not enough that industry is checked by the confinement of its views; it is further discouraged by the limitation of its own direct object, profit. This is a

---

[1] **of all the other kinds** cf. Gibbon, *Decline and Fall*, ch. 8: 'all taxes must, at last, fall upon agriculture'.

[2] **thirty years** the *Tracts*, ch. 2 (IA, p. 11f) explained that Catholics might enjoy leases for terms of less than thirty-one years, subject to severe limitations.

[3] **free circulation** i.e. to Roman Catholics who were about 75 per cent of the population, but owned about 3 per cent of the land.

regulation extremely worthy of our attention, as it is not a consequential, but a direct discouragement to melioration; as directly as if the Law had said in express terms, 'Thou shalt not improve.'

But we have an additional argument to demonstrate the ill policy of denying the occupiers of land any solid property in it. Ireland is a country wholly unplanted. The farmers have neither dwelling-houses, nor good offices; nor are the lands almost any where provided with fences and communications; in a word, in a very unimproved state. The land owner there never takes upon him, as it is usual in this Kingdom, to supply all these conveniences, and to set down his tenant in what may be called a completely furnished farm. If the tenant will not do it, it is never done. This convenience shews how miserably and peculiarly impolitick it has been in Ireland to be down the body of the tenantry to short and unprofitable tenures. A finished and furnished house will be taken for any term, however short: if the repair lies on the owner, the shorter the better. But no one will take one not only unfurnished but half built, but upon a term which, on calculation, will answer with profit all his charges. It is on this principle that the Romans established their *Emphyteusis*[4] or Fee-farm. For though they extended the ordinary term of their location only to nine years; yet they encouraged a more permanent letting to farm, with the condition of improvement as well as of annual payment on the part of the tenant where the land had lain rough and neglected; and therefore invented this species of engrafted holding in the later times when property came to be worse distributed by falling into a few hands. This denial of landed property to the gross of the people has this further evil effect in preventing the improvement of land; that it prevents any of the property acquired in trade to be regorged as it were upon the land. They must have observed very little who have not remarked the bold and liberal spirit of improvement, which persons bred to trade have often exerted on their land purchases; that they usually come to them with a more abundant command of ready money than most landed men possess; and that they have in general a much better idea, by long habits of calculative dealings, of the propriety of expending in order to acquire. Besides, such men often bring their spirit of commerce into their estates with them, and make manufactures take a root where the

---

[4] *Emphyteusis* in Roman law, *emphyteuses* is a lease in perpetuity or for a long period. It resembled ownership more than an ordinary lease and was both inheritable and alienable.

mere landed gentry had perhaps no capital, perhaps no inclination, and most frequently not sufficient knowledge to effect any thing of the kind. By these means what beautiful and useful spots have there not been made about trading and manufacturing towns, and how has agriculture had reason to bless that happy alliance with commerce; and how miserable must that nation be whose frame of polity has disjoined the landing and the trading interests.[5]

****

The great prop of this whole system is not pretended to be its justice or its utility, but the supposed danger to the State which gave rise to it originally, and which they apprehend would return if this system were overturned. Whilst, say they, the Papists of this Kingdom were possessed of landed property, and of the influence consequent to such property, their allegiance to the Crown of Great Britain was ever insecure;[6] the publick peace was ever liable to be broken; and Protestants never could be a moment secure either of their properties or of their lives.[7] Indulgence[8] only made them arrogant, and power daring; confidence only excited and enabled them to exert their inherent treachery; and the times, which they generally selected for their most wicked and desperate rebellions,[9] were those in which they enjoyed the greatest ease and the most perfect tranquillity.

[5] **trading interests** the theme is taken up in *Reflections*, p. 209f, where it is suggested that the peculiarities of France's polity had prevented men of commercial wealth from acquiring land and so a position in society: this encouraged them to abet in the overthrow of the old regime. 'By the ancient usages which prevailed in that kingdom, the general circulation of property, and in particular the mutual convertibility of land into money, and money into land, had always been a matter of difficulty . . . these had kept the landed and monied interests more separated in France, less miscible, and the owners of the two distinct species of property not so well disposed to each other as they are in this country' (i.e. in England).

[6] **insecure** Roman Catholics were supposed to be politically unreliable because of their dual allegiance, to their sovereign and to the Pope. The latter was supposed to be the stronger because of his supposed ability to absolve them from the obligation of oaths and undertakings.

[7] **properties or . . . lives** a papal redistribution of land from Protestant settlers back to the Catholic Church might be feared, but here the adjustment seems to be a redressing of Protestant inroads on the property of Catholic laymen; 'lives' refers especially to the rising of 1641.

[8] **Indulgence** since the monarch was Supreme Governor in ecclesiastical affairs, what we call 'toleration' is technically an act of indulgence from a superior.

[9] **rebellions** Burke was keen to set the record straight about alleged Catholic misdemeanours. For instance, chapter 55 of Hume's *History of England* suggested that religious fervour demented the Romanists so far that they undermined civil society. See David Berman, 'Hume's *History* and the 1641 Rebellion', *Studies* (1976) with references for Hume and Burke's response.

Such are the arguments that are used, both publickly and privately, in every discussion upon this point. They are generally full of passion and of error, and built upon facts which in themselves are most false. It cannot, I confess, be denied, that those miserable performances which go about under the names of Histories of Ireland,[10] do indeed represent those events after this manner; and they would persuade us, contrary to the known order of Nature, that indulgence and moderation in Governors is the natural incitement in subjects to rebel. But there is an interior History of Ireland, the genuine voice of its records and monuments,[11] which speaks a very different language from these histories, from Temple and from Clarendon; these restore Nature to its just rights, and policy to its proper order. For they even now show to those who have been at the pains to examine them, and they may show one day to all the world, that these rebellions were not produced by toleration, but by persecution; that they arose not from just and mild government, but from the most unparralled oppression. These records will be far from giving the countenance to a doctrine so repugnant to humanity and good sense, as that the unity of any Establishment, civil or religious, can ever depend upon the misery of those who live under it, or that its danger can arise from their quiet and prosperity. God forbid that the history of this or any Country should give such encouragement to the folly or vices of those who govern. If it can be shewn that the great rebellions of Ireland have arisen from attempts to reduce the Natives to the state to which they

[10] **histories of Ireland** Sir John Temple, *The Irish Rebellion: or a history of the beginnings and first progress of the general rebellion of 1641. Together with the barbarous cruelties and bloody massacres which ensued thereupon* (1646); Edward Hyde, 1st earl of Clarendon, *The history of the rebellion and civil wars in Ireland* (1719); see also Edmund Borlase, *History of the execrable Irish rebellion* (1680). These three were reprinted, the last two at Dublin, during the eighteenth century (respectively: 1724, 1720 and 1743).

[11] **records and monuments** publication of the sort of papers Burke presumably intended had to wait for the nineteenth and twentieth centuries, with work of the Historic Manuscripts Commission, the Irish Manuscripts Commission and *Calendar of State Papers .. Ireland 1603–1670*, ed. C.W. Russell, J.P. Prendergast and R.P. Mahaffy, 13 vols. (1870–1910), as well as the publication of MSS. from the archives of Trinity College, Dublin, from the Carte collection in the Bodleian and other sources (for the latter, see esp. the pages of *Analecta Hibernica*). For a specimen of what was available in Burke's time, see Sir Richard Cox, *Hibernia Anglicana, or the history of Ireland, from the conquest thereof by the English to this present time*, 2 vols. (1689) and J. Lodge (ed.), *Desiderata Curiosa Hibernica*, 2 vols. (1722).

For Burke's own contribution to Irish historiography and his interest in manuscripts, see two articles by Walter D. Love, 'Edmund Burke and an Irish Historiographical Controversy', *History and Theory* 21 (1962), pp. 180–98, and 'Edmund Burke, Charles Vallancey, and the Seabright Manuscripts', *Hermathena*, 95 (1961) pp. 21–35.

are now reduced, it will shew that an attempt to continue them in that state will rather be disadvantageous to the publick peace than any kind of security to it. These things have in some measure began to appear already, and as far as regards the argument drawn from former rebellions it will fall readily to the ground. But, for my part, I think the real danger to every State is to render its subjects justly discontented; nor is there in politicks or science any more effectual secret for their security than to establish in their people a firm opinion that no change can be for their advantage. It is true that bigotry and fanaticism may for a time draw great multitudes of people from a knowledge of their true and substantial interest. But upon this I have to remark three things; first, that such a temper can never become universal, or last for a long time. The principle of religion is seldom lasting; the majority of men are in no persuasion bigots; they are not willing to sacrifice, on every vain imagination that superstition or enthusism holds forth, or that even zeal and piety recommend, the certain possession of their temporal happiness. And if such a spirit has been at any time roused in a society, after it has had its paroxysm, it commonly subsides and is quiet, and is even the weaker for the violence of its first exertion; security and ease are its mortal enemies. But, secondly, if any thing can tend to revive and keep it up, it is to keep alive the passions of men by ill usage. This is enough to irritate even those who have not a spark of bigotry in their constitution to the most desperate enterprises; it certainly will inflame, darken, and render more dangerous the spirit of bigotry in those who are possessed by it. Lastly, By rooting out any sect, you are never secure against the effects of fanaticism; it may arise on the side of the most favoured opinions; and many are the instances wherein the Established Religion of a State has grown ferocious, and turned upon its keeper, and has often torn to pieces the Civil Establishment that had cherished it, and which it was designed to support; France – England – Holland.[12]

But there may be danger of wishing a change, even where no relgious motive can operate; and every enemy to such a State comes as a friend to the subject; and where other countries are under terror they begin to hope.

---

[12] **France – England – Holland**   referring, presumably, the Huguenot League, to the religious inspiration of the English Civil War and to the pressure of Calvinists on the government of the United Provinces during the seventeenth century.

This argument *ad verecundium*[13] has as much force as any such have. But I think it fares but very indifferently with those who make use of it; for they would get but little to be proved abettors of tyranny, at the expence of putting me to an inconvenient acknowledgement. For if I were to confess that there are circumstances in which it would be better to establish such a religion ****************

With regard to the Pope's interest. This foreign Chief of their Religion cannot be more formidable to us, than to other Protestant Countries; to conquer that Country for himself, is a wild chimera; to encourage revolt in favour of foreign Princes, is an exploded idea in the politicks of that Court. Perhaps, it would be full as dangerous to have the people under the conduct of factious Pastors of their own, as under a foreign Ecclesiastical Court.[14]

****

****

In the second year of the reign of Queen Elizabeth,[15] were enacted also several limitations in the acquisition, or the retaining of property, which had, so far as regarded any general principles, hitherto remained untouched under all changes.

These Bills met no opposition either in the Irish Parliament or in the English Council, except from privat Agents, who were little attended to; and they passed into Laws with the highest and most general applauses, as all such things are in the beginning, not as a system of persecution, but as master-pieces of the most subtle and refined politics. And, to say the truth, these Laws at first view have rather an appearance of a plan of vexation litigation and crooked law-chicanery, than of a direct and sanguinary attack upon the rights of private conscience; because they did not affect life, at least with regard to the Laity; and making the Catholick opinions rather the subject of Civil regulations than of Criminal prosecutions, to those

---

[13] **ad verecundium**   to the decency at your opponent.

[14] **Court**   despite the status of Cardinal for the Old Pretender's younger son, Henry, Duke of York (later Henry IX in the Jacobite succession), there was never any very substantial backing for the Jacobite cause from the papacy.

[15] **Queen Elizabeth**   Burke refers to the meeting of the so-called second Irish Reformation Parliament (1560), which approved the Elizabethan church settlement for Ireland. *Inter alia* this involved the insistence that appointment to government office depended upon acknowledging the authority of the monarch in spiritual as well as temporal affairs. Alternatively, Burke or his editors wrote 'Elizabeth' where they meant 'Anne'. In this case Burke referred to the Act of 1704 against the increase of Popery. This reading fits the ensuing details.

who are not Lawyers, and read these Laws, they only appear to be a species of jargon. For the execution of Criminal Law has always a certain appearance of violence; being exercised directly on the persons of the supposed offenders, and commonly executed in the face of the publick, such executions are apt to excite sentiments of pity for the sufferers, and indignation against those who are employed in such cruelties; being seen as single acts of cruelty, rather than as ill general principles of government; but the operation of the Laws in question being such as common feeling brings home to every man's bosom, they operate in a sort of comparative silence and obscurity; and though their cruelty is exceedingly great, it is never seen in a single exertion, and always escapes commiseration, being scarce known except to those who view them in a general, which is always a cold and phlegmatick light. The first of these Laws being made with so general a satisfaction, as the Chief Governours found that such things were extremely acceptable to the leading people in that Country, they were willing enough to gratify them with the ruin of their fellow citizens; they were not sorry to divert their attention from other enquiries, and to keep them fixed to this, as if this had been the only real object of their national politics; and for many years there was no speech from the Throne, which did not with great appearance of seriousness recommend the passing of such Laws, and scarce a Session went over without in effect passing some of them; until they have by degrees grown to be the most considerable head in the Irish Statute Book. At the same time, giving a temporary and occasional mitigation to the severity of some of the harshest of those Laws, they appeared in some sort the protectors of those, whom they were in reality destroying by the establishment of general Constitutions against them. At length, however, the policy of this expedient is worn out; the passions of men are cooled; those Laws begin to disclose themselves, and to produce effects very different from those which were promised in making them; for crooked counsels are ever unwise; and nothing can be more absurd and dangerous than to tamper with the natural foundations of society, in hopes of keeping it up by certain countrivances.

Thoughts on the Cause of the Present Discontents

Introduction

It was natural for the despairing author of Burke's *Tracts on the Popery Laws* to look outside Ireland for a properly constituted society, just as one might expect the admiring author of *An Abridgement of English History* to find it on the other side of St George's Channel. Yet the intellectual energy Burke gave to English society assumed rather than expounded the role he attributed to the property and social leadership of the aristocracy. He came to develop a different concern: the view that England's political arrangement was under threat. When he came into Parliament, he wrote later, he found the House of Commons 'surrendering itself to the guidance of an authority not grown out of an experienced wisdom and integrity, but out of the accidents of Court favour'.[1] We must set this view in the history of English politics.

England prided itself on possessing a balanced constitution. The most striking theory, that of Montesquieu, identified the three parts of the legislature (King, Lords and Commons) as bodies which balanced one another for the benefit of the governed. In Paley's words, 'there is no power possessed by one part of the legislature, the abuse, or excess of which is not checked by some antagonist power,

---

[1] *Letter to Thomas Burgh* (1780), IA, p. 314.

103

residing in another part'.[2] But precisely how the balance should be constituted, as a matter of right, had been left vague. Its indistinct character permitted the disputes about the proper role of the monarchy in government which characterized the 1760s.

If an observer had viewed England in 1760, he would have noted that whatever the theory, in practice Whigs in general had monopolized the central government continuously since 1714 and that the representatives, dependents and allies of the Pelham family in particular had held its highest offices since 1744. This hegemony rested on both of the supports necessary to rule in eighteenth-century England, namely the dexterous management of Lords and Commons (through the fruits of office, the flowers of oratory, and the emollient of tact) and the concurrence of the monarch. Royal favour was necessary to any administration's hold on office, granted the direct patronage and the rather more extensive influence the king could exercise in Parliament: these would be made available only to the minister of his choice. 'Balance' under the first two Georges showed the king and his Whig ministers usually presenting a single front, under whose countenance the political system ran fairly smoothly. Outside the system were the descendants of the deposed James II. Their military attempts to displace the Georges (in 1714 and 1745) had failed; by 1760 their hopes had dwindled to nothing. Their political sympathizers, the Tories, were naturally unacceptable to both the Georges. Within the system, the occasional deviant could be marginalized (like Carteret) or, if he was indispensable, absorbed (like the elder Pitt).

The accession of George III changed this situation. He did not suppose that Whigs alone were loyal – there was indeed little practical scope for Tory disloyalty by 1760, or much about which to be a Tory – but he did think that the Pelham regime was unsatisfactory: and he acted on his supposition. Within two years he had ousted the old corps and installed the minister of his choice, Lord Bute.

If we view these transactions in a neutrally uninquiring way, concerned only with registering events, we see the king first removing the ministers whom he distrusted in favour of his preferred candidate: we see Bute retiring, surprised by the difficulties of political life (1763): and then, until 1770, we see no ministry capable consistently of both

---

[2] Paley, *Principles of Moral and Political Philosophy*, VI. vii (edn 14, 1803, vol. II, p. 212f).

keeping royal favour and winning majorities from the Commons. Grenville (1763–65) and Rockingham (1765–66) failed to retain George's support. The elder Pitt (1766–67), who might have done, lost his reason and Grafton (1767–70) lost his nerve. Finally there emerged in North a man whose political dexterity extended to keep the favour of both king and Commons (1770–82). But this is not the only perspective possible. If we enquire into the intellectual environment in which these events occurred we find two aspects of major interest, the moral and the constitutional.

The constitutional question lay in the penumbra of ambiguity surrounding the idea of balance. Where precisely was a just balance found? It could be argued, for the royal point of view, that the king could choose his own servants – including his political servants. This there was no denying, and critics fastened on other considerations. They suggested that the king's prerogative here, though theoretically right, was practically difficult: that the influence the crown happened to enjoy was very great; that it was exercised on private, not public grounds; and that public opinion was averse to such conduct. The public's good opinion could be regained only by the king being more obviously motivated by respect for public considerations (which, decoded, meant that office should be held by its traditional custodians, who purported to have the confidence of the public.) In the duke of Devonshire's words to one of the king's supporters:

> You may fancy what you please about the power of the Crown, but believe me you will find yourself mistaken. If a King of England employs those people for his ministers, that the nation have a good opinion of, he will make a great figure; but if he chuses them merely through personal favour, it will never do, and he will be unhappy.[3]

The contrasting alternatives set out by the duke, if not necessarily an adherence to his choice between them, were found elsewhere. The *Annual Register* for 1763 gave a 'general idea of the principles, real or pretended, which have for some time unhappily divided the nation'. What was the end, it asked, which Bute and George preferred?

> Undoubtedly that . . . his majesty should, as the law intended, choose and retain his own Ministers . . . The friends of Lord

---

[3] Devonshire to Henry Fox, 14 Oct. 1762, in earl of Ilchester, *Henry Fox, first Lord Holland*, 2 vols. (1920), II, p. 203.

> Bute and of the ministry which succeeded, were for preserving
> to the crown the full exercise of a right, of which none disputed
> the validity, that of appointing its own servants. Those of the
> opposition did not deny this power in the crown, but they
> contended that the spirit of the constitution required, that the
> crown should be directed in the exercise of this public duty by
> public motives, and not private liking or friendship ... the
> observation of this rule would, and they were of opinion,
> nothing else could, in any degree, counterbalance that immense
> power, which the crown has acquired by the gift of such an
> infinite number of profitable places. Nothing but the very
> popular use of the prerogative can be sufficient to reconcile the
> nation to the extent of it.[4]

In short, there was opposed to the king's right the view that he should
exercise it only in a certain way, the way of 'public motives'.

This brings us to the moral dimension of the case. This was bound
to be prominent in an age which was anyway obsessed with moral
conduct and, at the same time, whose politics consisted almost
entirely of executive government, few of whose contingencies could
be determined beforehand by programmes. The moral dimension
had two aspects. The first was the theory of political morals; the other
the question of who would uphold them. The theory was quite simple.
It assumed that the good of the whole was to be preferred to the good
of the part, so that the public good must stand ahead of the private.
This accords with the European tradition of morality, with its regard
for others rather than the self. It assumes that on every question it is
possible to identify the good of the community or, minimally, hard to
mistake it for one's private benefit. Indeed the identification was
supposed to be easy, since failure to pursue it was attributed not to
intellectual error but to motives serving the self rather than the public.
Especially prominent amongst these were the temptations which
might turn judgement aside from the common good – a bribe, a
threat, any concern for personal advantage. Thus we find *The Auditor*
saluting a ministry 'who have no interests separate from the welfare of
the Kingdom' and hailing the king because 'he possesses property
enough to put him above temptation'.[5] The theory stated so simply
leaves no room for differences of principle.

---

[4] AR (1763), pp. 39, 42.   [5] *The Auditor*, no. 3, 17 June 1762, p. 18.

Dispute occurred in attributing political virtue or vice to one group or another. For instance, whilst *The Auditor* supposed that the king could be virtuous because too wealthy to be diverted by greed, the same merit could be attributed to some of his opponents, for (as an historian has noted) Rockingham was too rich to be offered a bribe. The location of vice was equally contestable. Lord Melcombe, whose experience had not left his innocence unspotted, thought that the Whigs of George II's reign 'under colour of making themselves responsible for the whole, have taken the sole direction of the royal interest and influence into their own hands, and applied it to their own creatures'.[6] On the other hand, those ousted early in George III's reign tended to see with Devonshire the destruction of a proper state of things by royal influence. But both sides were rarely too explicit in attributing vice to opponents: they were sufficiently preoccupied with appropriating virtue to themselves.

Where did Burke see political virtue? Let us consider him in terms of his own theory of the passions. If the affections of sympathy, imitation and ambition bonded men into society, to what society in particular did Burke adhere? In the early 1760s he was an impoverished if talented adventurer from the less convenient side of St George's Channel, looking for a patron to advance his fortunes in English politics. After false starts with W. G. Hamilton and Charles Townshend, he attached himself to Lord Rockingham in 1765. Rockingham, a nobleman of pure Whiggery and extensive wealth, was emerging as a considerable political figure. When Burke first served him, he was Prime Minister. Burke imitated his patron and his kind, setting up a landed estate and nurturing hopes of founding a dynasty. He exercised his ambition in their cause, not merely becoming a prominent speaker for the party in the Commons, but also developing its programme and stirring its leaders to action. Here his sympathies were strongest. How did his attachment affect his views?

To answer that question, we should turn first to the experience of his patron. Rockingham and his friends came to form a low opinion of George III. They were not unusual in suspecting the king's good faith. Shelburne, for a time his favoured minister, thought likewise and North at the end of his career voiced similar views. The dif-

---

[6] Melcombe to Bute (November 1760), in John Adolphus, *The History of England from the Accession of George III* (1802), i p. 27n.

ference lay in the firmness of their opinion. The eighteenth century sometimes had no very high view of aspirants to the title of political virtue. Marlborough's duchess observed that 'some of those people who call themselves *patriots* are certainly very good men';

> but I am very sure the whole party don't mean the same thing. They don't all go in a straight line to pursue steadily the right points; but they act coolly, sometimes one way and sometimes another, as they think will turn most to what they secretly have in view, some to keep places they are in possession of, and others to get into them.[7]

But it was acknowledged, even by an opponent, that the Rockinghams had constant views. William Knox saw that in the ordinary run of politics

> when an opposition gets into office, and the King trusts them with the exercise of his power, the farce is at an end, and, after a few aukward apologies, and a few ineffectual votes with old connections, by way of consistency, the business of Government is expected to be taken up, and carried on in the usual way.

'Such, however,' he acknowledged, 'was not the conduct of the old Whigs, when they came into office in 1765.'[8]

What moved them so? Their experience in the early 1760s was that the vagaries of royal favour made it difficult to conduct government with an eye to what they felt was virtue. Events soon hardened this opinion. Rockingham entered office in 1765 in the expectation of having both the supports a ministry needed. He felt sure of royal support, for his ministry was organized by the king's uncle, the duke of Cumberland. He was able to win the good opinion of the Commons by finding a sensible man of business in Dowdeswell and by popular policies. The difficulty began when these supports ceased to synchronise. Cumberland's death and the unwillingness of Rockingham to have truck with other political groups (especially Bute) did not create an impression of strength at court. The king's confidence seemed to diminish and placemen voted against the administration. This instability was surprising – Chesterfield called it 'an undecipherable state of affairs, which in fifty years' experience, I have never seen

---

[7] *The Opinions of Sarah, Duchess-Dowager of Marlborough* (1788), p. 67.
[8] William Knox, *Extra Official Papers* (1789), pp. 2–3.

anything like'.[9] Rockingham's demand for the removal of one deviant, Dyson, precipitated the fall of the ministry. George in fact was looking elsewhere for a stable administration. The interpretation natural to the dignity of those he ousted was that a ministry whose character had commanded the respect of Parliament had been undermined by court influence. It was as natural to identify their own character as virtuous and their opponent as villainous.

Why was it possible to maintain this stance? Rockingham and his closest friends were very wealthy and very determined to get their own way. Rockingham's wealth requires no emphasis. Unlike North he did not need to draw a salary as frequently as he drew breath. There were more subtle matters. He and his associates were not accustomed to habits of dependence, either personally or politically. Devonshire, Portland and Rockingham were quite young when they entered public life. By accidents of birth and death they gained independence through inherited wealth, title and position early in life. The fact that they were contemporaries of George III (or, in Devonshire's case, somewhat older) would not tend to make them naturally deferential to him, particularly as he had been set above them by a constitutional incident for which *their* ancestors had been responsible.[10] The date at which they had been born, moreover, meant that they were unaccustomed to administration as a way of life.

It was not merely a question of having views. Integral to their position was the claim to have the good opinion of the public. Devonshire's view that the king needed 'ministers, that the nation have a good opinion of' rested on the assumption that the country was governed ultimately by public opinion and that this was to be won by honourable conduct. Paley, as often, encapsulated the common view when he suggested that MPs were guided ultimately by the opinions of their electors, for

> The representative is so far dependent upon the constituent, and political importance upon public favour, that a member of parliament cannot more effectually recommend himself to eminence and advancement in the state, than by contriving and patronizing laws of public utility.

[9] Chesterfield to Philip Stanhope, 11 Feb. 1766, *Letters of Chesterfield*, 6 vols. (1932), ed. B. Dobree, vol. VI, p. 2, 712.

[10] *The North Briton*, no. 99, 8 April 1769, p. 605: "'Twas by their interest, chiefly, that that family was first placed upon the throne; 'tis by their interest, chiefly, that they have hitherto been supported in it'.

It was true, no doubt, that the electorate might be small and might be influenced by a peer too. But electoral influence would not always secure election of itself: and, in any case, peers are as much governed by public opinion as anyone else. Hence, it was needful to show evidence of the moral character which would win a merited honour: politicians should be the keepers of public virtue. The Rockinghams were quick to suggest that their opponents could not achieve this moral eminence. Richmond was happy to write to Rockingham that because North was 'a single man, no body' he would not do:

> I thought he ought not to be the minister of this country, for that as such a man did not depend upon the opinion of the world for his consequence but merely upon the king's pleasure, he could not follow his own opinions or those of the nation, and must be in too literal a sense the *servant* of the crown.

In some moods this appropriation of virtue encouraged the fond delusion that the backing of public opinion was a way of 'forcing the closet'. But they knew more soberly the realities of the eighteenth century in patronage and electoral organization made this unlikely. There were, however, other realities, amongst which not the least important was the deference of government to the opinion of Members of Parliament. In an age when whipping and the other coercive instruments of party control had scarcely arrived, when it was often easier to influence votes in Parliament by rewards rather than punishments and when anyhow many Members were not in the market for favours, the opinion of the House of Commons had to be courted and won. That opinion was correspondingly important. As North explained to George III in 1782, no ministry could defy the Commons with equanimity. He reminded the king that his predecessors had occasionally sacrificed 'their private wishes, and even their opinions' to the House and concluded that whilst

> Your Majesty has firmly and resolutely maintained what appeared to you essential to the welfare and dignity of this country, as long as this country itself thought proper to maintain it

yet

> The Parliament have altered their sentiments, and as their sentiments, whether just or erroneous, must ultimately prevail,

> Your Majesty having persevered, as long as possible, in what
> you thought right, can lose no honour if you yield at length ...
> to the opinion and wishes of the House of Commons.[11]

In short, everyone assumed that opinion ultimately ruled Britain, just as Burke's *Abridgement* had shown the passage from rule by force to an uncoerced obedience in the middle ages.

If Rockingham and his friends were eager to show themselves disinterested, they were keen by the same measure to win the opinion of the independent member of the Lower House and his freer electors in the country. They were naturally keen to show a backing for their views from those considered independent of the distortions of private interest. They were proud of the county vote (and had an especial regard for Sir George Savile, who sat for Yorkshire) and the representation of the great cities (Rockingham encouraged Burke to stand for Bristol, then England's second city).

The need to cultivate opinion necessarily involved the written word. We can see as much in the volume of publications which crowd the early years of George III's reign. Not the least of Burke's usefulness was as publicist, whether in newspapers and journals or as a pamphleteer. This activity culminated in his pamphlet *Present Discontents*.

The staple of Burke's case was the marriage of the commonly accepted tokens of virtue to a political cause. The former were found in articulating a concern for the liberty and property of the subject in matters like the Middlesex election, the revenue and the press. The latter lay partly in identifying the government as a threat to them and partly in advertising the Rockingham party's own virtues. There was a practical message implicit in this wedding of virtue and persons, that the latter were the antidote to the political difficulties of the second half of the 1760s.

These opinions were common to Burke's party. What they lacked was co-ordination into an ordered account. This is what the *Present Discontents* undertook. If we wished to summarize the book in a sentence, we could say that it argued that the government of England had

---

[11] Paley, *Principles*, p. 206f; Richmond to Rockingham, 22 Jan. 1771, Wentworth Woodhouse MSS. (Sheffield City Library) RI-1352; North to George III no. 3566 of J.W. Fortescue (ed.), *The Correspondence of King George the third from 1760 to December 1783*, 6 vols. (1927–28). v 395.

ceased to rest on a marriage of property and opinion, but had been grasped by a court faction; that it used these terms to explain the events of 1760–69; and suggested a return to the preceding state of affairs, through the agency of party. In short, it collected the elements of one school of political opinion as parts in a connected explanation. That explanation, as we shall now see, is simple but powerful in its architecture.

The obvious foundation was unusable. The simplest explanation of events was the ill nature of the king. This was thinkable, but could not be uttered publicly; certainly not where the object was to win unbiassed opinion. There was needed a device which pointed to that quarter, but indistinctly to an individual and so acceptably. This was found in a supposed plot to separate the parts which together composed the constitutional balance. The plot was said, in particular, to involve separating the king (or, as Burke said delicately, the court) from Parliament. The plot's fulcrum was the supposition of a double cabinet.

The double cabinet involved the separation of power from responsibility. The ministers responsible to Parliament were not in fact the people who controlled the conduct of the executive. Whilst the former were recognized officially as the king's cabinet, there was another, unofficial but active, which moved policy. Naturally it soon happened that the words of the ministers and the actions of the executive diverged. From this flowed numerous evils. Members who wished or needed to conciliate the crown became uncertain of how to act; so administrations became weak in Parliament, just as they were undermined behind the scenes.

Much scholarly ink has been devoted to showing that no court camarilla of this sort existed in fact: that it was only a heated fancy of Burke's. This may be true, but it overlooks the point of fantasizing in public. The double cabinet afforded a means of explaining events. It explained them, indeed, with specific point. It connected the political events of a decade in a way which reflected badly on the court and, by implicit contrast, hymned the merits of the opposition. The point was expressed in terms which the eighteenth century would recognize, for it represented England's favourite political values as under threat, in the reduction of liberty and destruction of virtue. Liberty was destroyed because the court system was said to aim at making all public men pliant to its will alone and so indisposed to resist its encroachments on liberty. Virtue decayed because the system worked by destroying those groups which already existed in politics; and these, Burke could allege, were bridges between private affection and public virtue.

The device of the double cabinet was not merely explanatory but also had a strong practical bearing. The bearing was both negative and positive. On the one hand it devalued the crown's claim to despise faction, whilst, on the other, it elevated Whig connection as a moral cause. In the 1760s George III aimed to improve public morals, just as he supposed that regius professors should be appointed for their learning alone. He preened himself particularly on destroying political combinations.[12] This developed the assumption that such groups aimed at their own good as distinct from the public's: in the language of the time, that they were factious. But if they could be dismissed as factions, there was also current the notion of party. Party, like faction, involved association, but was free of faction's connotation of conspiracy for private end.[13] Burke suggested that party was in fact the vehicle which reared and protected virtue.

Thus he gathered together the moral tokens of party and virtue for his political friends, and treated the court's proceedings as the inversion of the good. How could he treat party as an association in the interests of virtue? He exploited another piece of common coinage, the view that man was a social creature. His sociability implied that association was natural. It was more, Burke argued, it was a nursery of regard for others of like mind. These affections could be transferred to the public sphere. The transference, of course, depended on the material condition of the original association happening to be virtuous. Burke's constant hymn to the selflessness of his friends and

---

[12] For morals, see Romney Sedgwick (ed.), *Letters from George III to Lord Bute* (1939), p. 166; for regius professors, *Correspondence of King George the third*, nos. 928, 1, 117.

[13] The tone of the two words is caught in [Horace Walpole], *The Opposition to the Late Minister Vindicated* (1763), pp. 16–17:

They were called a FACTION, and the Word has been trumpted about the Kingdom. But mere Words are a feeble Support to a public Cause; and Invectives are, in this Case, the most impotent of all Words; If an Association of *wise* and *disinterested* Men, for the Purpose of delivering the King and Constitution from the dangerous Ambition of a Fellow-Subject, be a Faction, then the Opposers of the late Minister deserve that Name, and will be proud of it. But if a Party, composed of Men of different Views and Principles, united by manifest Motives of Interest, and conspiring to aggrandize one Man, against the known Interest of the King, at the Hazard of the Constitution, and at the Expence of public Tranquillity, be a FACTION, the Name will return naturally to its original Proprietors, notwithstanding the Virulence with which they cast it from themselves upon other Men.

to the 'hereditary virtue of the whole house of Cavendish'[14] are not accidental. By contrast, the court's desire to destroy 'faction' meant the destruction of virtue, whilst party would ensure its survival.

It may be worth admitting a little cool breeze into this affective atmosphere. The suggestion that government could be made virtuous by one sort of party had a practical bent, both general and particular. In general, it implied that if government could be redeemed by this method a more radical approach to its defects was superfluous. For instance, no major alterations in electoral arrangements would be necessary. Whether we should reduce this view entirely to the electoral influence of the marquess of Rockingham or the duke of Richmond is another question, but Burke's subsequent preference for the reform of executive government did stand in contrast to movements for parliamentary reform.

The more particular practical implication of this explanation is obvious. If party, in at least one case, was the bearer of political virtue and its protection against political vice, then this party should govern. What effects would it have? Burke assumed here, as he had in his *Tracts*, that good principles would produce beneficial consequences. The government of virtue would abridge the country's ills; those were the fruits of the court system, which separated people and decreased virtue: in short virtue would repair where vice had damaged.

Thus, Burke's *Present Discontents* assumed rather than developed his preceding conclusions about the beneficence of unequal societies and about free countries. Rather, it was compatible with both and developed a view of their relations in one country. It exemplified the assumption of inequality by adducing aristocratic virtue and leadership and by seeing a threat to freedom in the designs of the court. These identifications were quite contingent, and reflect Burke's personal location on the scene of party politics. They were meant to apply to one country in particular, at a specific juncture in its affairs. But Burke's position would inform his attitudes on other questions.

Analysis

Discontents in general: the statesman's duty to remove them (pp. 116–17).

---

[14] *Letter to . . . Sherriffs of Bristol*, W. ii 283.

(I) *The present discontents*: their exceptional gravity (pp. 118–19); the ministers' explanation of them unconvincing (pp. 119–21); the truth is that the old tyranny of the Crown has been revived in a new form (pp. 121–5).

(II) *The new form: the double cabinet*: its nature (pp. 125–7); how introduced (pp. 127–38); the party supporting it (pp. 138–41); the new system is at variance with the spirit of our constitution (pp. 141–7); a refutation of the view that in our constitution the Crown could not hear the true voice of the people (pp. 147–9).

(III) *Effects of the double cabinet*: on the executive, in both foreign and colonial affairs (pp. 149–52); on the temper of the people at home (pp. 152–4); on the interests of the Crown itself (pp. 154–9); on Parliament, by perverting its proper character from a check on the executive (including the Crown) to an arm of the executive (pp. 159–61), by weakening its control over the executive (pp. 161–2), by inducing it to exercise unlawful powers in respect of freedom of election (pp. 163–71) and surrendering the right of appropriation (pp. 171–7); the inefficiency of some proposed remedies for these defects, namely a Trienniel Bill and a Place Bill (pp. 177–81).

(IV) *The true remedy*: role of electors and representatives, especially in regard to Party (pp. 181–92); conclusion (p. 192).

Thoughts on the cause of the present discontents

Hoc vero occultum, intestinum, domesticum malum, non modo
non existit, verum etiam opprimit, antequam perspicere atque
explorare potueris.[1]   CIC.

It is an undertaking of some degree of delicacy to examine into the
cause of public disorders. If a man happens not to succeed in such an
enquiry, he will be thought weak and visionary; if he touches the true
grievance, there is a danger that he may come near to persons of
weight and consequence, who will rather be exasperated at the discovery of their errors, than thankful for the occasion of correcting
them. If he should be obliged to blame the favourites of the people, he
will be considered as the tool of power; if he censures those in power,
he will be looked on as an instrument of faction. But in all exertions of
duty something is to be hazarded. In cases of tumult and disorder, our
law[2] has invested every man, in some sort, with the authority of a
magistrate. When the affairs of the nation are distracted, private
people are, by the spirit of that law, justified in stepping a little out of
their ordinary sphere. They enjoy a privilege, of somewhat more
dignity and effect, than that of idle lamentation over the calamities of
their country. They may look into them narrowly; they may reason
upon them liberally; and if they should be so fortunate as to discover
the true source of the mischief, and to suggest any probable method

---

[1] **Hoc vero ... potueris** 'But this hidden, inner, domestic evil not only escapes
notice, but even surprises you before you can see and grasp it' (Cicero, *In Verrem
Actio Secunda*, I.xv.39). As often Burke's citation is inaccurate.

[2] **our law** 'All persons, noblemen and others (except women, clergymen, persons
decrepit, and infants under fifteen) are bound to attend the justices in suppressing
a riot' (William Blackstone, *Commentaries on the Laws of England*, 4 vols. (1765–9),
IV.xi.6 (vol. IV, p. 147).

of removing it, though they may displease the rulers for the day, they are certainly of service to the cause of Government. Government is deeply interested in every thing which, even through the medium of some temporary uneasiness, may tend finally to compose the minds of the subject, and to conciliate their affections. I have nothing to do here with the abstract value of the voice of the people. But as long as reputation, the most precious possession of every individual, and as long as opinion, the great support of the State, depend entirely upon that voice, it can never be considered as a thing of little consequence either to individuals or to Government. Nations are not primarily ruled by laws; less by violence. Whatever original energy may be supposed either in force or regulation; the operation of both is, in truth, merely instrumental. Nations are governed by the same methods, and on the same principles, by which an individual without authority is often able to govern those who are his equals or his superiors; by a knowledge of their temper, and by a judicious management of it; I mean, whenever public affairs are steadily and quietly conducted; not when Government is nothing but a continued scuffle between the magistrate and the multitude; in which sometimes the one and some times the other is uppermost; in which they alternately yield and prevail in a series of contemptible victories and scandalous submissions. The temper of the people[3] amongst whom he presides ought therefore to be the first study of a Statesman. And the knowledge of this temper it is by no means impossible for him to attain, if he has not an interest in being ignorant of what it is his duty to learn.

To complain of the age we live in, to murmur at the present possessors of power, to lament the past, to conceive extravagant hopes of the future, are the common dispositions of the greatest part of mankind; indeed the necessary effects of the ignorance and levity of the vulgar. Such complaints and humours have existed in all times; yet as all times have *not* been alike, true political sagacity manifests itself, in distinguishing that complaint which only characterizes the general infirmity of human nature, from those which are symptoms of the particular distemperature of our own air and season.

Nobody, I believe, will consider it merely as the language of spleen

---

[3] **the temper of the people**   cf. Tacitus, *Annals*, IV, 33: 'Noscenda tibi natura vulgi est, et quibus modis temperanter habeatur'.

or disappointment, if I say, that there is something particularly alarming in the present conjuncture. There is hardly a man in or out of power who holds any other language. That Government is at once dreaded and contemned; that the laws are despoiled of all their respected and salutary terrors; that their inaction is a subject of ridicule, and their exertion of abhorrence; that rank, and office, and title, and all the solemn plausibilities of the world, have lost their reverence and effect; that our foreign politicks are as much deranged as our domestic oeconomy; that our dependencies are slackened in their affection, and loosened from their obedience; that we know neither how to yield nor how to inforce; that hardly any thing above or below, abroad or at home, is sound and entire; but that disconnexion and confusion, in offices, in parties, in families, in Parliament, in the nation, prevail beyond the disorders of any former time: these are facts universally admitted and lamented.

This state of things is the more extraordinary, because the great parties[4] which formerly divided and agitated the kingdom are known to be in a manner entirely dissolved. No great external calamity has visited the nation; no pestilence or famine. We do not labour at present under any scheme of taxation new or oppressive in the quantity or in the mode. Nor are we engaged in unsuccessful war; in which, our misfortunes might easily pervert our judgement; and our minds, sore from the loss of national glory, might feel every blow of Fortune as a crime in Government.

It is impossible that the cause of this strange distemper should not sometimes become a subject of discourse. It is a compliment due, and which I willingly pay, to those who administer our affairs, to take notice in the first place of their speculation.[5] Our Ministers are of opinion, that the increase of our trade and manufactures, that our

---

[4] **the great parties** Henry Fox wrote to Horace Walpole in 1762, 'I do not know who are Whigs' (Walpole, *Memoirs of the Reign of George III*, ed. G.F. Russell Barker, 4 vols. (1894), I, p. 123. The idea can be found in Bolingbroke, *Dissertation on Parties*, Letter One, and even earlier. [John Douglas], *Seasonable Hints From an Honest Man on the present important crisis of a New Reign and a New Parliament* (1761), p. 32f exploited the dissolution of the distinction between Whig and Tory around 1760 to ask, 'Does any candid and intelligent man seriously believe that at this time there subsists any party distinction amongst us that is not merely nominal?'. Whilst Burke accepted that the Whig–Tory distinction had dissolved, he wished to argue that other differences were real.

[5] **speculation** similar views were held by North (PH, XVI, 717–20) and the elder Pitt (Speech in the Lords, 22 Jan. 1770).

growth by colonization and by conquest, have concurred to accumulate immense wealth in the hands of some individuals; and this again being dispersed amongst the people, has rendered them universally proud, ferocious, and ungovernable; that the insolence of some from their enormous wealth, and the boldness of others from a guilty poverty, have rendered them capable of the most atrocious attempts; so that they have trampled upon all subordination, and violently born down the unarmed laws of a free Government; barriers too feeble against the fury of a populace so fierce and licentious as ours. They contend, that no adequate provocation has been given for so spreading a discontent; our affairs having been conducted throughout with remarkable temper and consummate wisdom. The wicked industry of some libellers, joined to the intrigues of a few disappointed politicians, have, in their opinion, been able to produce this unnatural ferment in the nation.

Nothing indeed can be more unnatural than the present convulsions of this country, if the above account be a true one. I confess I shall assent to it with great reluctance, and only on the compulsion of the clearest and firmest proofs; because their account resolves itself into this short, but discouraging proposition, 'That we have a very good Ministry, but that we are a very bad people;' that we set ourselves to bite the hand that feeds us; that with a malignant insanity we oppose the measures, and ungratefully vilify the persons of those, whose sole object is our own peace and prosperity. If a few puny libellers, acting under a knot of factious politicians, without virtue, parts, or character (such they are constantly represented by these gentlemen), are sufficient to excite this disturbance, very perverse must be the disposition of that people, amongst whom such a disturbance can be excited by such means. It is besides no small aggravation of the public misfortune, that the disease, on this hypothesis, appears to be without remedy. If the wealth of the nation be the cause of its turbulence, I imagine, it is not proposed to introduce poverty, as a constable to keep the peace. If our dominions abroad are the roots which feed all this rank luxuriance of sedition, it is not intended to cut them off in order to famish the fruit. If our liberty has enfeebled the executive power, there is no design, I hope, to call in the aid of despotism, to fill up the deficiencies of law. Whatever may be intended, these things are not yet professed. We seem therefore to be driven to absolute despair; for we have no other materials to work upon, but those out of which God has been pleased to form the inhabitants of this island. If these be radically and essentially vitious, all that can be said is, that those men are very unhappy, to whose fortune or duty it falls to administer the affairs of this untoward people. I hear it indeed sometimes asserted, that a steady perseverance in the present measures, and a rigorous punishment of those who oppose them, will in course of time infallibly put an end to these disorders. But this, in my opinion, is said without much observation of our present disposition, and without any knowledge at all of the general nature of mankind. If the matter of which this nation is composed be so very fermentable as these gentlemen describe it, leaven never will be wanting to work it up, as long as discontent, revenge, and ambition, have existence in the world. Particular punishments are the cure for accidental distempers in the State; they inflame rather than allay those heats which arise from the settled mismanagement of the Government, or from a natural ill disposition in the people. It is of the utmost moment not to make mistakes in the use of strong measures; and firmness is then only a virtue when it accompanies the most perfect wisdom. In truth, inconstancy is a sort of natural corrective of folly and ignorance.

I am not one of those who think that the people are never in the wrong. They have been so, frequently and outrageously, both in other countries and in this. But I do say, that in all disputes between them and their rulers, the presumption is at least upon a par in favour of the people. Experience may perhaps justify me in going further. Where popular discontents have been very prevalent; it may well be affirmed and supported, that there has been generally something found amiss in the constitution, or in the conduct of Government. The people have no interest in disorder. When they do wrong, it is their error, and not their crime. But with the governing part of the State, it is far otherwise. They certainly may act ill by design, as well as by mistake. '*Les revolutions qui arrivent dans les grands etats ne sont point un effect du hazard, ni du caprice des peuples. Rien ne revolte les* Grands *d'un royaume comme* un Gouvernement foible et derangé. *Pour la* populace, *ce n'est jamais par envie d'attaquer qu'elle se souleve, mais par impatience de souffrir.*' *[6]These are the words of a great man; of a Minister of state;

---

* Mem. de Sully, vol. I, p. 133.

[6] *Les revolutions . . . souffrir* 'The revolutions that occur in great states are not the result of chance, or of the caprice of the people. Nothing rouses the great men

and a zealous assertor of Monarchy. They are applied to the *system of Favouritism* which was adopted by Henry the Third of France, and to the dreadful consequences it produced. What he says of revolutions, is equally true of all great disturbances. If this presumption in favour of the subjects against the trustees of power be not the more probable, I am sure it is the more comfortable speculation; because it is more easy to change an administration than to reform a people.

Upon a supposition, therefore, that in the opening of the cause the presumptions stand equally balanced between the parties, there seems sufficient ground to entitle any person to a fair hearing, who attempts some other scheme besides that easy one which is fashionable in some fashionable companies, to account for the present discontents. It is not to be argued that we endure no grievance, because our grievances are not of the same sort with those under which we laboured formerly; not precisely those which we bore from the Tudors, or vindicated on the Stuarts. A great change has taken place in the affairs of this country. For in the silent lapse of events as material alterations have been insensibly brought about in the policy and character of governments and nations, as those[7] which have been marked by the tumult of public revolutions.

It is very rare indeed for men to be wrong in their feelings concerning public misconduct; as rare to be right in their speculation upon the cause of it. I have constantly observed, that the generality of people are fifty years, at least, behind-hand in their politicks. There are but very few, who are capable of comparing and digesting what passes before their eyes at different times and occasions, so as to form the whole into a distinct system. But in books every thing is settled for them, without the exertion of any considerable diligence or sagacity. For which reason men are wise with but little reflexion, and good with little self-denial, in the business of all times except their own. We are very uncorrupt and tolerably enlightened judges of the transactions of past ages; where no passions deceive, and where the whole train of circumstances, from the trifling cause to the tragical event, is set in an orderly series before us. Few are the partizans of departed tyranny; and to be a Whig on the business of an hundred years ago, is very consistent with every advantage of present servility. This retrospective

of a kingdom like a weak and distempered government. As for the rabble, it never rises from a passion to attack, but from impatience of suffering.'
[7] **as those**   should be taken with 'as material'.

wisdom, and historical patriotism, are things of wonderful convenience; and serve admirably to reconcile the old quarrel between speculation and practice. Many a stern republican, after gorging himself with a full feast of admiration of the Grecian commonwealths and of our true Saxon constitution, and discharging all the splendid bile of his virtuous indignation on King John and King James, sits down perfectly satisfied to the coarsest work and homeliest job of the day he lives in. I believe there was no professed admirer of Henry the Eighth among the instruments of the last King James; nor in the court of Henry the Eighth, was there, I dare say, to be found a single advocate for the favourites of Richard of the Second.

No complaisance to our Court, or to our age can make me believe nature to be so changed, but that public liberty will be among us, as among our ancestors, obnoxious to some person or other; and that opportunities will be furnished, for attempting at least, some alteration to the prejudice of our constitution. These attempts will naturally vary in their mode according to times and circumstances. For ambition, though it has ever the same general views, has not at all times the same means, nor the same particular objects. A great deal of the furniture of ancient tyranny is worn to rags; the rest is entirely out of fashion. Besides, there are few Statesmen so very clumsy and awkward in their business, as to fall into the identical snare which has proved fatal to their predecessors. When an arbitrary imposition is attempted upon the subject, undoubtedly it will not bear on its forehead the name of *Ship-money*. There is no danger that an extension of the *Forest laws*[8] should be the chosen mode of oppression in this age. And when we hear any instance of ministerial rapacity, to the prejudice of the rights of private life, it will certainly not be the exaction of two hundred pullets, from a woman of fashion, for leave to lye with her own husband.*

Every age has its own manners, and its politicks dependent upon them; and the same attempts will not be made against a constitution fully formed and matured, that were used to destroy it in the cradle, or to resist its growth during its infancy.

---

* Uxor Hugonis de Nevill dat Domino Regi ducentors Gallinas, eo quod possit jacere una nocte cum Domino suo Hugone de Nevill,[9] Maddox, Hist. Exch. c. xiii, p. 326.

[8] **ship-money . . . Forest laws** Charles I attempted both (1634–7).

[9] **Uxor Hugonis . . . Nevill** 'The wife of Hugh de Nevill gives the king two hundred hens, that she can lie one night with her lord Hugh de Nevill.'

Against the being of Parliament, I am satisfied, no designs have
ever been entertained since the Revolution. Every one must perceive,
that it is strongly the interest of the Court, to have some second cause
interposed between the Ministers and the people. The gentlemen of
the House of Commons have an interest equally strong, in sustaining
the part of that intermediate cause. However they may hire out the
usufruct of their voices, they never will part with the *fee and
inheritance*.[10] Accordingly those who have been[11] of the most known
devotion to the will and pleasure of a Court, have at the same time
been most forward in asserting an high authority in the House of
Commons. When they knew who were to use that authority, and how
it was to be employed, they thought it never could be carried too far. It
must be always the wish of an unconstitutional Statesman, that an
House of Commons who are entirely dependent upon him, should
have every right of the people entirely dependent upon their pleasure.
It was soon discovered, that the forms of a free,[12] and the ends of an
arbitrary Government, were things not altogether incompatible.

The power of the Crown, almost dead and rotten as Prerogative,[13]
has grown up anew, with much more strength, and far less odium,
under the name of Influence.[14] An influence, which operated without
noise and without violence, an influence which converted the very
antagonist, into the instrument, of power, which contained in itself a
perpetual principle of growth and renovation, and which the distresses and the prosperity of the country equally tended to augment, was
an admirable substitute for a Prerogative, that being only the offspring
of antiquated prejudices, had moulded in its original stamina irresistible principles of decay and dissolution. The ignorance of the people
is a bottom but for a temporary system; the interest of active men in
the State is a foundation perpetual and infallible. However, some
circumstances, arising, it must be confessed, in a great degree from
accident, prevented the effects of this influence for a long time from

[10] *usufruct ... fee and inheritance*   respectively, the right of enjoying the use and
advantage of another's property, and the right of absolute ownership and of hand-
ing on to one's heirs.
[11] **those who have been**   Dyson may be meant here; cf. Grenville's speech, 2 April
1769 (PH, XVI, 550).
[12] **forms of a free**   cf. 'A constitution may be lost, whilst all its forms are preserved'
(*Annual Register*, 1763, p. 42).
[13] **Prerogative**   the discretionary power to act for the public good where the laws of
the land are silent.
[14] **name of Influence**   for the transition, cf. [Douglas], *Seasonable Hints*, p. 37.

breaking out in a manner capable of exciting any serious apprehensions. Although Government was strong and flourished exceedingly, the *Court* had drawn far less advantage than one would imagine from this great source of power.

At the Revolution, the Crown, deprived, for the ends of the Revolution itself, of many prerogatives,[15] was found too weak to struggle against all the difficulties which pressed so new and unsettled a Government. The Court was obliged therefore to delegate a part of its powers to men of such interest as could support, and of such fidelity as would adhere to, its establishment. Such men were able to draw in a greater number to a concurrence in the common defence. This connexion, necessary at first, continued long after convenient; and properly conducted might indeed, in all situations, be an useful instrument of Government. At the same time, through the intervention of men of popular weight and character, the people possessed a security for their just portion of importance in the State. But as the title to the Crown grew stronger by long possession, and by the constant increase of its influence, these helps have of late seemed to certain persons no better than incumbrances. The powerful managers for Government, were not sufficiently submissive to the pleasure of the possessors of immediate and personal favour sometimes from a confidence in their own strength natural and acquired;[16] sometimes from a fear of offending their friends, and weakening that lead in the country, which gave them a consideration independent of the Court. Men acted as if the Court could receive, as well as confer, an obligation. The influence of Government, thus divided in appearance between the Court and the leaders of parties, became in many cases an accession rather to the popular than to the royal scale; and some part of that influence which would otherwise have been possessed as in a sort of mortmain[17] and unalienable domain, returned again to the great ocean from whence it arose, and circulated among the people. This method therefore of governing, by men of great natural interest or great acquired consideration, was viewed in a very invidious light

---

[15] **many prerogatives** a convenient exaggeration; in 1689 the Crown lost only the capacities to embrace Roman Catholicism, and to raise a standing army without parliamentary approval.

[16] **strength natural and acquired** 'natural' could refer to the Whig aristocracy in general, 'acquired' to the elder Pitt.

[17] **mortmain** the character of lands or buildings held inalienably by corporations, i.e. bodies which never die (med. Latin *mortua manus*, dead hand).

by the true lovers of absolute monarchy. It is the nature of despotism to abhor power held by any means but its own momentary pleasure; and to annihilate all intermediate situations between boundless strength on its own part, and total debility on the part of the people.

To get rid of all this intermediate and independent importance, and *to secure to the Court the unlimited and uncontroulled use of its own vast influence, under the sole direction of its own private favour*, has for some years past been the great object of policy. If this were compassed, the influence of the Crown must of course produce all the effects which the most sanguine partizans of the Court could possibly desire. Government might then be carried on without any concurrence on the part of the people: without any attention to the dignity of the greater, or to the affections of the lower sorts. A new project was therefore devised, by a certain set of intriguing men, totally different from the system of Administration which had prevailed since the accession of the House of Brunswick. This project, I have heard, was first conceived by some persons in the court of Frederick Prince of Wales.[18]

The earliest attempt in the execution of this design was to set up for Minister, a person,[19] in rank indeed respectable, and very ample in fortune; but who, to the moment of this vast and sudden elevation, was little known or considered in the kingdom. To him the whole nation was to yield an immediate and implicit submission. But whether it was for want of firmness to bear up against the first opposition; or that things were not yet fully ripened, or that this method was not found the most eligible; that idea was soon abandoned.[20] The instrumental part of the project was a little altered, to accommodate it to the time, and to bring things more gradually and more surely to the one great end proposed.

The first part of the reformed plan was to draw *a line which should separate the Court from the Ministry*. Hitherto these names had been looked upon as synonymous; but for the future, Court and Administration were to be considered as things totally distinct. By this operation, two systems of Administration were to be formed; one which

---

[18] **Frederick, Prince of Wales**   for the whole subject of Leicester House and George III's early conduct, see the introduction to Romney Sedgwick (ed.), *Letters from George III to Lord Bute, 1756–66* (1939).

[19] **a person**   Bute.

[20] **soon abandoned**   Bute left office in a lurid glow during April 1763.

should be in the real secret and confidence;[21] the other merely ostensible, to perform the official and executory duties of Government. The latter were alone to be responsible; whilst the real advisers, who enjoyed all the power, were effectually removed from all the danger.

Secondly, *A party under these leaders was to be formed in favour of the Court against the Ministry*: this party was to have a large share in the emoluments of Government, and to hold it totally separate from, and independent of, ostensible Administration.

The third point, and that on which the success of the whole scheme ultimately depended, was *to bring Parliament to an acquiescence in this project*. Parliament was therefore to be taught by degrees a total indifference to the persons, rank, influence, abilities, connexions, and character, of the Ministers of the Crown. By means of a discipline, on which I shall say more hereafter, that body was to be habituated to the most opposite interests, and the most discordant politicks. All connexions and dependencies among subjects were to be entirely dissolved. As hitherto business had gone through the hands of leaders of Whigs or Tories, men of talents to conciliate the people, and to engage to their confidence, now the method was to be altered; and the lead was to be given to men of no sort of consideration or credit in the country. This want of natural importance was to be their very title to delegated power. Members of Parliament were to be hardened into an insensibility to pride as well as to duty. Those high and haughty sentiments, which are the great support of independence, were to be let down gradually. Point of honour and precedence were no more to be regarded in Parliamentary decorum, than in a Turkish army.[22] It was to be avowed as a constitutional maxim, that the King might appoint one of his footmen,[23] or one of your footmen, for Minister; and that he ought to be, and that he would be, as well followed as the first name for rank or wisdom[24] in the nation. Thus Parliament was to

---

[21] **In the real secret and confidence** i.e. of the king.

[22] **in a Turkish army** for the idea, cf. Algernon Sidney, *Discourses concerning Government*, III.28, in Sidney's *Works* (1772), p. 425.

[23] **footmen** Lord Holland is supposed to have remarked 'The king may make a page first minister' (Horace Walpole, *Memoirs of the Reign of George III*, III, p. 66). The suggestion inverted George II's complaints about being a prisoner of Newcastle's: 'he had not thought that he had so many of Newcastle's FOOTMEN about him; soon, he supposed, he should not be able to make a Page of the Backstairs' (cited in Aubrey Newman, *The World Turned Inside Out* (1988), p. 17).

[24] **rank or wisdom** presumably Newcastle and Pitt respectively are meant.

look on, as if perfectly unconcerned; while a cabal of the closet and back-stairs was substituted in the place of a national Administration.

With such a degree of acquiescence, any measure of any Court might well be deemed thoroughly secure. The capital objects, and by much the most flattering characteristicks of arbitrary power, would be obtained. Every thing would be drawn from its holdings in the country to the personal favour and inclination of the Prince. This favour would be the sole introduction to power, and the only tenure by which it was to be held: so that no person looking towards another, and all looking towards the Court, it was impossible but that the motive which solely influenced every man's hopes must come in time to govern every man's conduct; till at last the servility became universal, in spite of the dead letter of any laws or institutions whatsoever.

How it should happen that any man could be tempted to venture upon such a project of Government, may at first view appear surprizing. But the fact is, that opportunities very inviting to such an attempt have offered; and the scheme itself was not destitute of some arguments not wholly unplausible to recommend it. These opportunities and these arguments, the use that has been made of both, the plan for carrying this new scheme of government into execution, and the effects which it has produced, are in my opinion worthy of our serious consideration.

His Majesty came to the throne of these kingdoms with more advantages than any of his predecessors since the Revolution. Fourth in descent, and third in succession of his Royal family, even the zealots of hereditary right, in him, saw something to flatter their favourite prejudices; and to justify a transfer of their attachments, without a change in their principles. The person and cause of the Pretender were become contemptible; his title disowned throughout Europe, his party disbanded in England. His Majesty came indeed to the inheritance of a mighty war; but, victorious in every part of the globe, peace was always in his power, not to negociate, but to dictate.[25] No foreign habitudes[26] or attachments withdrew him from the cultivation of his power at home. His revenue for the civil establishment, fixed (as it was then thought) at a large, but definite sum, was

---

[25] **dictate**   for contemporary views on the ending of the Seven Years' War (1763), see Z.E. Rashed, *The Peace of Paris* (1951), esp. p. 201f.

[26] **foreign habitudes**   George III, unlike his predecessors, did not sojourn in Hanover.

ample, without being invidious.[27] His influence, by additions from conquests,[28] by an augmentation of debt,[29] by an increase of military and naval establishment, much strengthened and extended. And coming to the throne in the prime and full vigour of youth, as from affection there was a strong dislike, so from dread there seemed to be a general averseness, from giving any thing like offence to a Monarch, against whose resentment opposition could not look for a refuge in any sort of reversionary hope.[30]

These singular advantages inspired his Majesty only with a more ardent desire to preserve[31] unimpaired the spirit of that national freedom, to which he owed a situation so full of glory. But to others it suggested sentiments of a very different nature. They thought they now beheld an opportunity (by a certain sort of Statesmen never long undiscovered or unemployed) of drawing to themselves, by the aggrandisement of a Court faction, a degree of power which they could never hope to derive from natural influence or from honourable service; and which it was impossible they could hold with the least security, whilst the system of Administration rested upon its former bottom. In order to facilitate the execution of their design, it was necessary to make many alterations in political arrangement, and a signal change in the opinions, habits, and connexions of the greatest part of those who acted then in publick.

In the first place, they proceeded gradually, but not slowly, to destroy every thing of strength which did not derive its principal nourishment from the immediate pleasure of the Court. The greatest weight of popular opinion and party connexion were then with the Duke of Newcastle and Mr Pitt. Neither of these held their importance by the *new tenure* of the Court; they were not therefore thought

---

[27] **invidious** Langford notes that if there was a surplus on the duties yielding George III's civil list income (£800,000) it would go not to the crown but to the nation.

[28] **additions from conquests** Canada, Florida, Minorca, Cape Breton Island, Tobago, St Vincent, Dominica and Grenada, Senegal and the French had been virtually ejected from India.

[29] **debt** Langford notes that the increase in the National Debt was supposed to help the government. [Douglas], *Seasonable Hints*, pp. 15f, cf. 53f, 59f expressed disquiet over the growth of government expenditure.

[30] **reversionary hope** unlike his two predecessors, George III faced no threat from Jacobitism or from a male heir (the latter until the later 1780s).

[31] **only with a more ardent desire to preserve** Burke was less tactful in private; see William Hazlitt, *Conversations of Northcote* (1830), p. 40 for a case where his heatedness caused Goldsmith to leave the room.

to be so proper as others for the services which were required by that tenure. It happened very favourably for the new system, that under a forced coalition there rankled an incurable alienation and disgust between the parties which composed the Administration. Mr Pitt was first attacked. Not satisfied with removing him from power, they endeavoured by various artifices to ruin his character.[32] The other party seemed rather pleased to get rid of so oppressive a support; not perceiving, that their own fall was prepared by his, and involved in it. Many other reasons prevented them from daring to look their true situation in the face. To the great Whig families it was extremely disagreeable, and seemed almost unnatural, to oppose the Administration of a Prince of the House of Brunswick. Day after day they hesitated, and doubted, and lingered, expecting that other counsels would take place; and were slow to be persuaded, that all which had been done by the Cabal, was the effect not of humour, but of system. It was more strongly and evidently the interest of the new Court faction, to get rid of the great Whig connexions, than to destroy Mr Pitt. The power of that gentleman was vast indeed and merited; but it was in a great degree personal, and therefore transient. Theirs was rooted in the country. For, with a good deal less of popularity, they possessed a far more natural and fixed influence. Long possession of Government, vast property, obligations of favours given and received, connexion of office, ties of blood, of alliance, of friendship (things at that time supposed of some force), the name of Whig, dear to the majority of the people, the zeal early begun and steadily continued to the Royal Family; all these together formed a body of power in the nation, which was criminal and devoted. The great ruling principle of the Cabal, and that which animated and harmonized all their proceedings, how various soever they may have been, was to signify to the world, that the Court would proceed upon its own proper forces only; and that the pretence of bringing any other into its service was an affront to it, and not a support. Therefore, when the chiefs were removed, in order to go to the root, the whole party was put under a proscription,[33] so general and severe as to take their hard-

---

[32] **ruin his character**   there were a number of adverse newspaper comments, which could have been fabricated, but the barony of Chatham conferred on his wife and a pension of £3,000 a year for himself may have produced some reaction naturally.

[33] **under a proscription**   cf. Rockingham in the Lords 22 Jan. 1770 and Devonshire in *Memoirs of Rockingham*, I, p. 152.

earned bread from the lowest officers, in a manner which had never been known before, even in general revolutions. But it was thought necessary effectually to destroy all dependencies but one; and to shew an example of the firmness and rigour with which the new system was to be supported.

Thus for the time were pulled down, in the persons of the Whig leaders and of Mr Pitt (in spite of the services of the one at the accession of the Royal Family, and the recent services of the other in the war), the *two only securities for the importance of the people; power arising from popularity; and power arising from connexion.* Here and there indeed a few individuals were left standing, who gave security for their total estrangement from the odious principles of party connexion and personal attachment; and it must be confessed that most of them have religiously kept their faith. Such a change could not however be made without a mighty shock to Government.

To reconcile the minds of the people to all these movements, principles correspondent to them had been preached up with great zeal. Every one must remember that the Cabal set out with the most astonishing prudery, both moral and political. Those who in a few months after soused over head and ears into the deepest and dirtiest pits of corruption, cried out violently against the indirect practices in the electing and managing of Parliaments, which had formerly prevailed. This marvellous abhorrence which the Court had suddenly taken to all influence, was not only circulated in conversation through the kingdom, but pompously announced to the publick, with many other extraordinary things, in a pamphlet*[34] which had all the appearance of a manifesto preparatory to some considerable enter-prize. Throughout, it was a satire, though in terms managed and decent enough, on the politicks of the former Reign. It was indeed written with no small art and address.

In this piece appeared the first dawning of the new system; there first appeared the idea (then only in speculation) of *separating the Court from the Administration;* of carrying every thing from national connexion to personal regards; and of forming a regular party for that purpose, under the name of *King's men.*

To recommend this system to the people, a perspective view[35] of

---

* Sentiments of an honest Man.   [34] **pamphlet** [John Douglas], *Seasonable Hints.*
[35] **a perspective view** a device meant to produce an optical illusion, cf. *All's Well that Ends Well,* v.iii.49.

the Court gorgeously painted, and finely illuminated from within, was exhibited to the gaping multitude. Party was to be totally done away, with all its evil works. Corruption was to be cast down from Court, as *Atè*[36] was from Heaven. Power was thenceforward to be the chosen residence of public spirit; and no one was to be supposed under any sinister influence, except those who had the misfortune to be in disgrace at Court, which was to stand in lieu of all vices and all corruptions. A scheme of perfection to be realized in a Monarchy far beyond the visionary Republick of Plato. The whole scenery was exactly disposed to captivate those good souls, whose credulous morality is so invaluable a treasure to crafty politicians. Indeed there was wherewithall to charm every body, except those few who are not much pleased with professions of supernatural virtue, who know of what stuff such professions are made, for what purposes they are designed, and in what they are sure constantly to end. Many innocent gentlemen, who had been talking prose all their lives[37] without knowing any thing of the matter, began at last to open their eyes upon their own merits, and to attribute their not having been Lords of the Treasury and Lords of Trade many years before merely to the prevalence of party, and to the Ministerial power, which had frustrated the good intentions of the Court in favour of their abilities. Now was the time to unlock the sealed fountain of Royal bounty, which had been infamously monopolized and huckstered, and to let it flow at large upon the whole people. The time was come to restore Royalty to its original splendour. *Mettre le Roy hors de page*,[38] became a sort of watch-word. And it was constantly in the mouths of all the runners[39] of the Court, that nothing could preserve the balance of the constitution from being overturned by the rabble, or by a faction of the nobility, but to free the Sovereign effectually from that Ministerial tyranny under which the Royal dignity had been oppressed in the person of his Majesty's grandfather.

[36] *Atè* in Greek mythology, the goddess of mischief, who led gods and men into ill-considered actions; Zeus is supposed to have cast her out of Heaven for misleading him thus.

[37] **all their lives** the reminiscence of Molière was introduced into English literature in *Martinus Scriblerus*, ch. XII.

[38] **Mettre le Roy hors le page** i.e. make the king his own master. The French phrase was applied originally to Louis XI; see Sidney, *Discourses concerning Government*, II.30, *Works*, p. 253. It is quoted in Bolingbroke's sixth letter, *On the Study and Use of History*.

[39] **runners** messengers, cf. WSEB, ii, 448; 'the wretched runners for a wretched cause'.

These were some of the many artifices used to reconcile the people to the great change which was made in the persons who composed the Ministry, and the still greater which was made and avowed in its constitution. As to individuals, other methods were employed with them; in order so thoroughly to disunite every party, and even every family,[40] that *no concert, order, or effect, might appear in any future opposition*. And in this manner an Administration without connexion with the people, or with one another, was first put in possession of Government. What good effects followed from it, we have all seen; whether with regard to virtue, public or private; to the ease and happiness of the Sovereign; or to the real strength of Government. But as so much stress was then laid on the necessity of this new project, it will not be amiss to take a view of the effects of this Royal servitude and vile durance, which was so deplored in the reign of the late Monarch, and was so carefully to be avoided in the reign of his Successor. The effects were these.

In times full of doubt and danger to his person and family, George the Second maintained the dignity of his Crown connected with the liberty of his people, not only unimpaired, but improved, for the space of thirty three years. He overcame a dangerous rebellion, abetted by foreign force, and raging in the heart of his kingdoms;[41] and thereby destroyed the seeds of all future rebellion that could arise upon the same principle. He carried the glory, the power, the commerce of England, to an height unknown even to this renowned nation in the times of its greatest prosperity; and he left his succession resting on the true and only true foundations of all national and all regal greatness; affection at home, reputation abroad, trust in allies, terror in rival nations. The most ardent lover of his country cannot wish for Great Britain an happier fate than to continue as she was then left. A people emulous as we are in affection to our present Sovereign, know not how to form a prayer to Heaven for a greater blessing upon his virtues, or an higher state of felicity and glory, than that, that he should live, and should reign, and, when Providence ordains it, should die, exactly like his illustrious Predecessor.[42]

---

[40] **every family** Langford suggests that the Yorkes may be meant. Charles Yorke, in particular, had his loyalty divided between his family's long association with Newcastle and the natural home of a career lawyer in the ministry.

[41] **kingdoms** i.e. the Forty-Five, the last Jacobite rising, put down with brutal thoroughness by the king's younger son, the duke of Cumberland.

[42] **exactly like his illustrious predecessor** since George II suffered a heart attack

A great Prince may be obliged (though such a thing cannot happen very often) to sacrifice his private inclination[43] to his public interest. A wise Prince will not think that such a restraint implies a condition of servility; and truly, if such was the condition of the last reign, and the effects were also such as we have described, we ought, no less for the sake of the Sovereign whom we love, than for our own, to hear arguments convincing indeed, before we depart from the maxims of that reign, or fly in the face of this great body of strong and recent experience.

One of the principal topicks which was then, and has been since, much employed by that political* school, is an affected terror of the growth of an aristocratic power, prejudicial to the rights of the Crown, and the balance of the constitution. Any new powers exercised in the House of Lords, or in the House of Commons, or by the Crown, ought certainly to excite the vigilant and anxious jealousy of a free people. Even a new and unprecedented course of action in the whole Legislature, without great and evident reason, may be a subject of just uneasiness. I will not affirm, that there may not have lately appeared in the House of Lords a disposition to some attempts derogatory to the legal rights of the subject.[44] If any such have really appeared, they have arisen, not from a power properly aristocratic, but from the same influence which is charged with having excited attempts of a similar nature in the House of Commons; which House, if it should have been betrayed into an unfortunate quarrel with its constituents, and involved in a charge of the very same nature, could have neither power nor inclination to repell such attempts in others. Those attempts in the House of Lords can no more be called aristocratic

whilst attempting to perform a natural function, we had better not speculate on Burke's ambiguous intentions. For details of the event, see *Philosophical Transactions . . . of the Royal Society*, 52, 1 (1761), pp. 265–75.

* See the Political Writings of the late Dr. Brown,[45] and many others.

[43] **private inclination** George II tried to get rid of Walpole, despised Newcastle, had the elder Pitt forced on him in the forties by Pelham and in the fifties by necessity, and in 1744 was unable to keep his preferred minister, Carteret.

[44] **legal rights of the subject** as in the Lords' attempts to try Wilkes for inciting riot at the Middlesex election and their defence of the orders in council granting indemnity to those concerned in the Embargo on Wheat and Wheatflour, 1766 (see PH, XVI, 245–313). The elder Pitt as well as Northington defended the latter.

[45] **Dr Brown** his *Thoughts on Civil Liberty, Licentiousness and Faction* (second edition, 1765) aims 'to unite all honest men of all parties' (p. 124) and views bribery as necessary to free governments (p. 142).

proceedings, than the proceedings with regard to the country of Middlesex in the House of Commons can with any sense be called democratical.

It is true, that the Peers have a great influence in the kingdom, and in every part of the public concerns. While they are men of property, it is impossible to prevent it, except by such means as must prevent all property from its natural operation; an event not easily to be compassed, while property is power,[46] nor by any means to be wished, while the least notion exists of the method by which the spirit of liberty acts, and, of the means by which it is preserved. If any particular Peers, by their uniform, upright, constitutional conduct, by their public and their private virtues, have acquired an influence in the country; the people, on whose favour that influence depends, and from whom it arose, will never be duped into an opinion, that such greatness in a Peer is the despotism of an aristocracy, when they know and feel it to be the effect and pledge of their own importance.[47]

I am no friend to aristocracy, in the sense at least in which that word is usually understood.[48] If it were not a bad habit to moot cases on the supposed ruin of the constitution, I should be free to declare, that if it must perish, I would rather by far see it resolved into any

[46] **property is power** Harrington argued that political power tends to follow the location of property. After 1789 Burke did not place implicit faith in this view: 'That power goes with Property is not universally true, and the idea that the operation of it is certain and invariable may mislead us very fatally' *Thoughts on French Affairs* (1791), W, IV, p. 353 (and see the second of the *Letters on the proposals for Peace with the regicide Directory of France*, W, VI, p. 205). Burke was also suspicious of an elective senate of the kind he attributed to Harrington (W, IV, p. 353).

[47] **their own importance** Burke suggests in this paragraph that because the aristocracy were not powerful enough to govern by themselves, they must conciliate the people and so maintain the general interest e.g. liberty. The idea was not new to him: see his *Abridgement of English History*, III.viii, on *Magna Carta*

by which it is provided, that the barons shall grant to the tenants the same liberties which they had stipulated for themselves ... The English barons ... were not in a condition to set up for petty sovereigns by an usurpation equally detrimental to the crown and the people. They were able to act only in confederacy; and this common cause made it necessary to consult the common good, and to study popularity by the equity of their proceedings. This was a very happy circumstance to the growing liberty.

[48] **usually understood** i.e. 'austere and insolent domination'; at the same point in his *Abridgement*, Burke referred to 'the worst imaginable government, a feudal aristocracy'. See also *Annual Register* (1768), p. 272 (2nd pagination): 'aristocracy, the most oppressive of absolute governments'. Burke's argument that the aristocracy depends on the people and so will pursue the general interest countered the aspersions of [Douglas], *Seasonable Hints*, e.g. p. 11 about 'the dark and arbitrary influence of Aristocracy'.

other form, than lost in that austere and insolent domination. But, whatever my dislikes may be, my fears are not upon that quarter. The question, on the influence of a Court, and of a Peerage, is not, which of the two dangers is the most eligible, but which is the most imminent. He is but a poor observer, who has not seen, that the generality of Peers, far from supporting themselves in a state of independent greatness, are but too apt to fall into an oblivion of their proper dignity, and to run headlong into an abject servitude.[49] Would to God it were true, that the fault of our Peers were too much spirit! It is worthy of some observation, that these gentlemen, so jealous of aristocracy, make no complaints of the power of those Peers (neither few nor inconsiderable) who are always in the train of a Court, and whose whole weight must be considered as a portion of the settled influence of the Crown. This is all safe and right: but if some Peers (I am very sorry they are not as many as they ought to be) set themselves, in the great concern of Peers and Commons, against a back-stairs influence and clandestine government, then the alarm begins; then the constitution is in danger of being forced into an aristocracy.

I rest a little the longer on this Court topick, because it was much insisted upon at the time of the great change, and has been since frequently revived by many of the agents of that party: for, whilst they are terrifying the great and opulent with the horrors of mob-government, they are by other managers attempting (though hitherto with little success) to alarm the people with a phantom of tyranny of the Nobles. All this is done upon their favourite principle of disunion, of sowing jealousies amongst the different orders of the State, and of disjointing the natural strength of the kingdom; that it may be rendered incapable of resisting the sinister designs of wicked men, who have engrossed the Royal power.

Thus much of the topicks chosen by the Courtiers to recommend their system; it will be necessary to open a little more at large the nature of that party which was formed for its support. Without this, the whole would have been no better than a visionary amusement, like the scheme of Harrington's political club,[50] and not a business in

---

[49] **abject servitude** an allusion to the large number of placemen in the Lords. Phrases like 'thanes, high priests and household cavalry' are sometimes found in opposition criticism e.g. Lord John Russell (ed.), *Memorials and Correspondence of Charles James Fox*, 4 vols. (1853–7), II, p. 220.

[50] **political club** cf. *Rota* alluding to Harrington's group of associates under the Protectorate. The name is borrowed from a body of papal advisors.

which the nation had a real concern. As a powerful party, and a party constructed on a new principle, it is a very inviting object of curiosity.

It must be remembered, that since the Revolution, until the period we are speaking of, the influence of the Crown had been always employed in supporting the Ministers of State, and in carrying on the public business according to their opinions. But the party now in question is formed upon a very different idea. It is to intercept the favour, protection and confidence of the Crown in the passage to its Ministers; it is to come between them and their importance in Parliament; it is to separate them from all their natural and acquired dependencies; it is intended as the controul, not the support, of Administration. The machinery of this system is perplexed in its movements, and false in its principle. It is formed on a supposition that the King is something external to his government; and that he may be honoured and aggrandized, even by its debility and disgrace. The plan proceeds expressly on the idea of enfeebling the regular executory power. It proceeds on the idea of weakening the State in order to strengthen the Court. The scheme depending intirely on distrust, on disconnexion, on mutability by principle, on systematic weakness in every particular member; it is impossible that the total result should be substantial strength of any kind.

As a foundation of their scheme, the Cabal have established a sort of *Rota* in the Court. All sorts of parties, by this means, have been brought into Administration, from whence few have had the good fortune to escape without disgrace; none at all without considerable losses. In the beginning of each arrangement no professions of confidence and support are wanting, to induce the leading men to engage. But while the Ministers of the day appear in all the pomp and pride of power, while they have all their canvas spread out to the wind, and every sail filled with the fair and prosperous gale of Royal favour, in a short time they find, they know not how, a current, which sets directly against them; which prevents all progress; and even drives them backwards. They grow ashamed and mortified in a situation, which, by its vicinity to power, only serves to remind them the more strongly of their insignificance. They are obliged either to execute the orders of their inferiors, or to see themselves opposed by the natural instruments of their office. With the loss of their dignity, they lose their temper. In their turn they grow troublesome to that Cabal, which, whether it supports or opposes, equally disgraces and equally betrays them. It is soon found necessary to get rid of the heads of Administration; but it is of the heads only. As there always are many rotten members belonging to the best connexions, it is not hard to persuade several to continue in office without their leaders. By this means the party goes out much thinner than it came in; and is only reduced in strength by its temporary possession of power.[51] Besides, if by accident, or in course of changes, that power should be recovered, the Junto have thrown up a retrenchment of these carcases, which may serve to cover themselves in a day of danger. They conclude, not unwisely, that such rotten members will become the first objects of disgust and resentment to their antient connexions.

They contrive to form in the outward Administration two parties at the least;[52] which, whilst they are tearing one another to pieces, are both competitors for the favour and protection of the Cabal; and, by their emulation, contribute to throw every thing more and more into the hands of the interior managers.

A Minister of State will sometimes keep himself totally estranged from all his colleagues; will differ from them in their councils, will privately traverse, and publicly oppose, their measures.[53] He will, however, continue in his employment. Instead of suffering any mark of displeasure, he will be distinguished by an unbounded profusion of Court rewards and caresses; because he does what is expected, and all that is expected, from men in office. He helps to keep some form of Administration in being, and keeps it at the same time as weak and divided as possible.

However, we must take care not to be mistaken, or to imagine that such persons have any weight in their opposition. When, by them, Administration is convinced of its insignificancy, they are soon to be convinced of their own. They never are suffered to succeed in their opposition. They and the world are to be satisfied, that, neither office, nor authority, nor property, nor ability, eloquence, council, skill, or union, are of the least importance; but that the mere influence of the Court, naked of all support, and destitute of all management, is abundantly sufficient for all its own purposes.

[51] **temporary possession of power** a number of those who entered office with Rockingham in 1765 did not relinquish it in his company in 1766.

[52] **at the least** as Grafton's ministry was divided between his own followers and Bedford's.

[53] **their measures** Northington's conduct in Rockingham's ministry fits this description.

When any adverse connexion is to be destroyed, the Cabal seldom appear in the work themselves. They find out some person of whom the party entertains an high opinion.[54] Such a person they endeavour to delude with various pretences. They teach him first to distrust, and then to quarrel with his friends; among whom, by the same arts, they excite a similar diffidence of him; so that, in this mutual fear and distrust, he may suffer himself to be employed as the instrument in the change which is brought about. Afterwards they are sure to destroy him in his turn; by setting up in his place some person in whom he had himself reposed the greatest confidence, and who serves to carry off a considerable part of his adherents.

When such a person has broke in this manner with his connexions, he is soon compelled to commit some flagrant act of iniquitous personal hostility against some of them (such as an attempt to strip a particular friend of his family estate[55]), by which the Cabal hope to render the parties utterly irreconcilable. In truth, they have so contrived matters, that people have a greater hatred to the subordinate instruments than to the principal movers.

As in destroying their enemies they make use of instruments[56] not immediately belonging to their corps, so, in advancing their own friends, they pursue exactly the same method. To promote any of them to considerable rank or emolument, they commonly take care that the recommendation shall pass through the hands of the ostensible Ministry: such a recommendation might however appear to the world, as some proof of the credit of Ministers, and some means of increasing their strength. To prevent this, the persons so advanced

---

[54] **high opinion**   this could fit Grafton, who became secretary of state under Rockingham at thirty; his resignation, because the elder Pitt would not join, weakened the administration. When Grafton's own ministry fell he was succeeded by North, who had been his chancellor of the exchequer.

[55] **family estate**   Burke's later note ('Duke of Grafton to the Duke of Portland') referred to the attempt to strip Portland of Inglewood forest and the Manor and Castle of Carlisle (which had extensive electoral influence) by a crown grant to Sir James Lowther. These possessions had been enjoyed by Portland's family from the time of William III, though not specified in his grant of the honour of Penrith to them. The grant to Lowther was completed before Portland had any opportunity to establish his title, for the Treasury relied on the maxim *nullum tempus occurit regi* (the passage of time does not defeat crown claims). Savile's bill to abolish this maxim was initially rejected but subsequently passed into law, so that sixty years' possession would rebut a crown claim. It may be noted that Lowther was Bute's son-in-law.

[56] **instruments**   later identified by Burke as Charles Jenkinson.

are directed, in all companies, industriously to declare, that they are under no obligations whatsoever to Administration;[57] that they have received their office from another quarter; that they are totally free and independent.

When the Faction has any job of lucre to obtain, or of vengeance to perpetrate, their way is, to select, for the execution, those very persons to whose habits, friendships, principles, and declarations, such proceedings are publicly known to be the most adverse,[58] at once to render the instruments the more odious, and therefore the more dependent, and to prevent the people from ever reposing a confidence in any appearance of private friendship, or public principle.

If the Administration seem now and then, from remissness, or from fear of making themselves disagreeable, to suffer any popular excesses to go unpunished, the Cabal immediately sets up some creature of theirs to raise a clamour against the Ministers, as having shamefully betrayed the dignity of Government.[59] Then they compel the Ministry to become active in conferring rewards and honours on the persons who have been the instruments of their disgrace;[60] and, after having first vilified them with the higher orders for suffering the laws to sleep over the licentiousness of the populace, they drive them (in order to make amends for their former inactivity) to some act of atrocious violence, which renders them completely abhorred by the people.[61] They who remember the riots which attended the Middlesex Election; the opening of the present Parliament; and the transactions relative to Saint George's Fields,[62] will not be at a loss for an application of those remarks.

That this body may be enabled to compass all the ends of its

---

[57] **no obligations ... Administration**   later specified as 'Sir Fletcher Norton with many others'.

[58] **adverse**   possibly a reference to Shelburne's resignation in 1768, for which Grafton had pressed.

[59] **Government**   'Alderman Harley against the Duke of Grafton and Lord Camden' (Burke).

[60] **disgrace**   Burke noted 'Made a Privy Councillor'.

[61] **by the people**   'Lord Camden got to act a very foolish part about a pardon'. Edward MacQuirk was pardoned for a murder which allegedly occurred in one of the Middlesex by-elections. Langford suggests that the original wording would fit Weymouth's letter of 17 May 1768 encouraging the Surrey bench to deal firmly with rioters.

[62] **Saint George's Fields**   in March 1769, supporters of Wilkes clashed with troops, leading to a 'massacre'.

institution, its members are scarcely ever to aim at the high and responsible offices of the State.[63] They are distributed with art and judgement through all the secondary, but efficient, departments of office, and through the households of all the branches of the Royal Family: so as on one hand to occupy all the avenues to the Throne; and on the other to forward or frustrate the execution of any measure, according to their own interests. For with the credit and support which they are known to have, though for the greater part in places which are only a genteel excuse for salary, they possess all the influence of the highest posts; and they dictate publicly in almost every thing, even with a parade of superiority. Whenever they dissent (as it often happens) from their nominal leaders, the trained part of the Senate, instinctively in the secret, is sure to follow them;[64] provided the leaders, sensible of their situation, do not of themselves recede in time from their most declared opinions. This latter is generally the case. It will not be conceivable to any one who has not seen it, what pleasure is taken by the Cabal in rendering these heads of office thoroughly contemptible and ridiculous. And when they are become so, they have then the best chance for being well supported.

The members of the Court Faction are fully indemnified for not holding places on the slippery heights of the kingdom, not only by the lead in all affairs, but also by the perfect security in which they enjoy less conspicuous, but very advantageous situations. Their places are, in express legal tenure, or in effect, all of them for life. Whilst the first and most respectable persons in the kingdom are tossed about like tennis balls, the sport of a blind and insolent caprice, no Minister dares even to cast an oblique glance at the lowest of their body.[65] If an attempt be made upon one of this corps, immediately he flies to sanctuary, and pretends to the most inviolable of all promises. No conveniency of public arrangement is available to remove any of them

---

[63] **high and responsible . . . State** Elliot, Dyson and Stuart Mackenzie, for example, all enjoyed subordinate offices; Jenkinson disliked the prominence of the offices he later held.

[64] **sure to follow them** fifty-two placemen voted against the Rockingham ministry's Repeal of the Stamp Act.

[65] **lowest of their body** Burke noted 'Stewart Mackenzie among the higher, Dyson among the lesser'. Grenville got rid of Mackenzie in April 1765 (but he was restored by the elder Pitt); Rockingham tried to dismiss Dyson in June 1766, but was thwarted by the king (for Rockingham's animus against Dyson, see *Correspondence of George III*, nos. 333–4). Shortly after each occurrence the ministry fell.

from the specific situation he holds; and the slightest attempt upon one of them, by the most powerful Minister, is a certain preliminary to his own destruction.[66] Conscious of their independence, they bear themselves with a lofty air to the exterior Ministers.[67] Like Janissaries,[68] they derive a kind of freedom from the very condition of their servitude. They may act just as they please; provided they are true to the great ruling principle of their institution. It is, therefore, not at all wonderful, that people should be so desirous of adding themselves to that body, in which they may possess and reconcile satisfactions the most alluring, and seemingly the most contradictory; enjoying at once all the spirited pleasure of independence, and all the gross lucre and fat emoluments of servitude.

Here is a sketch, though a slight one, of the constitution, laws, and policy, of this new Court corporation. The name by which they chuse to distinguish themselves, is that of *King's men*, or the *King's friends*, by an invidious exclusion[69] of the rest of his Majesty's most loyal and affectionate subjects. The whole system, comprehending the exterior and interior Administrations, is commonly called, in the technical language of the Court, *Double Cabinet*; in French or English, as you choose to pronounce it.

Whether all this be a vision of a distracted brain, or the invention of a malicious heart, or a real Faction in the country, must be judged by the appearances which things have worn for eight years past.[70] Thus far I am certain, that there is not a single public man, in or out of office, who has not, at some time or other, born testimony to the truth of what I have now related. In particular, no persons have been more strong in their assertions, and louder and more indecent in their complaints, than those who compose all the exterior part of the

[66] **his own destruction** 'Grenville. Lord Rockingham' (Burke).
[67] **exterior Ministers** 'Sir Gilbert Elliot, Dyson, etc. frequently took a lead against Administration' (Burke).
[68] **Janissaries** the analogy seems first to have been applied to the King's friends by George Grenville 'a set of Janissaries, who might at any time be ordered to put the bowstring around his neck' (*Bedford Correspondence*, III, p. xxviii). Grenville was quoted by C.J. Fox on 17 Dec. 1783 (PH, XXIV, 213).
[69] **invidious exclusion** cf. the Machiavellian judgement that the king of France would permit no one to refer to a king's party, since that implied a party against him, *Discourses*, III. 27.
[70] **for eight years past** i.e. since Bute, when it was supposed to have been set up as a defence against Whiggery; see Charles Butler, *Reminiscences* (1827), II, p. 114.

present Administration;[71] in whose time that Faction has arrived at such an height of power, and of boldness in the use of it, as may, in the end, perhaps bring about its total destruction.

It is true, that about four years ago, during the administration of the Marquis of Rockingham, an attempt was made to carry on Government without their concurrence. However, this was only a transient cloud; they were hid but for a moment; and their constellation blazed out with greater brightness, and a far more vigorous influence, some time after it was blown over. An attempt was at that time made (but without any idea of proscription) to break their corps, to discountenance their doctrines, to revive connexions of a different kind, to restore the principles and policy of the Whigs, to reanimate the cause of Liberty by Ministerial countenance; and then for the first time were men seen attached in office to every principle they had maintained in opposition. No one will doubt, that such men were abhorred and violently opposed by the Court Faction, and that such a system could have but a short duration.

It may appear somewhat affected, that in so much discourse upon this extraordinary Party, I should say so little of the Earl of Bute, who is the supposed head of it. But this was neither owing to affectation nor inadvertence. I have carefully avoided the introduction of personal reflexions of any kind. Much the greater part of the topicks which have been used to blacken this Nobleman, are either unjust or frivolous. At best, they have a tendency to give the resentment of this bitter calamity a wrong direction, and to turn a public grievance into a mean personal, or a dangerous national, quarrel. Where there is a regular scheme of operations carried on, it is the system, and not any individual person who acts in it, that is truly dangerous. This system has not risen solely from the ambition of Lord Bute, but from the circumstances which favoured it, and from an indifference to the constitution which had been for some time growing among our gentry. We should have been tried with it, if the Earl of Bute had never existed;[72] and it will want neither a contriving head nor active members, when the Earl of Bute exists no longer. It is not, therefore, to rail at Lord Bute, but firmly to embody against this Court Party and

[71] **present Administration** Burke added 'Duke of Grafton, Lord Weymouth, Lord Gower, Rigby, etc.'

[72] **had never existed** correcting the *History of the late Minority* (1765), p. 10.

its practices, which can afford us any prospect of relief in our present condition.

Another motive induces me to put the personal consideration of Lord Bute wholly out of the question. He communicates very little in a direct manner with the greater part of our men of business. This has never been his custom. It enough for him that he surrounds them with his creatures. Several imagine, therefore, that they have a very good excuse for doing all the work of this Faction, when they have no personal connexion with Lord Bute. But whoever becomes a party to an Administration, composed of insulated individuals, without faith plighted, tie, or common principle; an Administration constitutionally impotent, because supported by no party in the nation; he who contributes to destroy the connexions of men and their trust in one another, or in any sort to throw the dependence of public counsels upon private will and favour, possibly may have nothing to do with the Earl of Bute. It matters little whether he be the friend or the enemy of that particular person. But let him be who or what he will, he abets a Faction that is driving hard to the ruin of his country. He is sapping the foundation of its liberty, disturbing the sources of its domestic tranquillity, weakening its government over its dependencies, degrading it from all its importance in the system of Europe.

It is this unnatural infusion of a *system of Favouritism* into a Government which in a great part of its constitution is popular, that has raised the present ferment in the nation. The people without entering deeply into its principles, could plainly perceive its effects, in much violence, in a great spirit of innovation, and a general disorder in all the functions of Government. I keep my eye solely on this system; if I speak of those measures which have arisen from it, it will be so far only as they illustrate the general scheme. This is the fountain of all those bitter waters[73] of which, through an hundred different conduits, we have drunk until we are ready to burst. The discretionary power of the Crown in the formation of Ministry, abused by bad or weak men, has given rise to a system, which, without directly violating the letter of any law, operates against the spirit of the whole constitution.

A plan of Favouritism for our executory Government is essentially at variance with the plan of our Legislature. One great end undoubt-

---

[73] **bitter waters**　Numbers 5:14.

edly of a mixed Government like ours, composed of Monarchy, and of controls, on the part of the higher people and the lower, is that the Prince shall not be able to violate the laws. This is useful indeed and fundamental. But this, even at first view, is no more than a negative advantage; an armour merely defensive. It is therefore next in order, and equal in importance, *that the discretionary powers which are necess-arily vested in the Monarch, whether for the execution of the laws, or for the nomination to magistracy and office, or for conducting the affairs of peace and war, or for ordering the revenue, should all be exercised upon public principles and national grounds, and not on the likings or prejudices, the intrigues or policies, of a Court.* This, I said, is equal in importance to the securing a Government according to law. The laws reach but a very little way. Constitute Government how you please, infinitely the greater part of it must depend upon the exercise of the powers which are left at large to the prudence and uprightness of Ministers of State. Even all the use and potency of the laws depends upon them. Without them, your Commonwealth is no better than a scheme upon paper; and not a living, acting, effective constitution. It is possible, that through negligence, or ignorance, or design artfully conducted, Ministers may suffer one part of Government to languish, another to be perverted from its purposes, and every valuable interest of the country to fall into ruin and decay, without possibility of fixing any single act on which a criminal prosecution can be justly grounded. The due arrangement of men in the active part of the State, far from being foreign to the purposes of a wise Government, ought to be among its very first and dearest objects. When, therefore, the abettors of the new system tell us, that between them and their opposers there is nothing but a struggle for power, and that therefore we are noways concerned in it; we must tell those who have the impudence to insult us in this manner, that of all things we ought to be the most con-cerned, who and what sort of men they are, that hold the trust of every thing that is dear to us. Nothing can render this a point of indifference to the nation, but what must either render us totally desperate, or soothe us into the security of ideots. We must soften into a credulity below the milkiness of infancy, to think all men virtuous. We must be tainted with a malignity truly diabolical, to believe all the world to be equally wicked and corrupt. Men are in public life as in private, some good, some evil. The elevation of the one, and the depression of the other, are the first objects of all true policy. But that form of Government, which, neither in its direct institutions, nor in their immediate tendency, has contrived to throw its affairs into the most trustworthy hands, but has left its whole executory system to be disposed of agreeably to the uncontrolled pleasure of any one man, however excellent or virtuous, is a plan of polity defective not only in that member, but consequentially erroneous in every part of it.

In arbitrary Governments, the constitution of the Ministry follows the constitution of the Legislature. Both the Law and the Magistrate are the creatures of Will. It must be so. Nothing, indeed, will appear more certain, on any tolerable consideration of this matter, than that *every sort of Government ought to have its Administration correspondent to its Legislature.* If it should be otherwise, things must fall into an hideous disorder. The people of a free Commonwealth, who have taken such care that their laws should be the result of general consent, cannot be so senseless as to suffer their executory system to be composed of persons on whom they have no dependence, and whom no proofs of the public love and confidence have recommended to those powers, upon the use of which the very being of the State depends.

The popular election of magistrates, and popular disposition of rewards and honours, is one of the first advantages of a free State. Without it, or something equivalent to it, perhaps the people cannot long enjoy the substance of freedom; certainly none of the vivifying energy of good Government. The frame of our Commonwealth did not admit of such an actual election: but it provided as well, and (while the spirit of the constitution is preserved) better for all the effects of it than by the method of suffrage in any democratic State whatsoever. It had always, until of late, been held the first duty of Parliament, *to refuse to support Government, until power was in the hands of persons who were acceptable to the people, or while factions predominated in the Court in which the nation had no confidence.* Thus all the good effects of popular election were supposed to be secured to us, without the mischiefs attending on perpetual intrigue, and a distinct canvass for every particular office throughout the body of the people. This was the most noble and refined part of our constitution. The people, by their representatives and grandees, were intrusted with a deliberative power in making laws; the King with the control of his negative. The King was instructed with the deliberative choice and the election to office; the people had the negative in a Parliamentary refusal to support. Formerly this power of controul was what kept Ministers in awe of Parliaments, and Parliaments in reverence with the people. If the use of this power of controul on the system and persons of Administration is gone, every thing is lost, Parliament and all. We may assure ourselves, that if Parliament will tamely see evil men take possession of all the strong-holds of their country, and allow them time and means to fortify themselves, under a pretence of giving them a fair trial, and upon a hope of discovering, whether they will not be reformed by power, and whether their measures will not be better than their morals; such a Parliament will give countenance to their measures also, whatever that Parliament may pretend, and whatever those measures may be.

Every good political institution must have a preventive operation as well as a remedial. It ought to have a natural tendency to exclude bad men from Government, and not to trust for the safety of the State to subsequent punishment alone: punishment, which has ever been tardy and uncertain; and which, when power is suffered in bad hands, may chance to fall rather on the injured than the criminal.

Before men are put forward into the great trusts of the State, they ought by their conduct to have obtained such a degree of estimation in their country, as may be some sort of pledge and security to the publick, that they will not abuse those trusts. It is no mean security for a proper use of power, that a man has shewn by the general tenor of his actions, that the affection, the good opinion, the confidence, of his fellow citizens have been among the principal objects of his life; and that he has owed none of the gradations of his power or fortune to a settled contempt, or occasional forfeiture of their esteem.

That man[74] who before he comes into power has no friends, or who coming into power is obliged to desert his friends, or who losing it has no friends to sympathize with him; he who has no sway among any part of the landed or commercial interest, but whose whole import-ance has begun with his office, and is sure to end with it; is a person who ought never to be suffered by a controuling Parliament to con-tinue in any of those situations which confer the lead and direction of all our public affairs; because such a man *has no connexion with the interest of the people.*

---

[74] **that man**   perhaps Bute or Shelburne.

Those knots or cabals[75] of men who have got together, avowedly without any party principle, in order to sell their conjunct iniquity at the higher rate, and are therefore universally odious, ought never to be suffered to domineer in the State, because they have *no connexion with the sentiments and opinions of the people.*

These are considerations which in my opinion enforce the necessity of having some better reason, in a free country, and a free Parliament, for supporting the Ministers of the Crown, than that short one, *That the King has thought proper to appoint them.* There is something very courtly in this. But it is a principle pregnant with all sorts of mischief, in a constitution like ours, to turn the views of active men from the country to the Court. Whatever be the road to power, that is the road which will be trod. If the opinion of the country be of no use as a means of power or consideration, the qualities which usually procure that opinion will be no longer cultivated. And whether it will be right, in a State so popular in its constitution as ours, to leave ambition without popular motives, and to trust all to the operation of pure virtue in the minds of Kings and Ministers, and public men, must be submitted to the judgement and good sense of the people of England.

Cunning men are here apt to break in, and, without directly controverting the principle, to raise objections from the difficulty under which the Sovereign labours, to distinguish the genuine voice and sentiments of his people, from the clamour of a faction, by which it is so easily counterfeited. The nation, they say, is generally divided into parties, with views and passions utterly irreconcileable. If the King should put his affairs into the hands of any one of them, he is sure to disgust the rest; if he select particular men from among them all, it is an hazard that he disgusts them all. Those who are left out, however divided before, will soon run into a body of opposition; which, being a collection of many discontents into one focus, will without doubt be hot and violent enough. Faction will make its cries resound through the nation, as if the whole were in an uproar, when by far the majority, and much the better part, will seem for a while as it were annihilated by the quiet in which their virtue and moderation incline them to enjoy the blessings of Government. Besides that the opinion of the meer vulgar is a miserable rule even with regard to themselves, on

---

[75] **Those knots or cabals**   perhaps Bedford and his followers.

account of their violence and instability. So that if you were to gratify them in their humour to-day, that very gratification would be a ground of their dissatisfaction on the next. Now as all these rules of public opinion are to be collected with great difficulty, and to be applied with equal uncertainty as to the effect, what better can a King of England do, than to employ such men as he finds to have views and inclinations most conformable to his own; who are least infected with pride and self-will, and who are least moved by such popular humours as are perpetually traversing his designs, and disturbing his service; trusting that, when he means no ill to his people, he will be supported in his appointments, whether he chooses to keep or to change, as his private judgement or his pleasure leads him? He will find a sure resource in the real weight and influence of the Crown, when it is not suffered to become an instrument in the hands of a faction.

I will not pretend to say that there is nothing at all in this mode of reasoning; because I will not assert, that there is no difficulty in the art of Government. Undoubtedly the very best Administration must encounter a great deal of opposition; and the very worst will find more support than it deserves. Sufficient appearances will never be wanting to those who have a mind to deceive themselves. It is a fallacy in constant use with those who would level all things, and confound right with wrong, to insist upon the inconveniencies which are attached to every choice, without taking into consideration the different weight and consequence of those inconveniencies. The question is not concerning *absolute* discontent or *perfect* satisfaction in Government; neither of which can be pure and unmixed at any time, or upon any system. The controversy is about that degree of good humour in the people, which may possibly be attained, and ought certainly to be looked for. While some politicians may be waiting to know whether the sense of every individual be against them, accurately distinguishing the vulgar from the better sort, drawing lines between the enterprizes of a faction and the efforts of a people, they may chance to see the Government, which they are so nicely weighing, and dividing, and distinguishing, tumble to the ground in the midst of their wise deliberation. Prudent men, when so great an object as the security of Government, or even its peace, is at stake, will not run the risque of a decision which may be fatal to it. They who can read the political sky will see an hurricane in a cloud no bigger than an hand[76] at the very

---

[76] **than an hand** I Kings 18:44.

edge of the horizon, and will run into the first harbour. No lines can be laid down for civil or political wisdom. They are a matter incapable of exact definition. But, though no man can draw a stroke between the confines of day and night, yet light and darkness are upon the whole tolerably distinguishable. Nor will it be impossible for a Prince to find out such a mode of Government, and such persons to administer it, as will give a great degree of content to his people; without any curious and anxious research for that abstract, universal, perfect harmony, which while he is seeking, he abandons those means of ordinary tranquillity which are in his power without any research at all.

It is not more the duty than it is the interest of a Prince, to aim at giving tranquillity to his Government. But those who advise him may have an interest in disorder and confusion. If the opinion of the people is against them, they will naturally wish that it should have no prevalence. Here it is that the people must on their part shew themselves sensible of their own value. Their whole importance, in the first instance, and afterwards their whole freedom, is at stake. Their freedom cannot long survive their importance. Here it is that the natural strength of the kingdom, the great peers, the leading landed gentlemen, the opulent merchants and manufacturers, the substantial yeomanry, must interpose, to rescue their Prince, themselves, and their posterity.

We are at present at issue upon this point. We are in the great crisis of this contention; and the part which men take one way or other, will serve to discriminate their characters and their principles. Until the matter is decided, the country will remain in its present confusion. For while a system of Administration is attempted, entirely repugnant to the genius of the people, and not comfortable to the plan of their Government, every thing must necessarily be disordered for a time, until this system destroys the constitution, or the constitution gets the better of this system.

There is, in my opinion, a peculiar venom and malignity in this political distemper beyond any that I have heard or read of. In former times the projectors of arbitrary Government attacked only the liberties of their country; a design surely mischievous enough to have satisfied a mind of the most unruly ambition. But a system unfavourable to freedom may be so formed, as considerably to exalt the grandeur of the State; and men may find in the pride and splendor of that prosperity some sort of consolation for the loss of their solid privileges. Indeed the increase of the power of the State has often been urged by artful men, as a pretext for some abridgement of the public liberty. But the scheme of the junto under consideration, not only strikes a palsy into every nerve of our free constitution, but in the same degree benumbs and stupifies the whole executive power; rendering Government in all its grand operations languid, uncertain, ineffective; making Ministers fearful of attempting, and incapable of executing, any useful plan of domestic arrangement, or of foreign politicks. It tends to produce neither the security of a free Government, nor the energy of a Monarchy that is absolute.[77] Accordingly the Crown has dwindled away, in proportion to the unnatural and turgid growth of this excrescence on the Court.

The interior Ministry are sensible, that war is a situation which sets in its full light the value of the hearts of a people; and they well know, that the beginning of the importance of the people must be the end of theirs. For this reason they discover upon all occasions the utmost fear of every thing, which by possibility may lead to such an event. I do not mean that they manifest any of that pious fear which is backward to commit the safety of the country to the dubious experiment of war. Such a fear, being the tender sensation of virtue, excited, as it is regulated, by reason, frequently shews itself in a seasonable boldness, which keeps danger at a distance, by seeming to despise it. Their fear betrays to the first glance of the eye, its true cause, and its real object. Foreign powers, confident in the knowledge of their character, have not scrupled to violate the most solemn treaties; and, in defiance of them, to make conquests in the midst of a general peace, and in the heart of Europe. Such was the conquest of Corsica,[78] by the professed enemies of the freedom of mankind, in defiance of those who were formerly its professed defenders. We have had just claims upon the same powers; rights which ought to have been sacred to them as well as to us, as they had their origin in our lenity and generosity towards France and Spain in the day of their great humiliation. Such I call the ransom of Manilla, and the demand on France for the East India

[77] **that is absolute**   cf. Montesquieu, *Spirit of the Laws*, v.10.
[78] **Corsica**   ruled by Genoa, Corsica had revolted in 1755. Britain's mediterranean fleet had in the past given assistance to Corsica, but in 1762 a royal proclamation forbade British subjects to help her. France then concluded an alliance with Genoa. In 1768 France absorbed the island. Britain thus helped to ensure that Napoleon would be a French subject.
[79] **Manilla ... East India prisoners**   Manilla was captured in October 1762, the garrison being allowed to withdraw by promising a million pounds in ransom. The East India prisoners were the garrison of Pondicherry, of whom about 1,400 were

prisoners.[79] But these powers put a just confidence in their resource of the *double Cabinet*. These demands (one of them at least) are hastening fast towards an acquittal by prescription. Oblivion begins to spread her cobwebs over all our spirited remonstrances. Some of the most valuable branches of our trade are also on the point of perishing from the same cause. I do not mean those branches which bear without the hand of the vine-dresser; I mean those which the policy of treaties had formerly secured to us; I mean to mark and distinguish the trade of Portugal, the loss of which, and the power of the Cabal, have one and the same area.

If, by any chance, the Ministers who stand before the curtain possess or affect any spirit, it makes little or no impression. Foreign Courts and Ministers, who were among the first to discover and to profit by this invention of the *double Cabinet*, attend very little to their remonstrances. They know that those shadows of Ministers have nothing to do in the ultimate disposal of things. Jealousies and animosities are sedulously nourished in the outward Administration, and have been even considered as a *causa sine qua non* in its constitution: thence foreign Courts have a certainty, that nothing can be done by common counsel in this nation. If one of those Ministers officially takes up a business with spirit, it serves only the better to signalize the meanness of the rest, and the discord of them all. His colleagues in office are in haste to shake him off, and to disclaim the whole of his proceedings. Of this nature was that astonishing transaction, in which Lord Rochford, our Ambassador at Paris, remonstrated against the attempt upon Corsica, in consequence of a direct authority from Lord Shelburne. This remonstrance the French Minister treated with the contempt that was natural; as he was assured, from the Ambassador of his Court to ours, that these orders of Lord Shelburne were not supported by the rest of the (I had like to have said British) Administration. Lord Rochford, a man of spirit, could not endure this situation. The consequences were, however, curious. He returns from Paris, and comes home full of anger. Lord Shelburne, who gave the orders, is obliged to give up the seals.[80] Lord Rochford, who

---

Europeans (*Annual Register* (1761), p. 54–8, esp. 56; cf. pp. 290–2 on Manilla and Pondicherry).

[80] **give up the seals** Shelburne did not resign in 1768 over Corsica, despite Burke's hint, and the divisions in the ministry did not relate to the King's friends. Langford observes that Burke's account in other respects is 'substantially' supported by official papers.

obeyed these orders, receives them. He goes, however, into another department of the same office, that he might not be obliged officially to acquiesce in one situation under what he had officially remonstrated against in another. At Paris, the Duke of Choiseul considered this office arrangement as a compliment to him: here it was spoke of as an attention to the delicacy of Lord Rochford. But whether the compliment was to one or both, to this nation it was the same. By this transaction the condition of our Court lay exposed in all its nakedness. Our office correspondence has lost all pretence to authenticity; British policy is brought into derision in those nations; that a while ago trembled at the power of our arms, whilst they looked up with confidence to the equity, firmness, and candour, which shone in all our negotiations. I represent this matter exactly in the light in which it has been universally received.

Such has been the aspect of our foreign politicks, under the influence of a *double Cabinet*. With such an arrangement at Court, it is impossible it should have been otherwise. Nor is it possible that this scheme should have a better effect upon the government of our dependencies, the first, the dearest, and most delicate objects, of the interior policy of this empire. The Colonies know, that Administration is separated from the Court, divided within itself, and detested by the nation. The *double Cabinet* has, in both the parts of it, shewn the most malignant dispositions towards them, without being able to do them the smallest mischief.

They are convinced, by sufficient experience, that no plan, either of lenity or rigour, can be pursued with uniformity and perseverance. Therefore they turn their eyes entirely from Great Britain, where they have neither dependence on friendship, nor apprehension from enmity. They look to themselves, and their own arrangements. They grow every day into alienation from this country; and whilst they are becoming disconnected with our Government, we have not the consolation to find, that they are even friendly in their new independence. Nothing can equal the futility, the weakness, the rashness, the timidity, the perpetual contradiction, in the management of our affairs in that part of the world. A volume might be written on this melancholy subject; but it were better to leave it entirely to the reflexions of the reader himself than not to treat it in the extent it deserves.

In what manner our domestic oeconomy is affected by this system, it is needless to explain. It is the perpetual subject of their own complaints.

The Court Party resolve the whole into faction.[81] Having said something before upon this subject, I shall only observe here, that when they give this account of the prevalence of faction, they present no very favourable aspect of the confidence of the people in their own Government. They may be assured, that however they amuse themselves with a variety of projects for substituting something else in the place of that great and only foundation of Government, the confidence of the people, every attempt will but make their condition worse. When men imagine that their food is only a cover for poison, and when they neither love nor trust the hand that serves it, it is not the name of the roast beef of Old England,[82] that will persuade them to sit down to the table that is spread for them. When the people conceive that laws, and tribunals, and even popular assemblies, are perverted from the ends of their institution, they find in those names of degenerated establishments only new motives to discontent. Those bodies, which, when full of life and beauty, lay in their arms, and were their joy and comfort, when dead and putrid, become but the more loathsome from remembrance of former endearments. A sullen gloom, and furious disorder, prevail by fits; the nation loses its relish for peace and prosperity, as it did in that season of fullness which opened our troubles in the time of Charles the First. A species of men to whom a state of order would become a sentence of obscurity, are nourished into a dangerous magnitude by the heat of intestine disturbances; and it is no wonder that, by a sort of sinister piety, they cherish, in their turn, the disorders which are the parents of all their consequence. Superficial observers consider such persons as the cause of the public uneasiness, when, in truth, they are nothing more than the effect of it. Good men look upon this distracted scene with sorrow and indignation. Their hands are tied behind them. They are despoiled of all the power which might enable them to reconcile the strength of Government with the rights of the people. They stand in a most distressing alternative. But in the election among evils they hope better things from temporary confusion, than from established

[81] **resolve the whole into faction** 'In all political disputes the word *faction* is much in esteem, and generally applied to the weaker side' (*North Briton*, no. 30).
[82] **Old England** alluding to the song in Henry Fielding, *Grub-street Opera*, III, 3.

servitude. In the mean time, the voice of law is not to be heard. Fierce licentiousness begets violent restraints. The military arm is the sole reliance; and then, call your constitution what you please, it is the sword that governs. The civil power, like every other that calls in the aid of an ally stronger than itself, perishes by the assistance[83] it receives. But the contrivers of this scheme of Government will not trust solely to the military power; because they are cunning men. Their restless and crooked spirit drives them to rake in the dirt of every kind of expedient. Unable to rule the multitude, they endeavour to raise divisions amongst them. One mob is hired to destroy another; a procedure which at once encourages the boldness of the populace, and justly increases their discontent. Men become pensioners of state on account of their abilities in the array of riot, and the discipline of confusion. Government is put under the disgraceful necessity of protecting from the severity of the laws that very licentiousness, which the laws had been before violated to repress. Every thing partakes of the original disorder. Anarchy predominates without freedom, and servitude without submission or subordination. These are the consequences inevitable to our public peace, from the scheme of rendering the executory Government at once odious and feeble; of freeing Administration from the constitutional and salutary controul of Parliament, and inventing for it a *new controul*, unknown to the constitution, an *interior Cabinet*; which brings the whole body of Government into confusion and contempt.

After having stated, as shortly as I am able, the effects of this system on our foreign affairs, on the policy of our Government with regard to our dependencies, and on the interior oeconomy of the Commonwealth; there remains only, in this part of my design, to say something of the grand principle which first recommended this system at Court. The pretence was, to prevent the King from being enslaved by a faction, and made a prisoner in his closet. This scheme might have been expected to answer at least its own end, and to indemnify the King, in his personal capacity, for all the confusion into which it has thrown his Government. But has it in reality answered this purpose? I am sure, if it had, every affectionate subject would have one motive for enduring with patience all the evils which attend it.

[83] **by the assistance** cf. Burke *Abridgement*, II.i on the Britons and the Saxons.

In order to come at the truth in this matter, it may not be amiss to consider it somewhat in detail. I speak here of the King, and not of the Crown; the interests of which we have already touched. Independent of that greatness which a King possesses merely by being a representative of the national dignity, the things in which he may have an individual interest seem to be these: wealth accumulated; wealth spent in magnificence, pleasure, or beneficence; personal respect and attention; and above all, private ease and repose of mind. These compose the inventory of prosperous circumstances, whether they regard a Prince or a subject; their enjoyments differing only in the scale upon which they are formed.

Suppose then we were to ask, whether the King has been richer than his predecessors in accumulated wealth, since the establishment of the plan of Favouritism? I believe it will be found that the picture of royal indigence which our Court has presented[84] until this year, has been truly humiliating. Nor has it been relieved from this unseemly distress, but by means which have hazarded the affection of the people, and shaken their confidence in Parliament. If the public treasures had been exhausted in magnificence and splendour, this distress would have been accounted for, and in some measure justified. Nothing would be more unworthy of this nation, than with a mean and mechanical rule, to mete out the splendour of the Crown. Indeed I have found very few persons disposed to so ungenerous a procedure. But the generality of people, it must be confessed, do feel a good deal mortified, when they compare the wants of the Court with its expences. They do not behold the cause of this distress in any part of the apparatus of Royal magnificence. In all this, they see nothing but the operations of parsimony, attended with all the consequences of profusion. Nothing expended, nothing saved. Their wonder is increased by their knowledge, that besides the revenue settled on his Majesty's Civil List to the amount of 800,000*l.* a year, he has a farther aid, from a large pension list, near 90,000*l.* a year, in Ireland; from the produce of the Dutchy of Lancaster (which we are told has been greatly improved); from the revenue of the Dutchy of Cornwall; from the American quit-rents; from the four and a half *per cent.* duty in the

[84] **has presented** an allusion to the £513,511 debt on the Civil List removed by the Commons in 1769, after some speculation about the reasons for the king's poverty. The catalogue which follows should be taken *cum grano salis*; the Irish revenue, for instance, was for use in Ireland only.

Leeward Islands; this last worth to be sure considerably more than 40,000*l.* a year. The whole is certainly not much short of a million annually.

These are revenues within the knowledge and cognizance of our national Councils. We have no direct right to examine into the receipts from his Majesty's German Dominions, and the Bishoprick of Osnabrug.[85] This is unquestionably true. But that which is not within the province of Parliament, is yet within the sphere of every man's own reflexion. If a foreign Prince resided amongst us, the state of his revenues could not fail of becoming the subject of our speculation. Filled with an anxious concern for whatever regards the welfare of our Sovereign, it is impossible, in considering the miserable circumstances into which he has been brought, that this obvious topick should be entirely passed over. There is an opinion universal, that these revenues produce something not inconsiderable, clear of all charges and establishments. This produce the people do not believe to be hoarded, nor perceive to be spent. It is accounted for in the only manner it can, by supposing that it is drawn away, for the support of that Court Faction, which, whilst it distresses the nation, impoverishes the Prince in every one of his resources. I once more caution the reader, that I do not urge this consideration concerning the foreign revenue, as if I supposed we had a direct right to examine into the expenditure of any part of it; but solely for the purpose of shewing how little this system of Favouritism has been advantageous to the Monarch himself; which, without magnificence, has sunk him into a state of unnatural poverty; at the same time that he possessed every means of affluence, from ample revenues, both in this country, and in other parts of his dominions.

Has this system provided better for the treatment becoming his high and sacred character, and secured the King from those disgusts attached to the necessity of employing men who are not personally agreeable? This is a topick upon which for many reasons I could wish to be silent; but the pretence of securing against such causes of uneasiness, is the corner-stone of the Court Party. It has however so happened, that if I were to fix upon any one point, in which this

---

[85] **Osnabrug** The nomination the bishopric alternated, under the terms of the Peace of Westphalia, between the Roman Catholic Church and the House of Hanover. George III bestowed it upon his second son, Frederick, aged one, and let the revenues accumulate until the latter attained his majority.

system has been more particularly and shamefully blameable, the effects which it has produced would justify me in choosing for that point its tendency to degrade the personal dignity of the Sovereign, and to expose him to a thousand contradictions and mortifications.[86] It is but too evident in what manner these projectors of Royal greatness have fulfilled all their magnificent promises. Without recapitulating all the circumstances of the reign, every one of which is more or less a melancholy proof of the truth of what I have advanced, let us consider the language of the Court but a few years ago, concerning most of the persons now in the external Administration: let me ask, whether any enemy to the personal feelings of the Sovereign, could possibly contrive a keener instrument of mortification, and degradation of all dignity, than almost every part and member of the present arrangement?[87] nor, in the whole course of our history, has any compliance with the will of the people ever been known to extort from any Prince a greater contradiction to all his own declared affections and dislikes than that which is now adopted, in direct opposition to every thing the people approve and desire.

An opinion prevails, that greatness has been more than once advised to submit to certain condescensions towards individuals, which have been denied to the entreaties of a nation. For the meanest and most dependent instrument of this system knows, that there are hours when its existence may depend upon his adherence to it; and he takes his advantage accordingly. Indeed it is a law of nature, that whoever is necessary to what we have made our object, is sure in some way, or in some time or other, to become our master. All this however is submitted to, in order to avoid that monstrous evil of governing in concurrence with the opinion of the people. For it seems to be laid down as a maxim, that a King has some sort of interest in giving uneasiness to his subjects: that all who are pleasing to them, are to be of course disagreeable to him: that as soon as the persons who are odious at Court are known to be odious to the people, it is snatched at as a lucky occasion of showering down upon them all kinds of emolu-

---

[86] **mortifications** cf. *Letters of Junius* (ed. John Cannon, 1978) no. xxii on Bedford's treatment of the king, but for one example in detail, *Bedford Correspondence*, III, p. 289f and, for an exculpation by one rude through heredity rather than design, see Lord John Russell, *ibid.* p. 290n.; for George Grenville, see his own account of the king's complaints, *Grenville Papers*, II, p. 210.

[87] **present arrangement** of course it is arguable that Grenville, Pitt and Rockingham had become more distasteful to the king than Bedford, Grafton and North.

ments and honours. None are considered as well-wishers to the Crown, but those who advise to some unpopular course of action; none capable of serving it, but those who are obliged to call at every instant upon all its power for the safety of their lives. None are supposed to be fit priests in the temple of Government, but the persons who are compelled to fly into it for sanctuary. Such is the effect of this refined project; such is ever the result of all the contrivances which are used to free men from the servitude of their reason, and from the necessity of ordering their affairs according to their evident interests. These contrivances oblige them to run into a real and ruinous servitude, in order to avoid a supposed restraint that might be attended with advantage.

If therefore this system has so ill answered its own grand pretence of saving the King from the necessity of employing persons disagreeable to him, has it given more peace and tranquillity to his Majesty's private hours? No, most certainly. The father of his people cannot possibly enjoy repose, while his family is in such a state of distraction. Then what has the Crown or the King profited by all this fine-wrought scheme? Is he more rich, or more splendid, or more powerful, or more at his ease, by so many labours and contrivances? Have they not beggared his Exchequer, tarnished the splendor of his Court, sunk his dignity, galled his feelings, discomposed the whole order and happiness of his private life?

It will be very hard, I believe, to state in what respect the King has profited by that faction which presumptuously choose to call themselves *his friends*.

If particular men had grown into an attachment, by the distinguished honour of the society of their Sovereign; and, by being the partakers of his amusements,[88] came sometimes to prefer the gratification of his personal inclinations to the support of his high character, the thing would be very natural, and it would be excusable enough. But the pleasant part of the story is, that these *King's friends* have no more ground for usurping such a title, than a resident freeholder in Cumberland or in Cornwall. They are only known to their Sovereign by kissing his hand, for the offices, pensions, and grants, into which

[88] **his amusements** Bute is supposed to have met Frederick, Prince of Wales at a racecourse. Burke was not above suggesting that kings liked low company, *Speech on Oeconomical Reform*, W, II, p. 363; but see *Thoughts on French Affairs*, W, IV, p. 362, for a kinder interpretation of this propensity.

they have deceived his benignity. May no storm ever come, which will put the firmness of their attachment to the proof; and which, in the midst of confusions, and terrors, and sufferings, may demonstrate the eternal difference between a true and severe friend to the Monarchy, and a slippery sycophant of the Court! *Quantum infido scurrae distabit amicus.*[89]

So far I have considered the effect of the Court system, chiefly as it operates upon the executive Government, on the temper of the people, and on the happiness of the Sovereign. It remains, that we should consider, with a little attention, its operation upon Parliament.

Parliament was indeed the great object of all these politicks, the end at which they aimed, as well as the instrument by which they were to operate. But, before Parliament could be made subservient to a system, by which it was to be degraded from the dignity of a national council, into a mere member of the Court, it must be greatly changed from its original character.

In speaking of this body, I have my eye chiefly on the House of Commons. I hope I shall be indulged in a few observations on the nature and character of that assembly; not with regard to its *legal form and power*, but to its *spirit*, and to the purposes it is meant to answer in the constitution.

The House of Commons was supposed originally to be *no part of the standing Government of this country*. It was considered as a *controul*, issuing *immediately* from the people, and speedily to be resolved into the mass from whence it arose. In this respect it was in the higher part of Government what juries are in the lower.[90] The capacity of a magistrate being transitory, and that of a citizen permanent, the latter capacity it was hoped would of course preponderate in all discussions, not only between the people and the standing authority of the Crown, but between the people and the fleeting authority of the House of Commons itself. It was hoped that, being of a middle nature between subject and Government, they would feel with a more tender and a nearer interest every thing that concerned the people, than the other remoter and more permanent parts of Legislature.

---

[89] *Quantum . . . amicus* 'how a friend will differ from a faithless parasite' (Horace, *Epistles*, I.xviii.4).

[90] **what juries are in the lower** cf. *Annual Register* (1768), p. 268, where the decline of trial by jury on the continent is correlated with the decline of free government.

Whatever alterations time and the necessary accommodation of business may have introduced, this character can never be sustained, unless the House of Commons shall be made to bear some stamp of the actual disposition of the people at large. It would (among public misfortunes) be an evil more natural and tolerable, that the House of Commons should be infected with every epidemical phrensy of the people, as this would indicate some consanguinity, some sympathy of nature with their constituents, than that they should in all cases be wholly untouched by the opinions and feelings of the people out of doors. By this want of sympathy they would cease to be an House of Commons. For it is not the derivation of the power of that House from the people, which makes it in a distinct sense their representative. The King is the representative of the people; so are the Lords; so are the Judges. They all are trustees for the people, as well as the Commons; because no power is given for the sole sake of the holder; and although Government certainly is an institution of Divine authority, yet its forms, and the persons who administer it, all originate from the people.

A popular origin cannot therefore be the characteristical distinction of a popular representative. This belongs equally to all parts of Government, and in all forms. The virtue, spirit, and essence of a House of Commons consists in its being the express image[91] of the feelings of the nation. It was not instituted to be a controul *upon* the people, as of late it has been taught, by a doctrine of the most pernicious tendency. It was designed as a controul *for* the people. Other institutions have been formed for the purpose of checking popular excesses; and they are, I apprehend, fully adequate to their object. If not, they ought to be made so. The House of Commons, as it was never intended for the support of peace and subordination, is miserably appointed for that service; having no stronger weapon than its Mace, and no better officer than its Serjeant at Arms, which it can command of its own proper authority. A vigilant and jealous eye over executory and judicial magistracy; an anxious care of public money, an openness, approaching towards facility, to public complaint: these seem to be the true characteristics of an House of Commons. But an addressing House of Commons, and a petitioning nation;[92] an House

[91] **express image** Hebrews 1:3.
[92] **a petitioning nation** see Johnson, *The False Alarm* (1770) in *Political Writings*, pp. 55ff, for a rather less respectful account.

of Commons full of confidence, when the nation is plunged in despair; in the utmost harmony with Ministers, whom the people regard with the utmost abhorrence; who vote thanks, when the public opinion calls upon them for impeachments; who are eager to grant, when the general voice demands account; who, in all disputes between the people and Administration, presume against the people; who punish their disorders, but refuse even to enquire into the provocations to them; this is an unnatural, a monstrous state of things in this constitution. Such an Assembly may be a great, wise, awful Senate; but it is not to any popular purpose an House of Commons. This change from an immediate state of procuration and delegation to a course of acting as from original power, is the way in which all the popular magistracies in the world have been perverted from their purposes. It is indeed their greatest and sometimes their incurable corruption. For there is a material distinction between that corruption by which particular points are carried against reason (this is a thing which cannot be prevented by human wisdom, and is of less consequence) and the corruption of the principle itself. For then the evil is not accidental, but settled. The distemper becomes the natural habit.

For my part, I shall be compelled to conclude the principle of Parliament to be totally corrupted, and therefore its ends entirely defeated, when I see two symptoms: first, a rule of indiscriminate support to all Ministers; because this destroys their very end as a controul, and is a general previous sanction to misgovernment: and secondly, the setting up any claims adverse to the right of free election; for this tends to subvert the legal authority by which the Parliament sits.

I know that, since the Revolution, along with many dangerous, many useful powers of Government have been weakened. It is absolutely necessary to have frequent recourse to the Legislature. Parliaments must therefore sit every year, and for great part of the year. The dreadful disorders of frequent elections have also necessitated a septennial instead of a triennial duration.[93] These circumstances, I mean the constant habit of authority, and the unfrequency of elections, have tended very much to draw the House of Commons towards the character of a standing Senate. It is a disorder which has arisen from the cure of greater disorders; it has arisen from the

---

[93] **duration** the Septennial Act of 1716 lengthened the possible length of Parliament from three to seven years.

extreme difficulty of reconciling liberty under a monarchical Government, with external strength and with internal tranquillity.

It is very clear that we cannot free ourselves entirely from this great inconvenience; but I would not increase an evil, because I was not able to remove it; and because it was not in my power to keep the House of Commons religiously true to its first principles, I would not argue for carrying it to a total oblivion of them. This has been the great scheme of power in our time. They who will not conform their conduct to the public good, and cannot support it by the prerogative of the Crown, have adopted a new plan. They have totally abandoned the shattered and old-fashioned fortress of prerogative, and made a lodgement in the strong hold of Parliament itself. If they have any evil design to which there is no ordinary legal power commensurate, they bring it into Parliament. In Parliament the whole is executed from the beginning to the end. In Parliament the power of obtaining their object is absolute; and the safety in the proceeding perfect; no rules to confine, no after reckonings to terrify. Parliament cannot with any great propriety punish others, for things in which they themselves have been accomplices. Thus the controul of Parliament upon the executory power is lost; because Parliament is made to partake in every considerable act of Government. *Impeachment,*[94] *that great guardian of the purity of the Constitution, is in danger of being lost, even to the idea of it.*

By this plan several important ends are answered to the Cabal. If the authority of Parliament supports itself, the credit of every act of Government which they contrive, is saved; but if the act be so very odious that the whole strength of Parliament is insufficient to recommend it, then Parliament is itself discredited; and this discredit increases more and more that indifference to the constitution, which it is the constant aim of its enemies, by their abuse of Parliamentary powers, to render general among the people. Whenever Parliament is persuaded to assume the offices of executive Government, it will lose all the confidence, love, and veneration, which it has ever enjoyed whilst it was supposed the *corrective and controul* of the acting powers of the State. This would be the event, though its conduct in such a

---

[94] *Impeachment* before 1770 the last had been made in 1747 against Lord Lovat for treason and in 1725 against Lord Chancellor Macclesfield for corruption. Burke later employed it against Hastings, with a negligible impact on the constitution.

perversion of its functions should be tolerably just and moderate; but if it should be iniquitous, violent, full of passion, and full of faction, it would be considered as the most intolerable of all the modes of tyranny.

For a considerable time this separation of the representatives from their constituents went on with a silent progress; and had those, who conducted the plan for their total separation, been persons of temper and abilities any way equal to the magnitude of their design, the success would have been infallible: but by their precipitancy they have laid it open in all its nakedness; the nation is alarmed at it; and the event may not be pleasant to the contrivers of the scheme. In the last session, the corps called the *King's friends* made an hardy attempt all at once, *to alter the right of election*[95] *itself;* to put it into the power of the House of Commons to disable any person disagreeable to them from sitting in Parliament, without any other rule than their own pleasure; to make incapacities, either general for descriptions of men, or particular for individuals; and to take into their body, persons who avowedly had never been chosen by the majority of legal electors, nor agreeably to any known rule of law.

The arguments upon which this claim was founded and combated, are not my business here. Never has a subject been more amply and more learnedly handled,[96] nor upon one side in my opinion more satisfactorily;[97] they who are not convinced by what is already written would not receive conviction *though one arose from the dead.*

I too have thought on this subject: but my purpose here, is only to consider it as a part of the favourite project of Government; to observe on the motives which led to it; and to trace its political consequences.

A violent rage for the punishment of Mr Wilkes was the pretence of the whole. This gentleman, by setting himself strongly in opposition

---

[95] **the right of election** i.e. in seating Colonel Luttrell as member for Middlesex instead of Wilkes. Wilkes was properly elected in 1768, but expelled in February, 1769 for disseminating seditious and obscene libels. He was re-elected and re-ejected three times. Luttrell was then induced to stand against him. He obtained 296 votes to Wilkes' 1,143. Wilkes was returned, but in April the Commons declared Luttrell elected.

[96] **learnedly handled** see Grenville's speech, 3 Feb. 1769 (PH, xvi 546); *Annual Register* (1769), e.g. pp. 197–8; Anon., *An Enquiry into the Doctrine of Libels* (1769).

[97] **more satisfactorily** perhaps a compliment to William Dowdeswell, on his *The Sentiments of an English Freeholder* (1769).

to the Court Cabal, had become at once an object of their persecution, and of the popular favour. The hatred of the Court Party pursuing, and the countenance of the people protecting him, it very soon became not at all a question on the man, but a trial of strength between the two parties. The advantage of the victory in this particular contest was the present, but not the only, nor by any means the principal, object. Its operation upon the character of the House of Commons was the great point of view. The point to be gained by the Cabal was this; that a precedent should be established, tending to shew, *That the favour of the People was not so sure a road as the favour of the Court even to popular honours and popular trusts.* A strenuous resistance to every appearance of lawless power; a spirit of independence carried to some degree of enthusiasm; an inquisitive character to discover, and a bold one to display, every corruption and every error of Government; these are the qualities which recommend a man to a seat in the House of Commons, in open and merely popular elections. An indolent and submissive disposition; a disposition to think charitably of all the actions of men in power, and to live in a mutual intercourse of favours with them; an inclination rather to countenance a strong use of authority, than to bear any sort of licentiousness on the part of the people; these are unfavourable qualities in an open election for Members of Parliament.

The instinct which carries the people towards the choice of the former, is justified by reason; because a man of such a character, even in its exorbitancies, does not directly contradict the purposes of a trust, the end of which is a controul on power. The latter character, even when it is not in its extreme, will execute this trust but very imperfectly; and, if deviating to the least excess, will certainly frustrate instead of forwarding the purposes of a controul on Government. But when the House of Commons was to be new modelled, this principle was not only to be changed, but reversed. Whilst any errours committed in support of power were left to the law, with every advantage of favourable construction, of mitigation, and finally of pardon; all excesses on the side of liberty, or in pursuit of popular favour, or in defence of popular rights and privileges, were not only to be punished by the rigour of the known law, but by a *discretionary* proceeding which brought on *the loss of the popular object itself.* Popularity was to be rendered, if not directly penal, at least highly dangerous. The favour of the people might lead even to a disqualification of representing them. Their odium might become, strained through the medium of two or three constructions, the means of sitting as the trustee of all that was dear to them. This is punishing the offence in the offending part. Until this time, the opinion of the people, through the power of an Assembly, still in some sort popular, led to the greatest honours and emoluments in the gift of the Crown. Now the principle is reversed; and the favour of the Court is the only sure way of obtaining and holding those honours which ought to be in the disposal of the people.

It signifies very little how this matter may be quibbled away. Example, the only argument of effect in civil life, demonstrates the truth of my proposition. Nothing can alter my opinion concerning the pernicious tendency of this example, until I see some man for his indiscretion in the support of power, for his violent and intemperate servility, rendered incapable of sitting in Parliament. For as it now stands, the fault of overstraining popular qualities, and, irregularly if you please, asserting popular privileges, has led to disqualification; the opposite fault never has produced the slightest punishment. Resistance to power, has shut the door of the House of Commons to one man; obsequiousness and servility, to none.

Not that I would encourage popular disorder, or any disorder. But I would leave such offences to the law, to be punished in measure and proportion. The laws of this country are for the most part constituted, and wisely so, for the general ends of Government, rather than for the preservation of our particular liberties. Whatever therefore is done in support of liberty, by persons not in public trust, or not acting merely in that trust, is liable to be more or less out of the ordinary course of the law; and the law itself is sufficient to animadvert upon it with great severity. Nothing indeed can hinder that severe letter from crushing us, except the temperaments it may receive from a trial by jury. But if the habit prevails of *going beyond the law*, and superseding this judicature, of carrying offences, real or supposed, into the legislative bodies, who shall establish themselves into *courts of criminal equity* (so the *Star Chamber*[98] has been called by Lord Bacon), all the evils of the *Star Chamber* are revived. A large and liberal construction in ascertaining offences, and a discretionary power in punishing them, is

---

[98] **Star Chamber** the highest secular court of prerogative under the Tudors and Stuarts was abolished in 1641. For Bacon, see his *History of Henry VII*.

the idea of *criminal equity*; which is in truth a monster in Jurisprudence. It signifies nothing whether a court for this purpose be a Committee of Council, or an House of Commons, or an House of Lords; the liberty of the subject will be equally subverted by it. The true end and purpose of that House of Parliament which entertains such a jurisdiction will be destroyed by it.

I will not believe, what no other man living believes, that Mr Wilkes was punished for the indecency of his publications, or the impiety of his ransacked closet. If he had fallen in a common slaughter of libellers and blasphemers, I could well believe that nothing more was meant than was pretended. But when I see that, for years together, full as impious, and perhaps more dangerous writings to religion and virtue and order, have not been punished, nor their authors discountenanced; that the most audacious libels on Royal Majesty have passed without notice; that the most treasonable invectives against the laws, liberties, and constitution of the country, have not met with the slightest animadversion; I must consider this as a shocking and shameless pretence. Never did an envenomed scurrility against every thing sacred and civil, public and private, rage through the kingdom with such a furious and unbridled licence. All this while the peace of the nation must be shaken, to ruin one libeller, and to tear from the populace a single favourite.

Nor is it that vice merely skulks in an obscure and contemptible impunity. Does not the publick behold with indignation, persons not only generally scandalous in their lives, but the identical persons who, by their society, their instruction, their example, their encouragement, have drawn this man into the very faults[99] which have furnished the Cabal with a pretence for his persecution, loaded with every kind of favour, honour and distinction which a Court can bestow? Add but the crime of servility (the *foedum crimen servitutis*)[100] to every other crime, and the whole mass is immediately transmuted into virtue, and becomes the just subject of reward and honour. When therefore I reflect upon this method pursued by the Cabal in distributing rewards and punishments, I must conclude that Mr Wilkes is the object of

[99] **the very faults** Wilkes had earlier been a companion of Dashwood, Bute's chancellor of the exchequer, in the Medmenham Club. Another member, Lord Sandwich had laid a complaint in the Lords against Wilkes' obscene writings. Sandwich was first lord of the Admiralty from 1771.

[100] *foedum crimen servitutis* 'the imputation of servility' (Tacitus *Histories*, I.1).

persecution, not on account of what he has done in common with others who are the objects of reward, but for that in which he differs from many of them: that he is pursued for the spirited dispositions which are blended with his vices; for his unconquerable firmness, for his resolute, indefatigable, strenuous resistance against oppression.

In this case, therefore, it was not the man that was to be punished, nor his faults that were to be discountenanced. Opposition to acts of power was to be marked by a kind of civil proscription. The popularity which should arise from such an opposition was to be shewn unable to protect it. The qualities by which court is made to the people, were to render every fault inexpiable, and every error irretrievable. The qualities by which court is made to power, were to cover and to sanctify every thing. He that will have a sure and honourable seat in the House of Commons, must take care how he adventures to cultivate popular qualities; otherwise he may remember the old maxim, *Breves et infaustos populi Romani amores.*[101] If, therefore, a pursuit of popularity expose a man to greater dangers than a disposition to servility, the principle which is the life and soul of popular elections will perish out of the constitution.

It behoves the people of England to consider how the House of Commons under the operation of these examples must of necessity be constituted. On the side of the Court will be, all honours, offices, emoluments; every sort of personal gratification to avarice or vanity; and, what is of more moment to most gentlemen, the means of growing, by innumerable petty services to individuals, into a spreading interest in their country. On the other hand, let us suppose a person unconnected with the Court, and in opposition to its system. For his own person, no office, or emolument, or title; no promotion, ecclesiastical, or civil, or military, or naval, for children, or brothers, or kindred. In vain an expiring interest in a borough calls for offices, or small livings, for the children of mayors, and aldermen, and capital burgesses. His Court rival has them all. He can do an infinite number of acts of generosity and kindness, and even of public spirit. He can procure indemnity from quarters. He can procure advantages in trade. He can get pardons for offences.[102] He can obtain a thousand

---

[101] **breves et infaustos . . .** 'shortlived and ill-starred are the darlings of the Roman people' (Tacitus, *Annals,* II.41).

[102] **offences** i.e. privileges in customs and excise, royal pardons for criminals and freedom from the quartering of troops.

favours, and avert a thousand evils. He may, while he betrays every valuable interest of the kingdom, be a benefactor, a patron, a father, a guardian angel, to his borough. The unfortunate independent member has nothing to offer but harsh refusal, or pitiful excuse, or despondent representation of an hopeless interest. Except from his private fortune, in which he may be equalled, perhaps exceeded, by his Court competitor, he has no way of shewing any one good quality, or of making a single friend. In the House, he votes for ever in a dispirited minority. If he speaks, the doors are locked.[103] A body of loquacious placemen go out to tell the world, that all he aims at, is to get into office. If he has not the talent of elocution, which is the case of many as wise and knowing men as any in the House, he is liable to all these inconveniences, without the eclat which attends upon any tolerably successful exertion of eloquence. Can we conceive a more discouraging post of duty than this? Strip it of the poor reward of popularity; suffer even the excesses committed in defence of the popular interest, to become a ground for the majority of that House to form a disqualification out of the line of the law, and at their pleasure, attended not only with the loss of the franchise, but with every kind of personal disgrace. – If this shall happen, the people of this kingdom may be assured that they cannot be firmly or faithfully served by any man. It is out of the nature of men and things that they should; and their presumption will be equal to their folly, if they expect it. The power of the people, within the laws, must shew itself sufficient to protect every representative in the animated performance of his duty, or that duty cannot be performed. The House of Commons can never be a controul on other parts of Government unless they are controuled themselves by their constituents; and unless these constituents possess some right in the choice of that House, which it is not in the power of that House to take away. If they suffer this power of arbitrary incapacitation to stand, they have utterly perverted every other power of the House of Commons. The late proceeding, I will not say, *is* contrary to law; it *must* be so; for the power which is claimed cannot, by any possibility, be a legal power in any limited member of Government.

The power which they claim, of declaring incapacities, would not

---

[103] **doors are locked**   any MP could ask to have the gallery of the House cleared and the doors locked, a device often used to deprive the opposition of a public hearing.

be above the just claims of a final judicature, if they had not laid it down as a leading principle, that they had no rule in the exercise of this claim, but their own *discretion*. Not one of their abettors has ever undertaken to assign the principle of unfitness, the species or degree of delinquency, on which the House of Commons will expel, nor the mode of proceeding upon it, nor the evidence upon which it is established. The direct consequence of which is, that the first franchise of an Englishman, and that on which all the rest vitally depend, is to be forfeited for some offence which no man knows, and which is to be proved by no known rule whatsoever of legal evidence. This is so anomalous to our whole constitution, that I will venture to say, the most trivial right which the subject claims, never was, nor can be, forfeited in such a manner.

The whole of their usurpation is established upon this method of arguing. We do not *make* laws. No; we do not contend for this power. We only *declare* law; and, as we are a tribunal both competent and supreme, what we declare to be law becomes law, although it should not have been so before. Thus the circumstance of having no *appeal* from their jurisdiction is made to imply that they have no *rule* in the exercise of it; the judgement does not derive its validity from its conformity to the law; but preposterously the law is made to attend on the judgement; and the rule of the judgement is no other than the *occasional will of the House*. An arbitrary discretion leads, legality follows; which is just the very nature and description of a legislative act.

This claim in their hands was no barren theory. It was pursued into its utmost consequences; and a dangerous principle has begot a correspondent practice. A systematic spirit has been shewn upon both sides. The electors of Middlesex chose a person whom the House of Commons had voted incapable; and the House of Commons has taken in a member whom the electors of Middlesex had not chosen. By a construction on that legislative power which had been assumed, they declared that the true legal sense of the country was contained in the minority, on that occasion; and might, on a resistance to a vote of incapacity, be contained in any minority.

When any construction of law goes against the spirit of the privilege it was meant to support, it is a vicious construction. It is material to us to be represented really and *bona fide*, and not in forms, in types, and shadows, and fictions of law. The right of election was not established merely as a *matter of form*, to satisfy some method and rule of technical reasoning; it was not a principle which might substitute a *Titius* or a *Maevius*, a *John Doe* or *Richard Roe*,[104] in the place of a man specially chosen; not a principle which was just as well satisfied with one man as with another. It is a right, the effect of which is to give to the people, that man, and *that man only*, whom by their voices, actually, not constructively given, they declare that they know, esteem, love, and trust. This right is a matter within their own power of judging and feeling; not an *ens rationis*[105] and creature of law: nor can those devices, by which any thing else is substituted in the place of such an actual choice, answer in the least degree the end of representation.

I know that the courts of law have made as strained constructions[106] in other cases. Such is the construction in common recoveries. The method of construction which in that case gives to the persons in remainder, for their security and representative, the door-keeper, cryer, or sweeper of the Court, or some other shadowy being without substance or effect, is a fiction of a very coarse texture. This was however suffered, by the acquiescence of the whole kingdom, for ages; because the evasion of the old statute of Westminster,[107] which authorized perpetuities, had more sense and utility than the law which was evaded. But an attempt to turn the right of election into such a farce and mockery as a fictitious fine and recovery, will, I hope, have another fate; because the laws which give it are infinitely dear to us, and the evasion is infinitely contemptible.

The people indeed have been told, that this power of discretionary disqualification is vested in hands that they may trust, and who will be sure not to abuse it to their prejudice. Until I find something in this argument differing from that on which every mode of despotism has been defended, I shall not be inclined to pay it any great compliment. The people are satisfied to trust themselves with the exercise of their

---

[104] *Titius . . . Richard Roe*   Burke lists the fictitious parties to actions at Roman and English law.

[105] *ens rationis*   that which is conceived to be before it is realized.

[106] **strained constructions**   refers to the method of barring entails by levying a fine and suffering a recovery, abolished in the 1830s.

[107] **statute of Westminster**   i.e. the Second Statute, 1285. 'Common recoveries' were practised in order to evade its provisions, which enacted that the holder of an estate had only a life interest in it, which, if his children were not alive at his decease, reverted to the original grantor of the estate. Power of entail was created thereby and the possessor's right of alienation curtailed. 'Sense and utility' pointed in another direction; a direct method of disentailing was substituted in the reign of William IV.

own privileges, and do not desire this kind intervention of the House of Commons to free them from the burthen. They are certainly in the right. They ought not to trust the House of Commons with a power over their franchises: because the constitution, which placed two other coordinate powers to controul it, reposed no such confidence in that body. It were a folly well deserving servitude for its punishment, to be full of confidence where the laws are full of distrust; and to give to an House of Commons, arrogating to its sole resolution the most harsh and odious part of legislative authority, that degree of submission which is due only to the Legislature itself.

When the House of Commons, in an endeavour to obtain new advantages at the expence of the other orders of the State, for the benefit of the *Commons at large*, have pursued strong measures; if it were not just, it was at least natural, that the constituents should connive at all their proceedings; because we were ourselves ultimately to profit. But when this submission is urged to us, in a contest between the representatives and ourselves, and where nothing can be put into their scale which is not taken from ours, they fancy us to be children when they tell us they are our representatives, our own flesh and blood, and that all the stripes they give us are for our good. The very desire of that body to have such a trust contrary to law reposed in them, shews that they are not worthy of it. They certainly will abuse it; because all men possessed of an uncontrouled discretionary power leading to the aggrandisement and profit of their own body have always abused it: and I see no particular sanctity in our times, that is at all likely, by a miraculous operation, to overrule the course of nature.

But we must purposely shut our eyes, if we consider this matter merely as a contest between the House of Commons and the Electors. The true contest is between the Electors of the kingdom and the Crown; the Crown acting by an instrumental House of Commons. It is precisely the same, whether the Ministers of the Crown can disqualify by a dependent House of Commons, or by a dependent court of *Star Chamber*, or by a dependent court of King's Bench. [108] If once Members of Parliament can be practically convinced, that they do not depend on the affection or opinion of the people for their political being; they will give themselves over, without even an appearance of reserve, to the influence of the Court.

[108] **court of King's Bench**   this had outlawed Wilkes in his absence.

Indeed, a Parliament unconnected with the people, is essential to a Ministry unconnected with the people; and therefore those who saw through what mighty difficulties the interior Ministry waded, and the exterior were dragged, in this business, will conceive of what prodigious importance, the new corps of *King's men* held this principle of occasional and personal incapacitation, to the whole body of their design.

When the House of Commons was thus made to consider itself as the master of its constituents, there wanted but one thing to secure that House against all possible future deviation towards popularity; an *unlimited* fund of money to be laid out according to the pleasure of the Court.

To compleat the scheme of bringing our Court to a resemblance to the neighbouring Monarchies, it was necessary, in effect, to destroy those appropriations of revenue, which seem to limit the property, as the other laws had done the powers, of the Crown. An opportunity for this purpose was taken, upon an application to Parliament for payment of the debts of the Civil List; which in 1769 had amounted to 513,000*l*.[109] Such applications had been made upon former occasions; but to do it in the former manner would by no means answer the present purpose.

Whenever the Crown had come to the Commons to desire a supply for the discharging of debts due on the Civil List; it was always asked and granted with one of the three following qualifications; sometimes with all of them. Either it was stated, that the revenue has been diverted from its puposes by Parliament: or that those duties had fallen short of the sum for which they were given by Parliament, and the intention of the Legislature had not been fulfilled: or that the money required to discharge the Civil List Debt, was to be raised chargeable on the Civil List duties. In the reign of Queen Anne, the Crown was found in debt. The lessening and granting away some part of her revenue by Parliament was alledged as the cause of that debt, and pleaded as an equitable ground, such it certainly was, for discharging it. It does not appear that the duties which were then applied to the ordinary Government produced clear above 580,000*l*. a year; because, when they were afterwards granted to George the First,

---

[109] **Civil List**   the precise sum was £513,511 (PH, XVI, 598). For the whole subject, see E. A. Reitan, 'The Civil List in Eighteenth-Century British Politics', *Historical Journal*, 9 (1966), pp. 318–37.

120,000*l.* was added, to complete the whole to 700,000*l.* a year. Indeed it was then asserted, and, I have no doubt, truely, that for many years the net produce did not amount to above 550,000*l.* The Queen's extraordinary charges were besides very considerable; equal, at least, to any we have known in our time. The application to Parliament was not for an absolute grant of money; but to empower the Queen to raise it by borrowing upon the Civil List funds.

The Civil List debt was twice paid in the reign of George the First. The money was granted upon the same plan which had been followed in the reign of Queen Anne. The Civil List revenues were then mortgaged for the sum to be raised, and stood charged with the ransom of their own deliverance.

George the Second received an addition to his Civil List. Duties were granted for the purpose of raising 800,000*l.* a year. It was not until he had reigned nineteen years, and after the last rebellion, that he called upon Parliament for a discharge of the Civil List debt. The extraordinary charges brought on by the rebellion, account fully for the necessities of the Crown. However, the extraordinary charges of Government were not thought a ground fit to be relied on.

A deficiency of the Civil List duties for several years before, was stated as the principal, if not the whole ground on which an application to Parliament could be justified. About this time the produce of these duties had fallen pretty low, and even upon an average of the whole reign they never produced 800,000*l.* a year clear to the Treasury.

That Prince reigned fourteen years afterwards: not only no new demands were made; but with so much good order were his revenues and expences regulated, that, although many parts of the establishment of the Court were upon a larger and more liberal scale than they have been since, there was a considerable sum in hand, on his decease, amounting to about 170,000*l.* applicable to the service of the Civil List of his present Majesty. So that, if this Reign commenced with a greater charge than usual, there was enough, and more than enough, abundantly to supply all the extraordinary expence. That the Civil List should have been exceeded in the two former reigns, especially in the reign of George the First, was not at all surprizing. His revenue was but 700,000*l.* annually; if it ever produced so much clear. The prodigious and dangerous disaffection to the very being of the establishment, and the cause of a Pretender then powerfully abetted from abroad, produced many demands of an extraordinary nature both abroad and at home. Much management and great expences were necessary. But the throne of no Prince has stood upon more unshaken foundations than that of his present Majesty.

To have exceeded the sum given for the Civil List, and to have incurred a debt without special authority of Parliament, was, *prima facie*, a criminal act: as such, Ministers ought naturally rather to have withdrawn it from the inspection, than to have exposed it to the scrutiny, of Parliament. Certainly they ought, of themselves, officiously to have come armed with every sort of argument, which, by explaining, could excuse, a matter in itself of presumptive guilt. But the terrors of the House of Commons are no longer for Ministers.

On the other hand, the peculiar character of the House of Commons, as trustee of the public purse, would have led them to call with a punctilious solicitude for every public account, and to have examined into them with the most rigorous accuracy.

The capital use of an account is, that the reality of the charge, the reason of incurring it, and the justice and necessity of discharging it, should all appear antecedent to the payment. No man ever pays first, and calls for his account afterwards; because he would thereby let out of his hands the principal, and indeed only effectual, means of compelling a full and fair one. But, in national business, there is an additional reason for a previous production of every account. It is a check, perhaps the only one, upon a corrupt and prodigal use of public money. An account after payment is to no rational purpose an account. However, the House of Commons thought all these to be antiquated principles; they were of opinion, that the most Parliamentary way of proceeding was, to pay first what the Court thought proper to demand, and to take its chance for an examination into accounts at some time of greater leisure.

The nation had settled 800,000*l.* a year on the Crown, as sufficient for the support of its dignity, upon the estimate of its own Ministers. When Ministers came to Parliament, and said that this allowance had not been sufficient for the purpose, and that they had incurred a debt of 500,000*l.* would it not have been natural for Parliament first to have asked, how, and by what means, their appropriated allowance came to be insufficient? Would it not have savoured of some attention to justice, to have seen in what periods of Administration this debt had been originally incurred? that they might discover, and, if need were, animadvert on the persons who were found the most culpable? To put their hands upon such articles of expenditure as they thought improper or excessive, and to secure, in future, against such misapplication or exceeding? Accounts for any other purposes are but a matter of curiosity, and no genuine Parliamentary object. All the accounts which could answer any of these purposes were refused, or postponed by previous questions. Every idea of prevention was rejected, as conveying an improper suspicion of the Ministers of the Crown.

When every leading account had been refused, many others were granted with sufficient facility.

But with great candour also, the House was informed, that hardly any of them could be ready until the next session; some of them perhaps not so soon. But, in order firmly to establish the precedent of *payment previous to account*, and to form it into a settled rule of the House, the god in the machine[110] was brought down, nothing less than the wonder-working *Law of Parliament*. It was alledged, that it is the law of Parliament, when any demand comes from the Crown, that the House must go immediately into the Committee of Supply; in which Committee it was allowed, that the production and examination of accounts would be quite proper and regular. It was therefore carried, that they should go into the Committee without delay, and without accounts, in order to examine with great order and regularity things that could not possibly come before them. After this stroke of orderly and Parliamentary wit and humour, they went into the Committee; and very generously voted the payment.

There was a circumstance in that debate too remarkable to be overlooked. This debt of the Civil List was all along argued upon the same footing as a debt of the State, contracted upon national authority. Its payment was urged as equally pressing upon the public faith and honour: and when the whole year's account was stated, in what is called *The Budget*, the Ministry valued themselves on the payment of so much public debt, just as if they had discharged 500,000*l.* of navy or exchequer bills.[111] Though, in truth, their payment, from the Sinking Fund, of debt which was never contracted by Parliamentary authority, was, to all intents and purposes, so much debt incurred. But

---

[110] **god in the machine** more usually quoted as the Latin *Deus ex machina* i.e. an unexpected intervention to resolve a situation.
[111] **navy or exchequer bills** were securities for raising cash to finance the public services, cf. Adam Smith, *Wealth of Nations*, v.iii.11.

such is the present notion of public credit, and payment of debt. No wonder that it produces such effects.

Nor was the House at all more attentive to a provident security against future, than it had been to a vindictive retrospect to past, mismanagements. I should have thought indeed that a Ministerial promise, during their own continuance in office, might have been given, though this would have been but a poor security for the publick. Mr Pelham gave such an assurance, and he kept his word.[112] But nothing was capable of extorting from our Ministers any thing which had the least resemblance to a promise of confining the expences of the Civil List within the limits which had been settled by Parliament. This reserve of theirs I look upon to be equivalent to the clearest declaration, that they were resolved upon a contrary course.

However, to put the matter beyond all doubt, in the Speech from the Throne, after thanking Parliament for the relief so liberally granted, the Ministers inform the two Houses, that they will *endeavour* to confine the expences of the Civil Government – within what limits think you? those which the law had prescribed? Not in the least – 'such limits as the *honour of the Crown* can possibly admit.'[113]

Thus they established an *arbitrary* standard for that dignity which Parliament had defined and limited to a *legal* standard. They gave themselves, under the lax and indeterminate idea of the *honour of the Crown*, a full loose for all manner of dissipation, and all manner of corruption. This arbitrary standard they were not afraid to hold out to both Houses; while an idle and unoperative Act of Parliament, estimating the dignity of the Crown at 800,000*l.* and confining it to that sum, adds to the number of obsolete statutes which load the shelves of libraries without any sort of advantage to the people.

After this proceeding, I suppose that no man can be so weak as to think that the Crown is limited to any settled allowance whatsoever. For if the Ministry has 800,000*l.* a year by the law of the land; and if by the law of Parliament all the debts which exceed it are to be paid previous to the production of any account; I presume that this is equivalent to an income with no other limits than the abilities of the subject and the moderation of the Court; that is to say, it is such an income as is possessed by every absolute Monarch in Europe. It

---

[12] **kept his word** history does not relate if this be true.
[13] **can . . . admit** a paraphrase of the speech of 9 May 1769 (CJ, XXXII, 453).

amounts, as a person of great ability said in the debate, to an unlimited power of drawing upon the Sinking Fund. Its effect on the public credit of this kingdom must be obvious; for in vain is the Sinking Fund the great buttress of all the rest, if it be in the power of the Ministry to resort to it for the payment of any debts which they may choose to incur, under the name of the Civil List, and through the medium of a Committee, which thinks itself obliged by law to vote supplies without any other account than that of the mere existence of the debt.

Five hundred thousand pounds is a serious sum. But it is nothing to the prolific principle upon which the sum was voted; a principle that may be well called, *the fruitful mother of an hundred more.* Neither is the damage to public credit of very great consequence, when compared with that which results to public morals and to the safety of the constitution, from the exhaustless mine of corruption opened by the precedent, and to be wrought by the principle, of the late payment of the debts of the Civil List. The power of discretionary disqualification by one law of Parliament, and the necessity of paying every debt of the Civil List by another law of Parliament, if suffered to pass unnoticed, must establish such a fund of rewards and terrors as will make Parliament the best appendage and support of arbitrary power that ever was invented by the wit of man. This is felt. The quarrel is begun between the Representatives and the People. The Court faction have at length committed them.

In such a strait the wisest may well be perplexed, and the boldest staggered. The circumstances are in a great measure new. We have hardly any land-marks from the wisdom of our ancestors, to guide us. At best we can only follow the spirit of their proceeding in other cases. I know the diligence with which my observations on our public disorders have been made; I am very sure of the integrity of the motives on which they are published: I cannot be equally confident in any plan for the absolute cure of those disorders, or for their certain future prevention. My aim is to bring this matter into more public discussion. Let the sagacity of others work upon it. It is not uncommon for medical writers to describe histories of diseases very accurately, on whose cure they can say but very little.

The first ideas which generally suggest themselves, for the cure of Parliamentary disorders, are, to shorten the duration of Parliaments;[114] and to disqualify all, or a great number of placemen, from a seat in the House of Commons.[115] Whatever efficacy there may in those remedies, I am sure in the present state of things it is impossible to apply them. A restoration of the right of free election is a preliminary indispensable to every other reformation. What alterations ought afterwards to be made in the constitution, is a matter of deep and difficult research.

If I wrote merely to please the popular palate, it would indeed be as little troublesome to me as to another, to extol these remedies, so famous in speculation, but to which their greatest admirers have never attempted seriously to resort in practice. I confess then, that I have no sort of reliance upon either a Triennial Parliament, or a Place-bill. With regard to the former, perhaps it might rather serve to counter-act, than to promote the ends that are proposed by it. To say nothing of the horrible disorders among the people attending frequent elections, I should be fearful of committing, every three years, the independent gentlemen of the country into a contest with the Treasury. It is easy to see which of the contending parties would be ruined first. Whoever has taken a careful view of public proceedings, so as to endeavour to ground his speculations on his experience, must have observed how prodigiously greater the power of Ministry is in the first and last session of a Parliament, than it is in the intermediate period, when Members sit a little firm on the seats. The persons of the greatest Parliamentary experience, with whom I have conversed, did constantly, in canvassing the fate of questions, allow something to the Court-side, upon account of the elections depending or imminent. The evil complained of, if it exists in the present state of things, would hardly be removed by a triennial Parliament: for, unless the influence of Government in elections can be entirely taken away, the more frequently they return, the more they will harrass private independence; the more generally men will be compelled to fly to the

---

[114] **duration of Parliaments**   the demands for the shortening of Parliament contained in the annual motions of Alderman Sawbridge. Catherine Macaulay, *Observations on a Pamphlet, entitled, Thoughts on the Cause of the Present Discontents* (1770) p. 25, suggests triennial parliaments and a rotation of members.

[115] **Commons**   the increase of offices under William III led to a place bill in 1693, proposing that no placeman should be allowed to sit in the Commons, and to an Act of 1705, which stated that the holder of any office created after 25 October must be excluded from Parliament and that any member of the House accepting any existing office of profit must vacate his seat and stand for re-election.

settled, systematic interest of Government, and to the resources of a boundless Civil List. Certainly something may be done, and ought to be done, towards lessening that influence in elections; and this will be necessary upon a plan either of longer or shorter duration of Parliament. But nothing can so perfectly remove the evil, as not to render such contentions, too frequently repeated, utterly ruinous, first to independence of fortune, and then to independence of spirit. As I am only giving an opinion on this point, and not at all debating it in an adverse line, I hope I may be excused in another observation. With great truth I may aver, that I never remember to have talked on this subject with any man much conversant with public business, who considered short Parliaments as a real improvement of the constitution. Gentlemen, warm in a popular cause, are ready enough to attribute all the declarations of such persons to corrupt motives. But the habit of affairs, if, on one hand, it tends to corrupt the mind, furnishes it, on the other, with the means of better information. The authority of such persons will always have some weight. It may stand upon a par with the speculations of those who are less practised in business; and who, with perhaps purer intentions, have not so effectual means of judging. It is, besides, an effect of vulgar and puerile malignity to imagine, that every Statesman is of course corrupt; and that his opinion, upon every constitutional point, is solely formed upon some sinister interest.

The next favourite remedy is a Place-bill. The same principle guides in both; I mean, the opinion which is entertained by many, of the infallibility of laws and regulations, in the cure of public distempers. Without being as unreasonably doubtful as many are unwisely confident, I will only say, that this also is a matter very well worthy of serious and mature reflexion. It is not easy to foresee, what the effect would be, of disconnecting with Parliament, the greatest part of those who hold civil employments, and of such mighty and important bodies as the military and naval establishments. It were better, perhaps, that they should have a corrupt interest in the forms of the constitution, than that they should have none at all. This is a question altogether different from the disqualification of a particular description of Revenue Officers from seats in Parliament; or, perhaps, of all the lower sorts of them from votes in elections.[116] In

---

[116] **votes in elections**   in 1782, Rockingham's second ministry succeeded in carrying such a measure.

the former case, only the few are affected; in the latter, only the inconsiderable. But a great official, a great professional, a great military and naval interest, all necessarily comprehending many people of the first weight, ability, wealth, and spirit, has been gradually formed in the kingdom. These new interests must be let into a share of representation, else possibly they may be inclined to destroy those institutions of which they are not permitted to partake. This is not a thing to be trifled with; nor is it every well-meaning man, that is fit to put his hands to it. Many other serious considerations occur. I do not open them here, because they are not directly to my purpose; proposing only to give the reader some taste of the difficulties that attend all capital changes in the constitution; just to hint the uncertainty, to say no worse, of preventing the Court, as long as it has the means of influence abundantly in its power, of applying that influence to Parliament; and perhaps, if the public method were precluded, of doing it in some worse and more dangerous method. Underhand and oblique ways would be studied. The science of evasion, already tolerably understood, would then be brought to the greatest perfection. It is no inconsiderable part of wisdom, to know how much of an evil ought to be tolerated; lest, by attempting a degree of purity impracticable in degenerate times and manners, instead of cutting off the subsisting ill practices, new corruptions might be produced for the concealment and security of the old. It were better, undoubtedly, that no influence at all could affect the mind of a Member of Parliament. But of all modes of influence, in my opinion, a place under the Government is the least disgraceful to the man who holds it, and by far the most safe to the country. I would not shut out that sort of influence which is open and visible, which is connected with the dignity and the service of the State, when it is not in my power to prevent the influence of contracts, of subscriptions, of direct bribery, and those innumerable methods of clandestine corruption, which are abundantly in the hands of the Court, and which will be applied as long as these means of corruption, and the disposition to be corrupted, have existence amongst us. Our constitution stands on a nice equipoise, with steep precipices, and deep waters upon all sides of it. In removing it from a dangerous leaning towards one side, there may be a risque of oversetting it on the other. Every project of a material change in a Government so complicated as ours, combined at the same time with external circumstances still more complicated, is a matter full of difficulties; in which a considerate man will not be too ready to decide; a prudent man too ready to undertake; or an honest man too ready to promise. They do not respect the publick nor themselves, who engage for more, than they are sure that they ought to attempt, or that they are able to perform. These are my sentiments, weak perhaps, but honest and unbiassed; and submitted entirely to the opinion of grave men, well affected to the constitution of their country, and of experience in what may best promote or hurt it.

Indeed, in the situation in which we stand, with an immense revenue, an enormous debt, mighty establishments, Government itself a great banker and a great merchant, I see no other way for the preservation of a decent attention to public interest in the Representatives, but *the interposition of the body of the people itself*, whenever it shall appear, by some flagrant and notorious act, by some capital innovation, that these Representatives are going to over-leap the fences of the law, and to introduce an arbitrary power. This interposition is a most unpleasant remedy. But, if it be a legal remedy, it is intended on some occasion to be used; to be used then only, when it is evident that nothing else can hold the constitution to its true principles.

The distempers of Monarchy were the great subjects of apprehension and redress, in the last century; in this, the distempers of Parliament. It is not in Parliament alone that the remedy for Parliamentary disorders can be compleated; hardly indeed can it begin there. Until a confidence in Government is re-established, the people ought to be excited to a more strict and detailed attention to the conduct of their Representatives. Standards, for judging more systematically upon their conduct, ought to be settled in the meetings of counties and corporations. Frequent and correct lists of the voters in all important questions ought to be procured.

By such means something may be done. By such means it may appear who those are, that, by an indiscriminate support of all Administrations, have totally banished all integrity and confidence out of public proceedings; have confounded the best men with the worst; and weakened and dissolved, instead of strengthening and compacting, the general frame of Government. If any person is more concerned for government and order, than for the liberties of his country; even he is equally concerned to put an end to this course of indiscriminate support. It is this blind and undistinguishing support, that feeds the spring of those very disorders, by which he is frighted into the arms of the faction which contains in itself the source of all disorders, by enfeebling all the visible and regular authority of the State. The distemper is increased by his injudicious and preposterous endeavours, or pretences, for the cure of it.

An exterior Administration, chosen for its impotency, or after it is chosen purposely rendered impotent, in order to be rendered subservient, will not be obeyed. The laws themselves will not respected, when those who execute them are despised; and they will be despised, when their power is not immediate from the Crown, or natural in the kingdom. Never were Ministers better supported in Parliament. Parliamentary support comes and goes with office, totally regardless of the man, or the merit. Is Government strengthened? It grows weaker and weaker; the popular torrent gains upon it every hour. Let us learn from our experience. It is not support that is wanting to Government, but reformation. When Ministry rests upon public opinion, it is not indeed built upon a rock of adamant; But when it stands upon private humour, its structure is of stubble, and its foundation is on quicksand. I repeat it again – He that supports every Administration, subverts all Government. As the whole business in which Courts usually take an interest goes on at present equally well, in whatever hands, whether high or low, wise or foolish, scandalous or reputable; there is nothing to hold it firm to any one body of men, or to any one consistent scheme of politicks. Nothing interposes, to prevent the full operation of all the caprices and all the passions of a Court upon the servants of the publick. The system of Administration is open to continual shocks and changes, upon the principles of the meanest cabal, and the most contemptible intrigue. Nothing can be solid and permanent. All good men at length fly with horrour from such a service. Men of rank and ability, with the spirit which ought to animate such men in a free state, while they decline the jurisdiction of dark cabal on their actions and their fortunes, will, for both, chearfully put themselves upon their country. They will trust an inquisitive and distinguishing Parliament; because it does enquire, and does distinguish. If they act well, they know, that in such a Parliament, they will be supported against any intrigue; if they act ill, they know that no intrigue can protect them. This situation, however aweful, is honourable. But in one hour, and in the self-same Assembly, without any assigned or assignable cause, to be precipitated from the highest authority to the most marked neglect, possibly into the greatest peril of life and reputation, is a situation full of danger, and destitute of honour. It will be shunned equally by every man of prudence, and every man of spirit.

Such are the consequences of the division of the Court from the Administration; and of the division of public men among themselves. By the former of these, lawful Government is undone; by the latter, all opposition to lawless power is rendered impotent. Government may in a great measure be restored, if any considerable bodies of men have honesty and resolution enough never to accept Administration, unless this garrison of *King's men*, which is stationed, as in a citadel, to controul and enslave it, be entirely broken and disbanded, and every work they have thrown up be leveled with the ground. The disposition of public men to keep this corps together, and to act under it, or to co-operate with it, is a touchstone by which every Administration ought in future to be tried. There has not been one which has not sufficiently experienced the utter incompatibility of that Faction with the public peace, and with all the ends of good Government: since, if they opposed it, they soon lost every power of serving the Crown; if they submitted to it, they lost all the esteem of their country. Until Ministers give to the publick a full proof of their entire alienation from that system, however plausible their pretences, we may be sure they are more intent on the emoluments than the duties of office. If they refuse to give this proof, we know of what stuff they are made. In this particular, it ought to be the electors business to look to their Representatives. The electors ought to esteem it no less culpable in their Member to give a single vote in Parliament to such an Administration, than to take an office under it; to endure it, than to act in it. The notorious infidelity and versatility of Members of Parliament in their opinions of men and things ought in a particular manner to be considered by the electors in the enquiry which is recommended to them. This is one of the principal holdings of that destructive system, which has endeavoured to unhinge all the virtuous, honourable, and useful connexions in the kingdom.

This Cabal has, with great success, propagated a doctrine which serves for a colour to those acts of treachery; and whilst it receives any degree of countenance, it will be utterly senseless to look for a vigorous opposition to the Court Party. The doctrine is this: That all political connexions are in their nature factious, and as such ought to be dissipated, and destroyed; and that the rule for forming

Administrations is mere personal ability (on the judgement of this Cabal upon it) taken by draughts from every division and denomination of public men. This decree was solemnly promulgated by the head of the Court corps, the Earl of Bute himself, in a speech which he made, in the year 1766, against the then Administration, the only Administration which he has ever been known directly and publicly to oppose.

It is indeed in no way wonderful, that such persons should make such declarations. That Connexion and Faction are equivalent terms, is an opinion which has been carefully inculcated at all times by unconstitutional Statesmen. The reason is evident. Whilst men are linked together, they easily and speedily communicate the alarm of any evil design. They are enabled to fathom it with common counsel, and to oppose it with united strength. Whereas, when they lie dispersed, without concert, order, or discipline, communication is uncertain, counsel difficult, and resistance impracticable. Where men are not acquainted with each other's principles, nor experienced in each other's talents, nor at all practised in their mutual habitudes and dispositions by joint efforts in business; no personal confidence, no friendship, no common interest, subsisting among them; it is evidently impossible that they can act a public part with uniformity, perseverance, or efficacy. In a connexion, the most inconsiderable man, by adding to the weight of the whole, has his value, and his use; out of it, the greatest talents are wholly unserviceable to the publick. No man, who is not inflamed by vain-glory into enthusiasm, can flatter himself that his single, unsupported, desultory, unsystematic endeavours are of power to defeat the subtle designs and united Cabals of ambitious citizens. When bad men combine, the good must associate; else they will fall, one by one, an unpitied sacrifice in a contemptible struggle.

It is not enough, in a situation of trust in the commonwealth, that a man means well to his country; it is not enough that in his single person he never did an evil act, but always voted according to his conscience, and even harangued against every design which he apprehended to be prejudicial to the interests of his country. This innoxious and ineffectual character, that seems formed upon a plan of apology and disculpation, falls miserably short of the mark of public duty. That duty demands and requires, that what is right should not only be made known, but made prevalent; that what is evil should not only be detected, but defeated. When the public man omits to put himself in a situation of doing his duty with effect, it is an omission that frustrates the purposes of his trust almost as much as if he had formally betrayed it. It is surely no very rational account of a man's life, that he has always acted right; but has taken special care, to act in such a manner that his endeavours could not possibly be productive of any consequence.

I do not wonder that the behaviour of many parties should have made persons of tender and scrupulous virtue somewhat out of humour with all sorts of connexion in politicks. I admit that people frequently acquire in such confederacies a narrow, bigoted, and proscriptive spirit; that they are apt to sink the idea of the general good in this circumscribed and partial interest. But, where duty renders a critical situation a necessary one, it is our business to keep free from the evils attendant upon it; and not to fly from the situation itself. If a fortress is seated in an unwholesome air, an officer of the garrison is obliged to be attentive to his health, but he must not desert his station. Every profession, not excepting the glorious one of a soldier, or the sacred one of a priest, is liable to its own particular vices; which, however, form no argument against those ways of life; nor are the vices themselves inevitable to every individual in those professions. Of such a nature are connexions in politicks; essentially necessary for the full performance of our public duty, accidentally liable to degenerate into faction. Commonwealths are made of families, free commonwealths of parties also; and we may as well affirm, that our natural regards and ties of blood tend inevitably to make men bad citizens, as that the bonds of our party weaken those by which we are held to our country.

Some legislators[117] went so far as to make neutrality in party a crime against the State. I do not know whether this might not have been rather to overstrain the principle. Certain it is, the best patriots in the greatest commonwealths have always commended and promoted such connexions. *Idem sentire de republica,*[118] was with them a principal ground of friendship and attachment; nor do I know any other capable of forming firmer, dearer, more pleasing, more honourable, and more virtuous habitudes. The Romans carried this principle a great way. Even the holding of offices together, the disposition of

---

[117] **some legislators**   the allusion is to Solon.
[118] *Idem sentire*   'to think alike about politics' (Cicero, *De Amicitia*, x; cf. xxvii).

which arose from chance not selection, gave rise to a relation, which continued for life. It was called *necessitudo sortis*,[119] and it was looked upon with a sacred reverence. Breaches of any of these kinds of civil relation were considered as acts of the most distinguished turpitude. The whole people was distributed into political societies, in which they acted in support of such interests in the State as they severally affected. For it was then thought no crime, to endeavour by every honest means to advance to superiority and power those of your own sentiments and opinions. This wise people was far from imagining that those connexions had no tie, and obliged to no duty; but that men might quit them without shame, upon every call of interest. They believed private honour to be the great foundation of public trust; that friendship was no mean step towards patriotism; that he who, in the common intercourse of life, shewed he regarded somebody besides himself, when he came to act in a public situation, might probably consult some other interest than his own. Never may we become *plus sages que les sages*,[120] as the French comedian has happily expressed it, wiser than all the wise and good men who have lived before us. It was their wish, to see public and private virtues, not dissonant and jarring, and mutually destructive, but harmoniously combined, growing out of one another in a noble and orderly gradation, reciprocally supporting and supported. In one of the most fortunate periods of our history this country was governed by a *connexion*; I mean, the great connexion of Whigs in the reign of Q Anne. They were complimented upon the principle of this connexion by a poet who was in high esteem with them. Addison, who knew their sentiments, could not praise them for what they considered as no proper subject of commendation. As a poet who knew his business, he could not applaud them for a thing which in general estimation was not highly reputable. Addressing himself to Britain,

Thy favourites grow not up by fortune's sport,
Or from the crimes or follies of a court.
On the firm basis of desert they rise,
From long-try'd faith, and friendship's holy ties.[121]

---

[119] **necessitudo sortis** the quaestor was bound to his superior, the praetor, in Roman practice by a quasi-filial tie, known by this name. The mention here picks up the epigraph (for Verres betrayed his praetor, C. Carbo) and so opposes party loyalty to court treachery. The idea was not new to Burke: see *Abridgement*, I.iii.

[120] **plus sages . . . sages** altered from Molière, *La critique de l'Ecole des Femmes*, 1.3.

[121] **Thy favourites . . . ties** Joseph Addison, *The Campaign*, ll. 37–40.

The Whigs of those days believed that the only proper method of rising into power was through hard essays of practised friendship and experimented fidelity. At that time it was not imagined, that patriotism was a bloody idol,[122] which required the sacrifice of children and parents, or dearest connexions in private life, and of all the virtues that rise from those relations. They were not of that ingenious paradoxical morality, to imagine that a spirit of moderation was properly shewn in patiently bearing the sufferings of your friends; or that disinterestedness was clearly manifested at the expence of other peoples fortune. They believed that no men could act with effect, who did not act in concert; that no men could act in concert, who did not act with confidence; and that no men could act with confidence, who were not bound together by common opinions, common affections, and common interests.

These wise men, for such I must call Lord Sunderland, Lord Godolphin, Lord Sommers, and Lord Marlborough, were too well principled in these maxims upon which the whole fabrick of public strength is built, to be blown off their ground by the breath of every childish talker. They were not afraid that they should be called an ambitious Junto; or that their resolution to stand or fall together should, by placemen, be interpreted into a scuffle for places.

Party is a body of men united, for promoting by their joint endeavours the national interest, upon some particular principle in which they are all agreed. For my part, I find it impossible to conceive, that any one believes in his own politicks, or thinks them to be of any weight, who refuses to adopt the means of having them reduced into practice. It is the business of the speculative philosopher to mark the proper ends of Government. It is the business of the politician, who is the philosopher in action, to find out proper means towards those ends, and to employ them with effect. Therefore every honourable connexion will avow it as their first purpose, to pursue every just method to put the men who hold their opinions into such a condition as may enable them to carry their common plans into execution, with all the power and authority of the State. As this power is attached to certain situations, it is their duty to contend for these situations. Without a proscription of others, they are bound to give to their own party the preference in all things; and by no means, for private con-

---

[122] **a bloody idol** a reference to Moloch, to whom the Israelites sacrificed their children, I Kings 11:7 etc.

siderations, to accept any offers of power in which the whole body is not included; nor to suffer themselves to be led, or to be controuled, or to be over- balanced, in office or in council, by those who contradict the very fundamental principles on which their party is formed, and even those upon which every fair connexion must stand.[123] Such a generous contention for power, on such manly and honourable maxims, will easily be distinguished from the mean and interested struggle for place and emolument. The very stile of such persons will serve to discriminate them from those numberless impostors, who have deluded the ignorant with professions incompatible with human practice, and have afterwards incensed them by practices below the level of vulgar rectitude.

It is an advantage to all narrow wisdom and narrow morals, that their maxims have a plausible air; and, on a cursory view, appear equal to first principles. They are light and portable. They are as current as copper coin; and about as valuable. They serve equally the first capacities and the lowest; and they are, at least, as useful to the worst men as the best. Of this stamp is the cant of *Not men, but measures*;[124] a sort of charm, by which many people get loose from every honourable engagement. When I see a man acting this desultory and disconnected part, with as much detriment to his own fortune as prejudice to the cause of any party, I am not persuaded that he is right; but I am ready to believe he is in earnest. I respect virtue in all its situations; even when it is found in the unsuitable company of weakness. I lament to see qualities, rare and valuable, squandered away without any public utility. But when a gentleman with great visible emoluments[125] abandons the party in which he has long acted, and tells you, it is because he proceeds upon his own judgement; that he acts on the merits of the several measures as they arise; and that he is obliged to follow his own conscience, and not that of others; he gives reasons which it is impossible to controvert, and discovers a character which it is impossible to mistake. What shall we think of him who never

---

[123] **must stand**   the principle on which Rockingham insisted; for his distaste for 'men who are ready to support all Administrations', see *Grenville Papers*, IV, p. 66.

[124] **not men but measures**   'As to my future conduct, your Lordship will pardon me if I say, "Measures, and not men," will be the rule of it', wrote Shelburne to Rockingham refusing office in 1765, *Memoirs of Rockingham*, I, p. 235.

[125] **great visible emoluments**   this would fit Henry Seymour Conway, who entered Rockingham's ministry as secretary of state and continued so under Pitt and Grafton.

differed from a certain set of men until the moment they lost their power, and who never agreed with them in a single instance afterwards? Would not such a coincidence of interest and opinion be rather fortunate? Would it not be an extraordinary cast upon the dice, that a man's connexions should degenerate into faction, precisely at the critical moment when they lose their power, or he accepts a place? When people desert their connexions, the desertion is a manifest *fact*, upon which a direct simple issue lies, triable by plain men. Whether a *measure* of Government be right or wrong, is *no matter of fact*, but a mere affair of opinion, on which men may, as they do, dispute and wrangle without end. But whether the individual *thinks* the measure right or wrong, is a point at still a greater distance from the reach of all human decision. It is therefore very convenient to politicians, not to put the judgement of their conduct on overt-acts, cognizable in any ordinary court, but upon such matter as can be triable only in that secret tribunal, where they are sure of being heard with favour, or where at worst the sentence will be only private whipping.

I believe the reader would wish to find no substance in a doctrine which has a tendency to destroy all test of character as deduced from conduct. He will therefore excuse my adding something more, towards the further clearing up a point, which the great convenience of obscurity to dishonesty has been able to cover with some degree of darkness and doubt.

In order to throw an odium on political connexion, these politicians suppose it a necessary incident to it, that you are blindly to follow the opinions of your party, when in direct opposition to your own clear ideas; a degree of servitude that no worthy man could bear the thought of submitting to; and such as, I believe, no connexions (except some Court Factions) ever could be so senselessly tyrannical as to impose. Men thinking freely, will, in particular instances, think differently. But still, as the greater part of the measures which arise in the course of public business are related to, or dependent on, some great *leading general principles in Government*, a man must be peculiarly unfortunate in the choice of his political company if he does not agree with them at least nine times in ten. If he does not concur in these general principles upon which the party is founded, and which necessarily draw on a concurrence in their application, he ought from the beginning to have chosen some other, more conformable to his opinions. When the question is in its nature doubtful, or not very material, the modesty which becomes an individual, and (in spite of our Court moralists) that partiality which becomes a well-chosen friendship, will frequently bring on an acquiescence in the general sentiment. Thus the disagreement will naturally be rare; it will be only enough to indulge freedom, without violating concord, or disturbing arrangement. And this is all that ever was required for a character of the greatest uniformity and steadiness in connexion. How men can proceed without any connexion at all, is to me utterly incomprehensible. Of what sort of materials must that man be made, how must he be tempered and put together, who can sit whole years in Parliament, with five hundred and fifty of his fellow citizens, amidst the storm of such tempestuous passions, in the sharp conflict of so many wits, and tempers, and characters, in the agitation of such mighty questions, in the discussion of such vast and ponderous interests, without seeing any one sort of men, whose character, conduct, or disposition, would lead him to associate himself with them, to aid and be aided in any one system of public utility?

I remember an old scholastic aphorism, which says, 'that the man who lives wholly detached from others, must be either an angel or a devil'.[126] When I see in any of these detached gentlemen of our times the angelic purity, power, and beneficence, I shall admit them to be angels. In the mean time we are born only to be men. We shall do enough if we form ourselves to be good ones. It is therefore our business carefully to cultivate in our minds, to rear to the most perfect vigour and maturity, every sort of generous and honest feeling that belongs to our nature. To bring the dispositions that are lovely[127] in private life into the service and conduct of the commonwealth; so to be patriots, as not to forget we are gentlemen. To cultivate friendships, and to incur enmities. To have both strong, but both selected: in the one, to be placable; in the other, immoveable. To model our principles to our duties and our situation. To be fully persuaded, that all virtue which is impracticable is spurious; and rather to run the risque of falling into faults in a course which leads us to act with effect and energy, than to loiter out our days without blame, and without use. Public life is a situation of power and energy; he trespasses

---

[126] **or a devil**   cf. Robert Burton, *Anatomy of Melancholy*, pt.1 s.2 mem.2 subs.7; the idea is from Aristotle, *Politics*, 1.i.
[127] **that are lovely**   Philippians 4:8.

against his duty who sleeps upon his watch, as well as he that goes over to the enemy.

There is, however, a time for all things.[128] It is not every conjuncture which calls with equal force upon the activity of honest men; but critical exigences now and then arise; and I am mistaken, if this be not one of them. Men will see the necessity of honest combination; but they may see it when it is too late. They may embody, when it will be ruinous to themselves, and of no advantage to the country; when, for want of such a timely union as may enable them to oppose in favour of the laws, with the laws on their side, they may, at length, find themselves under the necessity of conspiring, instead of consulting. The law, for which they stand, may become a weapon in the hands of its bitterest enemies; and they will be cast, at length, into that miserable alternative, between slavery and civil confusion, which no good man can look upon without horror; an alternative in which it is impossible he should take either part, with a conscience perfectly at repose. To keep that situation of guilt and remorse at the utmost distance, is, therefore, our first obligation. Early activity may prevent late and fruitless violence. As yet we work in the light. The scheme of the enemies of public tranquillity has disarranged, it has not destroyed us.

If the reader believes that there really exists such a Faction as I have described; a Faction ruling by the private inclinations of a Court, against the general sense of the people; and that this Faction, whilst it pursues a scheme for undermining all the foundations of our freedom, weakens (for the present at least) all the powers of executory Government, rendering us abroad contemptible, and at home distracted; he will believe also, that nothing but a firm combination of public men against this body, and that, too, supported by the hearty concurrence of the people at large, can possibly get the better of it. The people will see the necessity of restoring public men to an attention to the public opinion, and of restoring the constitution to its original principles. Above all, they will endeavour to keep the House of Commons from assuming a character which does not belong to it. They will endeavour to keep that House, for its existence, for its powers, and its privileges, as independent of every other, and as dependent upon themselves, as possible. This servitude is to an House of Com-

---

[128] **a time for all things**   cf. Ecclesiastes 3:1.

mons (like obedience to the Divine law) 'perfect freedom.'[129] For if they once quit this natural, rational, and liberal obedience, having deserted the only proper foundation of their power, they must seek a support in an abject and unnatural dependence somewhere else. When, through the medium of this just connexion with their constituents, the genuine dignity of the House of Commons is restored, it will begin to think of casting from it, with scorn, as badges of servility, all the false ornaments of illegal power, with which it has been, for some time, disgraced. It will begin to think of its old office of CONTROUL. It will not suffer, that last of evils, to predominate in the country; men without popular confidence, public opinion, natural connexion, or mutual trust, invested with all the powers of Government.

When they have learned this lesson themselves, they will be willing and able to teach the Court, that it is the true interest of the Prince to have but one Administration; and that one composed of those who recommend themselves to their Sovereign through the opinion of their country, and not by their obsequiousness to a favourite. Such men will serve their Sovereign with affection and fidelity; because his choice of them, upon such principles, is a compliment to their virtue. They will be able to serve him effectually; because they will add the weight of the country to the force of the executory power. They will be able to serve their King with dignity; because they will never abuse his name to the gratification of their private spleen or avarice. This, with allowances for human frailty, may probably be the general character of a Ministry, which thinks itself accountable to the House of Commons; when the House of Commons thinks itself accountable to its constituents. If other ideas should prevail, things must remain in their present confusion; until they are hurried into all the rage of civil violence; or until they sink into the dead repose of despotism.

[129] **'perfect freedom'** 'Whose service is perfect freedom' (*Book of Common Prayer*, Morning Prayer, Second Collect).

Conciliation with America

Introduction

'There is not a more difficult subject for the understanding of men than to govern a large Empire upon a plan of Liberty',[1] Burke observed early in the debate on America. The reconciliation of empire and liberty was the constant refrain in his speeches. To see that constancy in its proper setting we must understand how he mingled prepossession, principle and practicality. For his speeches provide a reflection at once of Burke's own experience and thought, of the requirements of public consistency and of political convenience.

To discuss the British empire in terms of liberty and subordination was a natural continuation of his interests. It flows not just from the proprietorial regard for liberty so congenial to the Rockinghams and the concern for the liberty of dependent bodies we expect from an Irishman addressing England. There is also Burke's view that obedience to political authority should be given freely. Obedience freely given accorded with the principles of imitation in human nature. It took place where the governors felt they could rely on the governed and so could dispense with coercion. That in its turn would happen when the governed were habituated to civilized behaviour.

[1] *Speech on Declaratory Resolution, 3rd February 1766*, WSEB, II, p. 47.

These were not Burke's only prepossessions. He also had a congruent view of America itself. There is a parallel with his concern that the England of George III should be governed by an unfettered opinion, for it was *that* sort of government he had in mind for America: if 'an Englishman must be subordinate to England', Burke observed, 'he must be governed according to the opinion of a free land'.[2] But how does this 'must', the necessity of governing in this way, arise? Burke believed that the colonists in America resembled the English in spirit. William Burke had written *An Account of the European Settlements in America*. William bore the nebulous but intimate relation of 'cousin' to Burke, who had a hand in the *Account*. The book described at length 'the effects of liberty' on the habits of the settlers. To conduct themselves independently was part of their character, for they revealed 'the work of a people guided by their own genius, and following the directions of their own natural temper in a proper path'.[3] So it was natural for Edmund to argue that America had to be governed according to 'a plan of Liberty', 'because it can be governed on no other'.[4]

Such thoughts were not only familial but also rang true. To view America on 'a plan of Liberty' was plausible. The colonists themselves described their case in the terms of liberty. So far as liberty was uppermost, Noah Welles declared in 1764, 'our lives, persons, and properties will be secure'. According to one group of colonists, British control implied 'the destruction of American liberty' and, for another, was 'subversive to the very idea of liberty'.[5]

What was understood by liberty? Though it may sound paradoxical, it was associated frequently with the British constitution. Liberty might be conceived as a natural attribute, as in James Duchals' declaration that because God 'hath endowed us with free-wills' it was evident that He 'intended we should be free'.[6] But more often it was conceived in relation to other entities, especially government. Here, liberty was supposed to depend on law, in that law could define the

---

[2] *Speech on Declaratory Resolution*, WSEB, II, p. 50.
[3] [William Burke], *An Account of the European Settlements in America*[3], 2 vols. (1760), pt. VI c.I (vol. II, p. 60).
[4] *Speech on Declaratory Resolution*, WSEB, II p. 50.
[5] Noah Welles, *Patriotism Described and Recommended* (1764), p. 17; Resolution of Accomack County, 27 July 1774, in *American Archives, Fourth Series* (1837), I, p. 639; Resolves of Chester County, 18 June 1774, *ibid.*, p. 428.
[6] James Duchals, *Sermons*[2] (1765), I, p. 170.

areas in which the citizen would be free of the government's action. Hence, law was a condition of liberty: 'liberty can exist no where, but by the protection of the laws'. This makes sense in that law implies a regular operation (in the words of Sir William Meredith, law 'deals out her Dispensations by the single Rule and Measure of Equality') as distinct from the caprice of a variable will, which might not respect settled arrangements concerning the subject as we find in Arthur Young's reference to 'the arbitrary power under which so great a part of the world at present groans'. His remark suggests that not all systems of law were felt to provide for the subject's liberty. The example of oriental despotism seemed clear: 'to do what the laws of Turky permit, certainly is *not* liberty'. Yet some governments supplied more liberty. Britain's was supposed to provide most of all, for it 'does actually bestow upon its subjects higher degrees of Liberty than any other people are known to enjoy'. Hence, liberty was often conceived in terms of the British constitution: such was its excellence, Caleb Evans asserted, 'that the voice of its laws is the voice of liberty'. The constitution's protection of liberty meant that it conformed with what was understood as the content of natural law. We find Camden suggesting that the constitution was one 'grounded on the eternal and immutable laws of nature; a constitution whose foundation and centre is liberty, which sends liberty to every subject'. The concern for liberty so understood was general in Britain and we find Lord North writing that 'our wish is not to impose on our fellow-subjects in America any terms inconsistent with the most perfect liberty'.[7]

The question in hand with America not about the idea of liberty, but, like the *Present Discontents*, concerned the furtherance and location of virtue. Who would uphold the liberty of the colonists? Burke had hinted that George III was not the guardian of Britain's constitution. The colonists were more explicit. They claimed the liberty of Englishmen and suggested that the proceedings of the British Parliament about the colonies were amiss. After all, the moral basis of the constitution suggested that it should be beyond serious alteration: as

[7] Anon., *Civil Liberty Asserted and the Rights of the Subject Defended* (1776), p. 138; [Sir William Meredith], *The Question Stated, Whether the Freeholders have lost their Right* (1769), p. 53f; Young, cited in *Monthly Review*, 46 (1772), 580; Anon., *The Case of Great Britain and America³* (1769) p. 6; [Adam Ferguson], *Remarks on a Pamphlet* (1776), p. 13; Caleb Evans, *British Constitutional Liberty* (1775), p. 20; Camden, debate in Lords, 24 Feb. 1766, P.H. XVI, 177; North to John Burgoyne 31 July 1775, in Alan Valentine, *Lord North*, 2 vols. (1967), I, p. 377.

Samuel Adams put it, there were 'fundamental rules of the constitution, which ... neither the supreme legislative nor the supreme executive can alter'.[8] The British Parliament, they thought, was innovating against the constitution. This followed from the view which we have just seen Camden take, that the constitution of Britain embodied the laws of nature. But if the truth was immutable, who was its advocate?

Since the question concerned virtue's location it could not be determined by conceptual considerations alone. If a concern for liberty was personally attractive to Burke and observationally accurate, it still remains for us to ask about his practical principles about America. This is particularly true, for to say America could 'be governed on no other' basis was perhaps to run a little ahead of the facts in 1766, when Burke spoke. The colonists' discontent in the 1760s was expressed in a manner calculated to gain relief from England rather than to eject the English. This was rather less true from 1773. Whilst it may be true that the colonies could have been held down by military strength, General Gage, the officer commanding in America, was never sanguine about governing by force. Burke's stance had at least one advantage, for he was able to see as much from England (and perhaps something more than was really visible) thanks to his own prepossessions.

His position was not only natural to his background of thought but also convenient for his political posture, for it made freedom the badge of his party abroad as much as at home. Having said so much, we should remember that the preservation of the empire was equally important to Burke. If he thought that 'without freedom, it would not be the British Empire', he also asserted that 'without subordination it would not be one Empire'[9]. The question before him was how best at once to preserve political liberty and to keep America within the empire.

This was a problem of constitutional elegance rather than practical conduct so long as the purposes of the imperial government were sensitive to American feeling. But the 1760s saw some insensitivity. For the difficulty of constitutional theory was laid bare by friction between Westminster and the colonies. After the Seven Years' War,

---

[8] Adams to Shelburne, 15 Jan 1768, in H. A. Cushing (ed.), *The Writings of Samuel Adams*, 4 vols. (1904–08), I, p. 166.
[9] *Speech on Declaratory Resolution*, WSEB, II, p. 50.

Britain settled down to peace and therefore to a reduction of war-time expenditure. America presented the obvious ground for gathering revenue, without offending the opinion of the British Parliament. In 1765 George Grenville, the pattern of financial rectitude, imposed the Stamp Act (which taxed legal and commercial documents, the papers of ships and merchants, as well as pamphlets and newspapers). The colonies objected, assembling in a congress at New York to protest. They felt that only taxation to maintain the government of North America was acceptable. The pattern of protest and justification was to be reproduced later, often augmented with physical violence, always at a more fevered tempo. The colonists would soon question the authority of the British Parliament to legislate for them in any respect. But in 1766 matters were at a more moderate temperature. The question of the day concerned Grenville's measures and their impact.

How did the Rockingham ministry, which succeeded Grenville, deal with it? Solutions, like greatness, are as often thrust on men as attained independently. The ministry arrived at the conclusion that America was best treated by matching theoretical assertion with practical tact. The latter they found in repealing the Stamp Act. The former lay in the Declaratory Act, which made explicit the British Parliament's right to make law for the colonies, especially laws with financial implications. As this was the position of Burke's connection, it is easy to see how his opinions fitted the situation. His references to subordination expressed the assertion of the Declaratory Act, whilst talk of liberty dignified the concession over the Stamp Act. This is not the less true because he articulated them before either measure was passed. The tasks to which political preposession can be applied are independent of its genesis.

How did these tasks develop in this case? The development of Burke's position was in general terms at first. His view was that a country could be governed only by respecting the disposition of its people. It was a view compatible with the common coin that government should be adapted to the good of the governed or that a politician should seek the good opinion of an unengaged electorate. It was also enshrined in Montesquieu. Not only did Burke thus advance a view acceptable to many, but also he did so in very general way. There is a decided shortage of specific comment from him in the surviving record for the 1760s.

His taciturn generality can be understood by reference to political circumstances. It was not the reflection merely of his view that Parliament could not superintend American detail, but one also of the convenience of this view. The Rockinghams always wished to continue on the trajectory from which they began, even if its impetus was not initially self-generated. The constancy that marked the pursuit of virtue demanded as much, particularly when it seemed popular. What had been thrust upon them was a policy whose ambiguity made it attractive to both Britons and Americans. Supremacy was a constant refrain in England, to which the Rockinghams lent their voice. A colonial agent noted in 1769 that they 'assert the supremacy of Parliament in almost as strong terms as the Ministerial party'.[10] At the same time they acquired the reputation of being friends of America, however inadvertently. The repeal of the Stamp Act had been neither self-generated nor much recollected by them subsequently. But that Rockingham's ministry had been its author placed them distinctly in the eye of the beholder. As Franklin noted, there were in England those who 'value themselves on being true to the interest of Britain', but there were also ' "*Americans*" ', amongst whom he included the Rockinghams.[11]

By the middle 1770s the Rockinghams took up a position which at once asserted Britain's legislative supremacy and was tender towards the colonists. But it was not always clear that they would. Tenderness, with which the events of 1766 had saddled them, was neither very popular in England during the seventies nor the natural inclination of all the party. The combination of supremacy and amiability was likely to become difficult with the movement of events, for between 1766 and 1775 relations between Britain and America were marked by a series of prods, increasing in viciousness reciprocally. Franklin's formulation underlines the problem in domestic politics which this implies. It posed alternatives which might seem disjunctive, *either* for America *or* for England. The Rockinghams were not unaware of the difficulty; and many of them in fact were not particularly well disposed towards the colonists. Burke himself at one point called them 'wild and absurd'.[12] His *Conciliation with America* was preceded by a coolness or, at best, an ambiguous smile towards them.

[10] W. S. Johnson to Governor Pitkin, 26 May 1769, *Collections of the Massachusetts Historical Society*, 5th series, IX, p. 338.
[11] *Franklin Papers*, XIV (1970), ed. L. W. Labaree, p. 229 (8 August, 1767).
[12] Corr, II, p. 77.

If the policy of 1766 was to be maintained it was questionable where precisely its emphasis would lie. Subordination, certainly, was always present to the Rockinghamite mind. But if tenderness was present its prominence varied with events. To maintain 1766 was a matter of consistency, especially since subordination was a token attractive to most Englishmen. But, as such, it was point common to politicians: something more was needed to differentiate a party. The question was just how the Rockinghams would present themselves. Naturally they were eager to be acceptable: subordination and liberty combined two tokens usually attractive to Englishmen. So, however, was bringing the colonists to heel. The Rockinghamite means of differentiating themselves from those in government was chiefly over matters of execution. For instance, the Rockinghams spoke indistinctly when in 1767 Townshend imposed duties on glass, lead, paper, paint and tea imported into America: and when violent protest in Boston led to all the duties, except that on tea, being withdrawn, they condemned not the principle but the conduct of ministerial designs. Dowdeswell went further than Townshend's calls for enforcement. Perhaps there was some personal inclination towards severity (later Lord John Cavendish would support North's coercion of Boston after the Tea Party), but the Rockinghams left the impression of intending to supplant the ministry. There was no claim to have a special line on America, as there had been a keenness to appropriate political virtue and the means to it in domestic politics.[13]

Burke's own position was one in which reticence balanced principle. His principles of subordination and liberty were sufficiently general to seem friendly both to British and American claims. When the repeal of Townshend's duties was debated in 1769 he 'spoke upon the subject, in a very general manner, but without giving any direct opinion whether they ought or ought not now to repeal'.[14] The need to maintain his balance was soon strengthened. In 1774 he became MP for Bristol, not least because he seemed acceptable to a merchant community keen to maintain a lucrative trade with America. Bristol was England's second city, and its representation made Burke

---

[13] For the substance of this paragraph, see Paul Langford, 'The Rockingham Whigs and America, 1767–1773', in Anne Whiteman et al. (eds.), Statesmen, Scholars and Merchants (1973), pp. 135–52; see also Henry Cruger's opinion of Burke, H.M.C. Dartmouth, II, p. 296 (also in H.C. Van Schaak Henry Cruger, the Colleague of Edmund Burke (1859), pp. 19–20).

[14] Johnson to Pitkin, 26 May 1769, Collections, 337.

a national figure. He became also agent in London for the province of New York. Whilst Burke's finances were probably too involved for even his understanding, he was aware of the bare fact of exigency. Friendliness to the colonies had its benefits, just as much as firmness.

This taciturn nurturing of principle depended on differences with America being no more than a family argument. A wider difference would entail more specificity. For armed conflict between Britain and America was unacceptable to the Marquess. Rockingham was always against war. In 1774 he observed that 'notwithstanding all that has passed, I can never give my assent to proceedings to actual force against the colonies'.[15]

So if generality was enough from Burke it was only so long as American discontent remained in the penumbra which shades the line between disobedience and resistance. Once the line was crossed and matters stood in a clearer light, a more sharply defined response would be necessary to show just what the Rockinghams thought. An explicit stance would be required from Burke in particular. For Dowdeswell, their leading man of business in the Commons, was first ailing and then dead of tuberculosis by the summer of 1774. Burke, in effect, succeeded to his place.

Events had transposed political tension into a sharper key by then. The growth of American claims, from demands for exemption from taxation to claims for effective self-government, was described by Thomas Hutchinson as one in which 'at first . . . the supreme authority seemed to be admitted, the case of taxes only excepted; but the exceptions gradually extended from one case to another, until it included all cases whatsoever'.[16] In the middle of January, 1774 news reached England of the Boston Tea Party. In 1773 Lord North's ministry had added to the East India Company Regulating Act a clause which exempted the Company from all import duties on tea brought into England and subsequently re-exported to America; American merchants feared that they would be undersold; American radicals recognized that the tea, being cheap, would sell and so involve the colonies in paying the Townshend duty on tea. That duty, alone of Townshend's measures, had been left in force as a symbol of Britain's right to legislate for colonial taxation. To drink the Com-

---

[15] Corr, II, p. 516 (30 Jan 1774).
[16] Thomas Hutchinson, *The History of the Province of Massachussets Bay from 1749–1774* (1828), p. 256.

pany's tea was to accept Britain's claim. On the night of 16 December, forty or so men boarded the ships which the Company had sailed into Boston harbour and hurled about 300 chests of tea into the sea. This act and the ministry's response altered the terms of Anglo-American relations. For North and his colleagues proposed to take sharp action against Boston by act of Parliament.

The ministry's response revived the constitutional question of the nature of Parliament's supremacy over the colonies. After the repeal of most of Townshend's duties, Britain's policy had been expressed through executive action, backed by existing legislation, and usually aimed at specific individuals. The Tea Party was met instead by Parliamentary measures. These, it is true, concentrated on imposing Britain's law in the colonies. The measures were essentially punitive, but their importance was less in their content than in their form. That they were legislation in effect suggested that no constitutional issue existed: that Britain was beyond doubt legislatively supreme. The American response was to resist the new legislation. Thus parliament's exercise of authority over the colonies was questioned. The authority itself was not yet disputed, merely an application which the colonists disliked. But, as Hutchinson noted, whilst 'a profession of "subordination" . . . still remained; it was a word without a precise meaning to it'.[17]

There was a choice before Britain. America could either be allowed its own way or be brought to heel by force. 'It is evident that our present situation with the Colonies is so critical that no effectual middle term can be found'; wrote the earl of Buckinghamshire in March, 1774, 'we must either insist upon their submission to the authority of the Legislature or give them up entirely to their own discretion.'[18] The alternatives were an exertion of legislative authority backed by force and reconciliation based on letting the right lie dormant. At this point British opinion, on the whole, preferred the former view: in Thurlow's words 'to say we have a right to tax America and never to exercise that right is ridiculous and a man must abuse his own understanding not to allow of that right'.[19] The view was easy to hold, for it was not yet obvious that American

[17] Hutchinson, *History*, p. 256.
[18] Buckinghamshire, in *H.M.C. Lothian*, pp. 290–1.
[19] Thurlow, in R. Gore-Brown, *Chancellor Thurlow* (1953), p. 85.

recalcitrance could muster military force or that such force could effect independence.

By the same token the situation was ambiguous for the Rockinghams, for they had not yet reached the place at which a distinct stand was possible. They agreed with the government on Britain's legislative superiority; it was not yet clear whether it was necessary to differ finally about its application. It was not immediately apparent that North's coercion would fail or would provoke war, so that calculation urged continued reticence or ambiguity. In any case they could hardly oppose the principle of the legislative superiority that the Declaratory Act had specified. In the debate of 7 March, 1774 Dowdeswell applauded 'the legislative authority of this country over America', and faced with North's resolutions about Boston merely refused to underwrite what he had not read. Burke reiterated his view that countries could be governed only in accordance with their dispositions: 'if . . . in all the operations, and effects, of Government . . . no man can extend them agreeable to our forms, and modes, you must change your modes . . . if such a government as this is universally discontented, no troops under Heaven [will] bring them to obedience'.[20] But he, as yet, waited the effects of a show of force to determine whether his accent should lie on liberty or on subordination, for it was unclear how the colonists would respond. On 25 March Burke reminded the Commons that 'universal discontent cannot be reconciled easily' but mentioned an alternative: that America might be taxed 'by Compulsion'.[21] Though his twin principles of liberty and subordination pointed more strongly to reconciliation than coercion, they still admitted of at least two policies.

Burke's speech on *American Taxation* reflects the same situation, albeit with his emphasis now inclining heavily towards tenderness. 'The popular current, both within doors and without,' he wrote on 6 April, 'at present sets strongly against America.' There was little hope of upsetting the coercive bills. Yet an opportunity presented itself to match them with something omitted by the government on this occasion: a conciliatory gesture. Rose Fuller wished to move the repeal of the Townshend tea duty. This proposal in effect balanced an exertion of legislative superiority (North's Acts against Boston) with a gesture

[20] Cavendish Diary, British Library Egerton MSS. 253 fols. 218–35, esp. 232f.
[21] *Speech on Boston Port Bill, 25th March 1774*, WSEB, II, p. 405.

agreeable to American feeling. There might be some chance of success, for Burke believed that MPs were wedded less to coercion than to the will to assert parliamentary superiority: the Boston Port Bill, he thought, won support 'not so much from any predilection, that I could observe,' but 'from a general notion that *some act* of power was become necessary.'[22] Hence, he balanced assertion of legislative superiority (especially the Declaratory Act) with magnanimous dismissals of the American policies of the great but troublesome dead (Grenville and Townshend) and suggested that a friendly America was Britain's strength, whether in commerce or war. He went further and suggested that American revenue was properly 'an instrument of empire, and not . . . a means of supply'.[23] But he did not question the wisdom of coercion: and North, who asserted 'convince your colonies that you are able, and not afraid to control them, and depend upon it, obedience will be the result of your deliberation',[24] won the day.

But circumstances were soon to alter. Firmness produced an unsteadying result. North began to hesitate or at least to become ambiguous. He complemented coercion with conciliatory suggestions in both private and public. The conciliatory line seemed practicable enough for Chatham to declare for a version of it. An explicitly friendly line was not only possible but needful for Burke. This was not just to outbid Chatham and North, but to soothe his employers. New York had declared its hand. The province professed warm loyalty to the Crown, but suggested that to effect 'a Restoration of Harmony and Affection' it was necessary to draw 'the line of Parliamentary Authority and American Freedom on just equitable and constitutional Grounds'.[25] Principle, as often, could be interpreted by political need. Events demanded a line interpreting principle in a decidedly amicable manner.

To preserve his posture Burke needed to differentiate a policy. It had become clear that coercion made the Americans not submissive but recalcitrant. In order to avoid war it was necessary to withdraw what they disliked. This retraction obviously required to be shaded by the assertion of principle. How was this to be managed? Liberty,

---

[22] Corr, II, p. 528 (to the Committee of Correspondence of the General Assembly of New York).
[23] *Speech on American Taxation, 19th April 1774*, WSEB, II, pp. 415, 429, 453, 460; 460.
[24] North in Almon, *Debates*, XI, p. 151.
[25] Excerpted in R. J. S. Hoffman, *Edmund Burke: New York Agent* p. 157.

Burke thought, was compatible with subordination. But now, because peace was needed, more was required than the theoretical reflection that they were congruent. A causal relationship had to be found. Burke needed to say liberty would *preserve* subordination. Where did he find this? His experience of Ireland and England furnished him with the contrast between a country governed against the prepossessions of its people and one governed in accordance with them; between the conquered and the free country. In this contrast liberty was thought to allow a voluntary subordination. Thus Burke had to hand a prescription which combined assertion of America's subordination to Britain with a balancing respect for the freedom he now announced, loudly enough, suited the Americans. It may be summed up in a sentence: that concessions to the spirit of liberty would quiet the colonial difficulty. He could structure his argument around a contrast: between governing by force, against the prepossessions of the ruled, and treating them in accordance with their character. This is the substance of *Conciliation with America*.

The retraction had to be executed delicately. For North's aggressive measures had been popular enough in the Commons. This need was met in the way that Burke introduced his resolutions. These, it is true to say, are less explained in the speech than appended to it. They are masterly by reason of inconsequence. This was because they consisted in extensive concession to the colonists: in the words of James Harris 'they were no more than a repetition of the American demands, claims and complaints.' But they had been prefaced by two-and-a-half hours of other things.

The clear expression of conciliation entailed political ineffectiveness. If the self-consciously virtuous congratulations of Rockingham did not evidence this, the course of the debate would have done so adequately. The replies of the government speakers, Jenkinson and Germain, bypassed rather than answered Burke. Jenkinson made 'a long, tedious speech, in which he thought fit to avoid the smallest attempt to answer or refute one of Mr Burke's arguments'. Germain was complimentary to Burke, declaring that 'as he was not convinced by him, he despaired of being ever convinced that his old opinion, of enforcing obedience from America, was ill-founded'. The ministry really had little need to answer. The view of the Commons is adequately reflected by its vote, which rejected Burke's proposals by 270 votes to 78. Two months later the news of Concord and Lexington reached England. 'All our prospects of American reconciliation are, I fear over', Burke wrote. 'Blood has been shed. The sluice is opend – Where, when, or how it will be stopped God only knows.'[26]

Analysis

Introduction: Variations in opinions about the colonies but Burke's views are consistent and a matter of principle (pp. 206–7). We need a plan of reconciliation (pp. 207–8). The principles of the scheme proposed. Its practicability (pp. 209–12).

(I) *Condition of America*, both prosperous and free: its population and trade expanding (pp. 212–18); its agriculture and fisheries (pp. 218–20); digression against the use of force [which belongs properly to (II), but placed here serves to prepare us for the description of the American character] (pp. 220–1); six facets of American character, all pointing to a free people, as its inherited devotion to liberty (pp. 221–3) and self-government (pp. 222–3), and these characteristics accentuated by slave-owning (pp. 224–5), legal training (pp. 225–6) and distance from London (pp. 226–7).

(II) *How to Deal with America*: the problem of governing such a people: the failure of past attempts (pp. 227–8). There are three alternatives: transformation, coercion, conciliation (pp. 229). (i) To alter the causes of the character of the colonists, as by restricting the growth of population & trade or by enfranchising slaves (pp. 229–33). (ii) Coercion (pp. 233–6). (iii) Conciliation, by laying to rest the question of the Right of Taxation, for the practice not the right is the source of friction (pp. 236–40). Such a concession would not encourage further demands (pp. 240–1) and would be modelled on constitutional precedents – Ireland, Wales, Chester and Durham – (pp. 241–6), which prove England's existing policies to be in the wrong (pp. 246–8).

(III) *Practical Application*: Burke's resolutions (pp. 248–56); the removal of objections (pp. 256–9); Lord North's plan of conciliation criticized (pp. 259–64); Conclusion (pp. 264–9).

[26] Harris to 2nd earl of Hardwicke, B.L. Add. Mss. 35612 fol. 191; *London Evening Post*, 23 March 1775; Corr, III, p. 160 (to Charles O'Hara, *c*.28 May 1775).

Speech of Edmund Burke, Esq., On Moving his Resolutions for Conciliation with the Colonies, March 22nd 1775 (third edition, 1775)

I HOPE, Sir, that, notwithstanding the austerity of the Chair, your good-nature will incline you to some degree of indulgence towards human frailty. You will not think it unnatural, that those who have an object depending, which strongly engages their hopes and fears, should be somewhat inclined to superstition. As I came into the house full of anxiety about the event of my motion, I found, to my infinite surprize, that the grand penal Bill, by which we had passed sentence[1] on the trade and sustenance of America, is to be returned to us from the other House. I do confess, I could not help looking on this event as a fortunate omen. I look upon it as a sort of providential favour; by which we are put once more in possession of our deliberative capacity, upon a business so very questionable in its nature, so very uncertain in its issue. By the return of this Bill, which seemed to have taken its flight for ever, we are at this very instant nearly as free to chuse a plan for our American Government, as we were on the first day of the Session. If, Sir, we incline to the side of conciliation, we are not at all embarrassed (unless we please to make ourselves so) by any incon-

---

[1] **passed sentence** 'The Act to restrain the Commerce of the Provinces of Massachuset's Bay and New Hampshire, and the Colonies of Connecticut and Rhode Island, and Providence Plantation, in North America, to Great Britain, Ireland, and the British Islands in the West Indies; and to prohibit such Provinces and Colonies from carrying on any Fishery on the Banks of Newfoundland, and other places therein mentioned, under certain conditions and limitations' (Burke).

gruous mixture of coercion and restraint.[2] We are therefore called upon, as it were by a superior warning voice, again to attend to America; to attend to the whole of it together; and to review the subject with an unusual degree of care and calmness.

Surely it is an awful subject: or there is none so on this side of the grave. When I first had the honour of a seat in this House, the affairs of that Continent pressed themselves upon us, as the most important and most delicate object of parliamentary attention. My little share in this great deliberation oppressed me. I found myself a partaker in a very high trust; and having no sort of reason to rely on the strength of my natural abilities for the proper execution of that trust, I was obliged to take more than common pains, to instruct myself in every thing which relates to our Colonies. I was not less under the necessity of forming some fixed ideas, concerning the general policy of the British Empire. Something of this sort seemed to be indispensable; in order, amidst so vast a fluctuation of passions and opinions, to concenter my thoughts; to ballast my conduct; to preserve me from being blown about by every wind of fashionable doctrine.[3] I really did not think it safe, or manly, to have fresh principles to seek upon every fresh mail which should arrive from America.

At that period, I had the fortune to find myself in perfect concurrence with a large majority[4] in this house. Bowing under that high authority, and penetrated with the sharpness and strength of that early impression, I have continued ever since, without the least deviation, in my original sentiments. Whether this be owing to an obstinate perseverance in error, or to a religious adherence to what appears to me truth and reason, it is in your equity to judge.

Sir, Parliament having an enlarged view of objects, made, during this interval, more frequent changes in their sentiments and their conduct, than could be justified in a particular person upon the contracted scale of private information. But though I do not hazard any thing approaching to a censure on the motives of former parliaments to all those alterations, one fact is undoubted; that under them the state of America has been kept in continual agitation. Every thing

---

[2] **coercion and restraint**   the former means attempting to break the resistance to the tea-duty, the latter refers to debarring the New Englanders from the Newfoundland fisheries.

[3] **fashionable doctrine**   cf. Ephesians 4:14.

[4] **a large majority**   275–161.

administered as remedy to the public complaint, if it did not produce, was at least followed by, an heightening of the distemper; until, by a variety of experiments, that important Country has been brought into her present situation; – a situation, which I will not miscall, which I dare not name; which I scarcely know how to comprehend in the terms of any description.

In this posture, Sir, things stood at the beginning of the session. About that time, a worthy member of great parliamentary experience,[5] who, in the year 1766, filled the chair of the American committee[6] with much ability, took me aside; and, lamenting the present aspect of our politicks, told me, things were come to such a pass, that our former methods of proceeding in the house would be no longer tolerated. That the public tribunal (never too indulgent to a long and unsuccessful opposition) would now scrutinize our conduct with unusual severity. That the very vicissitudes and shiftings of ministerial measures, instead of convicting their authors of inconstancy and want of system, would be taken as an occasion of charging us with a pre-determined discontent, which nothing could satisfy; whilst we accused every measure of vigour as cruel, and every proposal of lenity as weak and irresolute. The publick, he said, would not have patience to see us play the game out with our adversaries; we must produce our hand. It would be expected, that those who for many years had been active in such affairs should shew, that they had formed some clear and decided idea of the principles of Colony Government; and were capable of drawing out something like a platform of the ground, which might be laid for future and permanent tranquillity.

I felt the truth of what my Hon. Friend represented; but I felt my situation too. His application might have been made with far greater propriety to many other gentlemen. No man was indeed ever better disposed, or worse qualified, for such an undertaking than myself. Though I gave so far into his opinion, that I immediately threw my thoughts into a sort of parliamentary form, I was by no means equally ready to produce them. It generally argues some degree of natural impotence of mind, or some want of knowledge of the world, to hazard Plans of Government, except from a seat of Authority. Propositions are made, not only ineffectually, but somewhat disreputably,

---

[5] **experience** Rose Fuller.
[6] **American committee** i.e. a Committee of the whole House to consider American affairs.

when the minds of men are not properly disposed for their reception; and for my part, I am not ambitious of ridicule; not absolutely a candidate for disgrace.

Besides, Sir, to speak the plain truth, I have in general no very exalted opinion of the virtue of Paper Government;[7] nor of any Politicks, in which the plan is to be wholly separated from the execution. But when I saw, that anger and violence prevailed every day more and more;[8] and that things were hastening towards an incurable alienation of our Colonies; I confess, my caution gave way. I felt this, as one of those few moments in which decorum yields to an higher duty. Public calamity is a mighty leveller; and there are occasions when any, even the slightest, chance of doing good, must be laid hold on, even by the most inconsiderable person.

To restore order and repose to an Empire so great and so distracted as ours, is, merely in the attempt, an undertaking that would ennoble the flights of the highest genius, and obtain pardon for the efforts of the meanest understanding. Struggling a good while with these thoughts, by degrees I felt myself more firm. I derived, at length, some confidence from what in other circumstances usually produces timidity. I grew less anxious, even from the idea of my own insignificance. For, judging of what you are, by what you ought to be, I persuaded myself, that you would not reject a reasonable proposition, because it had nothing but its reason to recommend it. On the other hand, being totally destitute of all shadow of influence, natural or adventitious, I was very sure, that, if my proposition were futile or dangerous, if it were weakly conceived, or improperly timed, there was nothing exterior to it, of power to awe, dazzle, or delude you. You will see it just as it is; and you will treat it just as it deserves.

The proposition is Peace.[9] Not Peace through the medium of War; not Peace to be hunted through the labyrinth of intricate and endless negociations; not Peace to arise out of universal discord, fomented,

---

[7] **Paper Government**   Burke may have meant Carolina, in whose fundamental constitutions Locke had a hand (cf. [William Burke] *An Account of the European Settlements in America*, pt. VII, ch. 20). Burke's resolutions would have established a new charter for all the colonies.

[8] **more and more**   cf. Psalms 74:23.

[9] **The proposition is Peace**   'For after all, what is this Heaven-born pacific Scheme, of which we have heard so laboured an Encomium? Why truly; if we will grant the Colonies all that they shall require, and stipulate nothing in Return; then they will be at Peace with us' (Josiah Tucker, *A Letter to Edmund Burke* (1775), p. 44f).

from principle, in all parts of the Empire; not Peace to depend on the Juridical Determination of perplexing questions; or the precise marking the shadowy boundaries of a complex Government. It is simple Peace; sought in its natural course, and its ordinary haunts. – It is Peace sought in the Spirit of Peace; and laid in principles purely pacific. I propose, by removing the Ground of the difference, and by restoring the *former unsuspecting confidence of the Colonies in the Mother Country,*[10] to give permanent satisfaction to your people; and (far from a scheme of ruling by discord) to reconcile them to each other in the same act, and by the bond of the very same interest, which reconciles them to British Government.

My idea is nothing more. Refined policy ever has been the parent of confusion; and ever will be so, as long as the world endures. Plain good intention, which is as easily discovered at the first view, as fraud is surely detected at last, is, let me say, of no mean force in the Government of Mankind. Genuine Simplicity of heart is an healing and cemented principle. My Plan, therefore, being formed upon the most simple grounds imaginable, may disappoint some people, when they hear it. It has nothing to recommend it to the pruriency of curious ears. There is nothing at all new and captivating in it. It has nothing of the Splendor of the Project, which has been lately laid

---

[10] **Mother Country** the metaphor is important, because many British politicians conceived it as literally applicable. The colonists, like children, should obey those who knew better (note Burke's *'unsuspecting confidence'* and 'this child of your old age', below, p. 218). Some construed this is a harsh sense. On the side of tenderness, see Rockingham to the Speaker of the Massachusetts Assembly, 11 May 1767 (*Grenville Papers,* IV 13n):

> I shall always consider that this country, as the parent, should be tender and just; and that the colonies, as the children, ought to be dutiful. A system of arbitrary rule over the colonies I would not adopt on this side, nor would I do otherwise than strenuously resist when attempts were made to throw off that dependency to which the colonies ought to submit ... for their own real hapiness and safety.

[11] **upon your table** Burke noted the resolution moved by North in Committee and agreed by the Commons, 27 Feb. 1775:

> That when the Governor, Council, or Assembly, or General Court, of any of his Majesty's Provinces or Colonies in America, shall *propose* to make provision, *according to the condition, circumstances,* and *situation,* of such Province or Colony, for contributing their *proportion* to the *Common Defence* (such *proportion* to be raised under the Authority of the General Court, or General assembly, of such Province or Colony, and disposable by Parliament), and shall engage to make provision also for the support of the Civil Government, and the Administration of Justice, in such Province or Colony, it will be proper, *if such Proposal shall be approved by his Majesty, and the two Houses of Parliament,* and for so long as such Provision shall be made accordingly, to forbear, *in respect of such Province or Colony,* to levy any Duty, Tax, or Assessment, or to impose any further Duty, Tax, or Assessment, except such duties as it may be expedient to continue to levy or

upon your Table by the Noble Lord in the Blue Ribband.[11] It does
not propose to fill your Lobby with squabbling Colony Agents, who
will require the interposition of your Mace,[12] at every instant, to keep
the peace amongst them. It does not institute a magnificent Auction of
Finance, where captivated provinces come to general ransom by bidding against each other, until you knock down the hammer, and
determine a proportion of payments, beyond all the powers of Algebra
to equalize and settle.

The plan, which I shall presume to suggest, derives, however, one
great advantage from the proposition and registry of that Noble
Lord's Project. The idea of conciliation is admissible. First, the
House in accepting the resolution moved by the Noble Lord, has
admitted, notwithstanding the menacing front of our Address,[13]
notwithstanding our heavy Bill of Pains and Penalties – that we do not
think ourselves precluded from all ideas of free Grace and Bounty.

The House has gone farther; it has declared conciliation admissible, *previous* to any submission on the part of America. It has even
shot a good deal beyond that mark, and has admitted, that the complaints of our former mode of exerting the Right of Taxation were not
wholly unfounded. That right thus exerted is allowed to have had
something reprehensible in it; something unwise, or something
grievous; since, in the midst of our heat and resentment, we, of
ourselves, have proposed a capital alteration; and, in order to get rid
of what seemed so very exceptionable, have instituted a mode that is
altogether new; one that is, indeed, wholly alien from all the ancient
methods and forms of Parliament.

The *principle* of this proceeding is large enough for my purpose.
The means proposed by the Noble Lord for carrying his ideas into
execution, I think, indeed, are very indifferently suited to the end; and
this I shall endeavour to shew you before I sit down. But for the

impose, for the Regulation of Commerce; the Nett Produce of the Duties last mentioned
  to be carried to the account of such Province or Colony respectively.
Blue Ribband North was conspicuous in the Commons because he wore the
insignia of the Garter. The only previous commoner to have been KG was
Walpole. Their distinction is rare: they have since been joined by Castlereagh (the
heir to a peerage), Sir Edward Grey, Balfour, Eden and Wilson (who subsequently
became British peers) and by Palmerston, Churchill and Heath (who did not).
[12] **your Mace** i.e. the sergeant-at-arms, who carried the mace as a symbol of
authority.
[13] **our Address** i.e. the Commons' reply to the king's speech at the beginning of
the session, which had supported a forceful line.

present, I take my ground on the admitted principle. I mean to give peace. Peace implies reconciliation; and where there has been a material dispute, reconciliation does in a manner always imply concession on the one part or on the other. In this state of things I make no difficulty in affirming, that the proposal ought to originate from us. Great and acknowledged force is not impaired, either in effect or in opinion, by an unwillingness to exert itself. The superior power may offer peace with honour and with safety. Such an offer from such a power will be attributed to magnanimity. But the concessions of the weak are the concessions of fear. When such a one is disarmed, he is wholly at the mercy of his superior; and he loses for ever that time and those chances,[14] which, as they happen to all men, are the strength and resources of all inferior power.

The capital leading questions on which you must this day decide, are these two. First, whether you ought to concede; and secondly, what your concession ought to be. On the first of these questions we have gained (as I have just taken the liberty of observing to you) some ground. But I am sensible that a great deal more is still to be done. Indeed, Sir, to enable us to determine both on the one and the other of these great questions with a firm and precise judgement, I think it may be necessary to consider distinctly the true nature and the peculiar circumstances of the object[15] which we have before us. Because after all our struggle, whether we will or not, we must govern America, according to that nature, and to those circumstances; and not according to our own imaginations; not according to abstract ideas of right; by no means according to mere general theories of government, the resort to which appears to me, in our present situation, no better than arrant trifling. I shall therefore endeavour, with your leave, to lay before you some of the most material of these circumstances in as full and as clear a manner as I am able to state them.

The first thing that we have to consider with regard to the nature of the object is – the number of people in the Colonies.[16] I have taken for

---

[14] **those chances** cf. *Julius Caesar*, IV.ii.270ff.

[15] **object** America; the modern usage is subject.

[16] **people in the Colonies** Johnson remarked (*Taxation no Tyranny* (1775), *Political Writings* p. 102):

> We are soon told that the Americans, however wealthy, cannot be taxed; that they are the descendants of men who left all for liberty, and that they have constantly preserved the principles and stubborness of their progenitors; that they are too obstinate for persuasion, and too powerful for constraint; that they will laugh at argument, and defeat

some years a good deal of pains on that point. I can by no calculation justify myself in placing the number below Two millions of inhabitants of our own European blood and colour; besides at least 500,000 others, who form no inconsiderable part of the strength and opulence of the whole. This, Sir, is, I believe, about the true number. There is no occasion to exaggerate, where plain truth is of so much weight and importance. But whether I put the present numbers too high or too low, is a matter of little moment. Such is the strength with which population shoots in that part of the world, that, state the numbers as high as we will, whilst the dispute continues, the exaggeration ends. Whilst we are discussing any given magnitude, they are grown to it. Whilst we spend our time in deliberating on the mode of governing Two Millions, we shall find we have Millions more to manage. Your children do not grow faster from infancy to manhood, than they spread from families to communities, and from villages to nations.

I put this consideration of the present and the growing numbers in the front of our deliberation; because, Sir, this consideration will make it evident to a blunter discernment than yours, that no partial, narrow, contracted, pinched, occasional system will be at all suitable to such an object. It will shew you, that it is not to be considered as one of those *Minima* which are out of the eye and consideration of the law;[17] not a paltry excrescence of the state; not a mean dependant, who may be neglected with little damage, and provoked with little danger. It will prove, that some degree of care and caution is required in the handling such an object; it will shew, that you ought not, in reason, to trifle with so large a mass of the interests and feelings of the human race. You could at no time do so without guilt; and be assured you will not be able to do it long with impunity.

But the population of this country, the great and growing population, though a very important consideration, will lose much of its weight, if not combined with other circumstances. The commerce of your Colonies is out of all proportion beyond the numbers of the people. This ground of their commerce indeed has been trod some

---

violence; that the continent of North America contains three millions, not of men merely, but of Whigs, of Whigs fierce for liberty, and disdainful of dominion; that they multiply with the fecundity of their own rattle-snakes, so that every quarter of a century doubles their numbers.

[17] **out of the eye of the law** alluding to the maxim *De minimis non curat lex.*

days ago, and with great ability, by a distinguished person,[18] at your bar. This gentleman, after Thirty-five years[19] – it is so long since he first appeared at the same place to plead for the commerce of Great Britain – has come again before you to plead the same cause, without any other effect of time, than, that to the fire of imagination and extent of erudition, which even then marked him as one of the first literary characters of his age, he has added a consummate knowledge in the commercial interest of his country, formed by a long course of enlightened and discriminating experience.

Sir, I should be inexcusable in coming after such a person with any detail; if a great part of the members who now fill the House had not the misfortune to be absent, when he appeared at your bar. Besides, Sir, I propose to take the matter at periods of time somewhat different from his. There is, if I mistake not, a point of view, from whence if you will look at this subject, it is impossible that it should not make an impression upon you.

I have in my hand two accounts; one a comparative state of the export trade of England to its Colonies, as it stood in the year 1704, and as it stood in the year 1772. The other a state of the export trade of this country to its Colonies alone, as it stood in 1772, compared with the whole trade of England to all parts of the world (the Colonies included) in the year 1704. They are from good vouchers; the latter period from the accounts on your table, the earlier from an original manuscript of Davenant,[20] who first established the Inspector General's office,[21] which has been ever since his time so abundant a source of parliamentary information.

The export trade to the Colonies consists of three great branches. The African, which, terminating almost wholly in the Colonies,[22] must be put to the account of their commerce; the West Indian; and the North American. All these are so interwoven, that the attempt to separate them would tear to pieces the contexture of the whole; and, if

---

[18] **a distinguished person** Glover had appeared at the bar of the Commons (16 March) to support the petition of 2 February from the West Indian planters on the non-importation agreement (hoping that peace be concluded with the colonies); see PH XVIII, 461–78.

[19] **Thirty-five years** perhaps from the War of 1739 with Spain.

[20] **Davenant** Charles Davenant wrote a number of works on colonial trade; see his *Works*, ed. Charles Whitworth (5 vols., 1771).

[21] **office** i.e. of customs.

[22] **terminating almost wholly in the Colonies** because supposed to consist in slaves.

not entirely destroy, would very much depreciate the value of all the
parts. I therefore consider these three denominations to be, what in
effect they are, one trade.

The trade to the Colonies,[23] taken on the export side, at the beginning of this century, that is, in the year 1704, stood thus:

Exports to North America, and the
    West Indies, ... £483,265
To Africa, ... 86,665
                                                  569,930

In the year 1772, which I take as a middle year between the highest
and lowest of those lately laid on your table, the account was as
follows:

To North America and the West
    Indies, ... £4,791,734
To Africa, ... 866,398

    To which if you add the export
    trade from Scotland, which had   }   364,000
    in 1704 no existence, ...

                                       6,024,171

From Five Hundred and odd Thousand, it has grown to Six Millions. It has increased no less than twelve-fold. This is the state of the
Colony trade, as compared with itself at these two periods, within this
century; – and this is matter for meditation. But this is not all.
Examine my second account. See how the export trade to the Colonies alone in 1772 stood in the other point of view, that is, as
compared to the whole trade of England in 1704.

The trade with America alone is now within less than 500,000*l.* of
being equal to what this great commercial nation, England, carried on
at the beginning of this century with the whole world! If I had taken

[23] **trade to the Colonies** Burke's *Observations on a Late State of the Nation* (1769)
compared statistics of 1704 to illustrate the increase of the colonial trade. He noted
that the total exports of the colonies in 1704 were £483,265 and those of Jamaica
alone in 1767 were £467,681 (WSEB, II, p. 195).

The whole export trade of England, including that to the Colonies, in 1704, ...	£6,509,000
Export to the Colonies alone, in 1772, ...	6,024,000
Difference,	485,000

the largest year of those on your table, it would rather have exceeded. But, it will be said, is not this American trade an unnatural protuberance, that has drawn the juices from the rest of the body? The reverse. It is the very food that has nourished every other part into its present magnitude. Our general trade has been greatly augmented; and augmented more or less in almost every part to which it ever extended; but with this material difference; that of the Six Millions which in the beginning of the century constituted the whole mass of our export commerce, the Colony trade was but one- twelfth part; it is now (as a part of Sixteen Millions) considerably more than a third of the whole. This is the relative proportion of the importance of the Colonies at these two periods; and all reasoning concerning our mode of treating them must have this proportion as its basis; or it is a reasoning weak, rotten, and sophistical.

Mr. Speaker, I cannot prevail on myself to hurry over this great consideration. It is good for us to be here.[24] We stand where we have an immense view of what is, and what is past. Clouds indeed, and darkness, rest upon the future. Let us however, before we descend from this noble eminence, reflect that this growth of our national prosperity has happened within the short period of the Life of man. It has happened within Sixty- eight years. There are those alive whose memory might touch the two extremities. For instance, my lord Bathurst might remember all the stages of the progress. He was in 1704 of an age, at least to be made to comprehend such things. He was then old enough *acta parentum jam legere, et quae sit poterit cognoscere virtus*[25] – Suppose, Sir, that the angel of this auspicious youth, foreseeing the many virtues, which made him one of the most

---

[24] **to be here** Mark 9:5f.

[25] **acta parentum . . . virtus** 'to read now the acts of his ancestors and he could understand what virtue is' (Vergil, *Eclogues*, IV.26; the tense is altered to Burke's convenience).

amiable, as he is one of the most fortunate men of his age, had opened to him in vision, that when in the fourth generation,[26] the third Prince of the House of Brunswick had sat Twelve years on the throne of that nation, which (by the happy issue of moderate and healing councils) was to be made[27] Great Britain, he should see his son, Lord Chancellor of England, turn back the current of hereditary dignity to its fountain, and raise him to an higher rank of Peerage, whilst he enriched the family with a new one – If amidst these bright and happy scenes of domestic honour and prosperity, that angel should have drawn up the curtain, and unfolded the rising glories of his country, and whilst he was gazing with admiration on the then commercial grandeur of England, The Genius should point out to him a little speck, scarce visible in the mass of the national interest, a small seminal principle, rather than a formed body, and should tell him – 'Young man, There is America – which at this day serves for little more than to amuse you with stories of savage men,[28] and uncouth manners; yet shall, before you taste of death,[29] shew itself equal to the whole of that commerce which now attracts the envy of the world. Whatever England has been growing to by a progressive increase of improvement, brought in by varieties of people, by succession of civilizing conquests and civilizing settlements in a series of Seventeen Hundred years, you shall see as much added to her by America in the course of a single life!' If this state of his country had been foretold to him, would it not require all the sanguine credulity of youth, and all the fervid glow of enthusiasm, to make him believe it? Fortunate man, he has lived to see it! Fortunate indeed, if he lives to see nothing that shall vary the prospect and cloud the setting of his day![30]

---

[26] **in the fourth generation**   i.e. of the Hanoverian dynasty.

[27] **was to be made**   i.e. by the Union with Scotland in 1707.

[28] **stories of savage men**   cf. [William Burke], *Account*, pt. II, esp. ch. 4.

[29] **taste of death**   cf. Matthew 16:28; or *Julius Caesar*, II.ii.33.

[30] **setting of his day**   Johnson was merciless about this passage (see Mrs Piozzi, *Anecdotes of Dr Johnson*[2] (1786), p. 42f):

> Suppose, Mr Speaker, that to Wharton, or to Marlborough, or to any of the eminent Whigs of the last age, the devil had, not with any great impropriety, consented to appear; he would perhaps in somewhat like these words have commenced the conversation:
> 'You seem, my Lord, to be concerned at the judicious apprehension, that while you are sapping the foundations of loyalty at home, and propagating here the dangerous doctrine of resistance, the distance of America may secure its inhabitants from your arts, though active; but I will unfold to you the gay prospects of futurity. The people, now so innocent and harmless, shall draw the sword against their mother country, and bathe its point in the blood of their benefactors; this people, now contented with a little, shall then

Excuse me, Sir, if turning from such thoughts I resume this comparative view once more. You have seen it on a large scale; look at it on a small one. I will point out to your attention a particular instance of it in the single province of Pensylvania. In the year 1704 that province called for 11,459*l.* in value of your commodities, native and foreign. This was the whole. What did it demand in 1772? Why nearly Fifty times as much; for in that year the export to Pensylvania was 507,909*l.* nearly equal to the export to all the Colonies together in the first period.

I choose, Sir, to enter into these minute and particular details; because generalities, which in all other cases are apt to heighten and raise the subject, have here a tendency to sink it. When we speak of the commerce with our Colonies, fiction lags after truth; invention is unfruitful; and imagination cold and barren.

So far, Sir, as to the importance of the object in the view of its commerce, as concerned in the exports from England. If I were to detail the imports, I could shew how many enjoyments they procure, which deceive the burthen of life; how many materials which invigorate the springs of national industry, and extend and animate every part of our foreign and domestic commerce. This would be a curious subject indeed – but I must prescribe bounds to myself in a matter so vast and various.

I pass therefore to the Colonies in another point of view, their agriculture. This they have prosecuted with such a spirit, that, besides feeding plentifully their own growing multitude, their annual export of grain, comprehending rice, has some years ago exceeded a Million in value. Of their last harvest, I am persuaded, they will export much more. At the beginning of the century, some of these Colonies imported corn from the mother country. For some time past, the old world has been fed from the new. The scarcity which you have felt would have been a desolating famine; if this child of your old age, with a true filial piety, with a Roman charity,[31] had not put the full breast of

refuse to spare what they themselves confess they could not miss; and these men, now so honest and so grateful, shall, in return for peace and protection, see the vile agents in the house of Parliament, there to sow the seeds of sedition, and propagate confusion, perplexity, and pain. Be not dispirited, then, at the contemplation of their present happy state: I promise you that anarchy, poverty, and death shall, by my care, be carried even across the spacious Atlantic, and settle in America itself, the sure consequences of our beloved Whiggism.'

[31] **with a Roman charity** the story of Xanthippe and Cimon, related by Hyginus,

its youthful exuberance to the mouth of its exhausted parent.

As to the wealth which the Colonies have drawn from the sea by their fisheries, you had all that matter fully opened at your bar. You surely thought those acquisitions of value; for they seemed even to excite your envy;[32] and yet the spirit, by which that enterprizing employment has been exercised, ought rather, in my opinion, to have raised your esteem and admiration. And pray, Sir, what in the world is equal to it? Pass by the other parts, and look at the manner in which the people of New England have of late carried on the Whale Fishery. Whilst we follow them among the tumbling mountains of ice, and behold them penetrating into the deepest frozen recesses of Hudson's Bay, and Davis's Streights, whilst we are looking for them beneath the Arctic circle, we hear that they have pierced into the opposite region of polar cold, that they are at the Antipodes, and engaged under the frozen serpent of the south.[33] Falkland Island,[34] which seemed too remote and romantic an object for the grasp of national ambition,[35] is but a stage and resting-place in the progress of their victorious industry. Nor is the equinoctial heat more discouraging to them, than the accumulated winter of both the poles. We know that whilst some of them draw the line and strike the harpoon on the coast of Africa,

was known as the Roman Charity. Cimon was a prisoner, kept alive by the milk of his daughter Xanthippe. Pliny the elder (*Natural History*, VII, 36) and Valerius Maximus (V.47) have a mother instead of a father as the object of the story.

[32] **excite your envy** England and Holland had formerly divided the whaling industry, but Grenville's budget of 1764 freed the American colonies from restrictions on their whaling so that they took the first place.

[33] **frozen serpent of the South** the Hydrus is a small constellation within the Antarctic circle.

[34] **Falkland Island** 'Barren of everything except sea-lions and seals' (*Grenville Papers*, IV, p. 505). The correspondent continues 'there is not a stick so big as the pen I am writing with on any of them [the islands]'. This explains the scene in Samuel Foote's *The Cozeners* (1788), I.i, in which Mrs Fleece'em promises much to an applicant for the surveyorship of woods in Falkland's Island: 'Besides the salary, for perquisites you are to have all the loppings and Toppings' (p. 10f). Though estimates of the general character of the islands differed, no one mentioned trees.

[35] **too remote . . . national ambition** the islands were discovered at the end of the sixteenth century but not thought worth cultivating. In 1763 France built Port Louis on East Falkland and Britain soon after built Port Egmont on West Falkland, but soon abandoned it. The islands attained a new importance through whaling. They have since featured in the history of Britain and Argentina. 'That of which we were almost weary ourselves, we did not expect any one to envy; and therefore supposed that we should be permitted to reside in Falkland's Island, the undisputed lords of tempest-beaten barrenness' (Johnson *Thoughts on the Late Transactions respecting Falkland's Islands* (1771), *Political Writings* p. 67).

others run the longitude,[36] and pursue their gigantic game along the coast of Brazil. No sea but what is vexed by their fisheries. No climate that is not witness to their toils. Neither the perseverance of Holland, nor the activity of France, nor the dextrous and firm sagacity of English enterprize, ever carried this most perilous mode of hardy industry to the extent to which it has been pushed by this recent people; a people who are still, as it were, but in the gristle, and not yet hardened into the bone of manhood. When I contemplate these things; when I know that the Colonies in general owe little or nothing to any care of ours, and that they are not squeezed into this happy form by the constraints of watchful and suspicious government, but that through a wise and salutary neglect, a generous nature has been suffered to take her own way to perfection; when I reflect upon these effects, when I see how profitable they have been to us, I feel all the pride of power sink, and all presumption in the wisdom of human contrivances melt, and die away within me. My rigour relents. I pardon something to the spirit of Liberty.

I am sensible, Sir, that all which I have asserted in my detail, is admitted in the gross; but that quite a different conclusion is drawn from it. America, Gentlemen say, is a noble object. It is an object well worth fighting for. Certainly it is, if fighting a people be the best way of gaining them. Gentlemen in this respect will be led to their choice of means by their complexions and their habits. Those who understand the military art, will of course have some predilection for it. Those who wield the thunder of the state, may have more confidence in the efficacy of arms. But I confess, possibly for want of this knowledge, my opinion is much more in favour of prudent management, than of force; considering force not as an odious, but a feeble instrument, for preserving a people so numerous, so active, so growing, so spirited as this, in a profitable and subordinate connexion with us.

First, Sir, permit me to observe, that the use of force alone is but *temporary*. It may subdue for a moment; but it does not remove the necessity of subduing again: and a nation is not governed, which is perpetually to be conquered.

My next objection is its *uncertainty*. Terror is not always the effect of force; and an armament is not a victory. If you do not succeed, you are without resource; for, conciliation failing, force remains; but,

---

[36] **run the longitude**   sail down the South American coast.

force failing, no further hope of reconciliation is left. Power and authority are sometimes bought by kindness; but they can never be begged as alms, by an impoverished and defeated violence.

A farther objection to force is, that you *impair the object* by your very endeavours to preserve it. The thing you fought for, is not the thing which you recover; but depreciated, sunk, wasted, and consumed in the contest. Nothing less will content me, than *whole America*. I do not choose to consume its strength along with our own; because in all parts it is the British strength that I consume. I do not choose to be caught by a foreign enemy at the end of this exhausting conflict; and still less in the midst of it.[37] I may escape; but I can make no insurance against such an event. Let me add, that I do not choose wholly to break the American spirit, because it is the spirit that has made the country.

Lastly, we have no sort of *experience* in favour of force as an instrument in the rule of our Colonies. Their growth and their utility has been owing to methods altogether different. Our ancient indulgence has been said to be pursued to a fault. It may be so. But we know, if feeling is evidence, that our fault was more tolerable than our attempt to mend it; and our sin far more salutary than our penitence.

These, Sir, are my reasons for not entertaining that high opinion of untried force, by which many Gentlemen, for whose sentiments in other particulars I have great respect, seem to be so greatly captivated. But there is still behind a third consideration concerning this object, which serves to determine my opinion on the sort of policy which ought to be pursued in the management of America, even more than its Population and its Commerce, I mean its *Temper and Character*.

In this Character of the Americans, a love of Freedom is the predominating feature, which marks and distinguishes the whole: and as an ardent is always a jealous affection, your Colonies become suspicious, restive, and untractable, whenever they see the least attempt to wrest from them by force, or shuffle from them by chicane, what they think the only advantage worth living for. This fiece spirit of Liberty is stronger in the English Colonies probably than in any other people of the earth; and this from a great variety of powerful causes; which, to understand the true temper of their minds, and the direction which this spirit takes, it will not be amiss to lay open somewhat more largely.

[37] **caught . . . of it**   in 1778 France allied with the Americans against Britain.

First, the people of the Colonies are descendents of Englishmen. England, Sir, is a nation, which still I hope respects, and formerly adored, her freedom. The Colonists emigrated from you, when this part of your character was most predominant;[38] and they took this biass and direction the moment they parted from your hands. They are therefore not only devoted to Liberty, but to Liberty according to English ideas, and on English principles. Abstract Liberty, like other mere abstractions, is not to be found. Liberty inheres in some sensible object; and every nation has formed to itself some favourite point, which by way of eminence becomes the criterion of their happiness. It happened, you know, Sir, that the great contests for freedom in this country were from the earliest times chiefly upon the question of Taxing. Most of the contests in the ancient commonwealths turned primarily on the right of election of magistrates; or on the balance among the several orders of the state. The question of money was not with them so immediate. But in England it was otherwise. On this Point of Taxes the ablest pens, and most eloquent tongues have been exercised; the greatest spirits have acted and suffered. In order to give the fullest satisfaction concerning the importance of this point, it was not only necessary for those who in argument defended the excellence of the English constitution, to insist on this privilege of granting money as a dry point of fact, and to prove, that the right had been acknowledged in ancient parchments, and blind usages, to reside in a certain body called an House of Commons. They went much further; they attempted to prove, and they succeeded, that in theory it ought to be so, from the particular nature of a House of Commons, as an immediate representative of the people; whether the old records had delivered this oracle or not. They took infinite pains to inculcate, as a fundamental principle, that, in all monarchies, the people must in effect themselves mediately or immediately possess the power of granting their own money, or no shadow of liberty could subsist. The Colonies draw from you, as with their life-blood, these ideas and principles. Their love of liberty, as with you, fixed and attached on this specific point of taxing. Liberty might be safe, or might be endangered in twenty other particulars, without their being much

---

[38] **character was most predominant** 'The American freeholders at present are nearly, in point of condition, what the English Yeomen were of old, when they rendered us formidable to all Europe, and our name celebrated throughout the world. The former, from many obvious circumstances, are more enthusiastical lovers of liberty, than even our Yeomen were' (AR, 1775, p. 14).

pleased or alarmed. Here they felt its pulse; and as they found that beat, they thought themselves sick or sound. I do not say whether they were right or wrong in applying your general arguments to their own case. It is not easy indeed to make a monopoly of theorems and corollaries. The fact is, that they did thus apply those general arguments; and your mode of governing them, whether through lenity or indolence, through wisdom or mistake, confirmed them in the imagination, that they as well as you had an interest in these common principles.

They were farther confirmed in this pleasing error by the form of their provincial legislative assemblies. Their governments are popular[39] in an high degree; some are merely popular; in all, the popular representative is the most weighty; and this share of the people in their ordinary government never fails to inspire them with lofty sentiments, and with a strong aversion from whatever tends to deprive them of their chief importance.

If any thing were wanting to this necessary operation of the form of government, Religion would have given it a complete effect. Religion, always a principle of energy, in this new people, is no way worn out or impaired; and their mode of professing it is also one main cause of this free spirit. The people are protestants; and of that kind, which is the most adverse to all implicit submission of mind and opinion. This is a persuasion not only favourable to liberty, but built upon it. I do not think, Sir, that the reason of this averseness in the dissenting churches from all that looks like absolute Government is so much to be sought in their religious tenets, as in their history. Every one knows, that the Roman Catholick religion is at least coeval with most of the governments where it prevails; that it has generally gone hand in hand with them; and received great favour and every kind of support from authority. The Church of England too was formed from her cradle under the nursing care of regular government. But the dissenting interests have sprung up in direct opposition to all the ordinary powers of the world; and could justify that opposition only on a strong claim to natural liberty. Their very existence depended on the powerful and unremitted assertion of that claim. All protestantism, even the most cold and passive, is a sort of dissent. But the

---

[39] **popular** but Pennsylvania and Maryland were proprietary governments and the Carolinas, Georgia, Virginia, and New Jersey were royal colonies; cf. *Account*, pt. VII, ch. 30 (esp. vol. II, p. 296).

religion most prevalent in our Northern Colonies is a refinement on the principle of resistance; it is the dissidence of dissent;[40] and the protestantism of the protestant religion. This religion, under a variety of denominations, agreeing in nothing but in the communion of the spirit of liberty, is predominant in most of the Northern provinces; where the Church of England, notwithstanding its legal rights, is in reality no more than a sort of private sect, not composing most probably the tenth of the people. The Colonists left England when this spirit was high; and in the emigrants was the highest of all: and even that stream of foreigners, which has been constantly flowing into these Colonies, has, for the greatest part, been composed of dissenters from the establishments of their several countries, and have brought with them a temper and character far from alien to that of the people with whom they mixed.

Sir, I can perceive by their manner, that some Gentlemen object to the latitude of this description; because in the Southern Colonies the Church of England forms a large body, and has a regular establishment. It is certainly true. There is however a circumstance attending these Colonies, which in my opinion fully counterbalances this difference, and makes the spirit of liberty still more high and haughty than in those to the Northward. It is that in Virginia and the Carolinas, they have a vast multitude of slaves. Where this is the case in any part of the world, those who are free are by far the most proud and jealous of their freedom. Freedom is to them not only an enjoyment, but a kind of rank and privilege. Not seeing there, that freedom, as in countries where it is a common blessing, and as broad and general as the air,[41] may be united with much abject toil, with great misery, with all the exterior of servitude, Liberty looks amongst them like something that is more noble and liberal. I do not mean, Sir, to commend the superior morality of this sentiment, which has at least as much pride as virtue in it; but I cannot alter the nature of man. The fact is so; and these people of the Southern Colonies are much more strongly, and with an higher and more stubborn spirit, attached to liberty than those to the Northward. Such were all the ancient com-

---

[40] **dissidence of dissent** the idea is from Hooker, *Lawes of Ecclesiastical Polity*, iv.viii.4: 'seeketh to reform even the French reformation'. Tucker, *Letter*, p. 11, suggested that the religious enthusiasms of the original settlers had been replaced by a passion for Locke (cf. p. 18f).

[41] **as broad and general as the air** cf. *Macbeth*, iii.iv.22.

monwealths; such were our Gothick ancestors;[42] such in our days were the Poles;[43] and such will be all masters of slaves, who are not slaves themselves. In such a people the haughtiness of domination combines with the spirit of freedom, fortifies it, and renders it invincible.

Permit me, Sir, to add another circumstance in our Colonies, which contributes no mean part towards the growth and effect of this untractable spirit. I mean their education. In no country perhaps in the world is the law so general a study. The profession itself is numerous and powerful;[44] and in most provinces it takes the lead. The greater number of the Deputies sent to the Congress[45] were Lawyers. But all who read, and most do read, endeavour to obtain some smattering in that science. I have been told by an eminent Bookseller, that in no branch of his business, after tracts of popular devotion, were so many books as those on the Law exported to the Plantations. The Colonists have now fallen into the way of printing them for their own use. I hear that they have sold nearly as many of Blackstone's Commentaries[46] in America as in England. General Gage marks out this disposition very particularly in a letter on your table. He states, that all the people in his government are lawyers, or smatterers in law; and that in Boston they have been enabled, by successful chicane,[47] wholly to evade many parts of one of your capital penal constitutions. The smartness of debate will say, that this knowledge ought to teach them more clearly the rights of legislature, their obligations to obedience, and the penalties of rebellion. All this is might well. But my honourable and learned friend[48] on the floor, who

[42] **our Gothick ancestors** cf. Burke's *Abridgement*, II.vii on the Germans.

[43] **the Poles** 'Poland seems to be a country formed to give the most disadvantageous idea of liberty, by the extreme to which it is carried, and the injustice with which it is distributed' (AR, 1763, p. 42 (second pagination)).

[44] **numerous and powerful** cf. *Account*, pt. VII, ch. 30: 'In many . . . the lawyers have gathered to themselves the greatest part of the wealth of the country'. Tucker, *Letter*, p. 26, also commented on American legalism. Burke was to find one of the causes of the French Revolution in the predominance of lawyers in the National Assembly (*Reflections*, pp. 129–31).   [45] **Congress** at Philadelphia, 1774.

[46] **Blackstone's Commentaries** 1st edition 1765–69; for their influence, see G. Stouzh, 'William Blackstone: Teacher of Revolution', *Jahrbuch für Amerikastudien*, 15 (1970).

[47] **by successful chicane** Gage had prohibited the *calling* of town meetings after 1 August 1774. A town meeting occurred, on the pretence that it had not been called but merely succeeded an adjournment. See AR, 1775, p. 11.

[48] **honourable and learned friend** Thurlow, then attorney-general.

condescends to mark what I say for animadversion, will disdain that ground. He has heard as well as I, that when great honours and great emoluments do not win over this knowledge to the service of the state, it is a formidable adversary to government. If the spirit be not tamed and broken by these happy methods, it is stubborn and litigious. *Abeunt studia in mores.*[49] This study[50] renders men acute, inquisitive, dextrous, prompt in attack, ready in defence, full of resources. In other countries, the people, more simple and of a less mercurial cast, judge of an ill principle in government only by an actual grievance; here they anticipate the evil, and judge of the pressure of the grievance by the badness of the principle. They augur misgovernment at a distance; and snuff the approach of tyranny in every tainted breeze.

The last cause of this disobedient spirit in the Colonies is hardly less powerful than the rest, as it is not merely moral, but laid deep in the natural constitution of things. Three thousand miles of ocean lie between you and them. No contrivance can prevent the effect of this distance, in weakening Government. Seas roll, and months pass, between the order and the execution; and the want of a speedy explanation of a single point is enough to defeat an whole system. You have, indeed, winged ministers of vengeance, who carry your bolts in their pounces to the remotest verge of the sea. But there a power steps in,[51] that limits the arrogance of rageing passions and furious elements, and says, 'So far shalt thou go, and no farther.' Who are you, that should fret and rage, and bite the chains of Nature? – Nothing worse happens to you, than does to all Nations, who have extensive Empire; and it happens in all the forms into which Empire can be thrown. In large bodies, the circulation of power must be less vigorous at the extremities. Nature has said it. The Turk cannot govern Egypt, and Arabia, and Curdistan, as he governs Thrace;[52] nor has he the same dominion in Crimea, and Algiers, which he has at Brusa and Smyrna. Despotism itself is obliged to truck and huckster. The Sultan gets such obedience as he can. He governs with a loose rein, that he may govern at all; and the whole of the force and vigour of his authority in his centre, is derived from a prudent relaxation in all his

[49] **Abeunt studia in mores** 'studies inform character' (Ovid *Heroides*, xv.83).
[50] **This study** Burke's father was an attorney and he himself had studied law.
[51] **a power steps in** a reference to the story of Canute.
[52] **Thrace** European Turkey.

borders. Spain, in her provinces,[53] is, perhaps, not so well obeyed, as you are in yours. She complies too; she submits; she watches times. This is the immutable condition, the eternal Law, of extensive and detached Empire.

Then, Sir, from these six capital sources; of Descent; of Form of Government; of Religion in the Northern Provinces; of Manners in the Southern; of Education; of the Remoteness of Situation from the First Mover of Government; from all these causes a fierce Spirit of Liberty has grown up. It has grown with the growth of the people in your Colonies, and encreased with the encrease of their wealth; a Spirit, that unhappily meeting with an exercise of Power in England, which, however lawful, is not reconcileable to any ideas of Liberty, much less with theirs, has kindled this flame, that is ready to consume us.

I do not mean to commend either the Spirit in this excess, or the moral causes which produce it. Perhaps a more smooth and accommodating Spirit of Freedom in them would be more acceptable to us. Perhaps ideas of Liberty might be desired, more reconcileable with an arbitrary and boundless authority. Perhaps we might wish the Colonists to be persuaded, that their Liberty is more secure when held in trust for them by us (as their guardians during a perpetual minority) than with any part of it in their own hands. But the question is, not whether their spirit deserves praise or blame; – what, in the name of God, shall we do with it? You have before you the object; such as it is, with all its glories, with all its imperfections on its head.[54] You see the magnitude; the importance; the temper; the habits; the disorders. By all these considerations, we are strongly urged to determine something concerning it. We are called upon to fix some rule and line for our future conduct, which may give a little stability to our politics, and prevent the return of such unhappy deliberations as the present. Every such return will bring the matter before us in a still more untractable form. For, what astonishing and incredible things have we not seen already? What monsters have not been generated from this unnatural contention? Whilst every principle of authority and resistance has been pushed, upon both sides, as far as it would go, there is nothing so solid and certain, either in reasoning or in practice, that has been not shaken. Until very lately, all authority in America

[53] **in her provinces**   i.e. those in South America.
[54] **on its head**   cf. *Hamlet*, i.v.79.

seemed to be nothing but an emanation from yours. Even the popular part of the Colony Constitution derived all its activity, and its first vital movement, from the pleasure of the Crown. We thought, Sir, that the utmost which the discontented Colonists could do, was to disturb authority; we never dreamt they could of themselves supply it; knowing in general what an operose business it is, to establish a Government absolutely new. But having, for our purposes in this contention, resolved, that none but an obedient Assembly should fit, the humours of the people there, finding all passage through the legal channel stopped, with great violence broke out another way. Some provinces[55] have tried their experiment, as we have tried ours; and theirs has succeeded. They have formed a Government sufficient for its purposes, without the bustle of a Revolution, or the troublesome formality of an Election. Evident necessity, and tacit consent, have done the business in an instant. So well they have done it, that Lord Dunmore (the account is among the fragments on your table) tells you, that the new institution is infinitely better obeyed than the antient Government ever was in its most fortunate periods. Obedience is what makes Government, and not the names by which it is called; not the name of Governor, as formerly, or Committee, as at present. This new Government has originated directly from the people; and was not transmitted through any of the ordinary artificial media of a positive constitution. It was not a manufacture ready formed, and transmitted to them in that condition from England. The evil arising from hence is this; that the Colonists having once found the possibility of enjoying the advantages of order, in the midst of a struggle for Liberty, such struggles will not henceforward seem so terrible to the settled and sober part of mankind, as they had appeared before the trial.

Pursuing the same plan of punishing by the denial of the exercise of Government to still greater lengths, we wholly abrogated the ancient Government of Massachuset. We were confident, that the first feeling, if not the very prospect of anarchy, would instantly enforce a compleat submission. The experiment was tried. A new, strange, unexpected face of things appeared. Anarchy is found tolerable. A vast province has now subsisted, and subsisted in a considerable degree of health and vigour, for near a twelve-month, without Governor, without public Council, without Judges, without executive

---

[55] **some provinces**   e.g. Virginia and Massachusetts.

Magistrates. How long it will continue in this state, or what may arise out of this unheard-of situation, how can the wisest of us conjecture? Our late experience has taught us, that many of those fundamental principles, formerly believed infallible, are either not of the import-ance they were imagined to be; or that we have not at all adverted to some other far more important, and far more powerful principles, which entirely over-rule those we have considered as omnipotent. I am much against any further experiments, which tend to put to the proof any more of these allowed opinions, which contribute so much to the public tranquillity. In effect, we suffer as much at home, by this loosening of all ties, and this concussion of all established opinions, as we do abroad. For, in order to prove, that the Americans have no right to their Liberties, we are every day endeavouring to subvert the maxims, which preserve the whole Spirit of our own. To prove that the Americans ought not to be free, we are obliged to depreciate the value of Freedom itself; and we never seem to gain a paltry advantage over them in debate, without attacking some of those principles, or deriding some of those feelings, for which our ancestors have shed their blood.

But, Sir, in wishing to put an end to pernicious experiments, I do not mean to preclude the fullest enquiry. Far from it. Far from deciding on a sudden or partial view, I would patiently go round and round the subject, and survey it minutely in every possible aspect. Sir, if I were capable of engaging you to an equal attention, I would state, that, as far as I am capable of discerning, there are but three ways of proceeding relative to this stubborn Spirit, which prevails in your Colonies, and disturbs your Government. These are – To change that Spirit, as inconvenient, by removing the Causes. To prosecute it as criminal. Or, to comply with it as necessary. I would not be guilty of an imperfect enumeration; I can think of but these three. Another has indeed been started that of giving up the Colonies; but it met so slight a reception, that I do not think myself obliged to dwell a great while upon it. It is nothing but a little sally of anger; like forwardness of peevish children; who, when they cannot get all they would have, are resolved to take nothing.

The first of these plans, to change the Spirit as inconvenient, by removing the causes, I think is the most like a systematick proceeding. It is radical in its principle; but it is attended with great difficulties, some of them little short, as I conceive, of impossibilities. This will appear by examining into the Plans which have been proposed.

As the growing population in the Colonies is evidently one cause of their resistance, it was last session mentioned in both Houses, by men of weight, and received not without applause, that, in order to check this evil, it would be proper for the crown to make no further grants of land. But to this scheme, there are two objections. The first, that there is already so much unsettled land in private hands, as to afford room for an immense future population, although the crown not only withheld its grants, but annihilated its soil. If this be the case, then the only effect of this avarice of desolation, this hoarding of a royal wilderness, would be to raise the value of the possessions in the hands of the great private monopolists, without any adequate check to the growing and alarming mischief of population.

But, if you stopped your grants, what would be the consequence? The people would occupy without grants. They have already so occupied in many places. You cannot station garrisons in every part of these deserts. If you drive the people from one place, they will carry on their annual tillage, and remove with their flocks and herds to another. Many of the people in the back settlements are already little attached to particular situations. Already they have topped the Apalachian mountains.[56] From thence they behold before them an immense plain,[57] one vast, rich, level meadow; a square of five hundred miles. Over this they would wander, without a possibility of restraint; they would change their manners with the habits of their life; would soon forget a government, by which they were disowned; would become Hordes of English Tartars; and, pouring down upon your unfortified frontiers a fierce and irresistible cavalry, become masters of your Governors and your Counsellors, your collectors and comptrollers, and of all the Slaves that adhered to them. Such would, and, in no long time, must be, the effect of attempting to forbid as a crime, and to suppress as an evil, the Command and Blessing of Providence, 'Encrease and Multiply.'[58] Such would be the happy result of an endeavour to keep, as a lair of wild beasts, that earth, which God by an express Charter has given to the children of men.[59]

---

[56] **Apalachian mountains**   there is a reminiscence here of AR, 1758, p. 2.
[57] **an immense plain**   the other boundaries are the Mississippi and the lakes.
[58] **Encrease and Multiply**   this form is from *Paradise Lost*, x.730 rather than the Authorised Version.
[59] **children of men**   Psalms 115:16.

Far different, and surely much wiser, has been our policy hitherto. Hitherto we have invited our people, by every kind of bounty, to fixed establishments. We have invited the husbandman, to look to authority for his title. We have taught him piously to believe in the mysterious virtue of wax and parchment. We have thrown each tract of land, as it was peopled, into districts; that the ruling power should never be wholly out of sight. We have settled all we could; and we have carefully attended every settlement with government.

Adhering, Sir, as I do, to this policy, as well as for the reasons I have just given, I think this new project of hedging-in population to be neither prudent nor practicable.

To impoverish the Colonies in general, and in particular to arrest the noble course of their marine enterprizes, would be more easy task. I freely confess it. We have shewn a disposition to a system of this kind; a disposition even to continue the restraint after the offence; looking on ourselves as rivals to our Colonies, and persuaded that of course we must gain all that they shall lose. Much mischief we may certainly do. The power inadequate to all other things is often more than sufficient for this. I do not look on the direct and immediate power of the Colonies to resist our violence, as very formidable. In this, however, I may be mistaken. But when I consider, that we have Colonies for no purpose but to be serviceable to us, it seems to my poor understanding a little preposterous, to make them unserviceable, in order to keep them obedient. It is, in truth, nothing more than the old, and, as I thought, exploded problem of tyranny, which proposes to beggar its subjects into submission. But, remember, when you have compleated your system of impoverishment, that Nature still proceeds in her ordinary course; that discontent will encrease with misery; and that there are critical moments in the fortune of all states, when they, who are too weak to contribute to your prosperity, may be strong enough to complete you ruin. *Spoliatis arma supersunt.*[60]

The temper and character which prevail in our Colonies, are, I am afraid, unalterable by any human art. We cannot, I fear, falsify the pedigree of this fierce people, and persuade them that they are not sprung from a nation, in whose veins the blood of freedom circulates. The language in which they would hear you tell them this tale, would

[60] *Spoliatis arma supersunt* 'weapons remain to those who have been plundered' (Juvenal, *Satires*, VIII.124).

detect the imposition; your speech would betray you.[61] An Englishman is the unfittest person on earth, to argue another Englishman
into slavery.

I think it is nearly as little in our power to change their republican
Religion, as their free descent; or to substitute the Roman Catholick,
as a penalty;[62] or the Church of England, as an improvement. The
mode of inquisition and dragooning is going out of fashion in the old
world; and I should not confide much to their efficacy in the new. The
education of the Americans is also on the same unalterable bottom
with their religion. You cannot persuade them to burn their books of
curious science;[63] to banish their lawyers from their courts of law; or
to quench the lights of their assemblies, by refusing to choose those
persons who are best read in their privileges. It would be no less
impracticable to think of wholly annihilating the popular assemblies,
in which these lawyers sit. The army by which we must govern in their
place, would be far more chargeable to us; not quite so effectual; and
perhaps, in the end, full as difficult to be kept in obedience.

With regard to the high aristocratick spirit of Virginia and the
Southern Colonies, it has been proposed, I know, to reduce it, by
declaring a general enfranchisement of their slaves. This project has
had its advocates and panegyrists; yet I never could argue myself into
any opinion of it. Slaves are often much attached to their masters. A
general wild offer of liberty would not always be accepted. History
furnishes few instances of it. It is sometimes as hard to persuade
slaves to be free, as it is to compel freemen to be slaves; and in this
auspicious scheme we should have both these pleasing tasks on our
hands at once. But when we talk of enfranchisement, do we not
perceive that the American master may enfranchise too; and arm
servile hands in defence of freedom? A measure to which other
people have had recourse more than once, and not without success, in
a desperate situation of their affairs.[64]

Slaves as these unfortunate black people are, and dull as all men
are from slavery,[65] must they not a little suspect the offer of freedom

---

[61] **betray you**   St Matthew 26:73.

[62] **as a penalty**   presumably glances at Ireland; but Burke knew that Maryland was
predominantly Catholic, see *Account of the European Settlements*, pt. VII, ch. 18.

[63] **curious science**   Acts 19:19.

[64] **affairs**   the Athenians seem to have had armed slaves at Arginusae (Aristophanes,
Ranae, l.27); and after Cannae the Romans armed numerous slaves (Livy, XXIV.14).

[65] **slavery**   cf. VNS, above, p. 32 and note.

from that very nation which has sold them to their present masters?
From that nation, one of whose causes of quarrel with those masters
is their refusal to deal any more in that inhuman traffick? An offer of
freedom from England would come rather oddly, shipped to them in
an African vessel, which is refused an entry into the ports of Virginia
or Carolina, with a cargo of three hundred Angola negroes. It would
be curious to see the Guinea captain attempting at the same instant to
publish his proclamation of liberty, and to advertise his sale of
slaves.

But let us suppose all these moral difficulties got over. The Ocean
remains. You cannot pump this dry; and as long as it continues in its
present bed, so long all the causes which weaken authority by distance
will continue. 'Ye Gods annihilate but space and time, and make two
lovers happy!'[66] – was a pious and passionate prayer; – but just as
reasonable, as many of the serious wishes of very grave and solemn
politicians.

If then, Sir, it seems almost desperate to think of any alterative
course, for changing the moral causes (and not quite easy to remove
the natural), which produce prejudices irreconcileable to the late
exercise of our authority; but that the spirit infallibly will continue;
and, continuing, will produce such effects, as now embarrass us; the
second mode under consideration is, to prosecute that spirit in its
overt acts, as *criminal.*

At this proposition, I must pause a moment. The thing seems a
great deal too big for my ideas of jurisprudence. It should seem, to my
way of conceiving such matters, that there is a very wide difference in
reason and policy, between the mode of proceeding on the irregular
conduct of scattered individuals, or even of bands of men, who disturb order within the state, and the civil dissentions which may, from
time to time, on great questions, agitate the several communities
which compose a great Empire. It looks to me to be narrow and
pedantic, to apply the ordinary ideas of criminal justice to this great
public contest. I do not know the method of drawing up an indictment
against an whole people. I cannot insult and ridicule the feelings of
Millions of my fellow-creatures, as Sir Edward Coke insulted one

[66] **space and time**   Alexander Pope, *Peri Bathous: or Martinus Scriblerus His Treatise
of the Art of Sinking in Poetry,* in Rosemary Cowler (ed.), *The Prose Works of
Alexander Pope,* II, (1986), p. 211. For the use of *annihilate time and space,* cf. AR,
1761, p. 207.

excellent individual (Sir Walter Rawleigh[67]) at the bar. I am not ripe to pass sentence on the gravest public bodies, entrusted with magistracies of great authority and dignity, and charged with the safety of their fellow-citizens, upon the very same title that I am. I really think, that for wise men, this is not judicious; for sober men, not decent; for minds tinctured with humanity, not mild and merciful.

Perhaps, Sir, I am mistaken in my idea of an Empire, as distinguished from a single State or Kingdom. But my idea of it is this; that an Empire is the aggregate of many States, under one common head; whether this head be a monarch, or a presiding republic. It does, in such constitutions, frequently happen (and nothing but the dismal, cold, dead uniformity of servitude can prevent its happening) that the subordinate parts have many local privileges and immunities. Between these privileges, and the supreme common authority, the line may be extremely nice. Of course disputes, often too, very bitter disputes, and much ill blood, will arise. But though every privilege is an exemption (in the case) from the ordinary exercise of the supreme authority, it is no denial of it. The claim of a privilege seems rather, *ex vi termini*,[68] to imply a superior power. For to talk of the privileges of a State or of a person, who has no superior, is hardly any better than speaking nonsense. Now, in such unfortunate quarrels, among the component parts of a great political union of communities, I can scarcely conceive any thing more compleatly imprudent, than for the Head of the Empire to insist, that, if any privilege is pleaded against his will, or his acts, that his whole authority is denied; instantly to proclaim rebellion, to beat to arms, and to put the offending provinces under the ban. Will not this, Sir, very soon teach the provinces to make no distinctions on their part? Will it not teach them that the Government, against which a claim of Liberty is tantamont to high-treason, is a Government to which submission is equivalent to slavery? It may not always be quite convenient to impress dependent communities with such an idea.

We are, indeed, in all disputes with the Colonies, by the necessity of things, the judge. It is true, Sir. But, I confess, that the character of judge in my own cause is a thing that frightens me. Instead of filling me with pride, I am exceedingly humbled by it. I cannot proceed with

---

[67] **Rawleigh** see *Complete Collection of State Trials* (34 vols., 1809–28), ed. W. Cobbett *et al*, II, pp. 7ff.

[68] **ex vi termini** from the meaning of the term.

a stern, assured, judicial confidence, until I find myself in something more like a judicial character. I must have these hesitations as long as I am compelled to recollect, that, in my little reading upon such contests as these, the sense of mankind has, at least, as often decided against the superior as the subordinate power. Sir, let me add too, that the opinion of my having some abstract right in my favour would not put me much at my ease in passing sentence; unless I could be sure, that there were no rights which, in their exercise under certain circumstances, were not the most odious of all wrongs, and the most vexatious of all injustice. Sir, these considerations have great weight with me, when I find things so circumstanced; that I see the same party, at once a civil litigant against me in a point of right; and a culprit before me, while I sit as a criminal judge, on acts of his, whose moral quality is to be decided upon the merits of that very litigation. Men are every now and then put, by the complexity of human affairs, into strange situations; but Justice is the same, let the Judge be in what situation he will.

There is, Sir, also a circumstance which convinces me, that this mode of criminal proceeding is not (at least in the present stage of our contest) altogether expedient; which is nothing less than the conduct of those very persons who have seemed to adopt that mode, by lately declaring a rebellion in Massachuset's Bay, as they had formerly addressed to have Traitors brought hither under an act of Henry the Eighth, for Trial. For though rebellion is declared, it is not proceeded against as such; nor have any steps been taken towards the apprehension or conviction of any individual offender, either on our late or our former address; but modes of public coercion[69] have been adopted, and such as have much more resemblance to a sort of qualified hostility towards an independant power, than the punishment of rebellious subjects. All this seems rather inconsistent; but it shews how difficult it is to apply these juridical ideas to our present case.

In this situation, let us seriously and coolly ponder. What is it we have got by all our menaces, which have been many and ferocious? What advantage have we derived from the penal laws we have passed, and which, for the time, have been severe and numerous? What advances have we made towards our object, by the sending of a force, which, by land and sea, is no contemptible strength? Has the disorder

[69] **coercion** e.g. the Act of 1774 closing Boston harbour.

abated? Nothing less.[70] – When I see things in this situation, after such confident hopes, bold promises, and active exertions, I cannot, for my life, avoid a suspicion, that the plan itself is not correctly right.

If then the removal of the causes of this spirit of American Liberty be, for the greater part, or rather entirely, impracticable; if the ideas of Criminal Process be inapplicable, or, if applicable, are in the highest degree inexpedient, what way yet remains? No way is open, but the third and last – to comply with the American Spirit as necessary; or, if you please, to submit to it, as a necessary Evil.

If we adopt this mode; if we mean to conciliate and concede; let us see of what nature the concession ought to be? To ascertain the nature of our concession, we must look at their complaint. The Colonies complain, that they have not the characteristic Mark and Seal of British Freedom. They complain, that they are taxed in a Parliament, in which they are not represented. If you mean to satisfy them at all, you must satisfy them with regard to this complaint. If you mean to please any people, you must give them the boon which they ask; not what you may think better for them, but of a kind totally different. Such an act may be a wise regulation, but it is no concession: whereas our present theme is the mode of giving satisfaction.

Sir, I think you must perceive, that I am resolved this day to have nothing at all to do with the question of the right of taxation. Some gentlemen startle – but it is true: I put it totally out of the question. It is less than nothing in my consideration. I do not indeed wonder, nor will you, Sir, that gentlemen of profound learning are fond of displaying it on this profound subject. But my consideration is narrow, confined, and wholly limited to the Policy of the question. I do not examine, whether the giving away a man's money be a power excepted and reserved out of the general trust of Government; and how far all mankind, in all forms of Polity, are intitled to an exercise of that Right by the Charter of Nature. Or whether, on the contrary, a Right of Taxation is necessarily involved in the general principle of Legislation, and inseparable from the ordinary Supreme Power? These are deep questions, where great names militate against each other; where reason is perplexed; and an appeal to authorities only thickens the confusion. For high and reverend authorities[71] lift up their heads on

---

[70] **less** Isaiah 40:17.
[71] **reverend authorities** 'as to the right of taxation, the gentlemen who opposed it produced many learned authorities from Locke, Selden, Harrington, and Puf-

both sides; and there is no sure footing in the middle. This point is the *great Serbonian bog,*[72] *betwixt Damiata and Mount Casius old, where armies whole have sunk.* I do not intend to be overwhelmed in that bog, though in such respectable company. The question with me is, not whether you have a right to render your people miserable; but whether it is not your interest to make them happy? Is it not, what a lawyer tells me, I *may* do; but what humanity, reason, and justice, tell me, I ought to do. Is a politic act the worse for being a generous one? Is no concession proper, but that which is made from your want of right to keep what you grant? Or does it lessen the grace or dignity of relaxing in the exercise of an odious claim, because you have your evidence-room full of Titles, and your magazines stuffed with arms to enforce them? What signify all those titles, and all those arms? Of what avail are they, when the reason of the thing tells me that the assertion of my title is the loss of my suit; and that I could do nothing but wound myself by the use of my own weapons?

Such is stedfastly my opinion of the absolute necessity of keeping up the concord of this empire by a unity of Spirit, though in a diversity of operations,[73] that, if I were sure the Colonists had, at their leaving this country, sealed a regular compact of servitude; that they had solemnly abjured all the rights of citizens; that they had made a vow to renounce all ideas of Liberty for them and their posterity, to all generations; yet I should hold myself obliged to conform to the temper I found universally prevalent in my own day, and to govern two millions of men, impatient of Servitude, on the principles of Freedom. I am not determining a point of law; I am restoring tranquillity; and the general character and situation of a people must determine what sort of government is fitted for them. That point nothing else can or ought to determine.

My idea therefore, without considering whether we yield as matter of right, or grant as matter of favour, is *to admit the people of our Colonies into an interest in the constitution*; and, by recording that admis-

---

fendorf, shewing that the very foundation and ultimate point in view of all government, is the good of society ... These arguments were answered with great force of reason, and knowledge of the constitution, by the other side' (*AR*, 1766, p. 37).

[72] **Serbonian bog** the story is from Herodotus, *Histories*, III.5, and the quotation from *Paradise Lost*, II.592. Burke was fond of the passage (cf. WSEB, II, p. 86, and *Reflections*, p. 313), but its point here is to cover his silence about the Declaratory Act.

[73] **diversity of operations** cf. I Corinthians 12:4f.

sion in the Journals of Parliament, to give them as strong an assurance as the nature of the thing will admit, that we mean for ever to adhere to that solemn declaration of systematic indulgence.

Some years ago, the repeal of a revenue act, upon its understood principle, might have served to shew, that we intended an unconditional abatement of the exercise of a Taxing Power. Such a measure was then sufficient to remove all suspicion; and to give perfect content. But unfortunate events, since that time, may make something further necessary; and not more necessary for the satisfaction of the Colonies, than for the dignity and consistency of our own future proceeding.

I have taken a very incorrect measure of the disposition of the House, if this proposal in itself would be received with dislike. I think, Sir, we have few American Financiers.[74] But our misfortune is, we are too acute; we are too exquisite in our conjectures of the future, for men oppressed with such great and present evils. The more moderate among the opposers of Parliamentary Concession freely confess, that they hope no good from Taxation; but they apprehend the Colonists have further views; and, if this point were conceded, they would instantly attack the Trade-laws. These Gentlemen are convinced, that this was the intention from the beginning; and the quarrel of the Americans with Taxation was no more than a cloke and cover to this design. Such has been the language even of a Gentleman of real moderation,[75] and of a natural temper well adjusted to fair and equal Government. I am, however, Sir, not a little surprised at this kind of discourse, whenever I hear it; and I am the more surprized, on account of the arguments which I constantly find in company with it, and which are often urged from the same mouths, and on the same day.

For instance, when we alledge, that it is against reason to tax a people under so many restraints in trade as the Americans, the Noble Lord in the blue ribband shall tell you, that the restraints on trade are futile and useless; of no advantage to us, and of no burthen to those on whom they are imposed; that the trade to America is not secured by the acts of navigation, but by the natural and irresistible advantage of a commercial preference.

---

[74] **American Financiers** people who view the American question in a merely fiscal light.

[75] **Gentleman of real moderation** Rice.

Such is the merit of the trade-laws in this posture of the debate. But when strong internal circumstances are urged against the taxes; when the scheme is dissected; when experience and the nature of things are brought to prove, and do prove, the utter impossibility of obtaining an effective revenue from the Colonies; when these things are pressed, or rather press themselves, so as to drive the advocates of Colony taxes to a clear admission of the futility of the scheme; then, Sir, the sleeping trade laws revive from their trance; and this useless taxation is to be kept sacred, not for its own sake, but as a counter-guard and security of the laws of trade.

Then, Sir, you keep up revenue laws which are mischievous, in order to preserve trade laws that are useless. Such is the wisdom of our plan in both its members. They are separately given up as of no value; and yet one is always to be defended for the sake of the other. But I cannot agree with the Noble Lord, nor with the pamphlet from whence he seems to have borrowed[76] these ideas, concerning the inutility of the trade-laws. For without idolizing them, I am sure they are still, in many ways, of great use to us; and in former times, they have been of the greatest. They do confine, and they do greatly narrow, the market for the Americans. But my perfect conviction of this does not help me in the least to discern how the revenue laws form any security whatsoever to the commercial regulations; or that these commercial regulations are the true ground of the quarrel; or, that the giving way in any one instance of authority is to lose all that may remain unconceded.

One fact is clear and indisputable. The public and avowed origin of this quarrel, was on taxation. This quarrel has indeed brought on new disputes on new questions; but certainly the least bitter, and the fewest of all, on the trade laws. To judge which of the two be the real radical cause of quarrel, we have to see whether the commercial dispute did, in order of time, precede the dispute on taxation. There is not a shadow of evidence for it. Next, to enable us to judge whether at this moment a dislike to the Trade Laws be the real cause of quarrel, it is absolutely necessary to put the taxes out of the question by a repeal. See how the Americans act in this position, and then you will be able to discern correctly what is the true object of the controversy, or whether any controversy at all will remain. Unless you

[76] **seems to have borrowed** by Josiah Tucker, whom Burke had handled in American Taxation, WSEB, II, p. 446.

consent to remove this cause of difference, it is impossible, with decency, to assert that the dispute is not upon what it is avowed to be. And I would, Sir, recommend to your serious consideration, whether it be prudent to form a rule for punishing people, not on their own acts, but on your conjectures? Surely it is preposterous at the very best. It is not justifying your anger, by their misconduct; but it is converting your ill-will into their delinquency.

But the Colonies will go further. – Alas! alas! when will this speculating against fact and reason end? What will quiet these panic fears which we entertain of the hostile effect of a conciliatory conduct? Is it true, that no case can exist, in which it is proper for the sovereign to accede to the desires of his discontented subjects? Is there any thing peculiar in this case, to make a rule for itself? Is all authority of course lost, when it is not pushed to the extreme? Is it a certain maxim, that, the fewer causes of dissatisfaction are left by government, the more the subject will be inclined to resist and rebel?

All those objections being in fact no more than suspicions, conjectures, divinations, formed in defiance of fact and experience; they did not, Sir, discourage me from entertaining the idea of a conciliatory concession, founded on the principles which I have just stated.

In forming a plan for this purpose, I endeavoured to put myself in that frame of mind, which was the most natural, and the most reasonable; and which was certainly the most probable means of securing me from all error. I set out with a perfect distrust of my own abilities; a total renunciation of every speculation of my own; and with a profound reverence for the wisdom of our ancestors, who have left us the inheritance of so happy a constitution, and so flourishing an empire, and, what is a thousand times more valuable, the treasury of the maxims and principles which so med the one, and obtained the other.

During the reigns of the kings of Spain of the Austrian family,[77] whenever they were at a loss in the Spanish councils, it was common for their statesmen to say, that they ought to consult the genius of Philip the Second. The genius of Philip the Second might mislead them; and the issue of their affairs shewed, that they had not chosen the most perfect standard.[78] But, Sir, I am sure that I shall not be

---

[77] **family** the Hapsburgs.
[78] **standard** referring partly to the defeat of the Spanish Armada in 1588 and partly to Spain's loss of the Netherlands in 1648.

misled, when, in a case of constitutional difficulty, I consult the genius
of the English constitution. Consulting at that oracle (it was with all
due humility and piety) I found four capital examples in a similar case
before me: those of Ireland, Wales, Chester, and Durham.[79]

Ireland before the English conquest, though never governed by a
despotick power, had no Parliament. How far the English Parliament
itself was at that time modelled according to the present form, is
disputed among antiquarians.[80] But we have all the reason in the
world to be assured, that a form of Parliament, such as England then
enjoyed, she instantly communicated to Ireland; and we are equally
sure that almost every successive improvement in constitutional
liberty, as fast as it was made here, was transmitted thither. The
feudal Baronage, and the feudal Knighthood, the roots of our primitive constitution,[81] were early transplanted into that soil; and grew and
flourished there. Magna Charta, if it did not give us originally the
House of Commons, gave us at least an House of Commons of weight
and consequence. But your ancestors did not churlishly sit down
alone to the feast of Magna Charta. Ireland was made immediately a
partaker. This benefit of English laws and liberties, I confess, was not
at first extended to *all* Ireland. Mark the consequence. English authority and English liberties had exactly the same boundaries. Your
standard could never be advanced an inch before your privileges. Sir
John Davis[82] shews beyond a doubt, that the refusal of a general
communication of these rights was the true cause why Ireland was five
hundred years in subduing; and after the vain projects of a Military
Government, attempted in the reign of Queen Elizabeth,[83] it was soon

[79] **Ireland, Wales, Chester, and Durham** Chester, Wales and Durham had been
discussed earlier in the debate on America. George Grenville, speaking in 1766
(PH, XVI, 102, debate of 14 Jan. 1766) had insisted that the power to tax existed
over those 'who are not, who were never represented', as the East India Company,
Chester and Durham. In the same debate, Pitt said that he would have cited
Chester and Durham 'to have shewn that even under the most arbitrary reigns,
parliaments were ashamed of taxing people without their consent, and allowed
them representatives'. He added that Grenville could have 'taken a higher example
in Wales' (see the version in *Chatham Correspondence*, II, p. 369f; see also debate in
Lords, PH, XVI, 161ff, 10 Feb. 1766, especially Camden).
[80] **antiquarians** an interesting neutrality about the ancient constitution.
[81] **roots of our primitive constitution** for this period, see Burke, *Abridgement*, Bk.
II.vii, and III *passim*.
[82] **Sir John Davis** *Discoverie of the true Causes why Ireland was never entirely subdued
until the beginning of his Majestie's happy reign* (1612).
[83] **vain projects ... Elizabeth** the most determined of these, Essex's expedition,
ended as a fiasco in 1599.

discovered that nothing could make that country English, in civility and allegiance, but your laws and your forms of legislature. It was not English arms, but the English constitution, that conquered Ireland. From that time, Ireland has ever had a general Parliament, as she had before a partial Parliament. You changed the people;[84] you altered the religion;[85] but you never touched the form or the vital substance of free government in that kingdom. You deposed kings; you restored them;[86] you altered the succession to theirs as well as to your own crown;[87] but you never altered their constitution;[88] the principle of which was respected by usurpation;[89] restored with the restoration of Monarchy, and established, I trust for ever, by the glorious Revolution.[90] This has made Ireland the great and flourishing kingdom that it is;[91] and, from a disgrace and a burthen intolerable to this nation, has rendered her a principal part of our strength and ornament. This country cannot be said to have ever formally taxed her. The irregular things done in the confusion of mighty troubles, and on the hinge of great revolution, even if all were done that is said to have been done, form no example. If they have any effect in argument, they make an exception to prove the rule. None of your own liberties could stand a moment, if the casual deviations from them at such times were suffered to be used as proofs of their nullity. By the lucrative amount of

[84] **changed the people** a delicate allusion to the informal negligence of Elizabeth and the deliberate intent of Cromwell in not feeding the Irish, as well as to the plantation of Scots and others in Ulster and parts of Connacht, Leinster and Munster under James I.

[85] **altered the religion** see S.J. Connolly, 'Religion and History', *Irish Economic and Social History*, 10 (1983), pp. 66–80 for the historiography of the penal laws against Catholics.

[86] **deposed kings . . . restored them** presumably referring to Edward II, Richard II, Edward V and Charles I and more especially to the ups and downs of Henry VI and Edward IV.

[87] **crown** alluding to the succession of William & Mary in England (1689) before James II's forces were defeated at the Boyne (1690).

[88] **constitution** Burke conveniently overlooked Poynings' Act (1494) which subordinated the Irish to the English Parliament. But see below, p. 259.

[89] **usurpation** Burke avoids mentioning Cromwell by name. In *A Letter to a member of the National Assembly* (1791), W, IV, p. 307 and cf. p. 287f, he added 'his government, though military and despotic, had been regular and orderly'. There may also be an allusion to the support of the Geraldines for Lambert Simnel and Perkin Warbeck in their rebellions against Henry VII.

[90] **glorious Revolution** Burke both adopts an interpretation of 1688 compatible with his view in *Reflections*, that it conserved rather than added to the constitution, and displays the limit of the changes he desired in Ireland.

[91] **that it is** whether this quite squares with *Tracts on the Popery Laws* is for the reader to judge.

such casual breaches in the constitution, judge what the stated and fixed rule of supply has been in that Kingdom. Your Irish pensioners would starve, if they had no other fund to live on than taxes granted by English authority. Turn your eyes to those popular grants from whence all your great supplies are come; and learn to respect that only source of public wealth in the British empire.

My next example is Wales. This country was said to be reduced by Henry the Third. It was said more truly to be so by Edward the First.[92] But, though then conquered, it was not looked upon as any part of the realm of England. Its old constitution, whatever that might have been, was destroyed; and no good one was substituted in its place. The care of that tract was put into the hands of Lords March-ers – a form of Government of a very singular kind; a strange hetero-geneous monster, something between Hostility and Government: perhaps it has a sort of resemblance, according to the modes of those times, to that of commander in chief[93] at present, to whom all civil power is granted as secondary. The manners of the Welsh nation followed the Genius of the Government: The people were ferocious, restive, savage, and uncultivated; sometimes composed, never paci-fied. Wales within itself was in perpetual disorder; and it kept the frontier of England in perpetual alarm. Benefits from it to the state, there were none. Wales was only known to England, by incursion and invasion.

Sir, during that state of things, Parliament was not idle. They attempted to subdue the fierce spirit of the Welsh by all sorts of rigorous laws. They prohibited by statute the sending all sorts of arms into Wales, as you prohibit by proclamation (with something more of doubt on the legality) the sending arms to America. They disarmed the Welsh by statute, as you attempted (but still with more question on the legality) to disarm New England by an instruction. They made an act to drag offenders from Wales into England for trial, as you have done (but with more hardship) with regard to America. By another act, where one of the parties was an Englishman, they ordained, that his trial should be always by English. They made acts to restrain trade, as you do; and they prevented the Welsh from the use of fairs and markets, as you do the Americans from fisheries and foreign

[92] **Edward the First**   the Statute of Wales (1284) introduced the English system of government.
[93] **commander in chief**   glancing at America, where such powers had been vested in Gage.

ports. In short, when the statute book was not quite so much swelled as it is now, you find no less than fifteen acts of penal regulation on the subject of Wales.

Here we rub our hands – A fine body of precedents for the authority of Parliament and the use of it! – I admit it fully; and pray add likewise to these precedents, that all the while Wales rid this kingdom like an *incubus*; that it was an unprofitable and oppressive burthen; and that an Englishman travelling in that country could not go six yards from the high road without being murdered.

The march of the human mind is slow. Sir, it was not, until after Two Hundred years, discovered, that by an eternal law, Providence had decreed vexation to violence; and poverty to rapine. Your ancestors did however at length open their eyes to the ill husbandry of injustice. They found that the tyranny of a free people could of all tyrannies the least be endured; and that laws made against an whole nation were not the most effectual methods for securing its obedience. Accordingly, in the Twenty-seventh year of Henry VIII. the course was entirely altered. With a preamble stating the entire and perfect rights of the crown of England, it gave to the Welsh all the rights and privileges of English subjects. A political order was established; the military power gave way to the civil; the marches were turned into counties. But that a nation should have a right to English liberties, and yet no share at all in the fundamental security of these liberties, the grant of their own property, seemed a thing so incongruous; that Eight years after, that is, in the Thirty-fifth of that reign, a complete and not ill proportioned representation by counties and boroughs was bestowed upon Wales, by act of Parliament. From that moment, as by a charm, the tumults subsided; obedience was restored; peace, order, and civilization, followed in the train of liberty – When the day-star of the English constitution had arisen in their hearts,[94] all was harmony within and without –

> *Simul alba nautis*
> *Stella refulsit,*
> *Defluit saxis agitatus humor:*
> *Concidunt venit, fugiuntque nubes:*
> *Et minax (quòd sic voluere) ponto*
> *Unda recumbit.*[95]

[94] **arisen in their hearts** 2 Peter I.19.
[95] *Simul alba nautis* ... 'as soon as the white star shines for sailors, the water

The very same year the county palatine of Chester received the same relief from its oppressions, and the same remedy to its disorders. Before this time Chester was little less distempered than Wales. The inhabitants, without rights themselves, were the fittest to destroy the rights of others; and from thence Richard II. drew the standing army of Archers,[96] with which for a time he oppressed England. The people of Chester applied to Parliament in a petition penned as I shall read to you:

To the King our Sovereign Lord, in most humble wise shewn unto your Excellent Majesty, the inhabitants of your Grace's county palatine of Chester; That where the said county palatine of Chester is and hath been always hitherto exempt, excluded and separated out and from your high court of parliament, to have any knights and burgesses within the said court; by reason whereof the said inhabitants have hitherto sustained manifold disherisons, losses and damages, as well in their lands, goods, and bodies, as in the good, civil, and politick governance and maintenance of the commonwealth of their said country: (2.) And for as much as the said inhabitants have always hitherto been bound by the acts and statutes made and ordained by your said highness, and your most noble progenitors, by authority of the said court, as far forth as other counties, cities, and boroughs have been, that have had their knights and burgesses within your said court of parliament, and yet have had neither knight ne burgess there for the said county palatine; the said inhabitants, for lack thereof, have been oftentimes touched and grieved with acts and statutes made within the said court, as well derogatory unto the most ancient jurisdictions, liberties, and privileges of your said county palatine, as prejudicial unto the commonwealth, quietness, rest, and peace of your grace's most bounden subjects inhabiting within the same.

What did Parliament with this audacious address? – reject it as a libel? treat it as an affront to government? spurn it as a derogation from the rights of legislature? Did they toss it over the table? Did they burn it by the hands of the common hangman? – They took the petition of grievance, all rugged as it was, without softening or temperament, unpurged of the original bitterness and indignation of complaint; they made it the very preamble to their act of redress, and

---

flows down in a turbid stream from the rocks; the winds drop, the clouds disperse and (because they wish it so) the waves fall back on the sea' (Horace, *Odes*, I.xii.27).

[96] **army of Archers** Richard II in his later years wished to maintain his independence from his uncles and Parliament. A body of Welsh archers was one of his instruments.

consecrated its principle to all ages in the sanctuary of legislation.

Here is my third example. It was attended with the success of the two former. Chester, civilized as well as Wales, has demonstrated that freedom and not servitude is the cure of anarchy; as religion, and not atheism, is the true remedy for superstition. Sir, this pattern of Chester was followed in the reign of Charles II. with regard to the county palatine of Durham,[97] which is my fourth example. This county had long lain out of the pale of free legislation. So scrupulously was the example of Chester followed, that the style of the preamble is nearly the same with that of the Chester act; and without affecting the abstract extent of the authority of Parliament, it recognizes the equity of not suffering any considerable district in which the British subjects may act as a body, to be taxed without their own voice in the grant.

Now if the doctrines of policy contained in these preambles, and the force of these examples in the acts of Parliament, avail any thing, what can be said against applying them with regard to America? Are not the people of America as much Englishmen as the Welsh? The preamble of the act of Henry VIII. says the Welsh speak a language no way resembling that of his Majesty's English subjects. Are the Americans not as numerous? If we may trust the learned and accurate Judge Barrington's[98] account of North Wales, and take that as a standard to measure the rest, there is no comparison. The people cannot amount to above 200,000; not a tenth part of the number in the Colonies. Is America in rebellion? Wales was hardly ever free from it. Have you attempted to govern America by penal statutes? You made Fifteen for Wales. But your legislative authority is perfect with regard to America; was it less perfect in Wales, Chester, and Durham? But America is virtually represented.[99] What! does the electric force[100] of virtual representation more easily pass over the Atlantic, than pervade Wales, which lies in your neighbourhood; or than Chester and

---

[97] **palatine of Durham**   Burke omits to observe that in this period the government often rewrote the entitlements of the localities. The bishops of Durham, however, retained the status of prince-bishop until the death of William Van Mildert (1836).

[98] **Barrington**   the reference is obscure.

[99] **virtually represented**   Pitt had made this point about the East India Company (*Chatham Correspondence*, II, p. 370): 'They have connections with those that elect, and they have influence over them'.

[100] **electric force**   Franklin's experiment in the thunderstorm would spring to mind, since he had been the colonists' emissary shortly before. See *Thoughts on French Affairs*, W, IV, p. 333 for people being 'electrified' by their prospects and, for a similar reference, cf. *Letters on a Regicide Peace*, II, W, VI, p. 208.

Durham, surrounded by abundance of representation that is actual and palpable? But, Sir, your ancestors thought this sort of virtual representation, however ample, to be totally insufficient for the freedom of the inhabitants of territories that are so near, and comparatively so inconsiderable. How then can I think it sufficient for those which are infinitely greater, and infinitely more remote?

You will now, Sir, perhaps imagine, that I am on the point of proposing to you a scheme for a representation of the Colonies in Parliament. Perhaps I might be inclined to entertain some such thought; but a great flood stops me in my course. *Opposuit natura*[101] – I cannot remove the eternal barriers of the creation. The thing in that mode, I do not know to be possible. As I meddle with no theory, I do not absolutely assert the impracticability of such a representation. But I do not see my way to it; and those who have been more confident, have not been more successful. However, the arm of public benevolence is not shortened;[102] and there are often several means to the same end. What nature has disjoined in one way, wisdom may unite in another. When we cannot give the benefit as we would wish, let us not refuse it altogether. If we cannot give the principal, let us find a substitute. But how? Where? What substitute?

Fortunately I am not obliged for the ways and means of this substitute to tax my own unproductive invention. I am not even obliged to go to the rich treasury of the fertile framers of imaginary commonwealths; not to the Republick of Plato, not to the Utopia of More, not to the Oceana of Harrington.[103] It is before me – It is at my feet, *and the rude swain*[104] *treads daily on it with his clouted shoon.* I only wish you to recognize, for the theory, the ancient constitutional policy of this kingdom with regard to representation, as that policy has been declared in acts of parliament; and, as to the practice, to return to that mode which an uniform experience has marked out to you, as best; and in which you walked with security, advantage, and honour, until the year 1763.[105]

My resolutions therefore mean to establish the equity and justice of a taxation of America by *grant*, and not by *imposition*. To mark the *legal*

---

[101] **opposuit natura** 'nature says no' (Juvenal, *Satires*, x.152).
[102] **not shortened** Isaiah 59:1.
[103] **Harrington** for similar remarks, cf. PD, above, p. 135f.
[104] *and the rude swain* *Comus*, l.634, misquoted.
[105] **1763** i.e. until the end of the Seven Years War and the Stamp Act of 1764.

competency of the Colony assemblies for the support of their government in peace, and for public aids in time of war. To acknowledge that this legal competency has had *a dutiful and beneficial exercise*; and that experience has shewn the *benefit of their grants*, and the *futility of parliamentary taxation as a method of supply*.

These solid truths compose six fundamental propositions. There are three more resolutions corollary to these. If you admit the first set, you can hardly reject the others. But if you admit the first, I shall be far from sollicitous whether you accept or refuse the last. I think these six massive pillars will be of strength sufficient to support the temple of British concord.[106] I have no more doubt than I entertain of my existence, that, if you admitted these, you would command an immediate peace; and with but tolerable future management, a lasting obedience in America. I am not arrogant in this confident assurance. The propositions are all mere matters of fact; and if they are such facts as draw irresistible conclusions even in the stating, this is the power of truth, and not any management of mine.

Sir, I shall open the whole plan to you together, with such observations on the motions as may tend to illustrate them where they may want explanation. The first is a resolution – '*That the Colonies and Plantations of Great Britain in North America, consisting of Fourteen separate Governments, and containing Two Millions and upwards of free inhabitants, have not had the liberty and privilege of electing and sending any Knights and Burgesses, or others, to represent them in the high Court of Parliament.*' – This is a plain matter of fact, necessary to be laid down, and (excepting the description) it is laid down in the language of the constitution; it is taken nearly *verbatim* from acts of Parliament.

The second is like unto the first[107] – '*That the said Colonies and Plantations have been liable to, and bounden by, several subsidies, payments, rates, and taxes, given and granted by Parliament, though the said Colonies and Plantations have not their Knights and Burgesses, in the said high Court of Parliament, of their own election, to represent the condition of their country; by lack whereof they have been oftentimes touched and grieved by subsidies given, granted, and assented to, in the said court, in a manner prejudicial to the common wealth, quietness, rest, and peace of the subjects inhabiting within the same.*'

---

[106] **British concord** the figure would not have sounded fanciful in an age when classical allusions found their way into the landscape, cf. the Temple of Piety at Fountains Abbey. Gladstone called his library at Hawarden the Temple of Peace.

[107] **like unto the first** Matthew 22:39.

In this description too hot, or too cold, too strong, or too weak? Does it arrogate too much to the supreme legislature? Does it lean too much to the claims of the people? If it runs into any of these errors, the fault is not mine. It is the language of your own ancient acts of Parliament. *Non meus hic sermo, sed quæ præcepit Ofellus, rusticus, abnormis sapiens.*[108] It is the genuine produce of the ancient rustic, manly, home-bred sense of this country – I did not dare to rub off a particle of the venerable rust that rather adorns and preserves, than destroys the metal. It would be a profanation to touch with a tool the stones[109] which construct the sacred altar of peace. I would not violate with modern polish the ingenuous and noble roughness of these truly constitutional materials. Above all things, I was resolved not to be guilty of tampering, the odious vice of restless and unstable minds. I put my foot in the tracks of our forefathers; where I can neither wander nor stumble. Determining to fix articles of peace, I was resolved not to be wise beyond what was written;[110] I was resolved to use nothing else than the form of sound words; to let others abound in their own sense; and carefully to abstain from all expressions of my own. What the law has said, I say. In all things else I am silent. I have no organ but for her words. This, if it be not ingenuous, I am sure is safe.

There are indeed words expressive of grievance in this second resolution, which those who are resolved always to be in the right, will deny to contain matter of fact, as applied to the present case; although Parliament thought them true, with regard to the counties of Chester and Durham. They will deny that the Americans were ever 'touched and grieved' with the taxes. If they consider nothing in taxes but their weight as pecuniary impositions, there might be some pretence for this denial. But men may be sorely touched and deeply grieved in their privileges, as well as in their purses. Men may lose little in property by the act which takes away all their freedom. When a man is robbed of a trifle on the highway, it is not the Two-pence lost that constitutes the capital outrage. This is not confined to privileges. Even ancient indulgences withdrawn, without offence on the part of those who enjoyed such favours, operate as grievances. But were the

---

[108] *Non meus hic sermo . . . sapiens* 'it is not my opinion, but that which Ofellus teaches, a countryman, a man of uncommon good sense' (Horace, *Satires*, II.ii.3).
[109] **tool the stones** cf. Exodus 20:25.
[110] **what was written** cf. I Corinthians 4:6.

Americans then not touched and grieved by the taxes, in some measure, merely as taxes? If so, why were they almost all either wholly repealed or exceedingly reduced? Were they not touched and grieved, even by the regulating Duties of the Sixth of George II? Else why were the duties first reduced to one Third in 1764, and afterwards to a Third of that Third in the year 1766? Were they not touched and grieved by the Stamp Act? I shall say they were, until that tax is revived. Were they not touched and grieved by the duties of 1767, which were likewise repealed, and which Lord Hillsborough tells you (for the ministry) were laid contrary to the true principle of commerce? Is not the assurance given by that noble person to the Colonies of a resolution to lay no more taxes on them, an admission that taxes would touch and grieve them? Is not the resolution of the noble Lord in the blue ribband, now standing on your Journals, the strongest of all proofs that parliamentary subsidies really touched and grieved them? Else, why all these changes, modifications, repeals, assurances, and resolutions?

The next proposition is – '*That, from the distance of the said Colonies, and from other circumstances, no method hath hitherto been devised for procuring a representation in Parliament for the said Colonies.*' This is an assertion of a fact. I go no further on the paper; though in my private judgement, an useful representation is impossible; I am sure it is not desired by them; nor ought it perhaps by us; but I abstain from opinions.

The fourth resolution is – '*That each of the said Colonies hath within itself a body, chosen in part, or in the whole, by the freemen, freeholders, or other free inhabitants thereof, commonly called the General Assembly, or General Court, with powers legally to raise, levy, and assess, according to the several usage of such Colonies, duties and taxes towards defraying all sorts of public services.*'

This competence in the Colony assemblies is certain. It is proved by the whole tenour of their acts of supply in all the assemblies, in which the constant style of granting is, 'an aid to his Majesty;' and acts granting to the Crown have regularly for near a century passed the public offices without dispute. Those who have been pleased[111] paradoxically to deny this right, holding that none but the British parliament can grant to the Crown, are wished to look to what is done,

---

[111] **pleased** perhaps Grenville.

not only in the Colonies, but in Ireland, in one uniform unbroken tenour every session. Sir, I am surprized, that this doctrine should come from some of the law servants of the Crown. I say, that if the Crown could be responsible, his Majesty – but certainly the ministers, and even these law officers themselves, through whose hands the acts pass, biennially in Ireland, or annually in the Colonies, are in an habitual course of committing impeachable offences. What habitual offenders have been all Presidents of the Council, all Secretaries of State, all First Lords of Trade, all Attornies, and all Sollicitors General! However, they are safe; as no one impeaches them; and there is no ground of charge against them, except in their own unfounded theories.

The fifth resolution is also a resolution of fact – '*That the said General Assemblies, General Courts, or other bodies legally qualified as aforesaid, have at sundry times freely granted several large subsidies and public aids for his Majesty's service, according to their abilities, when required thereto by letter from one of his Majesty's principal Secretaries of State; and that their right to grant the same, and their chearfulness and sufficiency in the said grants, have been at sundry times acknowledged by Parliament.*' To say nothing of their great expences in the Indian wars; and not to take their exertion in foreign ones, so high as the supplies in the year 1695; not to go back to their public contributions in the year 1710; I shall begin to travel only where the Journals give me light; resolving to deal in nothing but fact, authenticated by parliamentary record; and to build myself wholly on that solid basis.

On the 4th of April 1748, a Committee of this House came to the following Resolution:

'Resolved,

That it is the opinion of this Committee, that it is just and reasonable that the several Provinces and Colonies of Massachuset's Bay, New Hampshire, Connecticut, and Rhode Island, be reimbursed the expences they have been at in taking, and securing to the crown of Great Britain, the Island of Cape Breton, and its dependencies.'

These expences were immense for such Colonies. They were above 200,000*l.* sterling; money first raised and advanced on their public credit.

On the 28th of January 1756, a message from the King came to us, to this effect – '*His Majesty, being sensible of the zeal and vigour with which his faithful subjects of certain Colonies in North America have exerted themselves in defence of His Majesty's just rights and possessions, recommends it to this House to take the same into their consideration, and to enable His Majesty to give them such assistance as may be a* proper reward and encouragement.'

On the 3d of February 1756, the House came to a suitable resolution, expressed in words nearly the same as those of the message: but with the further addition, that the money then voted was as an *encouragement* to the Colonies to exert themselves with vigour. It will not be necessary to go through all the testimonies which your own records have given to the truth of my resolutions. I will only refer you to the places in the Journals:

Vol. XXVII. – 16th and 19th May 1757.
Vol. XXVIII. – June 1st, 1758 – April 26th and 30th, 1759 – March 29th and 31st, and April 28th, 1760 – Jan. 9th and 20th, 1761.
Vol. XXIX. – Jan. 22nd and 26th, 1762 – March 14th and 17th, 1763.

Sir, here is the repeated acknowledgement of Parliament, that the Colonies not only gave, but gave to satiety. This nation has formally acknowledged two things; first, that the Colonies had gone beyond their abilities, Parliament having thought it necessary to reimburse them; secondly, that they had acted legally and laudably in their grants of money, and their maintenance of troops, since the compensation is expressly given as reward and encouragement. Reward is not bestowed for acts that are unlawful; and encouragement is not held out to things that deserve reprehension. My resolution therefore does nothing more than collect into one proposition what is scattered through your Journals. I give you nothing but your own; and you cannot refuse in the gross what you have so often acknowledged in detail. The admission of this, which will be so honourable to them and to you, will, indeed, be mortal to all the miserable stories, by which the passions of the misguided people have been engaged in an unhappy system. The people heard, indeed, from the beginning of these disputes, one thing continually dinned in their ears, that reason and justice demanded, that the Americans, who paid no Taxes, should be compelled to contribute. How did that fact of their paying nothing stand, when the Taxing System began? When Mr Grenville began to form his system of American Revenue, he stated in this House, that the Colonies were then in debt two millions six hundred thousand pounds sterling money; and was of opinion they would discharge that debt in four years. On this state, those untaxed people were actually subject to the payment of taxes to the amount of six hundred and fifty thousand a year. In fact, however, Mr. Grenville was mistaken. The funds given for sinking the debt did not prove quite so ample as both the Colonies and he expected. The calculation was too sanguine: the reduction was not compleated till some years after, and at different times in different Colonies. However, the Taxes after the war, continued too great to bear any addition, with prudence or propriety; and when the burthens imposed in consequence of former requisitions were discharged, our tone became too high to resort again to requisition. No Colony, since that time, ever has had any requisition whatsoever made to it.

We see the sense of the Crown, and the sense of Parliament, on the productive nature of a *Revenue by Grant*. Now search the same Journals for the produce of the *Revenue by Imposition* – Where is it? – let us know the volume and the page? – what is the gross, what is the nett produce? – to what service is it applied? – how have you appropriated its surplus? – What, can none of the many skilful Index-makers, that we are now employing, find any trace of it? – Well, let them and that rest together. – But are the Journals, which say nothing of the Revenue, as silent on the discontent? – Oh no! a child may find it. It is the melancholy burthen and blot of every page.

I think then I am, from those Journals, justified in the sixth and last resolution, which is – '*That it hath been found by experience, that the manner of granting the said supplies and aids, by the said General Assemblies, hath been more agreeable to the said Colonies, and more beneficial and conducive to the public service, than the mode of giving and granting aids in Parliament, to be raised and paid in the said Colonies.*'

This makes the whole of the fundamental part of the plan. The conclusion is irresistible. You cannot say, that you were driven by any necessity, to an exercise of the utmost Rights of Legislature. You cannot assert, that you took on yourselves task of imposing Colony Taxes, from the want of another legal body, that is competent to the purpose of supplying the Exigencies of the State without wounding the prejudices of the people. Neither is it true that the body so qualified, and having that competence, had neglected the duty.

The question now, on all this accumulated matter, is; – whether you will chuse to abide by a profitable experience, or a mischievous theory: whether you chuse to build on imagination or fact; whether you prefer enjoyment or hope; satisfaction to your subjects, or discontent?

If these propositions are accepted, every thing which has been made to enforce a contrary system must, I take it for granted, fall along with it. On that ground, I have drawn the following resolution, which, when it comes to be moved, will naturally be divided in a proper manner: '*That it may be proper to repeal an act, made in the seventh year of the reign of his present Majesty, intituled, An act for granting certain duties in the British Colonies and Plantations in America; for allowing a drawback of the duties of customs upon the exportation from this Kingdom, of coffee and cocoa-nuts of the produce of the said Colonies or Plantations; for discontinuing the drawbacks payable on China earthenware exported to America; and for more effectually preventing the clandestine running of goods in the said Colonies and Plantations. – And that it may be proper to repeal an act, made in the fourteenth year of the reign of his present Majesty, intituled, An act to discontinue, in such manner, and for such time, as are therein mentioned, the landing and discharging, lading or shipping, of goods, wares, and merchandize, at the town and within the harbour of Boston, in the Province of Massachuset's Bay, in North America. – And that it may be proper to repeal an act, made in the fourteenth year of the reign of his present Majesty, intituled, An act for the impartial administration of justice, in the cases of persons questioned for any acts done by them, in the execution of the law, or for the suppression of riots and tumults, in the province of Massachuset's Bay in New England. – And that it may be proper to repeal an act, made in the fourteenth year of the reign of his present Majesty, intituled, An act for the better regulating the Government of the province of the Massachuset's Bay in New England. – And also that it may be proper to explain and amend an act, made in the thirty-fifth year of the reign of King* Henry *the Eighth, intituled, An act of the Trial of Treasons committed out of the King's Dominions.*'

I wish, Sir, to repeal the Boston Port Bill, because (independently of the dangerous precedent of suspending the rights of the subject during the King's pleasure) it was passed, as I apprehend, with less regularity, and on more partial principles, than it ought. The corporation of Boston was not heard, before it was condemned. Other towns, full as guilty as she was, have not had their ports blocked up. Even the Restraining Bill of the present Session does not go to the length of the Boston Port Act. The same ideas of prudence, which induced you not to extend equal punishment to equal guilt, when even you were punishing, induce me, who mean not to chastise, but to reconcile, to be satisfied with the punishment already partially inflicted.

Ideas of prudence, and accommodation to circumstances, prevent you from taking away the Charters of Connecticut and Rhode-Island, as you have taken away that of Massachuset's Colony, though the Crown has far less power in the two former provinces than it enjoyed in the latter; and though the abuses have been full as great, and as flagrant, in the exempted as in the punished. The same reasons of prudence and accommodation have weight with me in restoring the Charter of Massachuset's Bay. Besides, Sir, the Act which changes the Charter of Massachuset's is in many particulars so exceptionable, that, if I did not wish absolutely to repeal, I would by all means desire to alter it; as several of its provisions tend to the subversion of all public and private justice. Such, among others, is the power in the Governor to change the sheriff at his pleasure; and to make a new returning officer for every special cause. It is shameful to behold such a regulation standing among English Laws.

The act for bringing persons accused of committing murder under the orders of Government to England for Trial, is but temporary. That act has calculated the probable duration of our quarrel with the Colonies; and is accommodated to that supposed duration. I would hasten the happy moment of reconciliation; and therefore must, on my principle, get rid of that most justly obnoxious act.

The act of Henry the Eighth, for the Trial of Treasons, I do not mean to take away, but to confine it to its proper bounds and original intention; to make it expressly for Trial of Treasons (and the greatest Treasons may be committed) in places where the jurisdiction of the Crown does not extend.

Having guarded the privileges of Local Legislature, I would next secure to the Colonies a fair and unbiassed Judicature; for which purpose, Sir, I propose the following resolution: '*That, from the time when the General Assembly, or General Court of any Colony or Plantation in North America, shall have appointed by act of Assembly, duly confirmed, a settled salary to the offices of the Chief Justice and other Judges of the Superior Court, it may be proper, that the said Chief Justice and other Judges of the Superior Court of such Colony, shall hold his and their office and offices during their good behaviour; and shall not be removed therefrom, but when the said removal shall be adjudged by his Majesty in Council, upon a hearing on complaint from the General Assembly, or on a complaint from the Governor, or Council, or the House of Representatives severally, of the Colony in which the said Chief Justice and other Judges have exercised the said offices.'*

The next resolution relates to the Courts of Admiralty.

It is this. *'That it may be proper to regulate the Courts of Admiralty, or Vice Admiralty, authorized by the 15th Chap. of the 4th of George the Third, in such a manner as to make the same more commodious to those who sue, or are sued, in the said Courts, and to provide for the more decent maintenance of the Judges in the same.'*

These Courts I do not wish to take away; they are in themselves proper establishments. This Court is one of the capital securities of the Act of Navigation. The extent of its jurisdiction, indeed, has been encreased; but this is altogether as proper, and is, indeed, on many accounts, more eligible, where new powers were wanted, than a Court absolutely new. But Courts incommodiously situated, in effect, deny justice; and a Court, partaking in the fruits of its own condemnation, is a robber. The congress complain, and complain justly, of this grievance.

These are the three consequential propositions. I have thought of two or three more; but they come rather too near detail, and to the province of executive Government, which I wish Parliament always to superintend, never to assume. If the first six are granted, congruity will carry the latter three. If not, the things that remain unrepealed will be, I hope, rather unseemly incumbrances on the building, than very materially detrimental to its strength and stability.

Here, Sir, I should close; but that I plainly perceive some objections remain, which I ought, if possible, to remove. The first will be, that, in resorting to the doctrine of our ancestors, as contained in the preamble to the Chester act, I prove too much; that the grievance from a want of representation, stated in that preamble, goes to the whole of Legislation as well as to Taxation. And that the Colonies grounding themselves upon that doctrine, will apply it to all parts of Legislative Authority.

To this objection, with all possible deference and humility, and wishing as little as any man living to impair the smallest particle of our supreme authority, I answer, that *the words are the words of Parliament, and not mine*; and, that all false and inconclusive inferences, drawn from them, are not mine; for I heartily disclaim any such inference. I have chosen the words of an act of Parliament, which Mr Grenville, surely a tolerably zealous and very judicious advocate for the sovereignty of Parliament, formerly moved to have read at your table, in consequence of his tenets. It is true that Lord Chatham considered these preambles as declaring strongly in favour of his opinions. He was a no less powerful advocate for the privileges of the Americans. Ought I not from hence to presume, that these preambles are as favourable as possible to both, when properly understood; favourable both to the rights of Parliament, and to the privilege of the dependencies of this crown? But, Sir, the object of grievance in my resolution, I have not taken from the Chester, but from the Durham act, which confines the hardship of want of representation to the case of subsidies; and which therefore falls in exactly with the case of the Colonies. But whether the unrepresented counties were *de jure*, or *de facto*, bound, the preambles do not accurately distinguish; nor indeed was it necessary; for, whether *de jure*, or *de facto*, the Legislature thought the exercise of the power of taxing, as of right, or as of fact without right, equally a grievance and equally oppressive.

I do not know, that the Colonies have, in any general way, or in any cool hour, gone much beyond the demand of immunity in relation to taxes. It is not fair to judge of the temper or dispositions of any man, or any set of men, when they are composed and at rest, from their conduct, or their expressions, in a state of disturbance and irritation. It is besides a very great mistake to imagine, that mankind follow up practically any speculative principle, either of government or of freedom, as far as it will go in argument and logical illation. We Englishmen stop very short of the principles upon which we support any given part of our constitution; or even the whole of it together. I could easily, if I had not already tired you, give you very striking and convincing instances of it. This is nothing but what is natural and proper. All government, indeed every human benefit and enjoyment, every virtue, and every prudent act, is founded on compromise and barter. We balance inconveniencies; we give and take; we remit some rights, that we may enjoy others; and we chuse rather to be happy citizens, than subtle disputants. As we must give away some natural liberty, to enjoy civil advantages; so we must sacrifice some civil liberties, for the advantages to be derived from the communion and fellowship of a great empire. But in all fair dealings the thing bought must bear some proportion to the purchase paid. None will barter away the immediate jewel of his soul.[112] Though a great house is apt to make slaves haughty,[113] yet it is purchasing a part of the artificial importance of a great empire too dear, to pay for it all essential rights, and all the intrinsic dignity of human nature. None of us who would not risque his life, rather than fall under a government purely arbitrary. But, although there are some amongst us who think our constitution wants many improvements, to make it a complete system of liberty, perhaps none who are of that opinion would think it right to aim at such improvement, by disturbing his country, and risquing every thing that is dear to him. In every arduous enterprize, we consider what we are to lose, as well as what we are to gain; and the more and better stake of liberty every people possess, the less they will hazard in a vain attempt to make it more. These are *the cords of man*.[114] Man acts from adequate motives relative to his interest; and not on metaphysical speculations. Aristotle,[115] the great master of reasoning, cautions us, and with great weight and propriety, against this species of delusive geometrical accuracy in moral arguments, as the most fallacious of all sophistry.

The Americans will have no interest contrary to the grandeur and glory of England, when they are not oppressed by the weight of it; and they will rather be inclined to respect the acts of a superintending legislature, when they see them the acts of that power, which is itself the security, not the rival, of their secondary importance. In this assurance, my mind most perfectly acquiesces; and I confess, I feel not the least alarm, from the discontents which are to arise, from putting people at their ease; nor do I apprehend the destruction of this empire, from giving, by an act of free grace and indulgence, to two millions of my fellow citizens, some share of those rights, upon which I have always been taught to value myself.

It is said indeed, that this power of granting, vested in American assemblies, would dissolve the unity of the empire; which was preserved, entire, although Wales, and Chester, and Durham, were added to it. Truly, Mr Speaker, I do not know what this unity means; nor has it ever been heard of, that I know, in the constitutional policy

---

[112] **jewel of his soul** cf. *Othello*, III.iii.161.
[113] **haughty** from Juvenal v.66.
[114] **cords of man** Hosea 11:4.
[115] **Aristotle** *Nicomachean Ethics*, I.3.

of this country. The very idea of subordination of parts excludes this
notion of simple and undivided unity. England is the head; but she is
not the head and the members too. Ireland has ever had from the
beginning a separate, but not an independent, legislature; which, far
from distracting, promoted the union of the whole. Every thing was
sweetly and harmoniously disposed through both Islands for the con-
servation of English dominion, and the communication of English
liberties. I do not see that the same principles might not be carried
into twenty Islands, and with the same good effect. This is my model
with regard to America, as far as the internal circumstances of the two
countries are the same. I know no other unity of this empire, than I
can draw from its example during these periods, when it seemed to
my poor understanding more united than it is now, or than it is likely
to be by the present methods.

But since I speak of these methods, I recollect, Mr. Speaker,
almost too late, that I promised, before I finished, to say something of
the proposition of the Noble Lord on the floor, which has been so
lately received, and stands on your Journals. I must be deeply concerned, whenever it is my misfortune to continue a difference with the
majority of this House. But as the reasons for that difference are my
apology for thus troubling you, suffer me to state them in a very few
words. I shall compress them into as small a body as I possibly can,
having already debated that matter at large, when the question was
before the Committee.

First, then, I cannot admit that proposition of a ransom by auction;
– because it is a meer project. It is a thing new; unheard of; supported
by no experience; justified by no analogy; without example of our
ancestors, or root in the constitution. It is neither regular parliamentary taxation, nor Colony grant. *Experimentum in corpore vili*,[116] is a
good rule, which will ever make me adverse to any trial of experiments
on what is certainly the most valuable of all subjects; the peace of this
Empire.

Secondly, it is an experiment which must be fatal in the end to our
constitution. For what is it but a scheme for taxing the Colonies in the
antichamber of the Noble Lord and his successors? To settle the

---

[116] **experimentum in corpore vili**   according to Payne, Muretus was once taken ill on
a journey; the doctors who attended him, supposing him of no account, agreed to
try a new remedy on him, remarking, 'faciamus periculum in anima vili'; Muretus
replied, 'vilem animam appellas, pro qua Christus non dedignatus est mori?'.

quotas and proportions in this House, is clearly impossible. You, Sir, may flatter yourself, you shall sit a state-auctioneer with your hammer in your hand, and knock down to each Colony as it bids. But to settle (on the plan laid down by the Noble Lord) the true proportional payment for four or five and twenty governments, according to the absolute and the relative wealth of each, and according to the British proportion of wealth and burthen, is a wild and chimerical notion. This new taxation must therefore come in by the back-door of the constitution. Each quota must be brought to this House ready formed; you can neither add not alter. You must register it. You can do nothing further. For on what grounds can you deliberate either before or after the proposition? You cannot hear the counsel for all these Provinces, quarrelling each on its own quantity of payment, and its proportion to others. If you should attempt it, the Committee of Provincial Ways and Means, or by whatever other name it will delight to be called, must swallow up all the time of Parliament.

Thirdly, it does not give satisfaction to the complaint of the Colonies. They complain, that they are taxed without their consent; you answer, that you will fix the sum at which they shall be taxed. That is, you give them the very grievance for the remedy. You tell them, indeed, that you will leave the mode to themselves. I really beg pardon: it gives me pain to mention it; but you must be sensible that you will not perform this part of the compact. For, suppose the Colonies were to lay the duties which furnished their Contingent, upon the importation of your manufactures; you know you would never suffer such a tax to be laid. You know too, that you would not suffer many other modes of taxation. So that, when you come to explain yourself, it will be found, that you will neither leave to themselves the quantum nor the mode; nor indeed any thing. The whole is delusion from one end to the other.

Fourthly, this method of ransom by auction, unless it be *universally* accepted, will plunge you into great and inextricable difficulties. In what year of our Lord are the proportions of payments to be settled? To say nothing of the impossibility that Colony agents should have general powers of taxing the Colonies at their discretion; consider, I implore you, that the communication by special messages, and orders between these agents and their constituents on each variation of the case, when the parties come to contend together, and to dispute on their relative proportions, will be a matter of delay, perplexity, and confusion, that never can have an end.

If all the Colonies do not appear at the outcry, what is the condition of those assemblies, who offer, by themselves or their agents, to tax themselves up to your ideas of their proportion? The refractory Colonies, who refuse all composition, will remain taxed only to your old impositions; which, however grievous in principle, are trifling as to production. The obedient Colonies in this scheme are heavily taxed; the refractory remain unburthened. What will you do? Will you lay new and heavier taxes by Parliament on the disobedient? Pray consider in what way you can do it? You are perfectly convinced that in the way of taxing, you can do nothing but at the ports. Now suppose it is Virginia that refuses to appear at your auction, while Maryland and North Carolina bid handsomely for their ransom, and are taxed to your quota; how will you put these Colonies on a par? Will you tax the tobacco of Virginia? If you do, you give its death-wound to your English revenue at home, and to one of the very greatest articles of your own foreign trade. If you tax the import of that rebellious Colony, what do you tax but your own manufactures, or the goods of some other obedient and already well-taxed Colony? Who has said one word on this labyrinth of detail, which bewilders you more and more as you enter into it? Who has presented, who can present you, with a clue, to lead you out of it? I think, Sir, it is impossible, that you should not recollect that the Colony bounds are so implicated in one another (you know it by your other experiments in the Bill for prohibiting the New-England fishery) that you can lay no possible restraints on almost any of them which may not be presently eluded, if you do not confound the innocent with the guilty, and burthen those whom, upon every principle, you ought to exonerate. He must be grosly ignorant of America, who thinks, that, without falling into this confusion of all rules of equity and policy, you can restrain any single Colony, especially Virginia and Maryland, the central, and most important of them all.

Let it also be considered, that, either in the present confusion you settle a permanent contingent, which will and must be trifling; and then you have no effectual revenue: or you change the quota at every exigency; and then on every new repartition you will have a new quarrel.

Reflect besides, that when you have fixed a quota for every Colony, you have not provided for prompt and punctual payment. Suppose one, two, five, ten years arrears. You cannot issue a treasury extent[117] against the failing Colony. You must make new Boston port bills, new restraining laws, new Acts for dragging men to England for trial. You must send out new fleets, new armies. All is to begin again. From this day forward the Empire is never to know an hour's tranquillity. An intestine fire will be kept alive in the bowels of the Colonies, which one time or other must consume this whole empire. I allow, indeed, that the empire of Germany raises her revenue and her troops by quotas and contingents; but the revenue of the empire, and the army of the empire, is the worst revenue, and the worst army, in the world.

Instead of a standing revenue, you will therefore have a perpetual quarrel. Indeed the noble Lord who proposed this project of a ransom by auction, seemed himself to be of that opinion. His project was rather designed for breaking the union of the Colonies, than for establishing a Revenue. He confessed, he apprehended that his proposal would not be to *their taste*. I say, this scheme of disunion seems to be at the bottom of the project; for I will not suspect that the noble Lord meant nothing but merely to delude the nation by an airy phantom which he never intended to realize. But whatever his views may be; as I propose the peace and union of the Colonies as the very foundation of my plan, it cannot accord with one whose foundation is perpetual discord.

Compare the two. This I offer to give you is plain and simple. The other full of perplexed and intricate mazes. This is mild; that harsh. This is found by experience effectual for its purposes; the other is a new project. This is universal; the other calculated for certain Colonies only. This is immediate in its conciliatory operation; the other remote, contingent, full of hazard.[118] Mine is what becomes the dignity of a ruling people; gratuitous, unconditional, and not held out as matter of bargain and sale. I have done my duty in proposing it to you. I have indeed tired you by a long discourse; but this is the misfortune of those to whose influence nothing will be conceded, and who must win every inch of their ground by argument. You have heard me with goodness: may you decide with wisdom! For my part, I feel my mind greatly disburthened, by what I have done to-day. I have

[117] **extent**   a writ for valuing lands to satisfy a Crown debt.
[118] **full of hazard**   'periculosae plenum opus aleae' (Horace, *Odes*, II.i).

been the less fearful of trying your patience, because on this subject I mean to spare it altogether in future. I have this comfort, that in every stage of the American affairs, I have steadily opposed the measures, that have produced the confusion, and may bring on the destruction, of this empire. I now go so far as to risque a proposal of my own. If I cannot give peace to my country; I give it to my conscience.

But what (says the Financier) is peace to us without money? Your plan gives us no Revenue. No! But it does – For it secures to the subject the power of REFUSAL; the first of all Revenues. Experience is a cheat, and fact a liar, if this power in the subject of proportioning his grant, or of not granting at all, has not been found the richest mine of Revenue ever discovered by the skill or by the fortune of man. It does not indeed vote you £152,752 : 11 : 2¼ths, nor any other paltry limited sum. – But it gives the strong box itself, the fund, the bank, from whence only revenues can arise amongst a people sensible of freedom: *Posita luditur arca*.[119] Cannot you in England; cannot you at this time of day; cannot you, an House of Commons, trust to the principle which has raised so mighty a revenue, and accumulated a debt of near 140 millions in this country? Is this principle to be true in England, and false every where else? Is it not true in Ireland? Has it not hitherto been true in the Colonies? Why should you presume that, in any country, a body duly constituted for any function will neglect to perform its duty, and abdicate its trust? Such a presumption would go against all government, in all modes. But, in truth, this dread of penury of supply, from a free assembly, has no foundation in nature. For first observe, that, besides the desire which all men have naturally of supporting the honour of their own government; that sense of dignity, and that security to property, which ever attends freedom, has a tendency to increase the stock of the free community. Most may be taken where most is accumulated. And what is the soil or climate where experience has not uniformly proved, that the voluntary flow of heaped-up plenty, bursting from the weight of its own rich luxuriance, has ever run with a more copious stream of revenue, than could be squeezed from the dry husks of oppressed indigence, by the straining of all the politic machinery in the world.

Next we know, that parties must ever exist in a free country. We know too, that the emulations of such parties, their contradictions,

---

[119] ***Posita luditur arca*** 'they play with their strong box before them' [i.e. they risk their whole fortune] (Juvenal, *Satires*, 1.90).

their reciprocal necessities, their hopes, and their fears, must send them all in their turns to him that holds the balance of the state. The parties are the Gamesters; but Government keeps the table, and is sure to be the winner in the end. When this game is played, I really think it is more to be feared, that the people will be exhausted, than that Government will not be supplied. Whereas, whatever is got by acts of absolute power ill obeyed, because odious, or by contracts ill kept, because constrained, will be narrow, feeble, uncertain, and precarious. '*Ease would retract vows made in pain, as violent and void.*'[120]

I, for one, protest against compounding our demands: I declare against compounding, for a poor limited sum, the immense, over-growing, eternal Debt, which is due to generous Government from protected Freedom. And so may I speed in the great object I propose to you, as I think it would not only be an act of injustice, but would be the worst œconomy in the world, to compel the Colonies to a sum certain, either in the way of ransom, or in the way of compulsory compact.

But to clear up my ideas on this subject – a revenue from America transmitted hither – do not delude yourselves – you never can receive it – No, not a shilling. We have experience that from remote countries, it is not to be expected. If, when you attempted to extract revenue from Bengal, you were obliged to return in loan what you had taken in imposition; what can you expect from North America? for certainly, if ever there was a country qualified to produce wealth, it is India; or an institution fit for the transmission, it is the East-India company. America has none of these aptitudes. If America gives you taxable objects, on which you lay your duties here, and gives you, at the same time, a surplus by a foreign sale of her commodities to pay the duties on these objects which you tax at home, she has performed her part to the British revenue. But with regard to her own internal establishments; she may, I doubt not she will, contribute in modera-tion. I say in moderation; for she ought not to be permitted to exhaust herself. She ought to be reserved to a war; the weight of which, with the enemies that we are most likely to have,[121] must be considerable in her quarter of the globe. There she may serve you, and serve you, and serve you essentially.

For that service, for all service, whether of revenue, trade, or

---

[120] *Ease would retract . . . void*   cf. *Paradise Lost*, IV.96.
[121] **likely to have**   France and Spain.

empire, my trust is in her interest in the British constitution. My hold of the Colonies is in the close affection which grows from common names, from kindred blood, from similar privileges, and equal protection. These are ties, which, though light as air, are as strong as links of iron.[122] Let the Colonies always keep the idea of their civil rights associated with your Government; – they will cling and grapple to you; and no force under heaven will be of power to tear them from their allegiance. But let it be once understood, that your Government may be one thing, and their Privileges another; that these two things may exist without any mutual relation; the cement is gone; the cohesion is loosened; and every thing hastens to decay and dissolution. As long as you have the wisdom to keep the sovereign authority of this country as the sanctuary of liberty, the sacred temple consecrated to our common faith, wherever the chosen race and sons of England worship freedom, they will turn their faces towards you. The more they multiply, the more friends you will have; the more ardently they love liberty, the more perfect will be their obedience. Slavery they can have any where. It is a weed that grows in every soil. They may have it from Spain, they may have it from Prussia. But until you become lost to all feeling of your true interest and your natural dignity, freedom they can have from none but you. This is the commodity of price, of which you have the monopoly. This is the true act of navigation, which binds to you the commerce of the Colonies, and through them secures to you the wealth of the world. Deny them this participation of freedom, and you break that sole bond, which originally made, and must still preserve, the unity of the empire. Do not entertain so weak an imagination, as that your registers and your bonds, your affidavits and your sufferances, your cockets and your clearances, are what form the great securities of your commerce. Do not dream that your letters of office, and your instructions, and your suspending clauses, are the things that hold together the great contexture of this mysterious whole. These things do not make your government. Dead instruments, passive tools as they are, it is the spirit of English communion that gives all their life and efficacy to them. It is the spirit of the English constitution, which, infused through the mighty mass, pervades, feeds, unites, invigorates, vivifies, every part of the empire, even down to the minutest member.

---

[122] **iron**   cf. *Othello*, III.iii.326, and *Julius Caesar*, I.iii.93.

Is it not the same virtue which does every thing for us here in England? Do you imagine then, that it is the land tax act[123] which raises your revenue? that it is the annual vote in the committee of supply, which gives you your army? or that it is the Mutiny Bill[124] which inspires it with bravery and discipline? No! surely no! It is the love of the people; it is their attachment to their government from the sense of the deep stake they have in such a glorious institution, which gives you your army and your navy, and infuses into both that liberal obedience, without which your army would be a base rabble, and your navy nothing but rotten timber.

All this, I know well enough, will sound wild and chimerical to the profane herd[125] of those vulgar and mechanical politicians, who have no place among us; a sort of people who think that nothing exists but what is gross and material; and who therefore, far from being qualified to be directors of the great movement of empire, are not fit to turn a wheel in the machine. But to men truly initiated and rightly taught, these ruling and master principles, which, in the opinion of such men as I have mentioned, have no substantial existence, are in truth every thing, and all in all.[126] Magnanimity in politicks is not seldom the truest wisdom; and a great empire and little minds go ill together. If we are conscious of our situation, and glow with zeal to fill our place as becomes our station and ourselves, we ought to auspicate all our public proceedings on America, with the old warning of the church, *Sursum corda!*[127] we ought to elevate our minds to the greatness of that trust to which the order of Providence has called us. By adverting to the dignity of this high calling,[128] our ancestors have turned a savage wilderness into a glorious empire; and have made the most extensive, and the only honourable conquests; not by destroying, but by promoting, the wealth, the number, the happiness of the human race. Let us get an American revenue as we have got an American empire. English privileges have made it all that it is; English privileges alone will make it all it can be.

In full confidence of this unalterable truth, I now (*quod felix*

---

[123] **land tax act**   in 1775 an important item in the revenue.
[124] **Mutiny Bill**   this was the legal instrument of maintaining order in the armed services, which had to be renewed annually by Parliament (until 1879).
[125] **profane herd**   an echo of *profanum vulgus* (Horace, *Odes*, III.i.1).
[126] **all in all**   I Corinthians 15:28.
[127] *Sursum corda*   'Lift up your hearts', the formula used just before the canon.
[128] **high calling**   Philippians 3:14.

faustumque sit[129]) – lay the first stone of the Temple of Peace; and I move you,

'That the Colonies and Plantations of Great Britain in North America, consisting of Fourteen separate governments, and containing Two Millions and upwards of free inhabitants, have not had the liberty and privilege of electing and sending any Knights and Burgesses, or others, to represent them in the high Court of Parliament.'

Upon this Resolution, the previous question was put, and carried; – for the previous question 270, – against it 78.

******

As the Propositions were opened separately in the body of the Speech, the Reader perhaps may wish to see the whole of them together, in the form in which they were moved for.

MOVED,

'That the Colonies and Plantations of Great Britain in North America, consisting of Fourteen separate Governments, and containing Two Millions and upwards of Free Inhabitants, have not had the liberty and privilege of electing and sending any Knights and Burgesses, or others, to represent them in the High Court of Parliament.'

'That the said Colonies and Plantations have been made liable to, and bounden by, several subsidies, payments, rates, and taxes, given and granted by Parliament; though the said Colonies and Plantations have not their Knights and Burgesses, in the said High Court of Parliament, of their own election, to represent the condition of their country; *by lack whereof, they have been oftentimes touched and grieved by subsidies given, granted, and assented to, in the said Court, in a manner prejudicial to the common wealth, quietness, rest, and peace, of the subjects inhabiting within the same.'*

'That, from the distance of the said Colonies, and from other circumstances, no method hath hitherto been devised for procuring a Representation in Parliament for the said Colonies.'

'That each of the said Colonies hath within itself a Body, chosen, in part or in the whole, by the Freemen, Freeholders, or other Free

[129] *quod . . . sit* 'may it be successful and fortunate'.

Inhabitants thereof, commonly called the General Assembly, or General Court; with powers legally to raise, levy, and assess, according to the several usage of such Colonies, duties and taxes towards defraying all sorts of public services*.'

'That the said General Assemblies, General Courts, or other bodies, legally qualified as aforesaid, have at sundry times freely granted several large subsidies and public aids for his Majesty's service, according to their abilities, when required thereto by letter from one of his Majesty's Principal Secretaries of State; and that their right to grant the same, and their chearfulness and sufficiency in the said grants, have been at sundry times acknowledged by Parliament.'

'That it hath been found by experience, that the manner of granting the said supplies and aids, by the said General Assemblies, hath been more agreeable to the inhabitants of the said Colonies, and more beneficial and conducive to the public service, than the mode of giving and granting aids and subsidies in Parliament to be raised and paid in the said Colonies.'

'That it may be proper to repeal an act made in the 7th year of the reign of his present Majesty, intituled, An Act for granting certain duties in the British Colonies and Plantations in America; for allowing a draw-back of the duties of Customs, upon the exportation from this kingdom, of coffee and cocoa-nuts, of the produce of the said Colonies or Plantations; for discontinuing the draw-backs payable on china earthen ware exported to America; and for more effectually preventing the clandestine running of goods in the said Colonies and Plantations.'

'That it may be proper to repeal an Act, made in the 14th year of the reign of his present Majesty, intituled, An Act to discontinue, in such manner, and for such time, as are therein mentioned, the landing and discharging, lading or shipping of goods, wares, and merchandize, at the Town, and within the Harbour, of Boston, in the province of Massachuset's Bay, in North America.'

'That it may be proper to repeal an Act made in the 14th year of the reign of his present Majesty, intituled, An Act for the impartial

---

* The first Four Motions and the last had the previous question put on them. The others were negatived.

The words in italicks were, by an amendment that was carried, left out of the motion; which will appear in the Journals, though it is not the practice to insert such amendments in the Votes.

administration of justice, in cases of persons questioned for any acts done by them in the execution of the law, or for the suppression of riots and tumults, in the province of Massachuset's Bay, in New England.'

'That it is proper to repeal an Act, made in the 14th year of the reign of his present Majesty, intituled, An Act for the better regulating the government of the province of the Massachuset's Bay, in New England.'

'That it is proper to explain and amend an Act, made in the 35th year of the reign of King Henry VIII. intituled, An Act for the trial of treasons committed out of the King's dominions.'

'That, from the time when the General Assembly, or General Court, of any Colony or Plantation, in North America, shall have appointed, by act of Assembly duly confirmed, a settled salary to the offices of the Chief Justice and Judges of the superior courts, it may be proper that the said Chief Justice and other Judges of the superior Courts of such Colony shall hold his and their office and offices during their good behaviour; and shall not be removed therefrom, but when the said removal shall be adjudged by his Majesty in Council, upon a hearing on complaint from the General Assembly, or on a complaint from the Governor, or Council, or the House of Representatives, severally, of the Colony in which the said Chief Justice and other Judges have exercised the said office.'

'That it may be proper to regulate the Courts of Admiralty, or Vice-admiralty, authorized by the 15th chapter of the 4th of George III, in such a manner, as to make the same more commodious to those who sue, or are sued, in the said courts; *and to provide for the more decent maintenance of the Judges of the same.*'

'Almas Ali Khan'

Introduction

Whilst Burke's interest in India was excited and, indeed, partially sustained by his connections, personal and political, the mind he applied to it was furnished with the doctrine and experience he had accumulated. Reflecting on India combined many facets of his thought and the combination was creative. For whilst it would be easy for the superficial reader to see in Burke on India merely another variation on the theme of conquest, it was more besides. His sympathies were extended to embrace a civilization different from the British; and because he conjured with a devastation in India far more terrible than the handicaps to liberty and improvement he had conceived in Ireland, England and America, his mind was focussed upon the foundations of society.

The Rockinghams took up Indian issues as a way of harrassing North's government during the later 1770s. In 1776 Lord Pigot, governor of Madras, was deposed illegally from his office by a cabal comprising discontented servants of the East India Company and a native ruler, Muhammed Ali (better known to history as the Nawab of Arcot). The components of this situation reflect the state of Britain's role in India. The Company was the principal agency of Britain's penetration of the sub-continent. The Company's primary aim was commercial, but commerce soon became inseparable from political affairs. For commercial opportunity was in the gift of government and so depended upon either conciliating or subduing the country's rulers. Though the Company's end was always gain, its means were variable, for its policy was decided ultimately by a board of directors, whose composition altered periodically. The greatest change, initiated in the 1750s, was to conquer and rule where necessary to secure Britain's commerce. This was directed firstly against the French, but after their ejection, was to be extended by Warren Hastings. Pigot's case began with a fluctuation on a more moderate scale. Previously British rule in Madras had favoured the Nawab: the Company now wished Pigot to balance this by restoring the Raja of Tanjore, previously ejected by the British for the Nawab's benefit. It is hardly surprising that Muhammed Ali and the British officials who had gained with him struck against Pigot.

The Pigot affair excited Burke's interest because the governor's brother, Admiral Hugh Pigot, was a parliamentary connection of the Rockinghams. The admiral met with a stony response from North. The Rockinghamite view assumed an anti-executive complexion. Burke and Fox alleged that the Nawab was suborning seven or eight MPs from their duty to the public by heavy bribery; and this at a time when he was unable to pay his household servants. Again, Burke was happy to suggest in 1781 that the government heavily influenced the directors of the East India Company.[1] This position, of course, continued the belief, expressed and exploited in Burke's *Present Discontents*, that executive power was too great for the constitution and was being exerted against the public interest. The belief appeared again in 1780, when Burke's *Speech on Oeconomical Reform* set out to limit the amount of power which could be abused by the executive.[2] Distrust of the executive, indeed, was the keynote of Burke's writings and speeches on India. Not only the British executive but also the government in India excited his wrath.

His concern, once excited, was sustained by external events. His

---

[1] *Speech on State of East India Company, 9th April 1781*, WSEB, v, p. 133. See also the view that to protect India was to safeguard England too, *Speech on Fox's East India Bill, 1st December, 1783*, WSEB, v, p. 383 and *ibid.*, p. 442 for the opinion that the legislation of 1773 and 1780 had increased the influence of the Crown. According to *Parliamentary Register*, XIII, 185. Burke objected to the control of India by 'the executive power of this country'.

[2] W, II, p. 355.

'cousin' William was employed as a London agent on behalf of the Raja, which must have drawn Burke's attention to the conduct of Britain's conquest. The knowledge he acquired, not least through writing about India in company with William, made him a natural member of parliamentary committees. These, in their turn, increased his grasp and informed his indignation about what he discovered. His acquaintance with Philip Francis gave him a decided (if not always balanced) view of Warren Hastings, who had become the chief agent of the further conquests the Company undertook in the seventies. This growing connection with India found its complement in a decided attitude to its conquest.

Ireland had seemed to Burke a country abused by its conquerors. America had been a country liable to conquest, but by 1779 looked likely to escape it: by 1781 it had done so. From the former year India became a public obsession for Burke. It was, as he wrote of Bengal, a conquered country, the victim of 'absolute Conquest putting an End to all Laws, Rights, and Privileges'.[3] Certainly, it was true beyond a doubt that parts of the sub-continent had been subdued by Britain in the course of the century and that Hastings was presently adding to them. But Burke meant something more. He meant that conquest abused Indian civilization. In 1779 it was 'a system of conquest by English arms' which in one case at least had 'brought innumerable and unspeakable calamities' to the country.[4] So India became focussed under Burke's eye as a country oppressed by its new rulers.

If this theme was to be made plausible, Burke needed to show that India's previous governments had been more beneficient. He began with a polarity in mind which helped him to this conclusion. He assumed that India, so far as under Muslim rule, had constitutional principles: on the other hand, British rule in Bengal was arbitrary.[5] Whilst he maintained the latter verdict, the former was not entirely tenable in his own mind.[6] If the pre-British governments were not all bearers of liberty, a new resource was needed to explain the evils of conquering India.

---

[3] *First Report of the Select Committee: 'Observations'* (1782), WSEB, v, p. 171.
[4] *The Policy of Making Conquests for the Mahometans* (1779), WSEB, v, p. 45.
[5] Speech of 30.3.1772, Egerton MS 239 fol 271, British Library; *Speech on Restoring Lord Pigot, 27th May 1777*, WSEB, v, p. 39.
[6] *First Report*, v, p. 171, where Burke noted that though there were clear principles of justice, there was not a mechanism to enforce them successfully.

Burke suggested that the existing regimes, whatever their defects, benefited India. He did not argue that they were perfect and, indeed, after a reverse in the Carnatic, declared that the proper foundation of government was purity.[7] Purity, however, was to be married to the habits of the native Indians. They needed a familar mode of government.[8] The familar comprised the standard items in the Burkean recipe for society, except liberty. Burke suggested that the familar was beneficent, for it embraced an hierarchical order and brought prosperity.[9] He would emphasize, in particular, the role of priests in securing prosperity.[10] If there was despotism, it co-existed with these benefits.[11]

So Burke could identify the British as the violators of a civilized order. It might not be fanciful to see Burke as an Irishman, alert to the wrongs of a conquered race, and free to express his indignation, as he was not free in respect of his native land. One objection to the treatment of India certainly fits. He drew attention to the depression of its economy through British rule.[12] This was precisely the charge he had made two decades earlier about Ireland.[13] But his general charges, elaborated in *Ninth Report*, were developed in a way calculated to appeal to English susceptibilities.

Burke's charges were divided under two heads, government and commerce. The British government of India was described as the enemy of liberty. For whilst the arrangements of Indian society were represented as comparable to Britain's, the laws imposed by the new government were not. The standard contrast between a preference for the good of the few, as against the good of the whole community appeared once more.

A parallel story was told about commerce. The commercial system in India favoured the interests of the Company's agents against the good of the natives. Where a properly directed flow of British investment might have boosted trade and agriculture, the Company reproduced in India the pattern seen in Ireland.[14]

[7] *Speech on Secret Committee, 30th April 1781*, WSEB, v, p. 138.
[8] *Speech on Bengal Judicature Bill, 27th June 1781*, WSEB, v, p. 141.
[9] See esp. *Speech on Fox's India Bill*, WSEB, v, p. 389f.
[10] *Speech on Fox's India Bill*, WSEB, v, p. 422.
[11] *Speech on Bengal Judicature Bill*, WSEB, v, p. 141.
[12] *Ninth Report of the Select Committee* (1783), WSEB, v, p. 231.
[13] Cf. above, *Tracts*, p. 96f.
[14] *Ninth Report of Select Committee* (1783), v, pp. 221f, 231.

The practical thrust of Burke's intent came to an ironic end. He and his political friends fell victim to the scepticism about the executive which they had so sedulously cultivated. They acquired office, but the way they gained it and the use they made of it were both damaging. When the American war was obviously lost, so too was North's government. Though North retained a large personal following, he had forfeited the confidence of the less committed MPs in 1782. Rockingham was able to form an administration; and died. The king sent for Shelburne, who was obnoxious to Charles Fox (who attained the greatest prominence amongst the Rockinghams) and Rockingham's following withdrew from the government. There were thus three significant groups of votes in the Commons: the followers of North, the Rockinghams, and the less committed, presently supporting Shelburne because he was the king's minister. In order to produce a majority, two out of the three had to coalesce. Shelburne failed to conciliate North: Fox and North formed a coalition. Unfortunately, it was a coalition hard to explain in the terms people were accustomed to use. The distrust for the creatures of executive power which Burke and his friends had done everything to encourage since 1766 synchronized poorly with embracing North, who had been in every government from 1761 to 1782 – with one short break, it was true, but that was when he refused to serve under Rockingham in 1765. By the same measure North too found some odd bedfellows.

The situation was not improved by the East India Bill which Fox produced. This would have placed his friends in a position of executive power over India virtually independent of the Commons' control. George III was too shrewd not to strike: the coalition was dismissed; the younger Pitt exhibited as the focus for loyalty at once to king and public interest; and the coalition trounced at a general election. Burke never held office again.

Hastings remained. Burke had identified him in 1783 as the great delinquent in India.[15] After 1784 he seemed to Burke's party a good means of striking at Pitt and, to Burke at least, an avenue to expose India's wrongs. For Pitt he provided an opportunity to divert the energies of the opposition: they were allowed to impeach Hastings, so that the question of Indian policy was narrowed into the responsibilities of an individual. Whilst Fox and others perceptibly lost interest in

[15] PH, xxiii, 800 (25 April 1783).

the case, Burke was moved to pursue it to the bitter end; in 1795 the trial of Hastings ended with his acquittal.

That, however, lay in the future when Burke gave his *Speech on Almas Ali Khan*. Almas Ali Khan was a revenue officer, who had been displaced for suspected malversation by Hastings. He figured in Burke's speech as an occasion for voicing his opinions about India. The speech expressed his indignation with a force which bespeaks a sense of ruin. When Burke spoke in 1784 the cause of his party in England and his hopes for India were alike defeated.

Burke's concern for India did no good to the sub-continent and little to himself. But it did touch many of his fundamental concerns, and implied a widening of them. It involved many of the principal motifs of his thought, more than any subject since he first considered Ireland. In India he saw a hierarchical society, with kings and nobles respected by their subjects, a benevolent priesthood and the riches of an industrious people violated by a conqueror. Its destruction was a complete violation of the providential order (though Burke did not suppose Indian civilization was progressive) and a very striking one: a whole civilization was threatened. The enroachments of the executive in England and America involved a narrower range of concerns. Burke's regard for India also embraced a new type of country within his sympathies. Ireland, England and America might be supposed alike in their aptitude for liberty: India could not, consistently with the natives' habituation to despotism. So whatever Burke's political disappointment, his concerns were exercised, both renewed and enlarged.

Thus, his motifs were fresh in Burke's mind at the coming of the French Revolution in 1789. In France too he saw the fall of a civilization, and sympathized with it, though it had not enshrined an English liberty. In 1783 he had compared Bengal to France.[16] The two cases differed, in that the subversion of France was internal rather than by conquest, but the principle of interpretation was identical.

Analysis

Introduction: the servants of the East India Company should be subjected to scrutiny, from which they are being protected (pp. 277–8).

---

[16] *Fox's India Bill*, WSEB, v, p. 425.

The government of India: obstacles to reform: the main shield of tyranny in India had been the claim of authority from home (pp. 278–80). Despite our best efforts substantial support for tyranny continued, because of corruption in Parliament (pp. 280–1). Illustrated in the case of Almas Ali Khan and others (pp. 281–5).

God would punish and was already punishing England for its dereliction of India (pp. 285–7).

Replies to critics: criticisms of fact rebutted (pp. 287–9) and the sorry condition of India reiterated (pp. 289–90); God's wrath on England re-emphasized (pp. 290–1); reiterated that influence protects tyranny and the chief agent of tyranny, Hastings, mentioned (pp. 291–6). Conclusion (pp. 296–7).

Speech on Almas Ali Khan
(30 July 1784)

Mr. *Burke* begged leave to call the attention of the House; he was aware how different it was to act from facts sufficiently substantiated, and from reports which might be either true or false. The matters he was now to lay before the House, were of great and pressing importance, and he doubted not would be found, upon trial, to depend on the best authority. The business he undertook would lead him to mention some articles of information, which, in his opinion, demanded, and even urged the most accurate, minute, and immediate investigation. He knew not how far his services as an informer might be liked: It was a character for which he professed no great predilection; and if he might judge of the present from the past, it was not likely that the part he was to act, was either an acceptable or a popular one.[1] There was at least this presumption against it, that it would readily prove offensive, in proportion as found to be true. For the mode of judging with a certain class of men, had of late been, not for, but against evidence; not because convicted of its reality, but because it was convenient to see no reality in any thing which had the most distant semblances of reality from that quarter. Here was the great stumbling-block which had undone India, and which would ultimately undo England.[2] A very large body of individuals were united and determined to protect the Company's servants from every sort of inquisition.[3] This was the only way by which the guilty could be screened from justice – by which those who deserved, could escape punishment! A confederacy was formed, for the sole purpose of extol-

[1] **popular** Burke was facing the House after the General Election of 1784, which had put himself and his friends in a minority.

[2] **England** because the wherewithal derived from Indian corruption would support whatever designs the executive had against English liberties.

[3] **inquisition** Burke exaggerates the size of the East India interest in the Commons, cf. above, p. 271.

ling the India government as a good one, and the Governor as unimpeachable. The whole drift of this crooked policy, was to keep the poor natives wholly out of sight. We might hear enough about what great and illustrious exploits were daily performing on that conspicuous theatre by Britons: But unless some dreadful catastrophe was to take place – unless some hero or heroine was to fall – unless the tragedy was to be a very deep and bloody one; – we were never to hear of any native's being an actor! No. The field was altogether engrossed by Englishmen; and those who were chiefly interested in the matter actually excluded. The extraordinary circumstance, to which the world owed so many unexampled transactions, was no other than a belief, industriously propaguted[4] in India, that all the measures of the Company's servants were approved and confirmed by authority *from home*. This had been long held up to that unfortunate race of men, as the radical principle of the Indian government: So that whether their English masters dealt in peculation, in oppression, in tyranny, or in murder, it was not to gratify their own unbounded avarice or ambition – it was not to render themselves independent of those who employed them – to amass enormous fortunes, and to return to this country, and, in the face of all law and justice, blazon the infamous trophies of extortion and rapine! No – These were none of their motives: they acted only by authority, and firmly relied on support *from home*. – Here he read an extract from some of Mr. Hastings' letters to the Directors, as transcribed into the Journals of Parliament, from the Reports of former Committees, in which an acknowledgement was explicitly made by that gentleman, of his having thus availed himself of such an expedient, even at a time when it was the current opinion, that all the power and authority of the Company were exerted in managing and controlling his proceedings. While, therefore, he was ravaging countries, depopulating kingdoms, reducing the gardens of the universe to a desert, plundering opulent towns, and consigning to atrocious cruelty and destruction the innocent and industrious inhabitants of whole empires, he laid the entire obloquy of his conduct to the authority under which he pretended to act. From this originated all those foul enormities, which had deluged the Indies in poverty and blood, and flung the British empire into one complete scene of animosity and distraction. Whatever projects ambi-

[4] **propaguted**   presumably a misprint for 'propagated'.

tion proposed, avarice grasped, or cruelty perpetrated; this apology was ready to cover, to extenuate, to authorise, to urge, or to sanction the whole! It was always support and protection *from home*, which gave operation and effect to rapacity, to peculation, and to bloodshed abroad! In this manner the English goverment was traduced, and the very name of Britons become infamous and execrable. There was a time, to be sure, when much was done in the House of Commons to counterwork the malignant influence of such an impolitic and merciless principle. He frequently heard a learned gentleman (Mr. Dundas[5]), whom he saw in his place, pour out a dreadful torrent of eloquence and invective, for the purpose of declaring to the whole world, that the servants of the Company were no longer the objects of support *at home*; that this country were not sharers in their guilt; and that justice would undoubtedly overtake delinquents, whose conduct had brought the foulest reproach on the British character! With what a catalogue of the blackest crimes had he not charged them, in the face of this House, and of the Public; and by a detail of evidence, which swelled the Journals of Parliament, and blackened the annals of the nation, which interested the curiosity, and roused the indignation of all Europe, and which would descend to posterity unbroken, unequivocal, and unimpeached, he demonstrated, to the complete satisfaction of all who understood the subject, that the English government in India had become almost as infamous *at home* as abroad – had lost all credit, even with its sovereigns in Leadenhall-street[6] – had not only refused compliance with the repeated orders of the Company, but uniformly contradicted them; and that therefore an immediate and universal reform was become indispensaable. The recall of Governor-general Hastings was the consequence of these bold and spirited exertions. This seemed the only expedient which the wisdom of Parliament thought adequate to the evil: And the measure undoubtedly possessed the confidence of the Public at large. Things were now brought to a crisis: whoever doubted but an order from the Court of Directors, or an order from the House of Commons, might singly, but especially when connected, have been able to bring from India a servant of the Company. No such thing. The experiment was made, and made with every prospect of success, on

---

[5] **Dundas**   the author of Pitt's East India Bill, which passed successfully into law.
[6] **Leadenhall-street**   where the headquarters of the East India Company were located.

the side of this country: But who can estimate the influence of corruption, when supported by all the treasures of India? This powerful and opulent country was evidently worsted in the struggle, and the sequel of the contest has proved, that the support *from home*, however secret and mysterious in its operation, was nevertheless real, and always at hand to answer the basest purposes, like prompt payment. The great question therefore, under such a series of misconduct, still was, How were the natives affected – what were their hardships – in what manner were they to be relieved –from whom were they ultimately to expect assistance? Was there no door of mercy left open for so many millions of our fellow-creatures, who had long groaned under every species of the grossest oppression? Or were the whole British possessions in India formally proscribed by act of Parliament, or consigned, however, to the scourge of the men, whose outrages had already rendered the finest and most fertile provinces on earth, one barren unhospitable solitude! He now appeared in behalf of those Indians, whom our barbarous policy had ruined and made desperate. Their grievances were unparallelled in history, and seemed to increase in proportion as they became unable to bear them. The English establishment among them appeared to have no other object, than to accumulate their oppression and distress. Was such a monstrous abuse of power – such a desolating calamity – so enormous a mischief, to continue its operations, without end or limitation Where were the innocent sufferers to appeal? Their tyrants were evidently invested with new powers. Those, at least, by which so much damage had been done, were approved, and received such a protection *from home*, as was enough to make every individual Indian tremble for his life, in proportion as his property rendered him an object of rapacity and destruction. And were men in such a predicament as this, to be under the necessity of demanding justice for the very authors of their wrongs – had they any thing like the mere forms of equity to expect from such as had injured them – Would not their heaviest complaints be treated as chimerical, and their most urgent petitions be rejected, as groundless and absurd? The people of Quebec had just brought forward a petition,[7] their requisition would be heard; public justice demanded it in their name, and they wanted[8] not friends in this country, who would faithfully represent, enforce, and facilitate their

[7] **petition** for an extension of representation and English law (CJ, xl, 384–6).
[8] **wanted** i.e. lacked.

claims. They, happy people! were not oppressed by a Governor General, over whom the British legislature had no power,[9] whose friends, both in Britain and India, triumphed in the plenitude of authority, and whose inhuman and execrable measures, proceeded on full security of protection *from home*. No. They were connected with many who were determined to see them righted, who generously made their cause their own – who were even interested in taking their parts. But the natives of India were universally abandoned to their fate: They had not only to struggle against the most dreadful odds, but were absolutely without friends or resource. Their riches were gone to make the fortunes of those, who now turned a deaf ear to all their complaints. Where was the friend of the Minister, or the favourite of the British Court, or the member of Parliament, whose influence promised success, who would stand up as advocate for the unfortunate Almas Ali Cawn? Alas! the situation and property of this man, like a great many of his countrymen, destroyed him, attracted the attention, stimulated the avarice, and brought down the vengeance of the British on his head. The crime of having money was imputed to this unfortunate prince, which, like the sin against the Holy Ghost[10] in Christian theology, in India politics can never be forgiven. It seemed impossible, in this instance, to plunder without murder. The bloody edict is therefore issued. Mark how soon the fatal science in that country is brought to perfection! No matter what is done, provided the manner of doing it be properly managed. Yet he had heard of a letter, and of a murder, or something very like it, recited in that letter; an extract of which had come to his hand.[11] From this extract he learned that orders had been sent to arrest Almas Ali Cawn: but this gentleman-like business must be done in the most gentleman-like manner. The Chief must be taken, and he must also be *put to death*; but all this must be so contrived as to imply no *treachery*. Here was honour of a very singular and nice description – Plunder, peculation, and even assassination, without treachery! – Such was the extreme refinement which distinguished the cruelties of the East. All possible delicacy was even to be shewn in the exercise of a ferocity, the foulest and the most atrocious that ever blackened the

[9] **no power** Burke means 'in practice', for the governor-general was legally answerable to the government of the day.
[10] **Holy Ghost** see Matthew 12:31; Mark 3:29; Luke 12:10.
[11] **hand** see Corr, v, p. 253.

prostitution of usurped authority. The reason of such extraordinary proceedings was not less extraordinary. The precaution is no compliment to the sensibility, but to the cunning and pusillanimity of the mind in whom the bloody mandate originated. There were persons to whom such a circumstance might procure a handle of reproach or invective. On this account, let Almas Ali Cawn be deprived of his life with as little indecency as possible. The proscription is absolute – he must die; but let his death be perpetrated honestly. This, however, was only one instance of many where the same wild and outrageous policy prevailed, and threatened an utter extermination of all our settlements in that part of the world. Every district almost in India daily exhibited marks or specimens of the same inhumanity and disclosed scenes of misery and degradation, by means of our mismanagement, of which few Europeans could have any conception. And what had been done to check the ravages and ambition of the Company's servants? Had Government interfered to prevent or put an end to those extravagancies? Was there any probability of things assuming another or a milder aspect? Had the system framed and matured by the wisdom of the new Parliament at home, or any late measures carried into execution by the Supreme Council[12] abroad, given hopes of better things? He wished to God these, and a thousand such questions, could be answered in the affirmative. He appealed to the Treasury Bench, who had all, undoubtedly, made themselves masters of the facts in debate. He would appeal to a Bench higher than the Treasury Bench: he meant the Indian Bench[13] behind it, where the agents of the Company and of the Company's servants sat, the honourary supporters of their own Administration. He asked what the House and the whole world were let to conclude from that impunity with which the most enormous transactions of those who had the good fortune to perpetrate them in India were treated? Could the House, without horror and indignation, recollect the barbarous usage which two unfortunate princesses had experienced? The tale which the history of these ladies, the mother and grandmother of the Vizier of Oude,[14] disclosed to Europe and to posterity, was enough to make

[12] **Supreme Council**   i.e. the governor-general and council of Bengal.
[13] **Indian Bench**   the friends of Hastings were unlikely to be found on Burke's side of the House, but those of the East India interest had made terms with Pitt chiefly because they lacked a more favourable alternative.
[14] **Oude**   the Begums or Begams of Oudh were the mother and wife of Sujah Dowlah, Nabob of Oudh. The latter was suspicious of his son and successor, Asaf

children yet unborn blush for the rapacity and brutality of their fathers, as well as flush the cheeks of Britons for the flagitious conduct of their countrymen. Were not the nearest relations of these illustrious women tempted to betray and ruin them? Were they not stripped of their all, and reduced, from the first situations which the country afforded, to a state of penury and beggary? Were not these dreadful sufferings inflicted because the women, who had on a former occasion smarted under that spirit of outrage and rapacity which hath stamped in blood the atrocious footsteps of the Indian Government, apprehending a repetition of the same depredations, assumed the courage which became their danger, and defended themselves to the utmost of their power. This happened during our residentiary commission for the government of that country. They were bereaved even of their jewels: their toilets, those altars of beauty, were sacrilegiously invaded, and the very ornaments of the sex foully purloined! No place, no presence, not even that of Majesty, was proof against the severe inquisition of the mercenary and the merciless. But where was all this immense booty? Was it placed to account? No. – Had it been occupied for investing any of the Company's ships? No. – Where then was it? Ought not some memorandum of it to exist? The fact was uncontrovertible; but the certain effect which it was meant to produce, and which it did produce, seemed oblitererated and vanished for ever. – Need he tell the House that Mahomed Caun[15] had written a letter on the ruin of his country, conceiving it his duty not to remain silent while a scene of such distress presented itself to his view wherever he turned his eye. This province was not able to produce a twelfth of what it had done but a short time before. Here nature had lately bloomed in luxuriance and bounty; the inhabitants had been rich, contented, and contributed their share to every burden proposed

al-Daula, and committed the Begams to the care of Hastings. The Begams controlled a considerable revenue from land grants and possessed a large hoard of treasure. Pressure from Hastings on Asaf al-Daula to pay his debts to the East India Company made the latter extract fifty-five *lakhs* of rupees and the forced cessation of the land grants from the Begams for a period. Violence was involved in the transaction. For Burke's view, see also *Speech on Fox's India Bill*, WSEB, v, p. 410ff. Burke here exemplifies suffering in the person of women of high rank in order to elicit sympathy, which he deployed classically with Marie Antionette in Ref, pp. 168ff.

[15] **Mahomed Caun** identified by Marshall as Mirza Muhammed Kazim Khan, who was an *amil* (revenue collector) in Rohilkhand and had written a report on conditions there.

with chearfulness and satisfaction. Now an armed force could not extort from them one twelfth part of what they had then granted voluntarily. Could any man be at a loss to conjecture the reason of so rapid a declension, since it appeared in this instance that the revenues decreased in proportion to the violence and force employed in collecting them. He wished from his heart any one would contradict the facts stated with regard to this wretched country. Reasons of State undoubtedly might be given in great abundance, and an apology made for every outrage which the strong could exercise over the weak: but facts were superior to sophistry, and would always speak for themselves. Was not this country, prior to the dirty and miserable interference of English politics, so plentiful, so well cultivated, and so rich, as to deserve the name of the Eden of the East. There was nothing like its fertility and luxuriance in those barren situations where we existed. It exhibited to Europeans a new spectacle of Nature putting forth all her strength. But where now was this beautiful paradise? It was no where to be found. This delightful spot, the joint effect of nature and art, the united work of God and man, was no more. The country was extirpated. *Haman Dowlah*,[16] the well-known appellation of Mr. Hastings in India, had reduced the whole to a waste, howling desert, where no human creature could exist. He challenged the abettors of such desolation to stand up and give him the lye. And how, or by what arguments, could a Government be defended, under which such a series of irreparable, unexampled, and uncontrovertible miseries existed? – He desired the Indian and Treasury Benches to look at Bengal, and to think, with horror, that while we were forging new chains for the wretched natives of that place, Heaven was rescuing them from our machinations by a famine,[17] which raged at this very moment in the environs of Calcutta. He called upon Major Scott, Mr. Atkinson, and several of the Company's friends who sat behind the Treasury Bench, to contradict any of his statements. It was from a country thus pillaged, depopulated, and deserted, hopes were entertained of retrieving the Company's affairs. And those men, whose dreadful delinquencies were notorious and unpardonable, were notwithstanding empowered by the British Government to act with more extensive authority than ever in that very capacity which they had already rendered the scourge of India and the opprobrium of

[16] **Haman Dowlah**   Marshall notes this = *Aman al-Dowleh*, 'the security of the state'.
[17] **famine**   the famine of 1783 had been severe in Oudh.

England. These were the men who had promised a revenue equivalent to all the necessities of the Company, and the arrears due from it to this country. Was the House aware of the magnitude of the sum to be raised, and of the situation of that country which was to produce it? In what state could they suppose that empire in which a famine reached, in its dreadful progress, the very gates of the capital? There was, he knew, a Committee watching the causes and effects of this dismal calamity, called the Committee of Famine: but this was no matter of surprise to him. The policy which had for some time prevailed in Bengal was adequate to the greatest evils which could befal its miserable inhabitants. That country was not more populous than this. There were, according to the best calculation that could be obtained, nearly the same number of inhabitants in both. Here, however, the duty on salt exceeded very little the sum of 250,000l.; but there it produced just twice that sum. The same sort of standard was in general applicable to every article of revenue. Whatever taxes we paid, it seemed to be the system of our Indian governors to impose the double of that burden on their subjects. Their Land tax,[18] where ours was only four, was not less than eight shillings in the pound. And what but a passion of the most flagitious rapacity could be the cause of such an enormous exaction. It was not, he found at last, altogether possible for either the Company or the Legislature to overlook such a system of delinquency. Some remains of decency compelled them to make occasional remonstrances on the subjects when their servants had incurred most blame. The orders which they issued were therefore replete with the best advice. Never did he see more sound morality than in these. In theory their sentiments were divine; but in their conduct how literally and awefully had the medal been reversed. – He had read somewhere, that *great were the company of preachers.*[19] He was sorry their labours had not been more successful, as most of the miseries they had brought on a harmless people originated in their preaching when they ought to have commanded. [Looking at Mr. Dundas, he exclaimed, but *Saul too was among the prophets;*[20] but he had proved one of those whose doctrines had *a Saviour of death unto death, and not of life unto life.*[21]] What then was to be the end of all this?

---

[18] **Land tax** an especially telling comparison, because most of Burke's audience would be at least connected with landed wealth.
[19] **great . . . preachers** cf. Psalms 68:11.
[20] **Saul too . . . prophets** cf. I Samuel 10:11.
[21] **Saviour . . . life** cf. II Corinthians 2:16.

It was now too plain the British Legislature would not interfere for the salvation or relief of people who had never injured them, though injured by them in the foulest manner. They would, however, find redress where neither the Company nor this country could prevent an attention to their wrongs; crimes which involved the sufferings, the ruin not of individuals only, but of nations and empires, could not ultimately escape the righteous judgement of God. The guilt and devastations we had carried into a country with which we had no concern, would be regarded as an insult on his conduct, who had the hearts of Kings, of Ministers, and of societies in his hand. In all these transactions he saw an over-ruling Providence[22] making such arrangements as should render it utterly impracticable for the criminal, however barricaded with power, however loaded with wealth, however extolled by flattery, finally to escape. A cry for vengeance had gone forth and reached his ears, who never could be inattentive to the distresses of his creatures; and we could expect as little mercy from him as we had shewn to them. We were still more in his power than the poor Indians were in ours. Should he but withdraw his finger, we should become as little among the nations as ever we were great. Did we not alaready exhibit marks of this aweful dereliction? Yes. – The country was devoted[23] to destruction: that House, the venerable palladium[24] of its liberties, was annihilated: the Constitution had received a shock, which it would never recover:[25] the empire was mutilated, and its very credit tottered to the foundation.[26] These were symptoms of a dissolution at hand. The decree was fixed; and as certainly as we had regarded the sufferings and grievances of the

---

[22] **Providence**   a particularly striking enunciation (and see too below, p. 290–1, 296) in the belief in particular providence which Burke had assumed from his youth, see above, p. xxiii.

[23] **devoted**   i.e. marked out for, with special reference usually to something or someone either judged by or sacrificed to a deity and perhaps to death. Cf. below, p. 289.

[24] **palladium**   in Athens the well-defended shrine of Pallas Athena, the patroness deity of the city, and so by transference any well-protected object of the highest value.

[25] **recover**   alluding to the dismissal of the Fox–North coalition by George III.

[26] **foundation**   alluding to the loss of America and to the greatly increased size of the National Debt consequent on the American war. The Debt had risen to just under £243 million, and required £3 million out of a revenue of £12–13 million to service. William Grenville, *Essay on the Supposed Advantages of a Sinking Fund* (1821), p. 19, recollected that 'the nation gave way ... to an almost universal panic on this subject'.

Indians without mercy, our punishment would come without mitigation. What are these men, said he, pointing to the Treasury Bench? Are they not the Ministers of vengeance to a guilty, a degenerated, and unthinking nation? Yes. – They are literally the executioners of that aweful and irreversible verdict which is registered in Heaven against us, and commissioned by the Great Sovereign of the world, who hath destined them his scourge, in loading with such a series of oppressive taxes as have no example, a people whose unprincipled ambition have rendered them infamous in both extremities of the globe. He concluded this part of his speech with moving *"That there be laid before this House copies of all letters, instructions, or minutes, relative to the seizure of the person of a native of India, resident in the country of Oude, called Almas Ali Cawn, and for putting the said native to death."*

Mr. *Burke* declared the honourable gentleman[27] had confirmed every word he had said – The famine which he had mentioned, was established beyond a controversy, by the best authority which could be obtained, and the fact could not be allowed without admitting the existence of those causes which unavoidably produced it. The honourable gentleman had also in effect confessed the government to have been so bad, that they were obliged to return it into the hands of its original owners, as not being able to make any thing of it themselves – but the wretched people, from whose territories they had withdrawn their Resident, they took care to make the prey of usury – What else was meant by the security of bankers to guarrantee the Company's acquisitions?[28] He desired to be contradicted and corrected if he mis-stated any particulars: but he acted on information which he knew to be sound, and every fact he advanced would thus reach the public ear under the sanction of the honourable gentleman's testimony. He was by no means conscious that the honourable gentleman's evidence was garbled or stated in any degree incorrectly; but if he thought it was, his redress was open. Why did he not complain to the House? He had a right to have made such an appeal – The House would have taken up his cause, and the matter undergone

---

[27] **gentleman** Scott, who had rebutted Burke's assertion that British India had suffered from famine.

[28] **acquisitions** Scott had argued that the British resident had withdrawn from Lucknow and that the payments from Oudh to the Company had been guaranteed by bankers in Lucknow.

a fresh investigation. Every one knew, that in framing Reports of Committees, it was not customary to state the entire evidence of every witness, but that part only which was most applicable to the point for which it was adduced; and whenever any doubt arose about the fairness of selection, the practice had always been to refer to the minutes. The honourable gentleman might therefore, if he chose, move for the minutes then; by them he was ready to abide. – But he foresaw all of those general and vague charges were only meant to blunt the force of his statements, and to hold up a specious but unmeaning language to the Public. He received with readiness and satisfaction the challenge which had been given on the subject of the Reports. It was easier to say they were false, than to prove it – He suspected the attempt would go no farther – It was not necessary – It might be impolitic – The multitude were not always in a capacity to distinguish between assertion and argument. He owned the Reports were libels, and libels of the bitterest sort, as they contained nothing but truths that were equally melancholy and alarming to the credit of this country. He had been urged to appeal to the Public; this appeal he was not much inclined to make; the Public were perhaps more disposed to listen to the honourable gentleman than to him, and he was averse to be tried by a tribunal which could give no judgement; but he demanded the judgement of the House, and the House only could come to a decision on the point. It was the cause of the House; the House were much more interested in the issue than he was, or any individual could be; and he was perfectly indifferent to the opinion of coffee houses and newspapers.

The papers were then ordered.

Mr. Burke then moved "*That there be laid before this House, copies of all letters relative to any demand of monies, or orders to take the same, from the mother or grandmother of the Soubah[29] of Oude, since the first of January, 1782,*"

Mr. *Burke* rose again, and moved, "That an account of what became of the jewels, and other valuables taken from the mother and grandmother of the Vizier of Oude, should be laid before the House."

Mr. *Burke* was astonished at the conduct of the Minister:[30] it was

[29] **Soubah** = *subahdar,* governor of a province in the Mogul empire: here the Nabob of Oudh.
[30] **Minister**   Pitt moved the order of the day in order to cut Burke off.

absurd, though not unaccountable. The right honourable gentleman had not given him time to state his grounds, for grounds he had, and would state – He did hope a time of reckoning would yet come, when he should be heard, and heard with a decency which the subject deserved. But the House of Commons was lost; its dignity, its energy, its utility, was no more – Did they imagine, because every thing went as they wished at present, the world was blind, or posterity would be blind to the evils they thus entailed on their country. The insensibility of Government to the foul enormities lately perpetrated, and now perpetrating by our countrymen in the East, was shocking – He deprecated the day the knowledge of them had ever come to his mind. The miserable objects it exhibited, countries extirpated, provinces depopulated, cities and nations all overwhelmed in one mass of destruction, constantly preyed upon his peace, and by night and day dwelt on his imagination. To relieve that devoted country from some of the many enormities under which it had groaned so many years, he had toiled many an hour, when others were amusing themselves in a way which was likely to serve them more substantially than his labours, however assiduous and unremitted, every had served him, or ever would. But the cries of the native Indians were never out of his ears – Their distresses roused his whole soul, and had kept him busy when those who now sneered at his earnestness, and sensibility were much more agreeably engaged. The facts related in papers, which, under the direction of Parliament, he was obliged to read, had left on his mind such an impression of horror, as had frequently deprived him of sleep; he was consequently desirous of seeing a conclusion to such barbarities, and such details, as the most savage or hardest heart could scarcely read without shuddering[31] – To put a stop to peculation, to tyranny, and to robberies and assassinations of the most daring and shameless description, he had exerted all his faculties; he was fully committed; his character was before the Public,[32] he risqued all the little popularity which his labours had procured from a grateful Public – It was in hopes of breaking the spirit, or checking the operations of that inhuman system, that he had so frequently and so patiently submitted to the scorn and derision of the House and of the world – Observing Mr. Macnamara, Mr. Rolle, Mr. Grenville, and

---

[31] **shuddering**   but Burke had acknowledged elsewhere that the unfamiliarity of the English with India tended to blunt their sympathies, see *Speech on Fox's India Bill*, WSEB, v, p. 403f.

[32] **Public**   an important protestation, see above, p. 109f.

others, laughing at his serious apprehensions, he said, the subject was a fit subject for levity – Millions of innocent individuals had been made the victims of our indiscretion, and what reason had he to complain being made the butt of juvenile statesmen;[33] who, like a young Emperor, of as much sense, and perhaps more sensibility than they, though in one unguarded moment, he fiddled at the fire which he had kindled[34] in the metropolis of the universe, could affect to be merry at recitals which ought to make them pale. He, for his own part, thought, the dreadful procedure of Providence was so strongly and obviously marked, as to have escaped no man but those who wished not to observe it – He believed from his heart, the vengeance of heaven to be raised against this country. By authorising the massacres which had been so foully perpetrated and repeated in India, Britain was now become a land of blood – Much innocent blood had been shed, and he doubted was still shedding – But an avenger would certainly appear and plead the cause of the wronged with those who had wronged them – Yes, the arm of God was abroad – His righteous visitation was already begun, and who could tell where it might end? He knew with accuracy how to discriminate the good from the bad, those who had, from those who had not, imbrued their hands in the blood of their fellow creatures. The instruments of his wrath were infinite, and would be exercised without ceasing or interval, till the redress of the wretched, and the punishment of the oppressors were completed. This great work Providence was visibly carrying on against a country, who, by its crooked policy, had ripened itself for destruction. What were the infatuation which seized us so generally, the debt which hung about our neck, with a weight which precipitated our downfal; our want of union, our want of principle, and our want of consequence, but certain indications of a malediction which the dreadful wretchedness we had entailed on a people much better than

---

[33] **juvenile statesmen** Burke's political difficulty in catching the ear of the new House was compounded by the fact that some members and several of its leading figures were young enough to be his children. William Grenville and Pitt, for instance, were both born in 1759. Rolle and Macnamara had both been born in 1756.

[34] **kindled** most ancient authors affirmed that Nero started the great fire of Rome (see Suetonius, *Nero*, 38; Dio Cassius 62.16.1, and Pliny, *Natural History*, 17.1,1,5) but Tacitus, *Annals*, xv.38 gives this merely as a report (but see 40). Likewise the story of Nero's performing the Fall of Troy at the time is reported by Suetonius and Dio (62.18.1) as fact, but by Tacitus (xv.39) as a rumour.

we, had brought at last on our own heads? After enforcing those beautiful and affecting sentiments, by a variety of pertinent and splendid passages from some of the Latin classics, nothing, he said, could be more striking and apposite than the following lines of our own poet:

> O wretched guardians of a charge too good!
> Ye mean deserters of your brother's blood!
> Know, if eternal justice rules the ball,
> Thus shall your wives and thus your children fall;
> On all the line a sudden vengeance wait,
> And frequent hearses shall besiege the gate.
> There passengers shall stand, and pointing, say,
> While the long funerals blacken all the way,
> Lo! these were they, whose souls the furies steel'd,
> And curs'd with hearts unknowing how to yield:
> Thus unlamented pass the proud away,
> The gaze of fools and pageants of a day,
> So perish all, whose breast ne'er learnt to glow,
> For others good, or melt at others woe![35]

The right honourable gentleman has answered these allegations, but how? His answers were before the Public, and the public would judge – The Reports[36] of the Committee had all their vouchers – The validity of these challenged the attention of the House and of the Public at large under the sanction of Parliament – Their reality had been impeached indeed, but impeached in a way which evidently shewed the impeachment was only made to serve a purpose, but never meant to provoke a trial. This was the great object of his wishes – Oh! he exclaimed, what would he not risque to find all the scenes of horror, to which no description was equal, but which were recited in those Reports, nothing but a fiction? He wished it for the honour of humanity; from sympathy to millions of hopeless individuals, and especially, from an anxiety which he had long felt, to retrieve this House, this country, this generation, and even the Company, from

---

[35] **O wretched guardians ... woe!** Pope, *Elegy to the Memory of an Unfortunate Lady*, 11.29–30, 35–46, with Burke's usual liberty of quotation. His chiefest alteration is from the singular to the plural in the first two lines.

[36] **Reports** i.e. the Eleven Reports of the Select Committee and Six of the Secret Committee.

infamy and execration. Why would not those men who had avowed so unequivocally convictions of their own falsehoods, come forward, and authenticate their allegations? He would meet them with alacrity, on the spot, and in the moment he was prepared to put the truths of every statement contained in seventeen volumes of Reports to the test. Where was the man who would take him at his word? He disclaimed all obstinacy of opinion – No member in the House would be more happy in the issue, should he fail in supporting his allegations, than he would be. It would, in fact, be to him a discovery more precious and grateful, than the discovery of a new world. Why did not they who possessed the secret, in compassion to mankind reveal it? To this precise, but desirable object, all his endeavours went. Did they not therefore deserve to be seconded? Much was said in the House, which tended to propagate an opinion that nothing was wrong in our India Government. He was eager to find such an opinion well established. Nothing was more likely to decide so material a question as a revisal of what had been reported, after three years laborious diligence, by Committees appointed for the sole purpose of arranging all the materials which had been produced on the subject. But whenever he urged the point, a thousand apologies were made, and his motions over-ruled. The *order of the day* was the only answer he could obtain to the most obvious and pertinent question he could put. Indeed the *order the the day* had its effect within these walls; but would the *order of the day* satisfy the world? Would the *order of the day* wipe away the disgrace which branded the character of the nation? Would the *order of the day* rescue the Minister from reproach for thus assiduously avoiding all inquiry into the grievances of India? To these ends the *order of the day* was not adequate; but the *order of the day*, while the Company had so many of their friends in the House, would always be able to suppress disagreeable truths, to screen a notorious delinquency, and, by a shocking medley of sophistry, impudence, and vague declamation, impose on the People of England, and keep them in the dark. He could excuse an honourable gentleman (Major Scott) for the part he took in the contest. He avowed an agency which required fidelity,[37] and he had always given him credit for his indefatigable exertions and honour in thus faithfully and openly adhering to the interest of his principal: but surely the same obligation did not

---

[37] **fidelity**   Scott was Hastings' agent.

extend to the House in general. How was he to account for the insensibility of the young Minister, who, at a time of life when compassion was in its prime, regarded the sufferers of India with so much indifference? He, more than any other, could afford them redress. The majorities[38] which had, during the present session, so ably supported his measures, were competent to the object. The other House was wholly his own.[39] He could not doubt but his heart would go with him. The right honourable gentleman had none of those connections to struggle with which bound the honourable gentleman (Major Scott) behind him: he had surely undertaken no agency, which it would be dishonour in any degree to relinquish. He did not represent, as personal, any great man, whom it might be dangerous to abandon or offend. The honourable gentleman, who filled this respectable situation, had executed his trust completely; and more ample powers had never been given to any man; for it seems his commission enabled him to do every thing, except one, and that single exception was, that he should not resign his government of Bengal. It astonished him to recollect the process, or, rather, the farce, which this man had exhibited to his countrymen for many years. The moment he is ordered to return, his friends all pledge themselves for his obedience. But still it has happened, and probably always will happen, at least till his object is perfectly obtained, that something invariably interferes, which renders his compliance with the command of his masters, and even the authority of this House, impracticable. Beyond this limitation, it was now obvious, the powers he delegated did not extend; and it was folly, after what had passed, not to see that the whole was the effect of system. It discovered to the world to what lengths this very extraordinary agency went. It accounted for the honourable gentleman's conduct: but who would say that it had any influence on the Minister? No: he was left to the freedom of his own will. His virtues, the consolation and hope of his countrymen, were not unknown. – His friends hailed him as the saviour, protector, and champion of the Constitution. What was there inconsistent with

[38] **majorities** it was estimated after the General Election of 1784 that Pitt had 306 supporters to the Opposition's 200 (and 38 Members doubtful) (see Cannon, *Fox-North Coalition*, p. 216). Pitt had a majority of 233–136 on the first division on the Westminister election.

[39] **his own** an allusion to the tendency of the Upper House to follow the government of the day (cf. above, p. 135), but especially to the rejection of Fox's Indian Bill by the Lords on the king's instructions.

the qualities so frequently ascribed to him, as a man and a statesman, in redressing the grievances of many millions of people, who had no other prospect of relief? Humanity and the Constitution were both on the side of the sufferers, and would co-operate with every effort he should make to relive them. Here stands the accuser and the accused – the latter by his agent, by his friends, and by his masters (the Directors), had pleaded not guilty. If any confidence was due to repeated and solemn declarations, he was ready, by these means, to disprove the charge. The judge (Mr. Pitt) sat on the bench, and was urged by every consideration which could affect the human heart, to give verdict on the cause. The indictment had no other evidence than those Reports, which had been so seriously and frequently reprobated as spurious, vindictive, and inconclusive: But even by these, such as they were, he was prepared to stand or fall. Every thing therefore was ready, and he would protest against any farther procrastination, in a business of such importance. He had no objections to a re-examination of the Reports, by a Committee appointed for that purpose; or to the institution of an inquiry into the conduct, which these Reports had so explicitly criminated. The *great God*, whose beautiful works, the finest countries in India, were defaced, were mangled and laid waste, demanded a trial of Haman Ul Dowlah – *man* who had been reduced to beggary, with all its concomitant wretchedness, called loud for justice. Great Britain, whose character and honour had received an indelible stain, waited the issue with solicitude and suspense! It became the Minister of a great and generous nation, instead of laughing at the miseries, of his fellow-creatures, to regard these important calls with all his attention. Good God! he exclaimed, What must the whole world think of a young man, who could hear of oppression, peculation, rapine, and even murder, not with insensibility only, but with levity – with laughter![40] Whatever sport it was to the Treasury Bench, it was, he could assure them, no sport to the poor helpless men, who daily saw the effects of their industry, the means of their subsistence, extorted from them, and their families reduced to abjection and want! Why then did they not either bring such an enormous delinquent to justice, or legally disprove the delinquency with which

---

[40] **laughter**   even in a more favourable House Burke's histrionics about India had provoked laughter (however he might try to carry it off); see *Speech on Fox's India Bill*, WSEB, v, p. 411.

he stood charged in the face of the public? He disclaimed every feeling of personal pique or aversion. Mr. Hastings had never injured or offended him. He possessed many qualities, of which he was as ready as any man to avow his admiration. He entered on the Select Committee with such a manifest partiality for this man, that the friends of Sir Elijah Impey often upbraided him for the prejudice which they thought he entertained in his favour.[41] He had been, like many of his betters, dazzled with the constant panegyrics, which attended the mention of his name. But the huge volumes of evidence which came under his inspection, effected a complete revolution in all his ideas of this celebrated character. The inquiries, which he thought it his duty to make, were laborious, and he soon foresaw would certainly subject him to a world of obloquy and infidious remark. He persevered, however; and what was the result? He found that plunder, murder, and desolation, had been systematically pursued; that the policy of India aimed only at rapacity; that no means, however foul and atrocious, which could facilitate this end, were omitted; and that the perpetrators of all these enormities, instead of being called to an account for their actions, were supported, protected, and cherished, by those, whose duty it was to prosecute and to punish them. He could not, therefore, but look upon Mr. Hastings as the scourge of India. It was his duty, and the duty of every man who thought and felt as he did, to deliver, if possible, any part of God's creation from such a scourge. His efforts he found were much too weak, though as strong as he could make them. This dreadful Colossus[42] was not to be shaken by any individual. He lorded it over every thing that was great and powerful and good in India, and in England. What was the present House of Commons but an engine to sanction whatever this daring man should do? But though the poor Indians were still destined to remain a prey to the Governor General; though in defending their cause against a power, which even Parliament dared not, could not pull down, he had exposed himself to such a torrent of reproach and obloquy, as afforded his enemies a momentary triumph; though every thing he had said was misconstrued, to feed the deception of the moment, he had this satisfaction to sweeten the cup of

[41] **favour** for Burke's attitude to Impey, see WSEB, v, pp. 143ff.
[42] **Colossus** from the Colossus of Rhodes, a very large statue of Apollo which had bridged the mouth of Rhodes harbour in classical antiquity.

disappointment, that he had fought the battle of humanity; and that as a British subject, he had laboured, though in vain, to rescue from ignominy and abhorrence the British name.

Mr. Burke rose to speak;[43] but there was a loud and confused clamour in opposition to him.

Mr. *Burke* said,[44] that he wished only to explain what he had thrown out. The order of the day was then called for, and the usual motion made, that the Speaker leave the chair.

Mr. *Burke* then observed, that as this was a new motion, he had a title to express his sentiments on it; and he could not do this without previously remarking, the rather indecent manner in which the order of the House had been enforced, respecting him, by a young member (Mr. Grenville) who sat opposite to him. There was, perhaps, a respect to years, which was not unbecoming a young man. He was now in order to insist, that every thing he had said concerning the outrages in India was true.

He denied having exaggerated a single circumstance: and protested, that exaggeration, with regard to the facts in discussion, was impossible. But this was the only mode by which his argument was to be attacked: It was always thus his reasoning was invalidated by general insinuation and surmise, which, like a stone in the hand of a David, might demolish the greatest giant on earth.[45] It was a weapon, which, as any one might wield with success, no man – no reasoning could repel. He hoped, therefore, no honourable gentleman could expect he would fight them at such fearful odds. He had no general assertions to make; the subject on which he made his stand, was incapable of insinuation. He stood committed – the Reports stood committed – the Governor General stood committed. The contest was not reduced to a few simple facts, which the meanest understanding could comprehend as well as the most accomplished. [And laying his hand on a volume of the Reports which lay on the table] I swear, said he, by this book, that the wrongs done to humanity in the eastern world, shall be avenged on those who have inflicted them: They will find, when the measure of their iniquity is full, that Providence was not asleep. The wrath of Heaven would sooner or later fall upon a

---

[43] **speak**   George Dempster had spoken for Hastings.
[44] **said**   William Grenville had objected to further contributions from Burke.
[45] **on earth**   alluding, of course, to Goliath, I Samuel 17:49.

nation, that suffers, with impunity, its rulers thus to oppress the weak and innocent. We had already lost one empire, perhaps, as a punishment for the cruelties authorised in another. And men might exert their ingenuities in qualifying facts as they pleased, but there was only one standard by which the Judge of all the earth would try them. It was not whether the interest of the East-India Company made them necessary, but whether they coincided with the prior interests of humanity, of substantial justice, with those rights which were *paramount to all others.*

He declared he had no manner of concern with the character of Mr. Hastings. The question was not, whether he was a good father, a good husband, or a good friend? But whether he made a good Governor? And whether those under his government, were *happy or miserable.* He said, as he had not on that day been permitted to go on in a string of motions which he had proposed to submit to the House, he would not read them as part of his speech to the House. Here he read a long string of motions, all tending to introduce inquiry respecting the peculations and outrages committed in India. These, he said, he would bring forward at another period, when he hoped they would not be precluded by an incessant clamour for the order of the day; and he particularly observed, that it was hard a Minister should oppose an inquiry, when the honourable gentleman (Major Scott) who sat above him, seemed so very desirous that it should immediately take place.[46]

[46] **place**   Grenville then replied and the order of the day was read.

Substance of The Speech ... In the Debate on the Army Estimates.

Introduction

Richard Burke, who followed his father's career closely, suggested in 1790 that Edmund's political opinions never arose suddenly. 'There is one thing ... which I know from an intimate experience of many Years', he wrote:

> It is, that my father's opinions are never hastily adopted; and that even those ideas, which have often appeared to me only the effect of momentary heat or casual impression, I have after-wards found, beyond a possibility of doubt, to be either the result of the systematick meditation perhaps of Years, or else if adopted on the spur of the occasion, yet formed upon the conclusions of long and philosophical experience.[1]

Nowhere is this reflection more fully realized than in Burke's view of the French Revolution.

When the summer of 1789 signalled the beginning of the French Revolution, Burke was about sixty years of age. His thought had developed continuously. Its basic stance had been established at an

---

[1] Corr, VI, p. 92.

early stage, as is usually the case if thought is to develop and mature. The assumption that the divine order was manifested through inequality is found in writings produced before Burke was thirty. He had praised revelation and considered the benefits of a propertied order when an undergraduate. He had explored the way in which nature tended to form societies, elevate some men above others and encourage improvement in his *Philosophical Enquiry* of 1757 and shown the benefits in liberty and civilization accruing from one such society, in the *Abridgement* he wrote soon afterwards. As Burke's life moved through the public scene after 1760, he developed a sense of the role of government in securing these benefits. The government of a conquered Ireland showed how far such a proper order could be suppressed and what bad consequences flowed from it. Burke, as he saw it, aimed to maintain Britain and establish America under a freer dispensation. He regarded India as a country conquered. His engagement with the sub-continent gave something more to his thought, for its reminder of the conditions on which civilization stood brought him to find room amongst his sympathies for a culture less respectful than Britain's of liberty. Whilst considering Bengal he likened it to France.

The Revolution presented itself to Burke as the negation of God and His order. The Revolution placed *égalité* amongst its ends. This implied to his way of thinking an end to the institutions that reflected nature. This was not strictly a matter of the concept of equality or of the entire programme of 1789. If we refer equality to parity of natural attributes or to equality of consideration in morals or at law, it is compatible with Burke's views. But if it denotes an opposition to the institutions which set one man above another in society, it was what the Third Estate meant by *égalité*, and this emphasis is plainly incompatible with Burke's views. However, this was not a denial of the whole range of his opinions. It says nothing about God, Christianity, property, civilization or the conditions of order in general. The interest of 1789 in political liberty was congruent enough with his position.

What was the source of Burke's opposition? He found in the Revolution tendencies which undermined every principle of his. Its apparent enemies were aristocratic and ecclesiastical distinctions. But behind its attitude to the aristocratic order was an enmity to established property in land; that enmity, by undermining the poor man's subordination to those above, would destroy respect for all property. The abolition of tithes and Church property was significant because its ultimate origin was a conspiracy of atheists, who intended an attack extending beyond the Church and even beyond Christianity to destroy all religion. Religion and property together sustained civilization. The Revolution, however modest its explicit programme, embodied the abolition of the entire providential order on Burke's reading.

In his thought, from erroneous principle bad consequences would flow. The Revolution's obsession with equality, because it would cut at social hierarchy and the Church, undermined the conditions of political liberty which he had identified long ago. Liberty was possible because obedience to government could be had without coercion; and this obedience was the fruit of a natural inequality: but to Burke's eyes the French were destroying the natural objects of their allegiance. As early as September 1789 he informed Windham that 'along with their political servitude' the revolutionaries 'have thrown off the Yoke of Laws and morals' and expressed 'great doubts whether any form of Government which they can establish will procure obedience'.[2] It was scarcely an accident that *Reflections* would begin with liberty, in order to suggest that the French had strayed so badly in seeking it that they were destroying the whole edifice of their civilization. Eventually Burke would describe the Revolution as 'the most extensive design that ever was carried on, since the beginning of the world against all property, all order, all religion, all law, and all real freedom'.[3]

Yet, as with any politician's declaration, there was more than meets the contemplative eye of principle. The Revolution presented an opportunity for Burke to reassert his political importance. His ejection from Bristol had diminished his national importance, whilst the death of Rockingham and the rise of a new generation had left him isolated within his party. Charles Fox was nearly two decades his junior, Sheridan slightly more. Grey was younger than Burke's own son. They had not much use for him after 1784: his concern for India seemed politically misconceived, his avuncular advice doubtless a bore and his plans for a regency (when they hoped in 1788 that George III was permanently unhinged) disagreed with their own. When Fox seemed to have a chance to form a government, he did not

---

[2] Corr, VI, p. 25.
[3] *Brissot's Address*, WSEB, VIII, p. 517.

send for Burke. Four days before the Bastille was stormed, Burke wrote mournfully that

> There is a time of Life, in which, if a man cannot arrive at a certain degree of authority, derived from a confidence from the Prince or the people, which may aid him in his operations, and make him compass useful Objects without a perpetual Struggle, it becomes him to remit much of his activity. Perpetual failure, ... will detract every day more and more from a mans Credit until he ends without Success and without reputation. In fact a constant pursuit even of the best Objects, without adequate instruments detracts something from the opinion of a mans Judgment.[4]

The coming of the Revolution presented an opportunity to redeem this situation. The means were Burke's own tongue and pen. These he could rely upon; and could hope to outstrip the Foxites in the eyes of the nation. Whether the English would approve of the Revolution depended on how it was interpreted. The political inclinations of the English were predominantly conservative, with a preference for political liberty. The two chimed together, for it was believed that liberty had long subsisted in England. Burke, writing in August, 1789, thought the country undecided, 'gazing with astonishment at a French struggle for Liberty' but, 'not knowing whether to blame or to applaud'.[5] Fox applauded the storming of the Bastille as the best event in human history, whilst Richard Price suggested that the Revolution instituted liberty in France.[6] Burke set out to persuade the nation to a different view.

The temper of the Foxites was seen in the two debates on the army estimates during February 1790. Fox himself suggested in the debate of the 5th that the 'new form which the government of France was likely to assume ... would render her a better neighbour'. In the debate of the 9th he told the Commons that he 'exulted' in the Revolution, 'from feelings and from principle'.[7] Faced with such views Burke made his declaration in the second debate.

His speech treated the Revolution as an attack on society as under-

---

[4] Corr, VI, p. 1f.
[5] Corr, VI, p. 10.
[6] Price, *A Discourse on the Love of our Country* (1789), in A.C. Ward (ed.) *A Miscellany of Tracts and Pamphlets* (1927), p. 458.
[7] PH, XXVIII, 332; 346.

stood by Burke and angled his presentation towards those features of English society his audience valued. He argued that the French were not improving their constitution towards an English liberty, but on the contrary destroying everything civilized. They acted for

> a cause, the real object of which was to level all those institutions, and to break all those connections, natural and civil, that regulate and hold together the community by a chain of subordination; to raise soldiers against their officers; servants against their masters . . . and children against their parents.

This cause, he decided, 'this cause of theirs was not an enemy to servitude, but to society'.[8] France was a conquered country, devastated far more effectively by the French than by England in the past: 'they had done their business . . . in a way which twenty Ramilies or Blenheims could never have done it'. The cause was also likely to infect England, because of her proximity to France. He felt free to ask

> the House to consider, how the members would like to have their mansions pulled down and pillaged, their persons abused, insulted, and destroyed; their title deeds brought out and burned before their faces, and themselves and their families driven to seek refuge in every nation throughout Europe, for no other reason than this; that without any fault of theirs, they were born gentlemen, and men of property, and were suspected of a desire to preserve their consideration and their estates.[9]

In short, the Revolution was represented as the end of society, and more particularly the end of the kind of society which his audience represented.

His appeal was well-calculated, as the response of members who spoke after Burke (except Sheridan) indicates. The younger Pitt, ever sensitive to the ambient temperature of politics, applauded.[10] The pained response of English radicals, as well as applause of those with other views, showed that he had hit the right note. Soon Burke's writings and speeches on the Revolution regained for him the place at

---

[8] Below, p. 315.
[9] Below, p. 309, 315.
[10] Sir George Howard (PH, xxviii, 373f) and Colonel Phipps (372); Pitt's approval (373) was all the more remarkable because just before Burke's speech he had observed cheerfully that the Revolution 'would provide freedom rightly understood' and that France 'would enjoy that just kind of liberty which he venerated, and the invaluable existence of which it was his duty, as an Englishman, peculiarly to cherish'.

centre stage that he had lost when he ceased to be member for Bristol in 1780. Now, perhaps, he stood under a brighter light. He had impressed upon many the belief that the Revolution in France was unenglish.

Though Burke may have won conservative sentiment to his side, we should not forget that his work proceeded from the particular cast of his own mind. His fundamental position, as we have noticed, rested on his previous thought. As was his habit, again, Burke's writings about the Revolution show the same marks of development we have seen in his earlier work. *Reflections on the Revolution in France*, which was on hand when he spoke in February, 1790, refined and developed his material. The Queen of France passage dwelt on the proper effects of sympathy and exposed the foundations of civilization more than this *Speech* had done. Burke inserted detailed observations, attributing the unsettlement of property to the pique of the commercial and literary classes.[11] His flexibility on detail continued after *Reflections*, for he soon revised this last opinion and withdrew his prediction that France would disintegrate; and correspondingly renewed his fear of her military force.[12] The list could be prolonged. Yet the fundamental lines of his arguments were the same, because proceeding from his basic assumptions about God, man and society.

Burke's position on the Revolution appears as very much his own from another angle. He was not very intelligible to his contemporaries. Just as Fox, Sheridan and Pitt addressed themselves to details of his *Speech on the Army Estimates* without scrutinizing his apocalyptic vision, so friend and foe alike seem not to have discovered the grounding of *Reflections* in his earlier thought. No doubt Paine's contempt for Burke's sympathetic description of the Queen of France expressed an interested disapproval but it also showed an ignorance of

---

[11] *Reflections*, esp. pp. 123f, 168–75, 185f, 209–14. He also enlarged on the notion that France had conquered herself:

> these pretended citizens treat France exactly like a country of conquest. Acting as conquerors, they have imitated the policy of the harshest of that harsh race. The policy of such barbarous victors, who contemn a subdued people, and insult their feelings, has ever been, as much as in them lay, to destroy all vestiges of the antient country, in religion, in polity, in laws, and in manners; to confound all territorial limits; to produce a general poverty; to put up all their properties to auction; to crush their princes, nobles, and pontiffs; to lay low every thing which had lifted its head above the level, or which could serve to combine or rally, in their distresses, the disbanded people, under the standard of old opinion. (p. 297f).

[12] See respectively, *Thoughts on French Affairs* (1791), W, IV, esp. p. 350, and *Four Letters on the proposals of peace with the regicide directory of France*, W, VI.

his *Philosophical Enquiry*,[13] just as it was ignorance of his view of civilization that Mary Wollstonecraft betrayed when she condemned his 'principles of natural subordination' as 'contemptible hardhearted sophistry'.[14] More conservative thinkers were equally insensitive to Burke's own particular views. Philip Francis stigmatized the Queen of France passage as 'pure foppery'.[15] When Gibbon applauded Burke's opposition to the Revolution he also described him as 'the most eloquent and rational madman I ever knew'.[16] George III's compliment to Burke, that he had defended the cause of gentlemen,[17] embodies a solid but not a penetrating assessment of his thought, whilst Pitt's later desire for reconciliation with France showed that he had opposed the Revolution on other grounds than Burke's. Those who were charmed by Burke's conclusions, seemed oblivious of their origins. Everyone saw that Burke offered an indictment of the Revolution they could not ignore, but few asked whence it came.

Burke illustrates the privilege of posterity in interpreting thought. Something is due to a thinker's situation and the traditions to which he has access, if such there be, in the views he articulates. But more than that, if we take a section of a man's thought at each period of his career we see that it is the outcome also of his own previous thought and of his preceding experience. His doctrines can be quite unintelligible without these. Burke, especially the Burke of the French Revolution, puzzled contemporaries: but *Reflections on the Revolution in France* reflects clearly its author's mind.

---

[13] Paine, *The Rights of Man*, pt. 1 in M. D. Conway (ed.), *The Writings of Tom Paine*, 4 vols. (1894–96), II, p. 288f. For Burke on sympathy, see above, p. 68f.

[14] Mary Wollstonecraft, *Vindication of the Rights of Man*, in *The Works of Mary Wollstonecraft*, ed. M. Butler and J. Todd, 7 vols. (1989), V, p. 55. Wollestonecraft, however, was a close student of Burke's *Philosophical Enquiry*. Godwin commented subsequently that her *Vindication* displayed 'a too contemptuous and intemperate treatment of the great man against whom its attack is directed'. *Memoirs of the Author of 'The Rights of Woman'*, ch. 6, ed. R. Holmes (1987), p. 230.

[15] Corr, VI, p. 86.

[16] J.E. Norton (ed.), *The Letters of Edward Gibbon* (3 vols., 1956), III, p. 229. Gibbon elsewhere described the revolutionaries as 'the fanatic missionaries of sedition', *Memoirs of my Life and Writings*, ed. G.A. Bonnard (1966), p. 185.

[17] Reported by Mrs Burke to William Burke in a letter of 21 March 1791, Corr, VI, pp. 237–39.

Analysis

Introduction: confidence in the executive would be the Commons' most dangerous attribute and jealousy of it their most tolerable vice. This was especially true of the size of the army (pp. 306–7).

(I) *Balance of Power in Europe*: size of our army should depend on need: need depends on threat from Europe (pp. 307–8). France had been the major threat in the past. (p. 308). Whilst we should not ignore France, she was presently no military danger at all (pp. 308–9).

(II) *True character of French menace*: her destruction of her own institutions – monarchy, church, nobility, law, revenue, army, navy, commerce, arts, manufactures (pp. 309–10) – and what lies behind it. Our proximity to France made us liable to its distempers in the past (pp. 310) and in the present: the present danger is the example of (i) destruction of good institutions, (ii) atheism and (iii) their military (pp. 310–11). (i) The French innovate in a way that makes improvement impossible (pp. 312–13), specifically by destroying balanced institutions (p. 313), which uphold property and liberty (pp. 313–14). (iii) The army had deserted its post in upholding society (pp. 314–15). Society depends upon subordination (pp. 315–16) and the new French army inverted this (p. 316).

(III) *England contrasted with France*: our army is obedient (p. 316); our Revolution of 1688 upset neither government (p. 317) nor society (pp. 317–18) nor church (p. 318); and because we did not abolish our institutions, but improved them, we prospered at home as well as abroad (pp. 318–19). Criticisms rebutted (pp. 319–20).

Substance of the Speech of the Right Honourable Edmund Burke, in the Debate on the Army Estimates, in the House of Commons, On Tuesday, the 9th Day of February, 1790. Comprehending a Discussion of the Present Situation of Affairs in France.

(Third edition, 1790)
(1790).

Mr. Burke's speech on the Report of the army has not been correctly stated in some of the public papers,[1] It is of consequence to him not to

---

[1] **papers**   the standard of parliamentary reporting was not high. Modern editors have not found it more satisfactory than contemporaries. Some MPs sent copies of their speeches to the newspapers, a practice which did not endear them to their colleagues. Burke preferred to publish his major efforts himself. The publication of this short piece emphasizes the importance he attached to his views on the French Revolution.

On parliamentary reporting, see John A. Woods *et al.* (eds.), *A Bibliography of Parliamentary Debates of Great Britain* (1956); P.D.G. Thomas 'Sources for the be misunderstood. The matter which incidentally came into discussion is of the most serious importance. It is thought that the heads and substance of the speech will answer the purpose sufficiently. If in making the abstract, through defect of memory, in the person who now gives it, any difference at all should be perceived from the speech as it was spoken, it will not, the editor imagines, be found in any thing which may amount to a retraction of the opinions he then maintained, or to any softening in the expressions in which they were conveyed.

Mr. Burke spoke a considerable time in answer to various arguments which had been insisted upon by Mr. Grenville and Mr. Pitt, for keeping an increased peace establishment,[2] and against an improper jealousy of the Ministers, in whom a full confidence, subject to responsibility, ought to be placed, on account of their knowledge of the real situation of affairs; the exact state of which it frequently happened, that they could not disclose, without violating the constitutional and political secresy, necessary to the well being of their country.

Mr. Burke said in substance, 'that confidence might become a vice, and jealousy a virtue, according to circumstances. That confidence, of all public virtues, was the most dangerous, and jealousy in an House of Commons, of all public vices, the most tolerable; especially where the number and the charge of standing armies, in time of peace, was the question.

That in the annual mutiny bill,[3] the annual army was declaredly to be for the purpose of preserving the balance of power in Europe.[4] The propriety of its being larger or smaller depended, therefore, upon the true state of that balance. If the increase of peace establishments demanded of Parliament agreed with the manifest appearance of the

Debates of the House of Commons, 1768–74', *Bulletin of the Institute of Historical Research* (special supplement, 4 (1959), and 'The Beginning of Parliamentary Reporting in Newspapers, 1768–1774', *English Historical Review*, 74 (1959), pp. 623–36; and Arthur Aspinall, 'The Reporting and Publishing of the House of Commons Debates, 1771–1834', pp. 227–57, in Richard Pares and A.J.P. Taylor (eds.) *Essays presented to Sir Lewis Namier* (1956).

[2] **establishment** William Grenville had suggested that 'it was not politic to alter our establishment on every alteration in the circumstances of rival powers' (PH, XVIII, 343f) and suggested that Britain should maintain a peacetime establishment adequate to deter any enemy (342f).

[3] **bill** see the note on CA, above p. 266. The necessity for an annual bill continued until 1879.

[4] **in Europe** Fox had reminded the House (PH, XXVIII, 348) that the Mutiny Act referred to the balance of power in Europe.

balance, confidence in Ministers, as to the particulars, would be very proper. If the increase was not at all supported by any such appearance, he thought great jealousy might, and ought to be, entertained on that subject.

That he did not find, on a review of all Europe, that, politically, we stood in the smallest degree of danger from any one state or kingdom it contained; nor that any other foreign powers than our own allies were likely to obtain a considerable preponderance in the scale.

That France had hitherto been our first object, in all considerations, concerning the balance of power. The presence or absence of France totally varied every sort of speculation relative to that balance.

That France is, at this time, in a political light, to be considered as expunged out of the system of Europe. Whether she could ever appear in it again, as a leading power, was not easy to determine: but at present he considered France as not politically existing; and most assuredly it would take up much time to restore her to her former active existence – *Gallos quoque in bellis floruisse audivimus,*[5] might possibly be the language of the rising generation. He did not mean to deny that it was our duty to keep our eye on that nation, and to regulate our preparation by the symptoms of her recovery.

That it was to her *strength*, not to her *form of government* which we were to attend; because Republics, as well as monarchies, were susceptible of ambition, jealousy, and anger, the usual causes of war.

But if, while France continued in this swoon, we should go on increasing our expences, we should certainly make ourselves less a match for her, when it became our concern to arm.

It was said, that as she had speedily fallen, she might speedily rise again. He doubted this. That the fall from an height was with an accelerated velocity; but to lift a weight up to that height again was difficult, and opposed by the laws of physical and political gravitation.

In a political view, France was low indeed. She had lost every thing, even to her name.

'Jacet ingens littere truncus
Avolsumque humeris *caput*, et sine *nomine* corpus'*

---

[5] **Gallos ... audivimus** 'We have heard that the Gauls also prospered in war' (Tacitus, *Agricola*, 5.2.3).

* Mr Burke, probably, had in his mind the remainder of the passage, and was filled with some congenial apprehensions:

He was astonished at it – he was alarmed at it – he trembled at the uncertainty of all human greatness.

Since the House had been prorogued in the summer[7] much work was done in France. The French had shewn themselves the ablest architects of ruin that had hitherto existed in the world. In that very short space of time they had completely pulled down to the ground, their monarchy; their church; their nobility; their law; their revenue; their army; their navy; their commerce; their arts; and their manufactures. They had done their business for us as rivals, in a way in which twenty Ramilies or Blenheims[8] could never have done it. Were we absolute conquerors, and France to lye prostrate at our feet, we should be ashamed to send a commission to settle their affairs, which could impose so hard a law upon the French, and so destructive of all their consequence as a nation, as that they had imposed upon themselves.

France, by the mere circumstance of its vicinity, had been, and in a degree always must be, an object of our vigilance, either with regard to her actual power, or to her influence and example. As to the former, he had spoken; as to the latter, (her example) he should say a few words: for by this example our friendship and our intercourse with that nation had once been, and might again, become more dangerous to us than their worst hostility.

In the last century, Louis the Fourteenth had established a greater and better disciplined military force than ever had been before seen in Europe, and with it a perfect despotism. Though that despotism was

'Haec finis Priami fatorum; hic exitus illum
Sorte tulit, Trojam incensam, & prolapsa videntem
Pergama; tot quondam populis, terrisque, superbum
Regnatorem Asiæ. Jacet ingens littore truncus,
Avolsumuque humeris caput, & fine nomine corpus.
At me tum primum sœvus circumstetit horror;
Obstupui: *subiit chari genitoris imago*' – [6]

[6] *Jacet ... imago* Vergil, *Aeneid*, ll. 557–8 and 554–60. The full passage runs: 'This was the end of Priam's destinies: this the death to which fate bore him, to see Troy in flames and in ruins; Troy the proud ruler of Asia, ruler over so many peoples and lands. He lies a huge lump on the foreshore, a body headless and nameless. Then rough horror seized me for the first time; I was speechless: there appeared the image of my dear father.'

[7] **the summer** i.e. of 1789.

[8] **Ramilies or Blenheims** Blenheim (1704) and Ramillies (1706) were two of Marlborough's four great victories over the French in the War of the Spanish Succession: they were preferred to Oudenarde (1708) and Malplaquet (1709) because more striking and less costly.

proudly arrayed in manners, gallantry, splendor, magnificence, and even covered over with the imposing robes of science, literature, and arts, it was, in government, nothing better than a painted and gilded tyranny; in religion, an hard stern intolerance,[9] the fit companion and auxiliary to the despotic tyranny which prevailed in its government. The same character of despotism insinuated itself into every court of Europe – the same spirit of disproportioned magnificence – the same love of standing armies, above the ability of the people. In particular, our then Sovereigns, King Charles and King James, fell in love with the government of their neighbour, so flattering to the pride of Kings. A similarity of sentiments brought on connections equally dangerous to the interests and liberties of their country. It were well that the infection had gone no farther than the Throne. The admiration of a government flourishing and successful, unchecked in its operations, and seeming therefore to compass its objects more speedily and effectually, gained something upon all ranks of people. The good patriots of that day, however, struggled against it. They sought nothing more anxiously than to break off all communication with France, and to beget a total alienation from its councils and its example; which, by the animosity prevalent between the abettors of their religious system and the assertors of ours, was, in some degree, effected.

This day the evil is totally changed in France: but there is an evil there. The disease is altered; but the vicinity of the two countries remains, and must remain; and the natural mental habits of mankind are such, that the present distemper of France it is far more likely to be contagious than the old one; for it is not quite easy to spread a passion for servitude among the people: but in all evils of the opposite kind our natural inclinations are flattered. In the case of despotism there is the *fœdum crimen servitutis*; in the last the *falsa* species *libertatis*; and accordingly, as the historian says, *pronis auribus accipitur.*[10]

In the last age we were in danger of being entangled by the example of France in the net of a relentless despotism. It is not necessary to say any thing upon that example. It exists no longer. Our present danger from the example of a people, whose character knows no medium, is,

---

[9] **intolerance**   e.g. the Revocation of the Edict of Nantes in 1685.
[10] ***fœdum crimen servitutis*** 'the imputation of servility ... the misleading appearance of liberty ... heard with willing ears' (Tacitus, *Histories*, i.i; cf. *Present Discontents*, above, p. 166.   -

with regard to government, a danger from anarchy; a danger of being led through an admiration of successful fraud and violence, to an imitation of the excesses of an irrational, unprincipled, proscribing, confiscating, plundering, ferocious, bloody, and tyrannical democracy. On the side of religion, the danger of their example is no longer from intolerance, but from Atheism; a foul, unnatural vice, foe to all the dignity and consolation of mankind;[11] which seems in France, for a long time, to have been embodied into a faction, accredited, and almost avowed.[12]

These are our present dangers from France: but, in his opinion, the very worst part of the example set is, in the late assumption of citizenship by the army, and the whole of the arrangement, or rather disarrangement of their military.

He was sorry that his right honourable friend (Mr. Fox[13]) had dropped even a word expressive of exultation on that circumstance; or that he seemed of opinion that the objection from standing armies was at all lessened by it. He attributed this opinion of Mr. Fox entirely to his known zeal for the best of all causes, Liberty. That it was with a pain inexpressible he was obliged to have even the shadow of a difference with his friend, whole authority would be always great with him, and with all thinking people – *Quæ maxima semper censetur nobis, et erit quæ maxima semper.*[14] – His confidence in Mr Fox was such, and

---

[11] **mankind** cf. Elizabeth Carter in 1763 on the Encyclopedists as trying 'to cheat mankind out of all that is worth living for, and all that is worth dying for' (*A Series of Letters from Mrs Elizabeth Carter to Mrs Vesey* (1819), III, p. 14).

[12] **avowed** cf. *Annual Register* (1762), p. 48, on a 'club of pretended sages' who had 'formed a sort of confederacy against the cause of Christianity, and are not a little anxious about making proselytes', and see *Reflections*, p. 211f, on the 'literary cabal' which 'formed something like a regular plan for the destruction of the Christian religion'; and cf. p. 185f. Cf. Mouffle d'Angerville, *Private Life of Louis XV* (English trans., 1781), II 350–1 for the *Encyclopedie* as 'a work ... requiring a great number of assistants' who 'would of course form a point of union for philosophers, who from this time would begin to grow into a sect and thus make one body'. These formulations enlarge unflatteringly to the opening sentence of d'Alembert's *Preliminary Discourse to the Encyclopedia* (1751). For that work's infidelity, see Laurence Sterne, *A Sentimental Journey*, ch. 3; Elizabeth Carter, *Letters from Mrs Elizabeth Carter to Mrs Montagu* (1817), II, p. 350 (11 Dec. 1775); and also *Select Essays from the Encyclopedia* (1772), p. iv, on the omission of all articles 'discovered to be offensive to religion, morality and consequently to the welfare of society in general'.

[13] **Fox** for similar compliments, see *Speech on Fox's East India Bill*, WSEB, V, p. 449.

[14] **Quæ ... semper** 'which always we hold great and always shall' (Vergil, *Aeneid*, VIII. 271–2).

so ample, as to be almost implicit. That he was not ashamed to avow that degree of docility. That when the choice is well made, it strengthens instead of oppressing our intellect. That he who calls in the aid of an equal understanding, doubles his own. He who profits of a superior understanding, raises his powers to a level with the height of the superior understanding he unites with. He had found the benefit of such a junction, and would not lightly depart from it. He wished almost, on all occasions, that his sentiments were understood to be conveyed in Mr. Fox's words; and that he wished, as amongst the greatest benefits he could with the country, an eminent share of power to that right honourable gentleman; because he knew that, to his great and masterly understanding, he had joined the greatest possible degree of that natural moderation, which is the best corrective of power; that he was of the most artless, candid, open, and benevolent disposition; disinterested in the extreme; of a temper mild and placable, even to a fault; without one drop of gall in his whole constitution.

That the House must perceive, from his coming forward to mark an expression or two of his best friend, how anxious he was to keep the distemper of France from the least countenance in England, where he was sure some wicked persons had shewn a strong disposition to recommend an imitation of the French spirit of Reform. He was so strongly opposed to any the least tendency towards the *means* of introducing a democracy like theirs, as well as to the *end* itself, that much as it would afflict him, if such a thing could be attempted, and that any friend of his could concur in such measures, (he was far, very far, from believing they could); he would abandon his best friends; and join with his worst enemies to oppose either the means or the end; and to resist all violent exertions of the spirit of innovation, so distant from all principles of true and safe reformation; a spirit well calculated to overturn states, but perfectly unfit to amend them.

That he was no enemy to reformation. Almost every business in which he was much concerned, from the first day he sat in that House to that hour, was a business of reformation; and when he had not been employed in correcting, he had been employed in resisting abuses. Some traces of this spirit in him now stand on their statute book.[15] In his opinion, any thing which unnecessarily tore to pieces the contex-

---

[15] **book** in particular, his reform of the Crown establishment in 1780 and again in 1782 as Paymaster-General.

ture of the state, not only prevented all real reformation, but introduced evils which would call, but, perhaps, call in vain, for new reformation.

That he thought the French nation very unwise. What they valued themselves on, was a disgrace to them. They had gloried (and some people in England had thought fit to take share in that glory[16]) in making a revolution; as if revolutions were good things in themselves. All the horrors, and all the crimes of the anarchy which led to their revolution, which attend its progress, and which may virtually attend it in its establishment, pass for nothing with the lovers of revolutions. The French have made their way through the destruction of their country, to a bad constitution, when they were absolutely in possession of a good one. They were in possession of it the day the States met in separate orders. Their business, had they been either virtuous, or wise, or had been left to their own judgement, was to secure the stability and independence of the States, according to those orders, under the Monarch on the Throne. It was then their duty to redress grievances.

Instead of redressing grievances, and improving the fabric of their State, to which they were called by their Monarch, and sent by their Country, they were made to take a very different course.[17] They first destroyed all the balances and counterpoises which serve to fix the state; and to give it a steady direction; and which furnish sure correctives to any violent spirit which may prevail in any of the orders. These balances existed in their oldest constitution; and in the constitution of this country; and in the constitution of all the countries in Europe.[18] These they rashly destroyed, and then they melted down the whole into one incongruous, ill-connected mass.

When they had done this, they instantly, with the most atrocious perfidy and breach of all faith among men, laid the axe to the root of all property, and consequently of all national prosperity, by the

---

[16] **glory** alluding to Richard Price, *A Discourse on the love of our country* (1789), shortly to be an especial object of Burke's enmity in *Reflections*.

[17] **course** Louis XVI, short on solvency, resorted to summoning the Estates-General (peers, churchmen and commoners) in order to obtain money for redress of grievance. The assembly had rather different ideas.

[18] **Europe** for European states sharing a common constitution, deriving from Christianity and the feudal system, see *Abridgement of English History*, III.i; *Letters on the proposals for peace with the regicide directory of France*, II, W, VI, p. 202f and IV, W, VI, p. 362.

principles they established, and the example they set, in confiscating all the possessions of the church. They made and recorded a sort of *institute* and *digest*[19] of anarchy, called the rights of man, in such a pedantic abuse of elementary principles as would have disgraced boys at school; but this declaration of rights was worse than trifling and pedantic in them; as by their name and authority they systematically destroyed every hold of authority by opinion, religious or civil, on the minds of the people. By this mad declaration they subverted the state; and brought on such calamities as no country, without a long war, has ever been known to suffer, and which may in the end produce such a war, and, perhaps, many such.

With them the question was not between despotism and liberty. The sacrifice they made of the peace and power of their country was not made on the altar of Freedom. Freedom, and a better security for freedom than that they have taken, they might have had without any sacrifice at all. They brought themselves into all the calamities they suffer, not that through them they might obtain a British constitution; they plunged themselves headlong into those calamities, to prevent themselves from settling into that constitution,[20] or into any thing resembling it.

That if they should perfectly succeed in what they propose, as they are likely enough to do, and establish a democracy, or a mob of democracies, in a country circumstanced like France, they will establish a very bad government – a very bad species of tyranny.

That, the worst effect of all their proceeding was on their military, which was rendered an army for every purpose but that of defence. That, if the question was, whether soldiers were to forget they were citizens, as an abstract proposition, he could have no difference about it; though, as it is usual, when abstract principles are to be applied, much was to be thought on the manner of uniting the character of citizen and soldier. But as applied to the events which had happened in France, where the abstract principle was cloathed with its circumstances, he thought that his friend would agree with him, that what was done there furnished no matter of exultation, either in the act or the example. These soldiers were not citizens; but base hireling mutineers, and mercenary sordid deserters, wholly destitute of any

[19] **institute, digest**   alluding to works as those of Gaius and Justinian, which gave organized form to the body of Roman law.
[20] **that constitution**   for a similar view, see Ref, p. 236.

honourable principle. Their conduct[21] was one of the fruits of that anarchic spirit, from the evils of which a democracy itself was to be resorted to by those who were the least disposed to that form as a sort of refuge. It was not an army in corps and with discipline, and embodied under the respectable patriot citizens of the state in resisting tyranny. Nothing like it. It was the case of common soldiers deserting from their officers, to join a furious, licentious populace. It was a desertion to a cause, the real object of which was to level all those institutions, and to break all those connections, natural and civil, that regulate and hold together the community by a chain of subordination; to raise soldiers against their officers; servants against their masters; tradesmen against their customers; artificers against their employers; tenants against their landlords; curates against their bishops; and children against their parents. That this cause of theirs was not an enemy to servitude, but to society.

He wished the House to consider, how the members would like to have their mansions pulled down and pillaged, their persons abused, insulted, and destroyed; their title deeds brought out and burned before their faces, and themselves and their families driven to seek refuge in every nation throughout Europe, for no other reason than this; that without any fault of theirs, they were born gentlemen, and men of property, and were suspected of a desire to preserve their consideration and their estates. The desertion in France was to aid an abominable sedition, the very professed principle of which was an implacable hostility to nobility and gentry, and whose savage war-whoop was '*a l'Aristocrate*,' by which senseless, bloody cry, they animated one another to rapine and murder; whilst abetted by ambitious men of another class, they were crushing every thing respectable and virtuous in their nation, and to their power disgracing almost every name, by which we formerly knew there was such a country in the world as France.

He knew too well, and he felt as much as any man, how difficult it was to accommodate a standing army to a free constitution, or to any constitution. An armed, disciplined body is, in its essence, dangerous to liberty; undisciplined, it is ruinous to society. Its component parts are, in the latter case, neither good citizens, nor good soldiers. What have they thought of in France, under such a difficulty as almost puts

---

[21] **their conduct** the army had not seemed sufficiently reliable in the summer of 1789 to be used against the National Assembly or Paris.

the human faculties to a stand? They have put their army under such a variety of principles of duty, that it is more likely to breed litigants, pettyfoggers, and mutineers, than soldiers.* They have set up, to balance their Crown army, another army, deriving under another authority, called a municipal army – a balance of armies, not of orders. These latter they have destroyed with every mark of insult and oppression. States may, and they will best, exist with a partition of civil powers.[23] Armies cannot exist under a divided command. This state of things he thought, in effect, a state of war, or, at best, but a truce instead of peace, in the country.

What a dreadful thing is a standing army, for the conduct of the whole, or any part of which, no man is responsible! In the present state of the French crown army, is the Crown responsible for the whole of it? Is there any General who can be responsible for the obedience of a Brigade? Any Colonel for that of a Regiment? Any Captain for that of a Company? And as to the municipal army, rein-forced as it is by the new citizen-deserters, under whose command are they? Have we not seen them, not led by, but dragging their nominal Commander with a rope about his neck,[24] when they, or those whom they accompanied, proceeded to the most attrocious acts of treason and murder? Are any of these armies? Are any of these citizens?

We have in such a difficulty as that of fitting a standing army to the state, he conceived, done much better. We have not distracted our army by divided principles of obedience. We have put them under a single authority, with a simple (our common) oath of fidelity; and we keep the whole under our annual inspection. This was doing all that could be safely done.

He felt some concern that this strange thing, called a Revolution in France, should be compared with the glorious event, commonly cal-led the Revolution in England;[25] and the conduct of the soldiery, on

---

* They are sworn to obey the King, the nation, and the law.[22]

[22] **the law** their oath differed pointedly from that of the ancien regime, which referred to the king only.
[23] **civil powers** cf. Montesquieu, *Espirit des Lois*, XI.6
[24] **about his neck** Louis XVI had been led in triumph on 6 October 1789; cf. Ref, pp. 164ff.
[25] **Revolution in England** Price had suggested that. Sheridan, speaking after Burke, remarked: 'He had never been accustomed to consider that transaction as

that occasion, compared with the behaviour of some of the troops of France in the present instance. At that period the Prince of Orange,[26] a prince of the blood royal in England, was called in by the flower of the English aristocracy[27] to defend its ancient constitution, and not to level all distinctions. To this Prince, so invited, the aristocratic leaders who commanded the troops went over with their several corps, in bodies, to the deliverer of their country. Aristocratic leaders brought up the corps of citizens who newly enlisted in this cause. Military obedience changed its object; but military discipline was not for a moment interrupted in its principle. The troops were ready for war, but indisposed to mutiny.

But as the conduct of the English armies was different, so was that of the whole English nation at that time. In truth, the circumstances of our revolution (as it is called) and that of France are just the reverse of each other in almost every particular, and in the whole spirit of the transaction. With us it was the case of a legal Monarch attempting arbitrary power – in France it is the case of an arbitrary Monarch, beginning, from whatever cause, to legalise his authority.[28] The one was to be resisted, the other was to be managed and directed; but in neither case was the order of the state to be changed, lest government might be ruined, which ought only to be corrected and legalised. With us we got rid of the man, and preserved the constituent parts of the state. There they get rid of the constituent parts of the state, and keep the man. What we did was in truth and substance, and in a constitutional light, a revolution, not made, but prevented. We took solid securities; we settled doubtful questions; we corrected anomalies in our law. In the stable fundamental parts of our constitution we made no revolution; no, nor any alteration at all. We did not impair the

merely the removal of one man and the substitution of another, but as the glorious æra that gave real and efficient freedom to this country, and established on a permanent basis, those sacred principles of government and that reverence for the rights of men, which he, for one, could not value here, without wishing to see diffused throughout the world' (PH, XXVIII, 360f).

[26] **Orange**   i.e. the future William III.
[27] **flower of the English aristocracy**   in fact, by a circular letter from a few peers, of whom some were first-generation creations, a bishop who was a peer's brother and two peers' sons.
[28] **legalise his authority**   the financial embarrassments of the monarchy necessitated complaisance towards the convocation at the Estates-General; its inability to control the Third Estate, once assembled, had permitted moves for the drafting of a constitution in June, 1789.

monarchy.[29] Perhaps it might be shewn that we strengthened it very considerably. The nation kept the same ranks, the same orders, the same privileges, the same franchises, the same rules for property, the same subordinations, the same order in the law, in the revenue, and in the magistracy; the same lords, the same commons, the same corporations, the same electors.

The church was not impaired. Her estates, her majesty, her splendor, her orders and gradations continued the same. She was preserved in her full efficiency, and cleared only of a certain intolerance,[30] which was her weakness and disgrace. The church and the state were the same after the revolution that they were before, but better secured in every part.

Was little done because a revolution was not made in the constitution? No! Every thing was done; because we commenced with reparation not with ruin. Accordingly the state flourished. Instead of lying as dead, in a sort of trance, or exposed as some others, in an epileptic fit, to the pity or derision of the world, for her wild, ridiculous, convulsive movements, impotent to every purpose but that of dashing out her brains against the pavement, Great Britain rose above the standard, even of her former self. An æra of a more improved domestic prosperity then commenced, and still continues, not only unimpaired, but growing, under the wasting hand of time. All the energies of the country were awakened. England never presented a firmer countenance, or a more vigorous arm, to all her enemies, and to all her rivals. Europe under her respired and revived. Every where she appeared as the protector, assertor, or avenger, of liberty. A war was made and supported against fortune itself. The treaty of Ryswick,[31] which first limited the power of France, was soon after made: the grand alliance[32] very shortly followed, which shook to the

---

[29] **the monarchy**   the Declaration of Rights, beyond prohibiting a standing army without parliamentary consent and barring Catholics from the throne, did not alter the monarch's powers.

[30] **intolerance**   the Toleration Act, 1689 suspended the penalties against Protestant dissent.

[31] **Ryswick**   the Treaty of Ryswick (1697) ended the war of 1689 (or the War of the English Succession, as it was sometimes called) in which Louis XIV, ostensibly aiming to restore James II to his throne, had tried the old tactic of attacking the Netherlands.

[32] **grand alliance**   between England, the Netherlands and the Empire, defeated France repeatedly in the War of the Spanish Succession. Cf. Burke's references to Ramillies and Blenheim, above, p. 309.

foundations the dreadful power which menaced the independence of mankind. The states of Europe lay happy under the shade of a great and free monarchy, which knew how to be great without endangering its own peace at home, or the internal or external peace of any of its neighbours.

Mr. Burke said he should have felt very unpleasantly if he had not delivered these sentiments. He was near the end of his natural, probably still nearer to the end of his political career; that he was weak and weary; and wished for rest. That he was little disposed to controversies, or what is called a detailed opposition. That at his time of life, if he could not do something by some sort of weight of opinion, natural or acquired, it was useless and indecorous to attempt any thing by mere struggle. *Turpe Senex Miles.*[33] That he had for that reason little attended the army business, or that of the revenue, or almost any other matter of detail for some years past. That he had, however, his task. He was far from condemning such opposition; on the contrary, he most highly applauded it, where a just occasion existed for it, and gentlemen had vigour and capacity to pursue it. Where a great occasion occurred, he was, and while he continued in Parliament, would be amongst the most active and the most earnest, as he hoped he had shewn on a late event. With respect to the constitution itself, he wished few alterations in it. Happy if he left it not the worse for any share he had taken in its service.

Mr. Fox then rose, and declared, in substance, that so far as regarded the French army, he went no farther than the general principle, by which that army shewed itself indisposed to be an instrument in the servitude of their fellow citizens, but did not enter into the particulars of their conduct. He declared, that he did not affect a democracy. That he always thought any of the simple, unbalanced governments bad; simple monarchy, simple aristocracy, simple democracy; he held them all imperfect or vicious: all were bad by themselves: the composition alone was good. That these had been always his principles, in which he had agreed with his friend, Mr. Burke, of whom he said many kind and flattering things, which Mr. Burke, I take it for granted, will know himself too well to think he

---

[33] ***Turpe Senex Miles*** 'an old man is a bad soldier' (Ovid, *Amores*, I.ix.4); let us hope that the continuation – *turpe senilis amor* – was inapplicable to the speaker. Burke had been feeling weary for some time; he had already used similar sentiments and the same quotation in a letter of July 1789 (Corr, VI, p. 1).

merits, from any thing but Mr. Fox's acknowledged good nature. Mr. Fox thought, however, that, in many cases, Mr. Burke was rather carried too far by his hatred to innovation.

Mr. Burke said, he well knew that these had been Mr. Fox's invariable opinions; that they were a sure ground for the confidence of his country. But he had been fearful, that cabals of very different intentions, would be ready to make use of his great name, against his character and sentiments, in order to derive a credit to their destructive machinations.

Mr. Sheridan then rose, and made a lively and eloquent speech against Mr. Burke; in which, among other things, he said that Mr. Burke had libelled the National Assembly of France, and had cast out reflections on such characters as those of the Marquis de la Fayette and Mr. Bailly.

Mr. Burke said, that he did not libel the National Assembly of France, whom he considered very little in the discussion of these matters.[34] That he thought all the substantial power resided in the republic of Paris, whose authority guided, or whose example was followed by all the Republics of France. The Republic of Paris had an army under their orders, and not under those of the National Assembly.

NB As to the particular gentlemen, I do not remember that Mr. Burke mentioned either of them – certainly not Mr. Bailly. He alluded, undoubtedly, to the case of the Marquis de la Fayette; but whether what he asserted of him be a libel on him, must be left to those who are acquainted with the business.

Mr. Pitt concluded the debate with becoming gravity and dignity, and a reserve on both sides of the question, as related to France, fit for a person in a ministerial situation. He said, that what he had spoken only regarded France when she should unite, which he rather thought she soon might, with the liberty she had acquired, the blessings of law and order. He, too, said several civil things concerning the sentiments of Mr. Burke, as applied to this country.

---

[34] **matters**   an omission remedied in *Reflections*.

Index of persons

Adams, Samuel, 196
Addison, Joseph, 66, 69, 186
Aemilius Paullus Macedonicus, L., 69
Agesilaus, xxxvi, 19
Agricola, Cn. Julius, 37
Alexander the Great, xxxvii, xxxviii, 19, 20, 31
Almas Ali Khan, xxxvii, 275, 281, 282, 283, 287
Anaxagoras, xxxvii, 39
Anne, Queen, xxxvii, xl, liv, lxiii, lxv, 101, 172, 173, 186
Antiochus, xxxviii, 23
Antoninus Pius, M., lxv, 34
Antony, Mark (M. Antonius), xlii
Archelaus, xxxviii, 23
Aristides, xxxviii, 36
Aristion, 23
Aristotle, xxxvii, 69, 71, 72, 190
Atkinson, Richard, xxxix, 284
Aubrey, John, lix
Augustus, C. Julius Caesar Octavianus, lxiv
Aurelius Antoninus, M., 34

Bacon, Francis, 165
Bailly, Jean Sylvain, xxxix, 320
Barrington, Judge, 246
Bathurst, Allen, first earl, xxxix, 216–17
Bathurst, Henry, second earl, xxxix, 217
Bedford, Francis Russell, fifth duke of, xxxix

Bedford, John Russell, fourth duke of, xi, xxxix, xlviii, lx, 137, 147, 157
Berkeley, George, bishop of Cloyne, 90
Blackburne, Francis, 15
Blackstone, Sir William, xxxix, 116, 225
Blount, Charles, 2, 5, 15
Boleyn, Anne, xlv
Bolingbroke, Henry St John, Viscount, xiii, xviii, xx, xxiv, xxxix–xl, liv, lix, lxv, 5–9, 12, 15, 30, 39, 41, 45, 81, 118, 131
Borlase, Edmund, 99
Boswell, James, lii
Brooke, Henry, 89
Brown, Rev. John, xl, 133
Burgh, Thomas, 4, 88, 103
Buckinghamshire, earl of, 201
Burke, Christopher (EB's son), xi
Burke, Jane (EB's wife), xi
Burke, Mary (EB's mother), 96
Burke, Richard (EB's son), xi, 298
Burke, Richard (EB's father), 96
Burke, William (EB's 'cousin'), 194, 272
Burton, Robert, 190
Bute, John Stuart, third earl of, xxxix, xl, xlv, xlvi, xlvii, xlviii, li, lii, liii, liv, lxii, 104, 105, 113, 125, 138, 146, 184
Butler, Joseph, bishop of Durham, 2

Caesar, C. Julius, xl, xli, xlii, 23
Caldwell, James, 90
Caligula, xli, 34, 39

Camden, Charles Pratt, first earl of, xli, 139
Caroline of Anspach, Queen, lxvi
Carter, Elizabeth, 9, 311
Carteret, John, baron (Earl Granville), 104, 133
Castillo, Bernal Diaz del, 25
Catilina, L. Sergius, xli, xlii
Cato, M. Porcius, xli, 70
Cavendish, Lord John, xli, 199
Charlemont, James Caulfield, first earl of, 91
Charles I, King, 122, 153
Charles II, King, xli–xlii, xlviii, li, liv, lxvi, 246, 310
Charles V (Holy Roman Emperor), lvii, lx, 25
Charles X (King of Sweden), 34
Charles XII (King of Sweden), 19–20
Choiseul, Etienne François, duc de, xlii
Chesterfield, Philip Dormer Stanhope, fourth earl of, xxxvii, 109
Chubb, Thomas, xviii, xlii
Churchill, Sir Winston, liv
Cicero, M. Tullius, xli, xlii, 53, 116, 185
Clarendon, Edward Hyde, first earl of, 99
Clarke, Samuel, 15
Clodius Pulcher, P., xlii
Coke, Sir Edward, Baron Coke, xlii–xliii, 10, 233
Collins, Anthony, xviii, xliii, 5, 81
Congreve, Richard, xxxix
Conway, Henry Seymour, xliii, 188
Cortes, 25
Crassus, M. Licinius, 23
Cromwell, Oliver, 242
Cumberland, Richard, bishop of Peterborough, 2
Cumberland, William Augustus, duke of, xliii, 108, 132

Damiens, Robert Francis, 64
Darius III, Emperor of Persia, lxvi
Dashwood, Sir Francis, 166
Davenant, Charles, 214
Davies, Sir John, xliii, 241
Dempster, George, xliv, 296
Dennis, William, 59
Devonshire, William Cavendish, fourth duke of, xxxix, xli, xliv, lix, lx, 105, 107, 109

Disraeli, Benjamin, earl of Beaconsfield, xl
Domitian, Emperor, Titus Flavius Domitianus, lxv, 37
Douglas, John, 118, 123, 128, 130, 134
Dowdeswell, William, xliv, 108, 163, 199, 200, 202
Dundas, Henry, Viscount Melville, xliv, 279, 285
Dunmore, John Murray, fourth earl of, xliv–xlv
Dyson, Jeremiah, xlv, 123, 140, 141

Edward I, King, xlv, 243
Edwards, John, 27
Elizabeth I, Queen, xlv, lix, 101, 241
Elliot, Sir Gilbert, xlv, 140, 141

Fielding, Henry, 20, 153
Fox, Henry, first baron Holland, xlvi, 105, 118, 126
Fox, Charles James, xxxi, xliv, xlvi, xlvii, lvi, lvii, lix, lxii, 135, 141, 274, 300, 301, 303, 307, 311, 312, 319, 320
Francis, Sir Philip, xlv, l, li, 272, 304
Franklin, Benjamin, 198, 246
Frederick, Prince of Wales, xiii, xl, xlvi, xlviii, lvi, 125, 158
Frederick Augustus, duke of York, 156
Frederick II (King of Prussia), 29
Frederick III (King of Denmark), 34
Fuller, Rose, xlvi, 202, 208

Gage, Thomas, xlvi, 196, 243
Garrick, David, xlvi–vii
George I, King, xl, lvi, lxiv, lxvi, 104, 173
George II, King, xiii, xliv, xlvi, xlvii, xlviii, l, liv, lv, lviii, lx, lxvi, 104, 126, 132–33, 173, 250, 251
George III, King, xiii, xv, xxix, xxxix, xl, xliii, xliv, xlv, xlvi, xlvii, xlix, lvi, lx, 104, 105, 106, 107, 109, 111, 113, 127, 128, 132, 194, 300, 304
Gibbon, Edward, lv, 17, 96, 304
Gloucester, William, duke of, xxxviii
Glover, Richard, xlvii, 214
Godolphin, Sidney, first earl of, xlviii, liv, 187
Godwin, William, 4, 64
Goldsmith, Oliver, xxix, xlviii, 64
Gordon, Thomas, 32

Gower, Granville Leveson-Gower, earl, xlviii, 142
Grafton, Henry Fitzroy, third duke of, xiv, xl, xlvii, xlviii, lvi, lx, lxii, 105, 137, 138, 142, 157
Grenville, George, xi, xiv, xxix, xxxix, xl, xlvii, xlviii, xlix, liv, lx, lxii, lxv, 105, 123, 140, 141, 157, 163, 197, 203, 250, 252f, 257
Grenville, William Wyndham, Baron Grenville, xlvi, lix, 289, 296, 307
Grey, Charles, second earl Grey, 300
Grotius, Hugo, 60
Guicciardini, Francesco, xlix, 17
Guilford, first earl of, lvi

Halifax, George Montagu Dunk, first earl of, xiii
Hamilton, W. G., xiii, xlix, 93, 107
Harley, Thomas, xlix, 139
Harrington, James, xlix, 134, 135, 247
Harris, James, 204
Hastings, Warren, xiv, xv, xxxi, xxxvii, xlv, xlix–l, li, lxi, lxii, 271–2, 274, 278, 279, 282, 283, 284, 294, 295
Henry III, King, xlv, 1
Henry IV, King, lix
Henry VIII, King, xlv, l, lv, 122, 235, 244, 254, 255
Herodotus, lxii
Hillsborough, Wills Hill, Viscount, 1, 250
Hobbes, Thomas, xliii, 1, 17
Holland, Henry Richard Fox, third baron, xlvi
Homer, l–li, 32
Hooker, Richard, 33
Horace (Q. Horatius Flaccus), 159
Hume, David, xxv, 6, 80, 98
Hutcheson, Francis, li, 59, 61
Hutchinson, Thomas, li, 200, 201

Impey, Sir Elijah, l, li, 295
Isocrates, 10

James I, King, xliii, lix
James II, King, xxxviii, xlii, xlvii, li, liv, lxvi, 89, 122, 310
James III (Old Pretender), 173f
Jenkinson, Charles, first earl of Liverpoool, li–lii, 138, 204, 205
John, King, l, lii, 122

Johnson, Samuel, xii, xlvi, lii, 160, 212, 217f, 219
Jugurtha, lii, 23
Junianus Justinus, M., lii, 18
Juvenal, D. Iunius Iuvenalis, 42, 46, 49

Knox, William, 108

Lafayette, M.-J. P. Y. R. G. du Motier, marquis de, lii, 320
Langrishe, Sir Hercules, xv
Livia, lxiv
Locke, John, xliii, liii, 2, 14, 32, 60, 66, 83, 86
Longinus, 74
Louis XI (King of France), 131
Louis XIV (King of France), liii, lxvi, 309
Louis XV (King of France), 64
Louis XVI (King of France), xv, 70, 313, 316
Lovat, Simon Fraser, twelfth baron, 71, 162
Lowther, Sir James, earl of Lonsdale, liii, 138
Lucullus, L. Licinius, xxxviii, 23
Luttrell, Colonel, 163
Lycurgus, liii, 28
Lysander, liii, 39

Macartney, George, 90
Macclesfield, earl of, 162
Macaulay, Catherine, 178
Machiavelli, Niccolo, liii, 17, 29, 141
Mackenzie, James Stuart, liii–liv, 140
Macnamara, John, liv, 289
Macquirk, Edward, 139
Mallet, David, 8
Marie Antoinette, Queen, 70
Marlborough, John Churchill, first duke of, xlvii, liv, lxiv, 187
Marlborough, Sarah, duchess of, 108
Mary I, Queen, xlv
Mary II, Queen, lxvi
Maxwell, John, 2
Mazarin, Cardinal, liii
Melcombe, Bubb Doddington, Baron, 107
Mildert, William Van, bishop of Durham, 246
Miltiades, liv, 39
Milton, John, 52

Minos, liv, lxiv, 28
Mirza Muhammed Kazim Khan, 283
Mithridates, xxxviii, xxix, liv–lv, 22
Molière, 131, 186
Montagu, Mrs Elizabeth, 9
Montesquieu, Charles le Secondat, Baron de, 103, 150, 197, 316
More, Sir Thomas, lv, 247
Morgan, Thomas, xviii, lv
Moses, lv, 28
Muhammed Ali (Nawab of Arcot), 270f

Nero Claudius Caesar, lv, 31, 38
Nerva, Emperor, M. Cocceius Nerva, lxv
Newcastle, Thomas Pelham-Holles, duke of, xxxix, xl, xliv, xlvi, xlviii, lv, lvii, lviii, 126, 128
Ninus, lvi, lxii
North, Frederick, Lord, xiv, xxviii, xxix, xxxi, xlv, xlvi, xlvii, xlviii, lvi, lvii, lviii, lix, lx, lxi, lxii, 105, 109, 110, 111, 118, 138, 157, 195, 199, 200, 210, 211, 238, 239, 259f, 262, 271, 274
Northington, Robert Henley, earl of, lvi, 137
Norton, Sir Fletcher, Baron Grantley, lvi, 139
Numa Pompilius, lvii, 28

O'Conor, Charles, 90
O'Hara, Charles, 89, 91
Orpheus, lvii, 28
Oxford, Robert Harley, first earl of, xlix

Paine, Thomas, 20, 303
Paley, William, 103, 109
Pelham, Henry, xiii, xxxix, lv, lvii, lviii, lxvi, 133, 176
Pericles, xxxvii, lvii, 38
Perseus V (King of Macedon), 69
Persius, A. Persius Flaccus, 76
Philip II (King of Spain), lvii, 240
Pigot, Sir George, Baron Pigot, lvii, 270f
Pigot, Admiral Hugh, lvii, 271
Pisistratus, lviii, 36
Pitt the elder, William, first earl of Chatham, xliii, xliv, xlv, xlvi, lv, lvi, lvii, lviii, lxii, lxv, 105, 118, 124, 128–30, 257
Pitt the younger, William, xxxix, xli, xliv,

xlvi, xlviii, xlix, liii, liv, lvi, lviii, lix, lxii, 105, 290, 293, 302, 303, 304, 320
Pizarro, 25
Plato, lviii, 39, 247
Plutarch, xxxviii, liii, lviii, lix, 23, 31, 38, 39
Pope, Alexander, lix, 5, 19, 54, 233, 291
Portland, William Cavendish-Bentinck, third duke of, liii, lix, 109, 138
Price, Richard, lix, 301, 313
Prior, Matthew, xxxix

Ralegh, Sir Walter, xliii, lix, 234
Rice, George, lix–lx, 238
Richard II, King, lix, 122, 245
Richelieu, Cardinal, liii
Richmond, Charles Lennox, third duke of, lx, 110, 111
Rigby, Richard, lx, 142
Robertson, Rev. William, xxxv, lx
Rochford, W. H. Zulestein de Nassau, earl of, lx, 151
Rockingham, Charles Wentworth-Watson, second marquess of, xii, xiv, xxix, xxx, xl, xli, xliii, xliv, xlv, xlvi, xlvii, xlviii, l, li, lvi, lvii, lx, lxi, lxii, lxv, 93, 105, 107, 109, 111, 129, 137, 140, 141, 142, 157, 179, 188, 210, 274
Rodney, Admiral George, lvii
Rolle, John, lxi, 289
Rousseau, J.-J., xx, xxii, xxiv, lxi, 6, 10, 12, 13, 14, 15, 16, 32, 33, 50, 52, 54, 58, 59, 61
Russell, Lord John, first earl Russell, xi, 135

Sammuramat, lxii
Sandwich, John Montagu, fourth earl of, 166
Savile, Sir George, lxi, 111
Scipio, P. Cornelius S. Africanus, lxi, 70
Scipio, P. Cornelius S. Aemilianus Africanus Numantinus, lxi, 70
Scott, Major John, lxi–lxii, 284, 287, 292
Semiramis, lvi, lxii, 19
Sesostris, lxii, 18
Shackleton, Abraham, xiii
Shackleton, Richard, 59

Shaftesbury, Anthony Ashley Cooper, third earl of, xl, li, 59, 61
Shakespeare, William, lii
Shamshi-Adad V, lxii
Shaw, George Bernard, 93
Shelburne, William Petty Fitzmaurice, second earl of, xiv, xliii, xlvii, xlviii, lvi, lviii, lxii, 107, 139, 151, 188, 196, 274
Sheridan, R. B., lxii, 300, 302, 303, 320
Sherlock, Thomas, bishop of London, 71
Sidney, Algernon, 126, 131
Smith, Adam, 6–7, 80, 175
Socrates, lxii–lxiii
Solon, lviii, lxiii, 36, 185
Somers, John, Baron, lxiii, 187
Sterne, Laurence, xxxix
Suetonius, 38
Sulla, L. Cornelius S. Felix, xxxviii, lxiii, 22–3
Sully, Maximilien de Bethune, duc de, lxiii, 120–1
Sunderland, Charles Spencer, third earl of, lxiii–lxiv, lxvi, 187
Swift, Jonathan, xxxix

Tacitus, Cn. Cornelius, 25, 31, 32, 117, 166, 167
Temple, Sir John, 99
Temple, Richard Grenville, second earl, xi
Tennyson, Alfred, first baron Tennyson, lix
Themistocles, xxxviii, lxiv, lxvi, lxvii, 36
Theseus, liv, lxiv
Thraesa Paetus, P. Clodius, 31
Thurlow, Edward, Baron Thurlow, lxiv, 201
Tiberius Julius Caesar Augustus, lxiv
Tigranes, xxxix, 23

Tindal, Matthew, xiii, xviii, lxiv, 81
Titus, Emperor, Titus Flavius Vespasianus, lxiv–lxv, 34
Toland, John, xviii, lxv, 5
Townshend, Charles, lxv, 93, 107, 199, 203
Townshend, Charles, second viscount, lxv
Trajan, M. Ulpius Traianus, lxv, 34
Trenchard, John, 32
Trogus Prompeius, lii
Tucker, Abraham, 239

Vergil, P. Vergilius Maro, 49, 69, 306–7
Vespasian, Emperor, T. Flavius Vespasianus, lxiv, lxv, 34

Walpole, Sir Robert, first earl of Orford, xiii, xxxix, lviii, lxiv, lxv–lxvi
Walpole, Horace, fourth earl of Orford, 113
Warburton, William, bishop of Gloucester, 81
Weymouth, Thomas Thynne, Viscount, 142
Wilkes, John, xiv, xli, xlix, lxiv, lxvi, 133, 139, 163, 165–6, 171
William II, Prince of Orange, lxvi
William III, King, li, liv, lix, lxiii, lxvi, 138, 317
William IV, King, 170
Windham, William, 300
Wollstonecraft, Mary, 304
Wortley Montagu, Lady Mary, 7

Xerxes, Emperor of Persia, lxvi–lxvii, 19

Yorke, Charles, 132
Young, Arthur, 88

Index of subjects and places

Aesthetics, xviii, 58–77
Africa, xli, lxii
Algiers, 226
Ambition, xxi, 68, 73–4
America, xxviii, xlvi, lx, lxiv, lxv, 193–269, 299
Apalachians, 230
Arabia, 226
Arcot, 270
Arginusae, 232
Aristocracy, xxx, 93
Armenia, xxxviii, xxxix, 23
Artemisium, lxiv, lxvii
Asia, lxii, lxiv, 19
Assyria, lxii, 24
Athens, liv, lvii, lviii, lxiii, lxiv, 20, 36–41
Atheism, xviii, 310

Babylon, lxii, 24
Bactria, xxxviii
Ballitore, xiii
Beaconsfield, xv
Beauty, 66f
Bedlam, 52
Bengal, l, li, 264, 272, 293, 299
Bithynia, xxxviii, 23
Blenheim, 302, 309, 318
Bologna, xlix
Boston, xiv, li, 199, 200, 202, 235, 254, 262, 268
Boston Tea Party, 200–1
Boyne, River, lxvi
Bridewell, 52
Bristol, xiv, 111

Britain, Great Britain, xl, 45, 51, 152, 213, 217, 267
Brusa, 226

Cabinet, Double, 125–81
Calcutta, 1
Cambridge, xlvi, xlviii, li
Canada, 128
Cannae, 232
Cape Breton Island, 128
Carmathenshire, lix
Carnatic, 273
Carolinas, 194, 223, 224, 261
Carthage, lxi, 20, 22, 40
Chaeronea, liii, 22
Chester, 241, 245–47, 249, 258
China, 45
Church of England, 223
Colchis, 18
Concord, 204
Connecticut, 255
Conquest, xxiv–xxix, xxxii, 220–1, 233–6, 270–97
Constitution, English, 103–92
Corinth, lxvii
Corsica, 150
Crete, liv
Crimea, 226
Culloden, xliii
Curdistan, 226
Cyzicus, 23

Dacia, 24
Davis' Straits, 219

Deism, xvii–xx, 1–57
Denmark, 34
Doab, xxxvii
Dominica, 128
Dublin, xiii, xvi, xvii, xlviii, 2
Durham, 241, 246–47, 249, 258

Edinburgh, xlviii, lx
Egypt, lxii, 18, 20, 38, 226
Empire, British, 88–102, 193–297
England, xxv–xxxi, xxxviii, xlv, lx, lxiii,
    100, 263, 316, 318
Etruria, 22

Falklands, 219
Florence, 40
Florida, 128
France, xxxi, xxxii, liii, 24, 100, 150,
    298–320

Gaul, xl
Genoa, 34, 150
Germany, 262
Glasgow, li
Government, xxv–xxviii, 4–57
Grecia-Magna, 21
Greece, xxxviii
Grenada, 128

Hanover, lviii, 156
Hastenbeck, xliii
Holland, 100
Hudson's Bay, 219

Imitation, xxi, 68, 72–3
Improvement, xxi, xxvii
India, xxvii, l, lx, lxi, 128, 264, 270–97
Inequality, xvi–xxxii, 4–57, 298–320
Ireland, xxvii, xlix, lix, lxvi, 88–102, 103,
    155, 241–3, 273
Italy, liii, 22, 24

Jamaica, xlvi
Jerusalem, lxiv
Judaea, lxiv, 24

Kora, xxxvii

Lauffelt, xliii
Leicester, liv
Lemnos, liv

Lexington, 204
Leyden, xlvi, xlviii
Liberty, xxii–xxiv, xxvii, 193–269
Lisbon, 17
London, xiii, xlvi, xlix
Lucknow, 287

Macedon, xxxvii, 20
Madras, l, lvii, 270
Madrid, lx
Malplaquet, 309
Manilla, 150, 151
Marathon, liv
Maryland, 223, 232, 261
Massachusetts, li, 228, 235, 255, 268,
    269
Middlesex, 169
Minden, lx
Modena, xlix
Montreal, xlvi

Nature, 1–57, 226
Newgate, 52
New York, xiv, 203
Normandy, lii
Numidia, lii

Oudh, xxxvii
Oxford, xlix, lxiv
Osnabrug, 156
Oudenarde, 309
Oudh, 282, 287, 288

Paris, xxxix, lx, 151, 320
Parliament, British, 152–76, 198
Parthia, xxxviii, xxxix
Party, 108–14, 181–92
Pennsylvania, 218
Pergamus, 20
Persia, xxxvii, liv, lxiv
Poland, 34
Pondicherry, 150, 151
Pontus, liv
Portugal, 151
Property, xxii–xxiv, xxxii, 89–93, 95–98
Providence, xxiii, 286, 290–1, 296
Pydna, 69

Quebec, 280

Ramilies, 302, 309, 318

Religion, xix–xx, 78–87
Revolution, 298–320
Rhode-Island, 255
Rhodes, 295
Roman Catholicism, 88–102, 223
Rome, xxxviii, lv, lvii, lxiii, 20, 40, 41

St Vincent, 128
Salamis, lxiv
Scotland, xxxviii, xlv, lix, lx, lxiii
Senegal, 128
Sicily, 21
Slavery, 232–33
Smyrna, 226
Spain, xli, xlv, lvii, 24, 240
Sparta, liii, lvii, lxiv, 41
Sublime, 58–65
Sympathy, xxi, 68–70
Syria, 20

Tanjore, lvii, 271

Thrace, liv
Ticonderoga, xlvi
Tobago, 128
Troy, 69
Turin, liv

Ukraine, 24

Venice, 34, 35
Virginia, 223, 224, 228, 232, 261

Wales, xlv, 241, 243–4, 258
Wendover, xiv
West Indies, 214, 215
Westminster, 170
Whitehaven, liii

Yorkshire, lxi

Zama, lxi

Cambridge Texts in the History of Political Thought

Titles published in the series thus far
Aristotle *The Politics* (edited by Stephen Everson)
Bakunin *Statism and Anarchy* (edited by Marshall Shatz)
Bentham *A Fragment on Government* (introduction by Ross Harrison)
Bodin *On Sovereignty* (edited by Julian H. Franklin)
Bossuet *Politics Drawn from the Very Words of Holy Scripture* (edited by Patrick Riley)
Burke *Pre-Revolutionary Writings* (edited by Ian Harris)
Cicero *On Duties* (edited by M.T. Griffin and E.M. Atkins)
Constant *Political Writings* (edited by Biancamaria Fontana)
Diderot *Political Writings* (edited by John Hope Mason and Robert Wokler)
Filmer *Patriarcha and Other Writings* (edited by Johann P. Sommerville)
Harrington *A Commonwealth of Oceana* and *A System of Politics* (edited by J.G.A. Pocock)
Hegel *Elements of the Philosophy of Right* (edited by Allen W. Wood and H.B. Nisbet)
Hobbes *Leviathan* (edited by Richard Tuck)
Hooker *Of the Laws of Ecclesiastical Polity* (edited by A.S. McGrade)
John of Salisbury *Policraticus* (edited by Cary Nederman)
Kant *Political Writings* (edited by H.S. Reiss and H.B. Nisbet)
Lawson *Politica sacra et civilis* (edited by Conal Condren)
Leibniz *Political Writings* (edited by Patrick Riley)
Locke *Two Treatises of Government* (edited by Peter Laslett)
Luther and Calvin on Secular Authority (edited by Harro Höpfl)
Machiavelli *The Prince* (edited by Quentin Skinner and Russell Price)
Malthus *An Essay on the Principle of Population* (edited by Donald Winch)
James Mill *Political Writings* (edited by Terence Ball)
J.S. Mill *On Liberty*, with *The Subjection of Women* and *Chapters on Socialism* (edited by Stefan Collini)
Milton *Political Writings* (edited by Martin Dzelzainis)
Montesquieu *The Spirit of the Laws* (edited by Anne M. Cohler, Basia Carolyn Miller and Harold Samuel Stone)

More *Utopia* (edited by George M. Logan and Robert M. Adams)
Nicholas of Cusa *The Catholic Concordance* (edited by Paul E. Sigmund)
Paine *Political Writings* (edited by Bruce Kuklick)
Price *Political Writings* (edited by D.O. Thomas)
Pufendorf *On the Duty of Man and Citizen according to Natural Law* (edited by James Tully and Michael Silverthorne)
The Radical Reformation (edited by Michael G. Baylor)
Vitoria *Political Writings* (edited by Anthony Pagden and Jeremy Lawrence)
William of Ockham *A Short Discourse on Tyrannical Government* (edited by A.S. McGrade and John Kilcullen)